English Manuscript Studies

English Manuscript Studies

Studies

1100–1700

VOLUME 9

Writings by Early Modern Women

Edited by

Peter Beal & Margaret J.M. Ezell

THE BRITISH LIBRARY

© 2000 The British Library Board

First published in 2000 by
The British Library
96 Euston Road
London NW1 2DB

British Library Cataloging in Publication Data

A cataloguing record for this publication is
available from The British Library

ISBN 0-7123-4674-0

Typeset in Monotype Baskerville by
Hope Services (Abingdon) Ltd.
Printed in England by
St Edmundsbury Press, Suffolk

Contents

Women, Writing and Scribal Publication in the Sixteenth Century

Jane Stevenson

The preliminary work for the forthcoming *Oxford Book of Early Modern Women Poets* which I have been undertaking in collaboration with Peter Davidson has been a serious attempt to find out how much verse by early modern women there in fact is (interpreting the term 'verse' rather liberally). It therefore seemed to us that it might be useful to review the question of what can reasonably be said about women and manuscripts in the sixteenth century, since we have a better idea than has hitherto been possible of what actually survives. In brief, our findings are that there were in the region of fifty English and Scottish women who wrote some kind of verse before 1600 which still survives in some form or other (and also a number of women composing in Welsh, Scottish Gaelic, or Irish, whose work falls outside this discussion). Of these fifty, about half printed at least some of what they wrote. Moreover, this half includes all of those with a substantial surviving oeuvre except Mary, Queen of Scots,[1] leading us to conclude that women and print in the sixteenth century is at least as important a topic as women and manuscripts.

What constitutes a private text?

It is natural for us now to identify anything handwritten as private, anything printed as public, with typescripts lying somewhere between, since they are generally intended for an audience other than the original writer even if it is an audience of one. But an immense amount of recent work on the context of literary production and the circulation of poetry in the sixteenth century disrupts these categories. Some kinds of manuscript text are private, others are intended to circulate, and the degree of publicity attaching to print also varies. Since the question of whether writing is 'public' or 'private' is so relevant to what women could or could not do, I want to use this paper to look at early modern women's verse in its social context, and to try and offer some conclusions as to whether it was essentially in the private domain.

A well-known story about Queen Elizabeth illustrates how a poem could originate as a private document on a tablet.

> Good Madam. Herewith I commit a precious jewel, not for your ear, but your eye; and doubt not but you will rejoyce to wear it even in your heart: It is of her Highness own enditing, and doth witness, how much her wisdom and great learning do outweigh even the perils of state, and how little all worldly dangers do work any change in her mynde. My Lady Wilougby did covertly get it on her Majesty's tablet, and had much hazard in so doing; for the Queen did find out the thief, and chid for spreading evil bruit of her writing such toyes, when other matters did so occupy her employment at this time; and was fearful of being thought too lightly of for so doinge. [2]

But truly private writing, in this period, normally stays private. Few women other than Elizabeth would find outsiders taking such interest in their 'tablets'. [3] A few women's commonplace books survive from the sixteenth century, a handful of which contain original verse; but no absolutely private books of the type implied here, not even Elizabeth's. [4] However, a number of works survive, including this one, which were originally *copied* from private notebooks. [5]

I also want to recall a couple of cautionary tales. One of the most internationally famous literary women of sixteenth-century England was (and is), Margaret Roper, née More, daughter of Sir Thomas More. Thomas Stapleton, More's biographer, notes that he saw Greek and Latin prose and verse by Margaret, and also mentions her treatise on the Four Last Things, written in friendly competition with her father, though only his unfinished treatment was published. [6] A letter of More's to Margaret is about a letter of hers which he showed to John Veysey: he had read one of her Latin letters and some Latin verses, and expressed himself charmed. [7] All this writing is lost: the normal fate for material which is not deliberately made public. Yet the odds for the survival of Margaret Roper's poetry were infinitely better than most, for specific historical reasons. In the aftermath of More's execution and canonisation, More 'books, letters and other writings, printed and unprinted' were being collected by a number of highly literate and concerned individuals, many of them women. [8] Margaret's own daughter, Mary Basset, was educated in Latin and Greek, and highly conscious of her heritage: she translated her grandfather Sir Thomas More's *History of The Passion* from Latin to English, and was considered one of the learned lights of Queen Mary's court; she would therefore have been well placed to preserve her mother's writings. [9] Although the family understandably kept a low profile for three generations thereafter, in the seventeenth century educated, female Mores and Ropers abounded in the English convents of the Low Countries, most of them Benedictines, the most intellectual of the orders open to women. They included Dame Mary Roper, who founded a new monastery in Ghent in 1623,[10] Dame Gertrude More, poet and mystic, and her sister Dame Bridget, and they were proud to trace a connection to Margaret More as well as to her father. But not even the combination of piety and family *pietas* led to the preservation of any of Margaret's writing other than the letters to Erasmus (which were kept, of course, in *his* archive), and her one published work.[11]

Another, less well known woman whose writing was respected in her own family was Elizabeth Holles, mother of the antiquary (and therefore, obsessive keeper of paper) Gervase Holles. She was born in 1578, her parent's only child, heir to a considerable fortune, and her father's pride and joy. In consequence,

> [she had] the best and choysest education, wch render'd hir, who had judgment beyond most of her sex, aequally accomplisht with the best of them . . . Shee wrote a hand far better than most weomen usually write, and (which in ye sex is strange) exact ortography, . . . Her stile was better than hir hand, weighty and unaffected. And to prove that a great fancy may sometimes accompany great virtues, shee compiled in verse the passages of hir whole life.[12]

We cannot know if this was 'Annals of my Life and Times', or self-exploration, like the seventeenth-century autobiographical poem of Martha Moulsworth,[13] since 'my uncle Holles (after hir death) borrowed [it] from my father wth importunity, and lost [it] as negligently.' This serves to remind us that even poetry which people have a strong interest in keeping can easily disappear, since books, then as now, were often treated carelessly, and fell into the hands of people who did not value them. In his account of the poet John Hoskyns, John Aubrey notes that, 'he had a booke of Poems, neatly written by one of his Clerkes, bigger than Dr Donne's Poemes, which his sonn Benet lent to he knowes not who, about 1633, and could never heare of it since.' Thus even a carefully prepared, large, professional manuscript, intended to be kept as an heirloom, could and did simply vanish, if the enthusiasm of the original compiler did not happen to meet with an equivalent enthusiasm in his or her heirs. Giles Dawson and Laetitia Kennedy-Skipton's book on Elizabethan handwriting reminds us, ominously, that 'used paper was a marketable commodity, much in demand for a great variety of uses . . . Housewives and cooks were prime consumers of waste paper.'[14] *Habent sua fata libelli*. Pope in the *Dunciad* describes the ordinary fate of obsolete or ephemeral books with heartless clarity: some suffer 'the martyrdom of jakes and fire' (B.I.143), while a few lucky exceptions are 'redeem'd from tapers and defrauded pies' (B.I.155).[15] Pope is, as usual, realistic in the details of his satire. An eighteenth-century antiquary, one John Warburton, who left a pile of manuscripts in a corner of his kitchen, discovered to his chagrin some time later that the cook had used them to line baking dishes—so even reaching the apparent haven of an antiquarian household was not necessarily sufficient to keep a document safe. Before thinking about women in particular, therefore, I think we have to remember how high the odds are stacked against the survival of *any* sixteenth century document written on paper (legal documents on parchment had a greater chance of survival).

All the same, a small amount of surviving verse apparently by women suggests that in the sixteenth century, a number of women of the rank of gentlewoman or above participated in the writing of ephemeral poetry as a social activity. There was very little consensus in the sixteenth century as to the scope or social purpose of a gentlewoman's education; but it seems virtually certain that a family whose sons attended the Inns of Court would at least teach its daughters to read, and probably rather more than that.[16] Verse composition was a virtually essential social grace to an extent which we find it hard to grasp now: the most unlikely people could and did write verse when required (William Cecil, for example). And although much literature of advice enjoins silence on women, there is often a gap between precept and practice. The examples which follow will, I hope, demonstrate that verbal facility and wit was in some contexts actually expected of gentlewomen, or at the least, was perceived as a desirable accomplishment.

Since practically no women's private notebooks survive from the sixteenth century, the evidence which I have for this has necessarily been extracted from writings by men, both manuscript and print, which record the social context in which verse was produced. Women's verse could, and sometimes did, end up in male friends' collections of loose papers, and subsequently find its way to some kind of repository. Here is a simple example, from the collected papers of a man who seems to have been at Cambridge, or had Cambridge connections:

> One of the Feminine kind, in a morning I lying in bed, sent me these two verses written on a Trencher for my breakfast:
>
> > Thy love that thou to one hast lent
> > In labour lost thy time was spent
>
> To which perusing [I] presently replyed these ensuing Distichs . . .

The jilted lover then proceeded to try out several appropriately witty replies to this brush-off, and notes which of them he finally decided to send: 'these verses as an answere to the former, which I had comp[osed] I sent backe to their Patronesse'.[17]

George Gascoigne includes in his *Hundred Sundrie Flowers* more sophisticated exchanges of verse with at least two gentlewomen.[18] Verse exchange, of course, is a kind of writing which women could engage in with some propriety, at least, when they answered rather than initiated the exchange. In many of the poems in *A Hundred Sundrie Flowers*, Gascoigne goes out of his way to sketch the precise social context from which a poem emerged. It is this concern with milieu which allows us to see how women in his circle interacted with him. What I want to focus on here is a piece of narrative in which a gentlewoman is not only praised for the quickness of her wit, but shown exercising it.

> And for a further proof of this Dames quick understanding, you shall now understand, that soone after this aunswer of hirs, the same author chaunced to be at a Supper in hir company, where were also hir brother, hir husband, and an old louer of hirs by whom she had bin long suspected. Nowe, although there were wanted no delicate viands, to cont<ent> them, yit their chief repast was by entreglancing of lookes. For GG being stoong with hot affection, could not otherwise relieve his passion but by gazing. And the Dame of a curteous enclinacion deigned (now and then) to require the same with glancing at him. Hir old louer occupied his eyes with watching: and hir brother perceyuing all this could not absteyne from winking, whereby he might put his Sister in remembrance least she shold too much forget herself. But most of all hir husband beholding the first and being euill pleased with the second, scarse contented with the third, and misconstruing the fourth, was constrained to play the fifth part in froward frowning. This royall banquet thus passed over, GG knowing that after supper they should passe the time in propounding of Riddles . . . contriued all this conceipt in a Riddle as followeth . . . She made a reply.

Although the answer to the riddle was obvious to the lady, and to most if not all of the men, manners dictated that nobody answer it. The lady dealt with the resulting social impasse very deftly, by turning it back on Gascoigne, with a counter-riddle as embarrassing to him as his had been to her.

Hir Question

> What thing is that which swimmes in blisse
> And yit consumes in burning grief

> Which being plast where pleasure is
> Can yit recouer no relief
> Which sees to sighe, and sighes to see
> All this in one, what may I bee?

Later on in their friendship, there was another contretemps, again of Gascoigne's making. He rummaged in her pocket, and found in it a letter from the old lover mentioned in the previous exchange. He chose to pass it off, though not without sarcasm, by getting hold of a lemon, and presenting it to her with a poem punning rather obviously on lemons and lemans. The life of educated men with pretensions to gentility was one in which literary challenges were readily offered and accepted: this narrative suggests that the same might also be true of educated women, since Gascoigne's poem, like the distich I quoted earlier, was clearly a challenge, to which as it turned out, the lady was more than equal. 'The Dame within very short space did aunswere it thus'—in terms which suggest that the lemon had done nothing to sweeten her disposition.

> A Lymone (but no Lemmane) Sir you found,
> For Lemmans beare their name to broad before
> The which since it hath giuen you such a wound
> That you seeme now offended very sore
> Content your self you shall find (there) no more
> But take your Lemmans henceforth where you lust
> For I will shew my letters where I trust.

It could be argued of course that Gascoigne wrote both sides of these interchanges; that the social world of his poetry is actually a dramatic fiction.[19] But even if this were so, it is a kind of fiction which is presented as a mirror of social realities. A young gentlewoman reading *A Hundrie Sundrie Flowers* would learn from it that witty rhyming was considered graceful and appropriate to a woman of her class. It is interesting, also, that Gascoigne, who has it in his power to control this narrative, does not represent himself as getting the better of either of these exchanges.

The participation of women in social versification is also a marked feature of a less literary text: the *Autobiography* of the musician, music-master and poetaster Thomas Whythorne. Whythorne's naive and overweening sexual vanity might make us sceptical of his version of why events turned out as they did, but I do not see why we should therefore doubt him as a witness to the private uses of verse. Both the stories told here probably date from the 1550s.

> I being now in place where were divers young women, one of the which
> . . . seemed to bear me very much good will; the which, through maid-

enly shamefastness, was not by her uttered unto me in word and deed in such sort as I perceived it, but she uttered it by writing . . . she devised certain verses in English, writing them with her own hand, and did put them between the strings of a gittern, the which . . . I then used to play on very often . . . The which verses did begin:

> Words that ye have rehearsed
> Hath my heart oppressed,
> And causeth me to die,
> Without remedy.
> But I wish you did know my mind,
> If you would not be to me unkind.
> My mind is
> That W. shall have this.

And where the W. standeth alone, there she wrote my name.

The woman's status is not clear. She is described as 'a young girl, rather than 'a young woman', and is sufficiently of the servant class to be dismissed when her forward behaviour is discovered by her mistress, but she may well have been a 'waiting gentlewoman'.[20]

Another episode in Whythorne's career which I find even more interesting is one where he was in a dependent position. 'There was a gentlewoman (who was a widow) that was desirous to have me to be both her servant and also her schoolmaster . . . to be a schoolmaster I did not mislike; but to be a serving-creature or servingman, it was so like the life of a water-spaniel . . . that I could not like of that life . . . I was behindhand of my wealth as of my health . . . .[so] I forced my will to yield to reason.'[21] The widow turned out to be a woman who revelled in the power which her wealth and independence permitted her: 'her joy was to have men in to be in love with her'. Whythorne fell in with her whims, and despised her, but was clearly reluctant to offend her: 'thus much may I say, that I, being loath that she should withdraw her good will from me, was very serviceable to please her . . . she would sometimes tell me in a scoffing manner that I was but a huddypick and lacked audacity'.[22] The post-Petrarchan tradition of love-poetry served him well as a defence against his mistress's complicated games of thus-far-and-no-further since he was able to take refuge in writing riddling verses, which she could take, if she wished, as compliment, or which he could disown if she pretended indignation. Whythorne, ever optimistic about his personal charms, began to evolve a hopeful theory that he might be able to talk her into marriage—it does not seem to have struck him that she was having far too much fun as things were. The story proceeds. 'One day, coming into my mistress' chamber and finding there a pen, ink and paper'—which I find quite interesting in itself—

I wrote in a piece of the paper as thus following:

> When pain is pleasure and joy is care
> Then shall good will in me wax rare.

This writing I left where I found the said implements to write withal; and coming the next day to her chamber, I found written as followeth:

> For your good will look for no meed
> Till that a proof you show by deed.

Unto the which when I had seen it, I replied as followeth:

> When opportunity of time serveth,
> Then shall you see how my heart swerveth.

After this I understood that the answer to my foresead rhythm was not made by my mistress, but by a waiting gentlewoman of hers . . . I repented me of that which I had then done, because I like not to make love to two at once . . . Then this young gentlewoman . . . thought I disdained her writing . . .

We can leave Whythorne to extricate himself from the pickle he has got himself into, scattering verses on all sides. I am struck by the *dramatic* quality of both Whythorne's and Gascoigne's narratives: either would make an excellent scene in a situation comedy. And in both, verse is used, lightly, ephemerally, to grease the wheels of social intercourse. Dropping into verse, for these men and women, indicates a measure of seriousness: not solemnity, but an indication that the interlocutor is worth a little trouble; perhaps rather as we distinguish between registers of correspondence such as scribbling information in ballpoint on a post-card, or writing a formal note on laid paper using a fountain pen. The use of verse also, of course, indicates a degree of education and culture.

We have to ask, I think, whether Whythorne was unusual in coming across women who flirted or wooed in rhyme, or whether it is simply unusual that this kind of stuff is recorded.[23] I would think the second more probable. In which case, the complicated structure of an English gentlewomen's social and intellectual formation included some important double messages about writing: were they always expected to be chaste, silent and obedient,[24] or were they actually supposed to be chaste, obedient and the mistress of an appropriate public discourse on occasion? I am also interested by Whythorne's widow's control over language, which extends beyond her own discourse: because she is economically powerful, she can and does control what is said to her, and the terms in which it is said. Whythorne, who is a gentleman, is one of several men in her vicinity tying himself into Petrarchan knots at her say-so.

A surviving example of private correspondence which seems to show a different aspect of the social use of verse is that of Gabriel Harvey's sister Marie. The Harveys were a family of artisans; while they were not poor, they were not gentlefolk.[25] The following story has been dismissed as fiction, though recent commentators seem inclined to treat it as factual, as I do.[26] Virginia Stern has suggested very sensibly that a possible reason why Harvey transcribed the two sets of letters into his private letter-book[27] (a manuscript which he did *not* circulate) is that he may have wanted to keep copies in case of future trouble, perhaps slanders against his sister.[28] It is hard to think why, if he wanted to write fiction, he should have chosen to write a very circumstantial account of the attempted seduction and rape of his sister (who is not a fiction: she is otherwise attested historically; and she could have been materially damaged by any such behaviour).

If we take the view that the letters are *not* fiction, therefore, their interest, with respect to the social history of versification, is that Marie Harvey, who was not even of gentlewoman status, seems to have dropped unselfconsciously into verse for the sake of emphasis. I must briefly describe what happened: the events took place around Christmas 1574, and the two parties were Marie Harvey, and Philip Howard, Earl of Surrey. Both of them were about seventeen. Harvey's account notes a series of meetings, the first accidental, the following engineered by Howard, and a series of gifts from him to her. Marie was determined not to surrender her virginity, but was far from indifferent to such gifts as a gold ring.[29] At one point, Marie was induced to write her dangerous admirer a letter, which took her some time. Harvey notes:[30]

> P. Cummes me the next night for her letter.
> It was not finnishid.
> He cummes againe ye next daye.
> She could not be spoke with at all.
> Bye the third day she had addressid her this letter, and gave it unto P. at his cumming.

P. is Howard's confidential servant. Letters are then fired to and fro, carried by P. Finally,[31]

> The maide being resolvid to write no more, yit upon ye receipt of so looving a letter, thought good to make an end with these fewe lines.

You knowe full well, Milord, faier words make fooles faine, and you weene of a like. Maides will refuse and take; but I would not you should thinke me a chaungelinge. Wary would I faine be: cruell can I not be; and your Lordship is unsatisfied, but not unhappie. Unhappie am I rather, that — ——, but there a strawe. Tis not inke and paper, your man telles me, that can content Milord.

> What, then, but put up mie pen,
>   And pray God amende you?
> An that be crueltie tooe, I know not what to dooe,
>   But pray God sende you.
>
> Yours as she may,
> And not as you say,
>   Though it greeve ye.
> Yours as she can,
> And not as you scan,
>   You may beleeve me.
>
> And thus I pray you stay.
>
> Pore M.

In this, and subsequent verses, dropping into simple rhyme seems to be a way of saying, 'please believe I mean what I say'. Later in this one-sided affair, when Howard had talked her into a meeting which she dodged, she left him a thirty-six-line poem by way of diplomatic apology.

> Milord I thanke you hartely
> For your late liberalitie;
> I would I were hable to requite
> Your lordships bowntie with ye like.
> Marry, mie hart is not so franke
> But mie habilitie is as scante;
> Therefore, in steade of a liefer gift,
> I bequeath you this paper for a shift.
> You se I am disposid to rime,
> Though it be cleen out of time.
> I hope your L. will have me excusid
> As longe as you feel not yourself abusid.
> To be short, Milord, thus it is, Iwis,
> I could not be at home according to prommis.
> I would not, perhaps it may to you seem,
> I pray you, Milord, do not so misdeem.
> Truly I was sent for to spend this good time
> A fewe miles of with a kinsman of mine.

Whether mi father in hast wuld so faine have me goe,
That I could not nor durst not for mielife say noe.

> So that I was faint [fain]
>   At his commaundiment
> To take a iornye
>   That I litle ment.
> I pray you, Milord,
>   Have me excusid,
> Though by mie frends
>   I be thus rulid.

The truth is, I am not mine owne maide,
My frends to disobey I am afraide.

> An other time as good
>   To speake your minde;
> In ye meane time if you seeke
>   You can not but finde.

Your honors to commaund
In anie honest demaund.

M.

The tone of transparent simplicity is misleading: this is a pack of lies: 'ye maide purposely tooke a iorny a seven miles of, in ye morning before six a clocke, dreading ye wurst if mie lord should chaunce to cum.' The poem is an excuse, an apology, and an attempt at temporizing,[32] since the week before this was sent, Howard had actually tried to rape her.[33] A few days later, Harvey himself intervened tactfully but firmly to put a stop to the whole affair.

Marie's verse, in this narrative, is used by her to deflect or disarm Howard's lust, anger, or rapacity. Generally, her stratagems for keeping this relationship in her control rather than Howard's are fascinating,[34] but language is the only one which is of present concern. Verse may be a poor weapon against an aristocratic seventeen-year-old male bent on sexual gratification, but it was a weapon of sorts. I would also suggest that she is using verse to indicate that she has a point of view, she is a speaking subject, not just a female object—perhaps making a Pamela-like bid through her very facility with words to be recognised as a woman of sufficient social status not to be used and discarded even by a Howard. Marie Harvey was not a lady, but these painfully indited letters imply that she was not a wench, and hint that she should not be treated as one.

Manuscript miscellanies

Now I want to turn from the kind of verse which survives fortuitously to the kind of verse which was kept on purpose. When we look at miscellany manuscript anthologies of the sixteenth century, women are clearly involved both as compilers and composers. Women played an active role in the literary coterie which surrounded Anne Boleyn, whose most salient figure is Thomas Wyatt.[35] The most important evidence for this is London, British Library Add. MS 17492 ('The Devonshire Manuscript'). [36] It was probably owned by Mary Fitzroy (née Howard), Duchess of Richmond, whose initials are on the original binding, but it seems to have been kept by Mary Shelton, a connection of the Howard family. She acted as overseer of this manuscript, which was returned to her at intervals: there are at least twenty-three hands at work in it.[37] It circulated among a group of friends who were mostly in the service of Anne Boleyn in the early 1530s, and contains a number of women's poems of obvious Howard interest: these include poems exchanged between Lady Margaret Douglas (later to become Duchess of Lennox and the mother of Lord Darnley) and her first husband, Lord Henry Howard. The Duchess of Richmond may be another author. Another poem from the circle of Wyatt which is apparently by a woman survives in two manuscripts.[38] Anne Boleyn herself could at least turn a couplet, on the evidence of BL King's MS 9, f. 66v, and may have written verse,[39] though the attribution of the lyric 'O death rock me asleep' to her seems to me to be made on insufficient evidence.[40] But it certainly looks as though the women of the Henrician court were active participants in literary games; while at least one woman, Lady Margaret Douglas, was also expressing serious emotion in verse.

Later in the century, women who were associated with University poets might find that some of their verse entered the pool of verse which passed between the notebooks of University men, and was thus made public within a particular coterie, since though manuscript miscellanies were obviously kept as private books, they could be, and often were, passed round within a social circle, and poems, sometimes even groups of poems, are copied from one to another.[41] John Donne is the most salient example of a poet who wrote for this kind of circulation: 'virtually all of the basic features of Donne's poetic art are related to its coterie character . . . Donne was obviously most comfortable when he knew his readers personally and they knew him'.[42] One such book is British Library Harley MS 7392, Humphrey Coningsby's manuscript, complied in the late sixteenth century.[43] Coningsby matriculated at Christ Church, Oxford, in 1581 and was MP for St Albans in 1584. It includes a poem attributed to Queen Elizabeth and an unfinished draft poetic translation by a woman identified as Mrs C.N. on f. 60v,[44] a version of the 'French Primero' (politics-as-a-card-game), which was one of the most popular poems circulating round the court and the Inns of Court in manuscript form.[45] The presence of a couple of poems attributed to women in this manuscript is far from unusual. Though women, of course, did not attend either Universities or the Inns of Court, they had friends who did; and a few women's verses make it into circulation in university and Inns of Court miscellanies.

One such poet and associate of poets was Anne Vavasour, a maid of honour (technically speaking), the mistress of the Earl of Oxford, to whom she bore a son in 1581, and subsequently of the Queen's Champion, Sir Henry Lee. The poem 'Thoughe I seem straunge sweet friend be thou not so' seems to reflect Anne Vavasour's somewhat peculiar situation in the early 1580s. It appears in four manuscripts, three men's commonplace books,[46] and also in Anne Cornwallis's short collection of verse from the late Elizabethan period.[47] In this last manuscript, it is subscribed *vavaser*.[48] The poem reflects an emotionally and practically complex situation; and whether it was written by Vavasour or about her, lines 23–24 suggest that it dates from 1580/81, since at this point, like the speaking voice of this poem, she had a lover and a 'champion', and may conceivably have also had a fiancé (who, understandably, made no attempt to claim her). Her love for Oxford was necessarily clandestine, since he was married: her 'hande' would obviously refer to a betrothal, or at least to a relationship sponsored by her family, while the possession of her 'glove' must refer to some individual choosing her as his lady in the game of courtly love: the obvious candidate for this role is Sir Henry Lee, whose attraction to her predates the disastrous affair with Oxford, on the incontrovertible evidence of his tilting armour, one suit of which was decorated with the initials AV accompanied by true-love knots.[49]

> Thoughe I seeme straunge sweete freende be thou not so
>   Do not annoy thy selfe with sullen will
> Myne harte hathe voude allthoughe my tongue saye noe
>   To be thyne owne in freendly liking styll
> 5   Thou seeste me liue amongest the Lynxes eyes
>   That pryes innto the priuy thoughte of mynde
> Thou knowest ryghte well what sorrows may aryse
>   Ife once they chaunce my setled lookes to fynde
> Contente thy selfe that once I made an othe
> 10   To sheylde my selfe in shrowde of honest shame
> And when thou lyste make tryall of my trouthe
>   So that thou [hast?] the ho^{n}oure of my name

And let me seme althoughe I be not coye
To cloak my sadd conceyts wth smylinge cheere
15   Let not my iestures showe wherein to ioye
Nor by my lookes let not my louee [sic] appeere.
We seely dames that falles suspecte, do feare
And liue within the moughte of envyes lake   mouth
Muste in oure heartes a secrete meaning beare
20   Far from the reste whiche outwardlye we make
Go were I lyke, I lyste not vaunte my love
where I desyre there moste I fayne debate
One hathe my hande an other hathe my glove,
But he my harte whome I seeme now to hate
25   Then farewell freende I will continue straunge
Thou shalt not heere by worde or writinge oughte
Let it suffice my vowe shall never chaunge
As for the rest I leave yt to thy thoughte.[50]

6   F: pryes innto the] pries and spies eche
13   F: hast] saue

I am inclined to accept the attribution to Vavasour: the construction of *heroides*: *i.e.* poems modelled on those of Ovid written in the person of an amorous woman, was a popular literary game of the period,[51] but as a genre, *heroides* tend to be far more explicit: the riddling quality of this poem is in its favour.

Beside Anne Cornwallis's book, we may put a somewhat later, but important women's manuscript from the Folger, Lady Anne Southwell's commonplace book, which contains poetry by herself, Sir Walter Ralegh and Henry King,[52] as well as a variety of prose. The paper in this notebook dates from before 1600: since she includes accounts for the rent of her house in Acton which she took in 1631, she was actually writing in it towards the end of her life (1573–1636), though I hope I may be forgiven for mentioning it here.[53] A probably earlier manuscript which contains a draft of a poem addressed to the King by Lady Anne Southwell, British Library Lansdowne MS 740, is important in that it suggests that her circle overlapped with that of Donne and his literary friends: this manuscript (which Helen Gardner suggests was copied out at different times by a single individual), contains sacred and secular poems written by Donne before 1610, and poems by Sir Thomas Overbury, Sir Thomas Roe, Sir John Roe, and John Hoskyns.[54] Lucy Harington, Countess of Bedford, is another extremely important woman in the milieu of Donne who may have left a single poem in circulation in this type of manuscript: the *Elegie on the Ladye Markham*

('Death, be not proud, thy hand gave not this blow': datable to 1609, and surviving in a number of miscellanies) was sometimes attributed to Donne himself, and circulates with his work, but is possibly of her composition.[55]

I will come back to Lucy Harington in a moment, but before I do, I would like to observe that the island's other court shows a similar pattern of women's involvement with court poetry in the later sixteenth century: aristocratic Scotswomen were active as both compilers and composers of verse. The Maitland Quarto,[56] a manuscript written for or partially by the daughter of the diplomat Maitland of Lethington, contains an overtly homoerotic woman's poem of which Marie Maitland herself is the most probable author.[57] At least one of the anonymous poems in the 1568 Bannatyne manuscript is by a woman: its unnamed writer was a patroness of Alexander Scott.[58] Two other identifiable women active in the court of James VI who were friendly with court poets, and had some of their verses preserved in consequence, are Christian Lindsay, patroness of Alexander Montgomerie,[59] and Elizabeth Douglas, friend or patroness of William Fouler, secretary to Queen Anne.[60]

Lucy, Countess of Bedford, one of the greatest ladies in the court of King James after the Queen herself, brings me to another point which I want to make. No one could possibly accuse the Countess of Bedford of lacking confidence. As Barbara Lewalski has suggested, we need to look elsewhere for reasons why she neither published nor publicised her verse—it is quite clear from 'Death be not proud', if indeed she wrote it, that she was a poet of some ability. To such a woman, writing was one of several means of self-expression, but if you got someone else to write for you, it was still self-expression.[61] In a hierarchical society, in which there are strong vertical relationships between writers and patrons, authorship can be thought of as *instigation*: the question of who actually strung the words together may have been considered all that material.[62] The Countess of Bedford was given considerable credit by contemporaries as the impresario of court masques; *rector chori*,[63] or Lady and Mistress of the Feast.[64]

A woman of the sixteenth century whose interactions with the written word illustrate this perception with some clarity is Mildred Cecil, née Cooke (1526–89). She and her sisters were famous in their time for their education. She married William Cecil in 1545, when he was a protégé of William Seymour, Duke of Somerset and Lord Protector.[65] After Somerset's fall and during the reign of Mary Tudor, William Cecil was as yet nothing more than a promising civil servant. During this period, some time in the 1550s (probably before 1551), Mildred

translated a Greek homily by Basil the Great, wrote it out in a fine, regular italic, and presented it to Lady Somerset, widow of Cecil's erstwhile
patron, with a humble dedication to 'yᵉ veray noble and vertuose
Duchess of Summarsid hir ryght good Lady and Mystres'.[66] This work,
existing, and probably intended to exist, in a single copy, is the product
of Mildred's learning and industry, but of the Cecils' common social
ambition.

In her middle years, after the accession of Elizabeth, and the abrupt
rise of Cecil to the top of his profession, we find Mildred engaged in
humanist exchange with a number of internationally famous poets. The
earliest piece of evidence for Mildred's changed status is the set of
poems to her by an important Low Countries humanist, Franciscus
Junius (père), preserved in a collection of state papers from 1558, the
year of Elizabeth's coronation, which suggests that she was seen as a
person worth cultivating from the very beginning of the Queen's
reign.[67] George Buchanan, the most famous contemporary Latin poet
to have been born in the British Isles, and like herself, a committed
Calvinist, was another of her correspondents, who seems actually to
have participated in a poetic exchange with her. Three poems 'Ad
Mildredam Gulielmi Cecilii uxorem matronam virtute et eruditione
praestantem' by George Buchanan (whose poems and correspondence
demonstrate his friendly acquaintance with her father, husband, sister,
and brother-in-law) make it clear that she sent him poetry of her own in
reply to his first, speculative, offering, a new-year *xenium* hinting that the
author might benefit from her taking an interest in him. His second
opens,

> Mildred, since you have sent me a poem more precious than gold,
> I rejoice continually in your wit.[68]

Her verses, if we may read between the lines of his reply, seem to have
said that she considered wealth a disease, which she might rid herself of
by sending it to Buchanan. Thus, she was writing 'great ladies' poetry',
graciously confirming that she will honour Buchanan's attention in
appropriate fashion. Buchanan's third poem in the series acknowledges
her generosity, and suggests that it might spur his Muse to greater
efforts.[69] It is unfortunate that none of the texts of Buchanan's works
preserve her verses, but all the same, they are indirect evidence for
Mildred as a writer, and direct evidence for her patronage of Buchanan,
independent of his relationship with William Cecil.

Mildred's relationship with the international humanist community
did not stop with Buchanan. The Cecils were also connected with one
of Buchanan's closest friends, Charles Utenhove of Ghent, a Protestant

who spent time in England, and who was a person of good standing at the English court.[70] Cecil himself was Utenhove's chief patron in England;[71] but an important piece of evidence for Mildred's *independent* relations with Utenhove is a letter which he wrote to Jean de Morel in 1564, from London, reporting that he had given a public lecture on Thucydides, well attended by English scholars, with Mildred Cecil as guest of honour. He then expatiates on Mildred, praising her writing in both Latin and Greek.[72]

It is clear from these interchanges with Junius, Buchanan and Utenhove, all of whom were international and well-known humanist poets and scholars, that during the reign of Elizabeth it was well worth courting Mildred Cecil separately from her husband. What we see in the writings of all three are traces of Mildred Cecil's high-profile participation in a literary world which is not merely public, but international, even though we now have so little of her actual writing. [73]

I want to focus specifically on an epigram titled 'Pro Mild. Ce.' published some years later in Utenhove's *Xenia*, an album of his court poetry (pp 69–70):

> I will do what your letter asks in anxious words,
> But the words are divorced from your actions.
> Scarcely, to you, scarcely shall I stoop to say 'Hail' to you in return,
> Whom it disgusts to say 'Farewell' in a pleasant voice.

The letter which evoked this is lost. This is apparently not a poem to Mildred: *pro* means 'on behalf of, acting for, in the place of'; if it was about, *i.e.* against her, the pronoun would be *ad* or *in*: so it was apparently something which she had asked him to write. But if Mildred Cecil wanted to send someone a disdainful Latin epigram, she was perfectly capable of writing it herself. Why get Utenhove to write on her behalf? I would suggest that people of either sex at the exalted level of Lady Burghley or the Countess of Bedford were quite as likely to ask a professional poet to compose what they wanted said as they were to ask a professional scribe to write it—as the Countess of Bedford, for example, asked Donne for an epitaph on her friend Cecilia Bulstrode before, apparently, writing one herself.

We have some direct evidence, in addition to the rather indirect evidence offered by Buchanan, that Mildred Cecil was seen as a potential patron. Utenhove's letter to Jean de Morel already mentioned, ends by saying that if Camille (his daughter) wanted to write to her, she would reply, and a most interesting and elegant correspondence would result. Camille was learned in Latin, Greek, and Hebrew, and a competent poet in the first of these languages, while Utenhove, as her tutor and a friend of the family, seems to have been trying to advance his ex-pupil in the English court.[74] Not only does he seek to interest Mildred Cecil in her, he also involved Camille in his approaches to Queen Elizabeth, publishing her Latin versions of his Hebrew and Greek poems rather than making his own, as well as sending separate poems to Elizabeth of her composition.[75]

What all this suggests is that the process by which women, or men, wrote, or perhaps, sought to publish and preserve what they wrote, is rather delicately calibrated. Mildred's own presentation manuscript made for the Duchess of Somerset was written when the Cecils were still clawing their way up. But from the beginning of the reign of Elizabeth, Cecil's vertiginous rise turned Mildred herself from client to potential patron, as we can see from the Buchanan and Utenhove interchanges, and this in turn is likely to have changed her attitude to writing.

In order to make sense of Mildred Cecil's relations with these people, we need, I think, to be aware of the kind of people they were. Jean de Morel, Utenhove and Buchanan were all members of the minor nobility (in France, Ghent and Scotland respectively), but all three were effectively of the 'noblesse de robe', which is to say that their social and financial advancement depended on their intellectual abilities. Utenhove, at least, seems to have hoped that the same might be true of Camille. It is not impossible that either Lady Burghley or the Queen might have taken up Camille de Morel.[76]

The only context in which verse by Lady Burghley actually survives is in a very remarkable manuscript in Cambridge University Library MS Ii.5.37, apparently commissioned in 1571 by her and her sisters acting as a group. We are again in a situation of vertical exchange, since the manuscript is aimed at Lord Leicester, and perhaps indirectly, at the Queen.[77] It is a stunningly beautiful piece of work, written by an extremely skilful Florentine scribe and illuminator called Petruccio Urbaldini who worked in London. In addition to the main text, the *Silvae* of Bartholo Silva, who was a Turinese doctor and surgeon resident in London, it includes Latin and Greek dedicatory verses on Silva and his work by Edward Dering, his wife Anne Locke, all four of the Cooke sisters, and an international group of male supporters.[78] Leicester was the principal supporter of Elizabethan Puritans, and it is clear from Silva's own dedicatory note 'all' illustrissimo signor . . . Roberto Dudleio, Conte di Lecestria' that he was seeking to attract Leicester's patronage. The manuscript is dated precisely 24 May 1571. It has been argued by Louise Schleiner that it was written in the hopes that Leicester might be persuaded to exert himself on behalf of Dering, who had insulted the Queen in a sermon of 1570, preached in her presence. I am inclined to wonder if the Cooke sisters' support for Dering was actually a minor feature of the project.[79] This book would have taken some time to make. Calligraphy, and probably illumination, were complete by 24 May 1571 (though the date when the book was started is unknown): Dering's changing fortunes presumably account for one of the book's interesting features, the deletion of Anne Bacon's name from her contribution, since it was her husband, Sir Nicholas Bacon, who was responsible for depriving Dering of his license to preach.[80] But, apart from the time taken for calligraphy and illumination, I would venture to suggest that if it was intended to please the Queen, it is very likely to have started off with an embroidered binding (its present binding is certainly not original), and such things also take time: therefore, it seems to me both possible that the book was begun before Dering's fall from grace—hence the inclusion within it of poetry by both Dering and his wife—and also that it was actually presented some considerable time later than May 1571, by which time Dering was, from a court viewpoint, ancient history.[81]

We might wonder, therefore, whether the principal aim of the book was to promote Bartholo Silva rather than Dering, whose fortunes may represent an incidental or secondary aspect of the project. The *Silva* (which is the subject of all the Cooke sisters' poems) and all the other commendatory poems, which in Schleiner's reading, have no obvious purpose, would thus be explicable, as would the inclusion of a portrait of the handsome young doctor himself.[82] Certainly Dr Silva, as an Italian Protestant in London, was badly in need of friends. We have no direct evidence of Mildred's patronage of the man, but Burghley himself sought to confer with Silva about Sir Francis Walsingham's illness in 1571, the same year the *Silvae* was written, suggesting that he was seen as trustworthy even by that most cautious of men.[83] In either case, the remarkable beauty of the manuscript perhaps implies the hope that Leicester, having absorbed its message, to which he was likely to be sympathetic, would then show, or give, the manuscript to Queen Elizabeth, who was not. The immense effort and investment represented by this beautiful book was intended for an audience of one, or ideally, two: it was aimed at a specific moment, to achieve a specific end, and its future thereafter was an irrelevant consideration.

Another classic example of the one-copy, presentation book is the manuscript of her own poetry presented by Jane Seager to Queen Elizabeth in 1589.[84] This little vellum manuscript is exquisitely written, and bound (by Jane Seager herself) in red velvet with gold braid and set-in *verre eglomisé* illuminations front and back, also her own work. Whatever she may have hoped to gain from this gift,[85] it is clear that it was adequately 'published', as far as its author was concerned, by existing (for all intents and purposes) in a single copy. Thus in both these cases, the making of an unique and beautiful single manuscript has everything to do with the intended function of the book, and nothing to do with considerations of whether print is inappropriately public for women.

Publication

To sum up: The distinction between a manuscript and a printed book is not a distinction between public and private writing. When women sought to publish their work, they did it for their own reasons. It is not true that all women saw publication as trespassing or intruding on the rights of men; and it is perhaps worth observing that a poem addressed by John Davies to the Countess of Bedford, the Countess of Pembroke and Elizabeth Cary, admonishes them not for their high visibility, but for their *reluctance* to publish: he complains, 'you presse the Presse with little you haue made'.[86] We have to ask ourselves, 'what public is intended?', as well as 'what is private?'—a variety of recent work by historians insists that ' "public" and "private", "outside" and "inside" the house were, in fact, terms no more easily separable than "domestic" and "political".'[87] If I may trespass again on the early seventeenth century, the literary career of Bathsua Makin, née Rainolds, is instructive in this respect. As a young girl of sixteen, Bathsua Rainolds collected together evidence for her precocious and multilingual brilliance in a printed book, *Musa Virginea Graeco-Latino-Gallica*, published in 1616 and containing poems in Latin, Greek, French, Hebrew and Italian.[88] Since this is dedicated to James VI and consists almost entirely of poems on members of the Royal Family, it seems virtually certain that she was doing so in order to attract a patron.[89] Her father wrote something very similar, a broadside of Latin poems praising James I, Charles I and Henrietta Maria, printed in 1625, the year of James's death and Charles's accession and marriage.[90] It seems probable that in 1616, Bathsua Rainolds had no court connections which would enable her to target one Stuart in particular. Print was thus an appropriate strategy; one book could be, and probably was, sent to each. In the short term, the project earned her presentation at court, and an often-quoted put-down from King James:[91]

> when a learned maid was presented to King James for an English rarity, because she could speake and rite pure Latine, Greeke and Hebrew, the King ask'd 'But can shee spin?'

In the longer term, it perhaps earned her the position of tutor to the Princess Elizabeth, though in the thick of the Civil War this was no longer worth what it might have been. Her husband, Richard Makin, whom she married in 1621, was a minor court servant in the 1620s and 30s, but then lost his place, which may explain why Bathsua herself was seeking court preferment in the 1640s.[92] The publication of *Musa Virginea* was no more transgressive or self-assertive than writing it in the first place; both were quite evidently done with the active assistance and co-operation of her father.

Bathsua Makin disappears from view in the decades in which her husband was apparently successful in keeping a roof over their heads, and emerges again only in the 1640s, perhaps as a widow. A few poems survive from this stage of her life, in both English and Latin. They are in manuscript, but it is easy to see why. She was actively seeking the patronage of Lucy Hastings, Countess Dowager of Huntingdon; and so the poems on the deaths of her two children, Lord Henry Hastings (d. 1649) and Lady Elizabeth Hastings (d. 1664) are addressed to the Countess alone, and are preserved as they were sent: as single-sheet fair copies. Her Latin poem to Sir Henry Vane was probably presented in similar form, though it survives only in a copy, in a manuscript owned by Paul and William Elyot, the nephews of Makin's friend and admirer, Sir Simonds D'Ewes, who had been one of her father's pupils.[93]

Mrs Makin's best-known work *Essay to Revive the Antient Education of Gentlewomen, in Religion, Manners, Arts & Tongues*, was published anonymously in 1673. But I do not think that the anonymity of this work indicates a lady-like shrinking from the printing press. As it is presented to students of women's history, the *Essay* is generally treated as a groundbreaking account of the glories of women's education in the past, contrasted with the regrettable academic wasteland of the present. Read with reasonable care, and in its entirety, its rhetorical strategy appears rather different. The speaking voice is male. The glories of women's education in the past are presented with a stress on the promotion of virtue and social stability. Having then depressed the reader as far as possible about the sorry state of education in the present day, the *Essay* then produces a solution: the concerned parent need have no fears, since for a mere £20 per annum, Mrs Makin is available to transform your daughter into an educated and virtuous gentlewoman. It seems to me that to read this as a disinterested study of women's educational opportunities over time is perverse: this is an advertisement. It argues a need, explains the background, denies the existence of any alternatives, and makes a pitch.[94] Anonymity is a vital part of the writing strategy since it is obviously essential that it appear that the essay was written by absolutely anyone except Mrs Makin herself. The conclusion which I would draw from Bathsua Makin's use of print or manuscript for her work, none of which can be described as private, is that whether she published or presented a handwritten copy, and whether she signed it, depended on who she was writing to and why. When we look at other works by women, they often tell similar stories.[95]

We distinguish sharply between script and print, but the idea that printed books were essentially different from manuscripts is one which not all sixteenth-century authors would have recognised.[96] As Marotti has recently pointed out, although print encouraged the notion of an authorised text (with or without the cooperation of actual authors), texts remained malleable.[97] With small print runs,[98] and an enormous amount of handwork involved anyway, printed books could be personalised in a variety of ways. Most obviously, a dedicatory poem could be added in manuscript, as Elizabeth Jane Weston does to the copy of *Parthenicon* now in the British Library (C 61 d 2, second flysheet r & v).[99] This is a particularly interesting example, since unusually, it is not a poem flattering the recipient (who is not named) so much as one blowing off steam about her editor Martin von Baldhoven, who as she sees it, has combined high-handedness with incompetence: I give the poem in my translation.

AD LECTOREM ('To the Reader')

Everything you see, Reader, in the little book before you
　　is published under my name.
I do not conceal that I have written; there is another reason
　　why I did not want to see these things committed to type:
Everything is incredibly jumbled together, with no order
　　and linked to the *Parthenicon*, which I gave out when newly married.
Here, there and everywhere, they are full of printers' errors
　　(and I fear idle malice will attribute them to me).
An un-friend, trusting I know not whom, at his own whim
　　has filled my pages, without justification.
In this book, there is superadded a series of learned Poets
　　which, while free, are also superfluous.
You must realise many of my poems have been left out:
　　you will find others' poems randomly mixed up with mine.
Do you want, I ask, a book of the days of Westonia
　　you, who have scarcely allotted any space *to* Westonia?
It would have been better to earn proper praises for an intact book
　　which we could both worthily have rejoiced in.
Since you have linked these poems with a woman's minor works
　　great things are diminished by contact with lesser.

However, I will not delay the Reader, if he takes the negative
  away from me, and reads the positive, with an open mind.
A time will come when without you (if Fate permits)
  the page will be filled up with Westonia's own poems.

Authorial intervention to create special copies could also take place
actually at the printing works. Two of the surviving copies of the
Countess of Falkland's *The Tragedie of Mariam* have a leaf (A 1) of dedicatory verse addressed to 'my worthye sister Mistris Elizabeth Carye'.
This leaf was subsequently cancelled (e.g. in the BL copy) and probably
only the presentation copies were issued with it.[100] In the case of this
particular work, it is only the dedicatory poem which gives away the
author's identity (the title-page has 'E.C.'). Similarly, the copy of
Aemilia Lanyer's *Salve, Rex Iudaeorum* which was given to Prince Henry
was 'tailored' for its recipient: the poem praising the family embarrass-
ment, his cousin Arbella Stuart, is omitted.[101] Men also did such things:
for example, a few copies of Owen Felltham's *Resolves*, 1661, were made
with his Form of Prayer included on a final gathering, which was then
cancelled and the rest printed without it.[102] I would conclude that
women's use of both print and manuscript, like men's, was flexible, and
reflects not so much a greater or lesser degree of authorial confidence,
but an accurate sense of the socially appropriate channel through which
to reach the intended audience.

NOTES

1 I would personally include monumental verse (such as that of Elizabeth Russell) as
   a form of publication, since it is undoubtedly *evulgatur*.
2 Sir John Harington, *Nugae Antiquae: Being a Miscellaneous Collection of Original Papers in
   Prose and Verse*, ed. Henry Harington, 2 vols (London, 1769), I, 58 [text pp. 58–59].
3 'Tablets' or a 'table book' could denote an unbound notebook, a pocket book, a
   kind of waxed writing pad from which entries could be easily erased, a more formal repository for original compositions, or even a drawing book: there is evidence
   for all these usages. See Peter Beal, 'Notions in Garrison: The Seventeenth-
   Century Commonplace Book', in *New Ways of Looking at Old Texts*, ed. W. Speed
   Hill (Binghamton, NY, 1993), pp. 131–47 (p. 132).
4 A few loose sheets of what do seem to be private papers of Elizabeth's survive: a
   partially-preserved early draft of a long, religious poem in French, kept among the
   Cecil papers at Hatfield, written in a swift, illegible scrawl with many crossings-out,
   missing the first page (Hatfield House, Cecil Papers 147, nos. 150–4, ff. 207–14).
   Burghley may perhaps have acquired it as a clue to his mistress's state of mind: the
   preservation of such rough draft is most unusual, and may be unique.
5 We have one such that I am fairly sure of from the early seventeenth century, a
   poem by Battina Cromwell, daughter of Sir Horatio Palavicino (1595/8–1618):
   'Verces made by Mrs Battina Cromwell wife to Henry Cromwell esq. S[r] Oliver

Cromwell's sone'. This is in *A Booke of severall devotions collected from good men by the worst of sinners, Anna Cromwell, 1656*, London, British Library Harley MS 2311, f. 21r–v, a personal notebook containing family material collected in the middle of the seventeenth century. This is the earliest woman's verse of this type I know of, and it does not survive in her autograph but in a private book of two generations later.

6 *The Life and Illustrious Martyrdom of Sir Thomas More*, trs. Philip E. Hallett, ed. E.E. Reynolds (London, 1966), pp. 103–4, 106–17.

7 E.M.G. Routh, *Sir Thomas More and his Friends 1477–1535* (London, 1934), pp. 133–4.

8 The quotation is from William Rastell's dedication to his edition of More's English works, *The Works of Sir Thomas More, Knyght*, (London, 1557), sig. Cii.

9 Roger Ascham, *Whole Works*, ed. J.A. Giles, 3 vols (London, 1864–5), I, ep. 166, to Mary Basset: 'Your remarkable love of virtue and zeal for learning, most illustrious lady, joined with such talent and perseverance, are worthy of great praise . . . It was I who was invited (by your mother Margaret Roper (in the house of your kinsman Lord Giles Alington, to teach you and her other children the Greek and Latin tongues, but at that time no offer could induce me to leave the University (you have (the aid of those two learned men, Cole and Christopherson, so that you need no help from me'. See also Maria Dowling, *Humanism in the Age of Henry VIII* (Beckenham, 1986), p. 222.

10 The Lady Abbess of St Scholastica's Abbey, Teignmouth, 'Abbess Neville's annals of five communities of English Benedictine nuns in Flanders, 1598–1687, *Catholic Record Society Miscellanea 5*, vol. 6 (London, 1909), pp. 1–72 (p. 12).

11 Elizabeth McCutcheon, 'Life and Letters: Editing the writing of Margaret More Roper', in *New Ways of Looking at Old Texts* (1993), pp. 111–17. By contrast, such More memorabilia as his hair shirt and the beaker he habitually drank from were kept, at considerable risk.

12 Gervase Holles, *Memorials of the Holles Family*, ed. A.C. Wood, Camden Society 3rd ser. 55 (1937), p. 219. Elizabeth Holles's mother, incidentally, was also an educated woman, who had been taught by the wife of John Stanhope, Archbishop of York.

13 Edited by Robert C. Evans and Barbara Wiedemann, *'My Name was Martha': A Renaissance Woman's Autobiographical Poem* (West Cornwall, Conn., 1993). See also Ann Depas-Orange and Robert C. Evans, eds, *'The Birthday of my Self: Martha Moulsworth, Renaissance Poet, Critical Matrix* (Princeton, 1996), and Robert C. Evans, *'The Muses Female Are': Martha Moulsworth and other woman writers of the English Renaissance*, Locust Hill Literary Studies 20 (West Cornwall, Conn., 1996).

14 Giles Dawson and Laetitia Kennedy-Skipton, *Elizabethan Handwriting, 1500–1650* (New York, 1966), p. 7.

15 For example, a poem of the Countess of Pembroke's was discovered by Samuel Woodford among books bought as wrapping paper by a coffee-merchant: see *The Triumph of Death and Other Unpublished and Uncollected Poems*, ed. Gary Waller (Salzburg, 1977), p. 24.

16 Dennis Kay, for example, has asserted that '*any* educated person in the sixty years leading up to the English Civil War is liable to have written verses of some kind': 'Poems by Sir Walter Aston and a date for the Donne/Goodyer verse epistle *Alternis Vicibus*', *Review of English Studies*, NS 37 (1986), p. 198. While Kay may be using 'person' as a synonym for 'man', as it happens, the survival of quantities of private papers from the Aston family itself strongly suggests a common culture between men and women, at least in this circle of provincial Recusant gentlefolk: see Jenijoy La Belle, 'The Huntington Aston Manuscript', *The Book Collector*, 29 (1980), 542–67.

17 BL Add. MS 15277, f. 28r, cited in Arthur F. Marotti, *Manuscript Print, and the English*

Renaissance Lyric (Ithaca, NY, 1995), p. 166. Thomas Whythorne records a similar use of rhyme to discourage an unwanted suitor: when he took to wearing hops in his hat (to indicate 'hope'), the woman he had in view responded with the rhyme, 'The suds of soap/Shall wash your hope'. Incidentally, this may not have been original: it occurs in an unpublished poem of about the same date; on f. 21 of the Braye Lute Book, in New Haven, Yale, Osborn Collection, Box 22, no. 10: *The Autobiography of Thomas Whythorne*, ed. J.M. Osborne (London, 1962), p. 41 (I quote the modern spelling edition of this text, since Whythorne's spelling is phonetic, and idiosyncratic in the extreme).

18 *A Hundred Sundrie Flowres bounde up in one small Poesie* (London, 1573). The first of these is on pp. 304–5, the second, from which I quote, is on pp. 307–10.

19 Arthur F. Marotti, *John Donne: Coterie Poet* (Madison & London, 1986), p. 10, comments: 'whether or not the poems Gascoigne included in his collection were ever part of the contexts he constructed for them, the act of social-narrative articulation in which he engaged is found, in shorter or longer form, in prose works like his own novella "A discourse of the adventures passed by Master F.J.", Sidney's *Arcadia*, and Thomas Whythorne's *Autobiography* as well as in a miscellany like Tottel's'.

20 *Autobiography*, p. 22.

21 *Autobiography*, p. 28.

22 *Autobiography*, p. 33.

23 Satirists by definition exaggerate, but perhaps we should note the complaint of Robert Anton:

> And I much wonder that this *lustie time*,
> That women can both *sing* and *sigh* in rime,
> *Weepe* and *dissemble* both in *baudie meetre*,
> Laugh in luxurious pamphlets . . .

Robert Anton, *The Philosophers Satyrs* (London, 1616), p. 52.

24 As Suzanne W. Hull's well-known work implies: *Chaste, Silent and Obedient: English Books for Women, 1475–1640* (San Marino, Ca., 1982).

25 Virginia F. Stern, *Gabriel Harvey: His Life, Marginalia and Library*, (Oxford, 1979), pp. 5–7. John Harvey (Gabriel's father) was a ropemaker, but a man of substantial property.

26 Stern, *Gabriel Harvey*, pp. 35–38.

27 London, BL Sloane MS 93, transcribed and printed by E.J.L Scott as *The Letter-Book of Gabriel Harvey, AD 1573–1580*, Camden Society, 1884.

28 Laura Gowing, *Domestic Dangers: Women, Words and Sex in Early Modern London* (Oxford, 1996), outlines the readiness of anyone disputing *anything* with a woman—or even with other members of her family—to drag in her sexual reputation; see particularly pp. 62–67. This can be directly illustrated with reference to the Harvey family, since Harvey's enmity with Thomas Nashe exposed his sister Mary to libel: in *Have with You to Saffron-Walden*, 1596 (*Works*, ed. R.B. McKerrow, 3 vols, London, 1904, III, 129), he gleefully reports, 'I will not present into the Arches or Commissaries Court what prinkum prankums Gentlemen (his nere neighbors) have whispred to me of his Sister, and how shee is as good a fellow as ever turned belly to belly; for which she is not to be blam'd, but I rather pitie her and thinke she cannot do withall, having no other dowrie to marie her . . . ' It is hard to believe that Harvey would have risked adding to the stock of damaging gossip apparently in circulation about his sister: it is plausible, however, that he might make a memorandum of what he believed to be the facts.

29 In this, she has probably put herself in the wrong, as Gowing makes plain: 'gifts operated as a form of communication in courtship, so that the occasion as well as the nature of the token furnished its significance. But that significance was potentially ambiguous, and at court, women and men fought carefully over the exact implications of every transaction in which they had taken part' (*Domestic Dangers*, p. 159). See also Diana O'Hara, ' "Ruled by my Friends": Aspects of Marriage in the Diocese of Canterbury, c.1540–c.1570', *Continuity and Change*, 6/1 (1991), 9–41.

30 *The Letter-Book*, f. 74r, Scott, p. 147.

31 *The Letter-Book*, f. 78r, Scott, p. 151.

32 *The Letter-Book*, f. 80r–v, Scott, pp. 154–5.

33 '[She] prommisd to speake with him on sutch a day, at sutch a neighbours house . . . Milord stud reddie in a litle parlour in his dublet and his hose, his points untrust, and his shirt lying out round about him. And after a short salutation, and a twoe or thre kisses would needs have laid ye maide on ye bed. The maide would none of that, but bad him fie for shame, and so by struggeling shiftid as well as she might.' *The Letter-Book*, f. 78v, Scott, p. 152.

34 She exploits very cleverly her own absence of privacy. Even in the instance above, when Howard had organised a private room for their assignation, she made a counter-arrangement with 'the good wife of ye howse' that if she was not out in a minute or two, the woman was to hammer on the door and call out that Marie's mother had sent for her ('whereuppon mi yung lord fill to swaring').

35 This is not the only early-sixteenth-century anthology in which women can be seen to participate. Oxford, Bodleian MS Rawlinson C 813, recently edited as *The Welles Anthology: MS Rawlinson C 813, A Critical Edition*, by Sharon L. Jansen and Kathleen H. Jordan (Binghamton, NY, 1991), contains anonymous poems by women. Another which contains at least one woman's poem is British Library Cotton MS Vespasian A.25, edited as *Tudor Songs and Ballads from MS Cotton Vespasian A 25* by Peter J. Seng (Cambridge, Mass., 1978).

36 Kenneth Muir, 'Unpublished Poems in the Devonshire Manuscript', *Proceedings of the Leeds Philosophical Society*, 6 (1947), No. 12, p. 264, No. 37, p. 276, No. 42, p. 277.

37 The hands are discussed by R. Southall, 'The Devonshire Manuscript Collection of Early Tudor Poetry, 1532–41', *Review of English Studies*, NS 15 (1964), 142–50; by Marotti, *Manuscript*, pp. 38–39, and more recently by Helen Baron, 'Mary (Howard) Fitzroy's hand in the Devonshire Manuscript', *Review of English Studies*, NS 45 (1994), 318–35.

38 'Aunswere': ['Of few wourdes sr you seme to be'], BL Egerton MS 2711, f. 24v, Dublin, Trinity College MS 160 (the Blage MS), f. 128r. The Blage MS is discussed by Helen Baron, 'The 'Blage' Manuscript: The original compiler identified', *English Manuscript Studies*, 1 (1989), 85–119

39 Her brother, Thomas Boleyn, was a recognised court poet: see *Tottel's Miscellany*, ed. H.E. Rollins (Cambridge, Mass., 1965), II, 83. On Anne's culture, see Dowling, *Humanism*, pp. 231–2.

40 BL Add. MS 15117, f. 3v, Add. MSS 18936–9, f. 70v, Add. MSS 10480–4, f. 37r. None of these manuscripts attribute the poem to the Queen: the attribution is found in William Chappell, *Old English Popular Music*, rev. ed. H.E. Wooldridge, 2 vols (London, 1893), I, 111, on unstated grounds. The line 'Oh death rock me asleepe' is quoted in a pornographic poem, *A Choice of Valentines*, by Thomas Nashe: see David O. Frantz, *Festum voluptatis: A Study of Renaissance Erotica* (Columbus, 1989), p. 196.

41 Peter Beal, 'Notions in Garrison', p. 133.

42 Marotti, *John Donne*, p. 19. Gentleman poets of the same kind include John Hoskyns and Sir John Roe.

43 A manuscript which has been recently discussed by Henry Woudhuysen, in his *Sir Philip Sidney and the Circulation of Manuscripts, 1550–1640* (Oxford, 1996), pp. 278–86.

44 Of which there is a text in BL Add. MS 38823, f. 30.

45 Steven W. May, 'Manuscript Circulation at the Elizabethan Court', in *New Ways of Looking at Old Texts*, ed. Speed Hill (1993), pp. 273–80 (p. 276), and Steven W. May, 'The French Primero: A Study in Renaissance Textual Transmission and Taste', *English Language Notes*, 9 (1971), 102–8.

46 BL Harley MS 6910, f. 145, 'finis qd La. B. to N'; Oxford, Bodleian Library MS Rawl. Poet. 85, f. 17; MS Rawl. Poet. 172, f. 5v (Crum T2362), discussed in L. G. Black, *Studies in Some Related Manuscript Poetic Miscellanies of the 1580s* (Oxford D.Phil, 1971).

47 Washington, D.C., Folger Shakespeare Library MS V.a.89. See William H. Bond, 'The Cornwallis-Lysons Manuscript and the Poems of John Bentley', in *Joseph Quincy Adams Memorial Studies*, ed. James G. McManaway, Giles E. Dawson, and Edwin E. Willoughby (Washington, D.C., 1948), pp. 683–93. Anne Cornwallis was daughter of Sir William Cornwallis and later wife to the seventh Earl of Argyll.

48 Marotti, *Manuscript*, p. 58, has a transcription of the Folger text. It is edited by Laurence Cummings, 'John Finet's Miscellany' (PhD Diss. Washington University, 1960) using 6 manuscripts: since the Finet MS dates from the 1580s it cannot be written later than this. Conversely, Cummings suggests (p. 225) that there are elements in the poem that conflict with the circumstances of Vavasour's life, though I see it as compatible with what we know of her.

49 E.K. Chambers, *Sir Henry Lee: An Elizabethan Portrait* (Oxford, 1936), p. 132.

50 From Bodleian Library MS Rawl. poet. 85, f. 17: a text to trust, since it is early (1588/90: within eight years or so of the poem's being written), and contains a group of five poems associated with the Earl of Oxford; with a couple of *varia* from Washington, D.C., Folger MS V. a. 89.
Folger MS V. a. 89 subscribes it *vavaser*.
BL Harley MS 6910 subscribes it 'qᵈ La. B. to N.'
BL Harley MS 7392, a shortened text, is subscribed 'Ball', perhaps for 'ballad'.

51 See, for example, Josephine A. Roberts, 'The Imaginary Epistles of Sir Philip Sidney and Lady Penelope Rich', *English Literary Renaissance*, 15 (1985), 59–77 (from Bodleian Library MS Eng. poet. f. 9, owned by Henry Champernowne).

52 We might note here that Henry King's sister Anne (1621–after 1671) wrote poetry which is preserved in Bodleian Library MS Rawlinson D. 398, f. 235 (a King family manuscript) and also in other contemporary miscellanies.

53 Folger MS V.b.198, edited as *The Southwell-Sibthorpe Commonplace Book*, by Jean Klene (Tempe, Arizona, 1997). Prose contents include a list of her belongings, her accounts for the house she rented in Acton, a mini-bestiary, scriptural and doctrinal commentary, and a collection of apothegms. See also the article by Jean Klene below.

54 *To the kinges most excellent Maᵗʸᵉ* ('Darest thou my muse present thy Battlike winge'), Klene, pp. 124–5. On the MS, see H.J.C. Grierson, *The Poems of John Donne* (Oxford, 1912), II, civ–v; Helen Gardner, *The Elegies and The Songs and Sonnets* (Oxford, 1965), pp. lxviii–ix.

55 Bodleian Library MS Rawl. Poet. 31, f. 39, which titles it 'Elegie on the Ladye Markham by L.C. of B.': see discussion in R.C. Bald, *John Donne: A Life* (New York & Oxford, 1970), p. 179; Marotti, *John Donne*; Claude Summers, 'Donne's 1609 Sequence of Grief and Comfort', *Studies in Philology*, 89 (1992), 211–31.

B.K. Lewalski, 'Lucy, countess of Bedford: Images of a Jacobean Courtier and Patroness', in *Politics of Discourse*, ed. Sharpe & Zwicker, pp. 52–77.

56 Cambridge, Magdalene College, Pepys Library MS 2253, ff. 78b–79b. *The Maitland Quarto Manuscript*, ed. W.A. Craigie, Scottish Text Society, NS 9 (Edinburgh & London, 1920), pp. 160–2 (No. xlix). The MS was written either by or for Marie Maitland. The bulk of the MS is written in two styles, 'a small but clear form of the old Scottish hand', and a large Italic lettering. As Marotti has pointed out (*Manuscript*, pp. 25–26), sixteenth-century women almost invariably used italic rather than secretary script: it is therefore possible that the italic hand is that of Marie Maitland.

57 There is an article on this poem by J. Farnsworth, 'Voicing Female Desire in "Poem XLIX" ' *Studies in English Literature*, 36 (1984), 57–72. A poem to her, 'To your self' (f. 126, p. 257), makes considerable claims for Maitland as a poet: stanza 1 is about Sappho, stanza 2 about the Renaissance Latin poet Olimpia Morata, stanza 3 puts 'Maistres Marie' in their illustrious company. This perhaps strengthens the attribution of 'As phoebus in his spheris hicht' to her, and conceivably, other anonymous poetry in this MS: No. lxxi, f. 116, p. 235, 'gif faithfulnes ζe find' might be another contender.

58 *The Bannatyne Manuscript, written in Tyme of Pest, 1568*, by George Bannatyne, f. 228a, ed. W. Tod Ritchie, 5 vols, Scottish Text Society (Edinburgh & London, 1934), IV, 293–4. There is an answer to this poem by the poet Alexander Scott in the same manuscript, (ff. 235b–36a), notably respectful in tone, in a way which suggests a reply to a patroness rather than a lover.

59 In *The Poems of Alexander Montgomerie*, ed. James Cranstoun, Scottish Text Society (Edinburgh & London, 1887), No. xxx. Christian Lindsay was part of a circle of court poets active in Scotland 1583–86, known as 'the Castalian Band'. Robert Hudson, on whose behalf she writes, was a musician and poet, 'court violar': see Helena M. Shire, *Song, Dance and Poetry of the Court of Scotland under King James VI* (London, 1969), p. 97. She appears in a poem by James VI, complaining that Montgomerie has given Christian grounds for her accusation that 'poets lie':

> Not yett woulde ye not call to memorie
> What grounde ye gave to Christian Lindsay by it
> For now she sayes, which makes us all full sorie
> Your craft to lie; with leave, now have I tried.

Another sonnet of Montgomerie's from 1580–86, addressing Robert Hudson, court violar, says:

> Ye can pen out tua cuple and ye pleis
> Yourself and I, old Scot and Robert Semple
> Quhen we are deid, that all our dayis bot daffis
> Let Christian Lyndesay wryte our epitaphis.

(*Montgomerie*, ed. Cranstoun, p. 101, sonnet xxv). This last suggests that Edinburgh poets regarded her as part of their circle, but did not take her verse seriously.

60 Edinburgh, National Library of Scotland, MS 2065, f. 4r–v. *The Works of William Fouler, Secretary to Queen Anne, wife of James VI*, ed. H.W. Meikle, Scottish Text Society (Edinburgh & London, 1914–40), I, 19. On p. 9 of the same volume is William Fouler's funeral sonnet, giving her full name as 'Elizabeth Dovvglas, spouse to M. Samuel Cobvvrne, Laird of Temple-Hall'.

61 As Lewalski argues in her 'Lucy, Countess of Bedford'.

62 Henry Woudhuysen has suggested that the literary career of Henry Howard, Earl of Northampton, illustrates something important about sixteenth-century aristocrats' attitude to writing. Howard used manuscript books through the first part of his life as gifts, and to try and advance his career. From 1600 onwards, once his position at court was established, he stopped producing texts, the flow was reversed, and a rich procession of dedications came his way: *Sir Philip Sidney*, p. 102. This suggests that the Countess of Bedford's attitude to her own writing had more to do with her class than with her gender.

63 Samuel Daniel describes her thus with respect to the Christmas masque of 1604: *i.e.* leader of the (women) masquers; the Duke of Lennox led the men. Andrew Sabol notes in *Four Hundred Songs and Dances from the Stuart Masques* (Providence, RI, 1978), pp. 231, 580, that a musical score for one of the dances from this masque, in BL Add. MS 10444, ff. 39r, 89v, is titled 'The Lady Lucies Masque' in reference to her role as *rector chori*.

64 John Chamberlain, with reference to Jonson's *Lovers Made Men*, in *The Letters of John Chamberlain*, ed. N.E. McClure, 2 vols (Philadelphia, 1939), II, 55.

65 Conyers Read, *Mr Secretary Cecil and Queen Elizabeth* (London, 1955), p. 34: 'the marriage of William Cecil to Mildred Cooke was fraught with political and religious significance . . . a group of significant public figures [were] drawn together into a family alliance, the catalytic being the Cooke sisters and the nucleus the Cecils'.

66 BL Royal MS 17 B. XVIII, f. IV.

67 London, Public Record Office, SP 12/47, ff. 14–20. Three poems to Cecil complain that the Queen is refusing to listen to him, and stress the urgency of his suit, which Cecil is asked to expedite. But there are also two poems to Mildred herself (ff. 17–18), the first of which begs her to soften her husband's heart, while the second flatters her as a second Sappho.

68 *Georgii Buchanani Scoti Poemata* (Amsterdam, 1687), pp. 395–6.

69 I.D. MacFarlane, *Buchanan* (London, 1981), p. 329:

> Quod Mildreda mihi carmen pretiosus auro
> Miseris, ingenio gratulor usque tuo.   .

70 Where he had a number of friends such as Daniel Rogers and Sir Philip Sidney. Utenhove was a Protestant, though of a notably liberal and humanist variety. He had London connections, since his uncle Jan was the pastor of the Dutch church in London, and he had a number of friends in the London Dutch community: see Leonard Foster, *Janus Gruter's English Years* (Leiden, 1967), pp. 44–48, and J.H. Hessels (ed.), *Ecclesiae Londino-Batavae Archivum* (Cambridge, 1887).

71 Which may also account for the link between the Cecils and Buchanan: MacFarlane, *Buchanan*, pp. 226–7.

72 Preserved in Munich, Staatsbibliothek Clm 10384, f. 206 (a copy). Mildred began learning Greek from her father and from Giles Lawrence of Christ Church, Oxford: see Retha M. Warnicke, *Women of the English Renaissance and Reformation* (Westport, Con., 1983), p. 105.

73 Jan van Dorsten, 'Mr Secretary Cecil: Patron of Letters', in his *The Anglo-Dutch Renaissance: Seven Essays* (Leiden, 1988), pp. 28–37 (p. 31): 'Unlike Dudley, [Cecil] was a scholar, a lover of books, and a man of great intellectual curiosity. He and his wife Mildred . . . had their children tutored to a high degree of erudition, and in their house Classical studies, philosophy and science, and at least certain kinds of poetry and music could seek refuge. *Indeed, Cecil House was England's nearest equivalent to a humanist salon since the days of More*' (my italics).

74 Camille de Morel's life and achievements are outlined by M. Gerard Davis, 'A Humanist Family in the Sixteenth Century', in *The French Mind: Studies in Honour of Gustave Rudler*, ed. W. Moore *et al.* (Oxford, 1952), pp. 1–16.

75 *Caroli Utenhovii F. patricii Gandavensis XENIA seu ad illustrium aliquot Europae hominum nomina, Allusionum (intertextis alicubi Ioach. Bellaii eiusdem arumenti versibus), liber primus* (Basel, 1568) This work is dedicated 'Ad Elizabetham Sereniss. Angl. Franc. Hib. &c. Reginam', and Camille de Morel's poem to Queen Elizabeth is on pp. 15–16.

76 Elizabeth, had she married, might have wanted a tutor for a princess (as Princess Eleanor of Prussia, for example, asked Utenhove's multilingual adopted daughter Anna Utenhovia to join her household in 1591 as French tutor to her daughters), and she employed one or two foreign women as ladies in waiting, e.g. the Swedish Helena Snakenborg, and the Belgian Mary Yetswiert. Mildred might also have wanted a tutor for daughters or wards at some stage of her life.

77 Louise Schleiner, *Tudor and Stuart Woman Writers* (Bloomington & Indianapolis, 1994), p. 40, suggests that 'the book was to be an intellectual and visual treat for Leicester and the Queen . . . the whole thing was calculated to please the Queen. She loved Italian things in general, and handsome, learned young Italian men in particular.'

78 The other writers of commendatory verse are Petrus Bizarus, Carolus Rogerius, Diego Ximines, George Stanley, and Pierre Penna.

79 It is probable that they did support Dering, whose religious views were similar to their own: Patrick Collinson, *A Mirror of Elizabethan Puritanism: the Life and Letters of Godly Master Dering* (London, 1964), shows a close relationship between Dering and Katherine Killigrew in particular. But this seems to me a subsidiary, not a principal concern of the volume.

80 Schleiner, *Tudor and Stuart Women*, p. 42.

81 Elizabeth was noted as a connoisseur of embroidered bindings, and amassed a notable collection, though from the time of Henry VIII onwards books presented to the ruler (whether male or female) were often decorated in this way: see Cyril Davenport, *English Embroidered Bookbindings* (London, 1899), esp. pp. 57–65. Davenport points out that such bindings have to be precisely fitted to the book, so cannot be undertaken until the book itself exists.

82 This, incidentally, is a hand-coloured engraving, very carefully tipped in, and almost undetectable, suggesting, perhaps, a strong desire for an accurate likeness (p. iv)

83 John Strype, *Annals of the Reformation* (Oxford, 1824), II, 119.

84 BL Add. MS 10037. She may perhaps have been a connection of Sir William Segar, Garter King at Arms, scribe, limner and calligrapher: Henry Woudhuysen, *Sir Philip Sidney*, pp. 58, 74, suggests she was his daughter, since her hand is identical to his.

85 Its intended purpose is perhaps related to its strangest feature: it is a parallel text with Segar's poems written in italic on the verso pages, and in an early form of shorthand invented by Timothe Bright on the facing recto. Why Jane Segar wished to publicise Bright's 'characterie' we can only guess. Bright's *Characterie: an Arte of Shorte, Swifte, and secrete writing by Character*, had appeared (dedicated to Queen Elizabeth) thirty years previously, in 1558. The manuscript is discussed by Werner Kramer, 'Zur englischen Kurzschrift im Zeitalter Shakespeares. Das Jane-Seager-Manuskript', *Shakespeare Jahrbuch*, 67 (1931), 26–61.

86 *The Muses Sacrifice* (1612), in *The Complete Works of John Davies*, ed. Alexander B. Grosart, 2 vols (Edinburgh, 1878), II, 1, line 4.

87 Gowing, *Domestic Dangers*, p. 26. See further David Cressy, 'Response: Private Lives, Public Performance, and Rites of Passage', in *Attending to Women in Early Modern England*, ed. Betty S. Travitsky and Adele F. Seeff (Newark, 1994), pp. 187–97 (p. 187): 'I propose to argue . . . that all life was public in early modern England, or at least had public, social or communal dimensions.'

88 This extremely rare book (there is a copy in Cambridge University Library) is forthcoming in facsimile, in *Neo-Latin Women Writers: Elizabeth Jane Weston and Bathsua Reginald [Makin]*, ed. Donald Cheney (Ashgate, 1999).

89 Bathsua's book is addressed to James I, and also includes poems to his queen, Anne of Denmark, his son Charles (later Charles I), and the Elector Palatine, his son in law.

90 STC 20840.

91 The Commonplace Book of John Collet, 1633 (BL Add. MS 3890), quoted in W.J. Thoms, *Anecdotes and Traditions Illustrative of Early English History and Literature*, Camden Society (London, 1839), p. 129.

92 Biographical details are from Francis Teague, 'The Identity of Bathsua Makin', *Biography*, 16.1 (1993), 1–17, and Jean R. Brink, 'Bathsua Rainolds Makin: "Most Learned Matron" ', *Harvard Language Quarterly*, 54 (1991), 313–26.

93 Bodleian Library Rawlinson MS poet. 116: Mary Hobbs, *Early Seventeenth-Century Verse Miscellany Manuscripts* (Aldershot, 1992), p. 2.

94 Compare an almost contemporary book: Edward Chamberlayne, *An Academy, or College, wherein Young Ladies and Gentlewomen may at a very moderate expence be educated in the true Protestant religion and in all virtuous qualities that may adorn that sex* (London, 1671): a different prescription for feminine perfection, but in itself, a very similar text. Note also that, as Peter Beal points out to me, Sarah Jinner's almanac praising women's achievements, *An Almanack or prognostication for the year of our Lord 1658*, adopts a similar strategy to that of Bathsua Makin: see his *In Praise of Scribes* (Oxford, 1998), pp. 151–3.

95 See, for example, Beal's very full account in *In Praise of Scribes* of Katherine Philips' strategies for the dissemination of her work (pp. 147–91).

96 This point is made by John Pitcher, 'Editing Daniel', in *New Ways of Looking at Old Texts*, pp. 57–73 (p. 61). See also A.F. Marotti, 'Malleable and Fixed Texts: Manuscript and printed miscellanies and the transmission of lyric poetry in the English Renaissance', in *ibid.*, pp. 159–73 (p. 170).

97 Marotti, 'Malleable and Fixed Texts', p. 161.

98 There is little direct evidence for the size of print runs. The Stationers' Company set a ceiling of 1,250, but there is some evidence for runs of as few as forty-five, and even this may not represent the lowest figure in the case of very modest books or pamphlets. See Rudolf Hirsch, *Printing, Selling and Reading, 1450–1550* (Wiesbaden, 1967), p. 126. John Dee's *General and Rare Memorials Pertaining to the Art of Navigation*, a handsome folio with an elaborate iconographic title-page, was printed in 1577 in a run of only 100 copies: Marjorie Plant, *The English Book Trade* (London, 1939), p. 93.

99 Compare Paul Melissus (a friend of Weston's), flyleaf autograph signed poem to George Gilpin, 'Reginae Angliae ad Imp. Rudolphum II legato, viro integro' in the BL copy of his *Ode Pindarica ad serenissimum potentissimumque dominam Elizabetham Britanniae, Franciae, Hiberniaeque reginam* (Vienna, 1578). A generation later, Elizabeth Cary, Lady Falkland, added a handwritten dedicatory sonnet to Queen Henrietta Maria to her published translation of the works of Cardinal Perron (this copy is now in the Beinecke Library, Yale).

100 The Harvard and Huntington copies have the extra leaf: see Samuel Halkett and Catherine Laing, *Dictionary of Anonymous and Pseudonymous Publications in the English Language, 1475–1644*, revised ed. by John Horden (London, 1980), p. 197 (T126).

101 London, National Art Library, Victoria and Albert Museum, Dyce 4to 5675. B.K. Lewalski, 'Of God and Good Women: The Poems of Aemilia Lanyer', in *Silent but for the Word: Tudor Women as Patrons, Translators, and Writers of Religious Works*, ed. M.P. Hannay (Kent, Ohio, 1985), pp. 203–24, note 6, p. 284, observes that the British Library copy was also tailored: she suggests for the Countess of Cumberland or the Countess of Dorset.

102 T.-L. Pebworth, 'An Anglican family worship service', *English Literary Renaissance*, 16 (1986), pp. 206–33 (p. 206).

Princess Elizabeth's Hand in
The Glass of the Sinful Soul

Frances Teague

When she was eleven years old, the Princess Elizabeth gave her step-mother, Katherine Parr, a small book as a New Year's gift: *The Glass of the Sinful Soul*.[1] The book is Elizabeth's handwritten prose translation of a French religious poem by Marguerite de Navarre, *Miroir de l'âme pécheresse* (1531), bound in a carefully embroidered cover, which Elizabeth also prepared. As monarch, Elizabeth I was, quite rightly, proud of her learning, and this 1544 work establishes her early interest in translation.

The manuscript presents a work self-consciously in process. In a dedicatory letter, the Princess Elizabeth acknowledges the work's imperfections when she writes to Katherine Parr (folio 3v–4r):

> And althoughe i knowe yᵗ as for my parte, wich i haue wrought in it: ~~the~~ (as well spirituall, as manuall) there is nothinge done as it shulde be nor els worthy to come in youre graces handes, but rather all vnperfytte and vncorecte: yet, do i truste also that aubeit it is like a worke wich is but newe begonne and shapen: yᵗ the syle of youre excellent witte and godly lerninge in the redinge of it (if so it vouchesafe your highnes to do) shall rubbe out, polishe, and mende (or els cause to mende) the wordes (or rather the order of my writting) the wich i knowe in many places to be rude, and nothinge done as it shuld be.

To some extent, this passage makes a conventional claim of modesty about her accomplishment, but throughout the manuscript Elizabeth crosses out, inserts, and corrects words, all changes suggesting that she did regard the work as incompletely done when she presented it to her stepmother.

In the first part of the manuscript, however, she works with great care. Anne Lake Prescott notes that 'The first 145 lines have, so far as I can tell, no serious errors or omissions . . . . At first glance Elizabeth's manuscript is neat and her handwriting pretty, but in fact the pages, especially in the second half, have some cancellations and corrections'.[2] One can reasonably argue that Princess Elizabeth began with the hope that her translation was finished. Realizing as she copied her work that her New Year's gift was not quite right, Elizabeth decided to proceed anyway, knowing that Katherine Parr would appreciate her efforts. If further work were done on the translation, no evidence of that work survives. John Bale obtained a copy of the manuscript, probably from Katherine Parr herself, and published it with relatively few changes as *A Godly Medytacyon of the Christen Sowle* . . . in 1548 (STC 17320). The lack of alteration in Bale's printed version of the manuscript suggests that Princess Elizabeth did little, if any, revision subsequent to her presentation of the work to Katherine Parr.

The Oxford, Bodleian Library's MS Cherry 36 is a small book of rough-hewn thick sheets or membranes of vellum (now somewhat yellowed and cockled) sewn into an embroidered cover, reinforced with boards at some later time (probably in the late seventeenth or early eighteenth century). The cover is described fully below. There are eleven quires, each of which has three sheets folded to create six pages. The lined large octavo or small quarto-sized pages are irregular in size, measuring 160–170 by 120–125mm.; the text is in faded black ink, filling fifteen lines per page with occasional references to Biblical passages in the margins, which are between 21 and 27mm. wide. Folio 1 is blank; folios 2–4v have a dedication to Katherine Parr, dated 1544. The translation begins on folio 5 with the epistle, 'To the Reader' (fols 5r–6r) and continuing to folio 63r. Folios 63v–64r have 'A praier made by her ma^{tie}' copied in an italic hand unlike Elizabeth's. According to Ames, 'The prayer, copied by another hand on folio 63 of the manuscript, was composed by Queen Elizabeth for her Navy in 1597, and is the third of "Three most excellent Prayers made by the late famous Queene Elizabeth . . ." ' (pp. 9–10). Folios 64v–65v are blank save for some scribbled numbers (1–8 and 9,9,9). The sheet marked as folio 66 is a piece of paper added at a later date; the vellum folio 66 has been cut out.

Traditionally, the manuscript is seen as a curiosity. Studies of *The Glass of the Sinful Soul* have generally praised the princess's industry and intention, but have less praise for the translation's quality, although scholars have speculated about its implications. In the first extended study, Percy Ames begins by commenting, 'If the question of literary merit alone had been considered, the publication [of this edition] would scarcely be justified'; yet while the work is 'admittedly not of high rank', as Ames points out, the translator is. Thus Ames says he concluded that 'any writing which brought us into closer touch with the mind of Glorious Queen Bess, at any period of her life, would be generally regarded as of value and importance' (pp. 3–4). Neale calls *The Glass of the Sinful Soul* 'an excessively dreary French poem in Elizabethan prose'. Of Elizabeth's translation, he comments: 'Thus early she began a habit which was to grow into a curse, making her studied writings insufferably obscure and involved'.[3] Yet he too regards the work as worth consideration because it serves as a link between the future queen and 'the Cambridge group of humanists', especially John Cheke, Roger Ascham, and William Grindall (pp. 14–15). Janel Mueller mentions Elizabeth's work in passing because Elizabeth prepared it for Katherine Parr and it may thus cast light on Parr's religious position.[4] These commentators on *The Glass of the Sinful Soul* regard the work as valuable for its associations with the monarch and her world.

Recent discussions have taken the princess's aspirations to learning more seriously. Yet even sympathetic critics of the work praise it in terms that suggest its weakness. Placing the work within the context of the world of learned sixteenth-century women, Prescott remarks that Elizabeth's translation 'is quite accurate, even dutiful' (p. 67), but goes on to analyze the mistranslations that exist. The most enthusiastic commentary about Elizabeth's work comes from Marc Shell. He argues that the work has 'an ideology both important and discomforting in its personal and historical aspects. Its treatment of bastardy and incest, for example, has potentially disconcerting ramifications for ideas of liberty and politics generally and illuminates the historical rise of the English nation and biographical role of Elizabeth herself' (p. 6). When he turns to the translation itself, however, he comments, 'Elizabeth's translation, though not without "inaccuracies," is generally "literal"' (p. 108), and his discussion, like Prescott's, emphasizes the work's errors.

Both Prescott and Shell find Elizabeth's errors personally revealing (Shell, pp. 107–109; Prescott, pp. 68–71). The princess consistently reduces the emotive force of Marguerite de Navarre's erotic language for a more controlled, less passionate text because that eroticism evidently embarrassed her. Elizabeth mistranslates familial words in passages that deal with a husband's punishing his adulterous wife; the potential parallel to the history of Henry VIII and Anne Boleyn make such errors understandable. Perhaps most tellingly, she translates the French word 'tour', not as 'tower', but as 'prison'.[5] Thus the work, considered as a translation, has weaknesses, as every commentator has explicitly acknowledged. Implicitly, they all reach the same conclusion: to assess it only as a translation is to misvalue it: the actual value lies in its associations.

What interests me is that while critics have found value in the manuscript for its associations with 'Glorious Queen Bess', the Cambridge humanists, other learned Tudor women, and Renaissance thought on bastardy and incest, no one seems to have considered certain practical questions. The work is one of several that Princess Elizabeth gave as gifts. Shell comments, 'At about this time [*i.e.*, of her translation of *The Glass of the Sinful Soul*] Elizabeth gave as gifts to members of her family other holograph translations as well—an English translation of John Calvin's *Institution Chrétienne* to Katherine Parr (1545[/6]); Latin, French, and Italian translations from Catherine Parr's *Prayers, or Meditations* to Henry VIII (1545[/6]); and a Latin translation of Bernardino Ochino's *De Christo sermo* to her brother, the ten-year-old Edward (1547)' (pp. 291–2).[6] Between the New Year's celebration in 1545 and that in 1546, then, Princess Elizabeth prepared three gift books of translation in embroidered covers. Her only other such gift translation was sent to her brother sometime in 1547, when she was in need of his support.[7] One might ask why she should prepare three translations within a year. I would like to argue that these works provide an interesting synecdoche for their creator, the Princess Elizabeth, as a commodity, a marriageable princess. First I shall discuss how such a synecdoche might function, and then I shall examine the actual circumstances under which this translation (as well as others) was prepared. As a synecdochic object, the manuscript of *The Glass of the Sinful Soul* undercuts some of the assumptions our own culture has made about Elizabeth Tudor.

From her birth in 1533, Elizabeth's value as a marriageable princess was recognized. Soon after her first birthday, Henry negotiated unsuccessfully to marry her to the Duke of Angoulême, third son to King François I and thus Marguerite de Navarre's nephew; another proposed husband was the Earl of Arran. Definite evidence exists for these negotiations, and others, which are rumoured, may also have taken place. Venetian and Spanish documents mention various candidates: 'a Frenchman' in 1540, 'Charles V, the Emperor of Germany' in 1542, and Emmanuel Philibert of Savoy, the Prince of Piedmont, also in 1542.[8] Nor were foreigners the only ones interested in Elizabeth: in 1547 when Henry VIII died, Thomas Seymour had proposed to the Council that he should marry her; he was refused by the Council and a few months later was married to Elizabeth's stepmother Katherine Parr (Neale, pp. 21–23). Seymour knew the princess personally, of course, but potential grooms who were foreign had to depend on descriptions, portraits, and synecdochic objects during negotiations.

It was standard practice to use such tokens as portraits or symbolic gifts during a marriage negotiation. Susan Doran speaks about Queen Elizabeth's courtship by Eric of Sweden; his embassy wore a rich 'livery, displaying some hearts pierced by a javelin on the lapels of their red velvet coats, symbolizing the passion of their sovereign' and a later ambassador won friends because he handed out 'sumptuous presents as bribes to courtiers'. Among the many gifts he offered was a ring presented to Elizabeth thought to be worth some five or six thousand crowns'.[9] Clearly Eric of Sweden's gifts were intended to demonstrate the man's eagerness, passion, and generosity. More commonly, courtship involved the exchange of portraits. Thus the representative of Emperor Ferdinand wrote in some excitement when one of Elizabeth's courtiers requested Ferdinand's portrait, for the request indicated that the negotiations were becoming serious.[10] As Roy Strong points out,

> Most portraits [of Elizabeth I] . . . reached the Continent in the way of diplomatic gifts, or in connection with the numerous marriage negotiations which cover twenty or more years of the reign.[11]

He is speaking, of course, about the portraits of Queen Elizabeth, not of Princess Elizabeth as she was in 1544. Only three portraits of Elizabeth prior to her accession survive: one is as a figure in a family group portrait at Hampton Court; another is an unflattering portrait done around 1550 by Levina Teerlinc (Strong, p. 52). A portrait from 1547–48 shows her as an attractive girl, richly dressed and jeweled, holding one book and standing next to a second. This portrait, prepared for her brother Edward VI, implies that the Princess Elizabeth is healthy, physically attractive, well-dowered, and interested in the sort of reading associated with Protestant Humanism.[12] In 1544, no such portrait existed and Holbein was dead. Nor was the princess's appearance of principal importance in a marriage negotiation. As Henry VIII would later remark of his daughters, they were 'both well educated and qualified for a prince of the greatest honor.'[13] In his eyes, in other words, their education gave them value, not their physical beauty, although both girls seem to have been attractive.

Rather than having a portrait of Elizabeth prepared for would-be suitors, then, someone involved in marriage negotiations—such as Katherine Parr who had assumed responsibility for training the princess, or secretary of state William Paget who was active in several negotiations, or even the king himself—could have suggested that the princess be set to work on a task that would both further her education and produce the sort of object that could be presented to potential husbands, should such negotiations conclude successfully and a synecdochic gift be required. If marriage negotiations provided the occasion for the book Princess Elizabeth gave to Katherine Parr (as well as her other gifts of translations), then how one assesses that book depends on how well it presents its producer as a royal bride.

In this context, the production of the manuscript becomes particularly important. Because of Marguerite's connections to the English court, as virtually every commentator notes, the choice of a text originally by Marguerite de Navarre is appropriate. The French work was probably specified by Katherine Parr in consultation with William Grindall, Elizabeth's tutor, possibly at the urging of William Paget or Henry himself.[14] These adults would be aware that Marguerite was on particularly good terms with Henry and his family in the 1540's (Ames, p. 31). Moreover, the text was one that suggested a religious doubleness: Marguerite was herself a Roman Catholic, although she was clearly sympathetic to the reformist movement. As one recent analyst remarks, the work positions Marguerite as a Roman Catholic:

> To the extent that [the text] precludes the possibility of preparing for justification in any way, this view distances Marguerite from the position of Erasmus and that adopted later by the Fathers of Trent. Nevertheless Marguerite is very much in line with the thought of Saint Augustine. Moreover, if modern scholarship is correct in discerning in Luther's thought the attribution of the will's slavery to sin not merely to man's Fall but to his creaturely status itself, Marguerite's view is in fact closer to that of Augustine than it is to that of Luther.[15]

Yet Ferguson also notes that in this work 'Marguerite employs many of the ideas and images emphasised by the Reformers and in particular by Luther' (Ferguson, p. 41). Small wonder, given this mixture of traditional Catholicism doctrine with Reformation techniques, that the work aroused anxiety: soon after its publication in 1533 the Sorbonne scrutinized it for heresy, although the accusation was quickly dropped and the deputies were forced by the king to say as much publicly (Ferguson, pp. 54–57). The work is especially suitable for a princess who might be sympathetic to new ideas about religion, but who would not dismiss marriage to a Roman Catholic out of hand.

The work's dedicatory epistle (fols 2r–4v) makes a second point about the Princess Elizabeth: her affiliation with Queen Katherine Parr, who was at that particular moment the most powerful woman in England. (Indeed the queen's power led to trouble. In the year after Elizabeth gave her book to Katherine Parr, a group of religious conservatives on the Privy Council tried unsuccessfully to implicate Queen Katherine and her circle in Anne Askew's heresy trial.[16]) Among her responsibilities, Katherine Parr evidently took on the task of supervising Princess Elizabeth's upbringing and education; presumably Parr was also concerned about her stepdaughter's future prospects. In 1544, Elizabeth's ascension to the throne seemed most unlikely, so her marriage seemed advisable. Thus anyone who was interested in how Henry VIII's wife might regard her stepdaughter, an important consideration given Henry VIII's poor health, needed only to look at the dedication to learn that stepdaughter and stepmother were on excellent terms. Moreover, the dedication, with its request for assistance, shows an altogether becoming modesty. The maid might be learned, but she did not think so herself.

If the curious observer were unable to read English, he still might learn much from the book. After all, any prince interested in obtaining the Princess Elizabeth's hand would find that the book offers a clear representation of that hand, both in the handwriting and in the

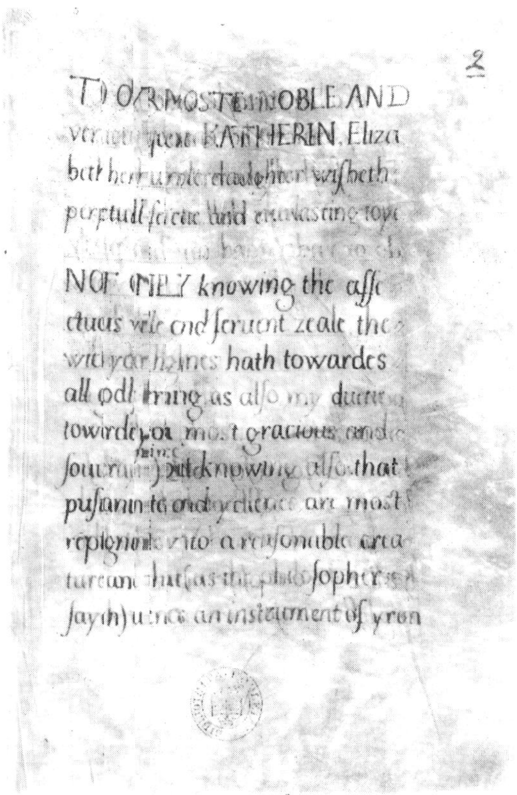
2
TO OUR MOST NOBLE AND
vertuous quene KATHERIN, Eliza
beth her humble daughter wissheth
perpetuall felicite and everlasting joye
NOT ONLY knowing the affe
ctuous wille and fervent zeale the
which your highnes hath towardes
all godly learning as also my duetie
towardes you (most gracious and
soveraigne princes) but knowing also that
pusillanimite and ydlenes are most
repugnante unto a reasonable crea
ture and that (as the philosopher
sayeth) even as an instrument of yron

PLATE I. *Princess Elizabeth's autograph dedication of* The Glass of the Sinful Soul *to Katherine Parr: Oxford, Bodleian Library* MS *Cherry 36, f. 2r (Original size 160 × 120mm.) Reproduced by permission of the Bodleian Library, University of Oxford.*

hand-embroidered cover. The manuscript is in an attractive hand, which Alfred Fairbank describes as 'an italic bookhand of Italian appearance'.[17] The handwriting, which Jean Belmain taught the princess, is a neat but amateur piece of calligraphy, slightly less controlled than is her writing in the autograph 'Poem on a French Psalter'.[18] Elizabeth's use of a form of italic writing, rather than a secretary hand, is telling. In the sixteenth century, roman and italic hands, associated with Humanism, came to England, where they became fashionable and served as an indicator of learning and class status. Thus Jonathan Goldberg observes ' . . . that increasingly in the sixteenth century, and invariably by the close of the period, English royalty wrote their private correspondence in an italic hand, but also that others, aspiring to this mark of privilege, signed their letters in italic, although the rest of their letter (whether written by themselves or by a secretary) usually remained in secretarial [*sic*] hand'.[19] Jenkinson comments that such handwriting was 'the special property of the learned or the travelled'.[20] The writing in the manuscript, because it is an elegant humanistic hand, is new and Continental. Elizabeth's hand in marriage is rendered more valuable by her hand in this manuscript, which is fashionable, clear, and controlled. Roger Ascham would later praise the Princess Elizabeth's handwriting in terms that suggest an equivalence between hand and head, between characters and character: ' . . .within the walles of her priuie chamber, she hath obteyned that excellencie of learnyng, to vnderstand, speake, and write, **both wittely with head, and faire with hand**, as scarce one or two rare wittes in both the Vniuersities haue in many yeares reached vnto'.[21] Ascham also remarks that her excellent hand ought to shame 'yong Ientlemen of England' (p. 67), so these attributes of her handwriting (her character, if you will) could be regarded as masculine ones, if her text were not contained within the feminine embroidered binding.

As many histories of embroidery make plain, Elizabeth prepared an unusual and feminine cover for her work. Cyril Davenport, for example, speaks of the work with enthusiasm.

> The book is now one of the great treasures of the Bodleian Library; it is bound in canvas, measures about 7 by 5 inches, and was embroidered in all probability by the hands of the Princess herself . . . The design is the same upon both sides. The ground is all worked over in a large kind of tapestry-stitch in thick pale blue silk, very evenly and well done, so well that it has been considered more than once to be a piece of woven material. On this is a cleverly designed interlacing scrollwork of gold and silver braid, in the centre of which are the joined initials K.P.

PLATE 2. *The upper cover and spine of the binding embroidered by Princess Elizabeth for* The Glass of the Sinful Soul: *Oxford, Bodleian Library MS Cherry 36 (Original size 189 × 155mm.) Reproduced by permission of the Bodleian Library, University of Oxford.*

In each corner is a heartsease worked in thick coloured silks, purple and yellow, interwoven with fine gold threads, and a small green leaflet between each of the petals. The back is very much worn, but it probably had small flowers embroidered upon it.[22]

In fact, the back or lower cover, while more worn than the upper or front cover, is clearly intended to duplicate it, while the spine has four small silver and blue flowers with gilt and yellow leaves. Commenting on a photograph of the cover Kerry Taylor, textiles expert at Sotheby's, London, offers this slightly different description of the embroidery:

> The linen ground is densely worked with interlocking pale blue threads in tent stitch worked to the corner with raised-work gold and silver thread pansies, the initials KP to the centre within raised embroidered plaited gold and silver threads forming a parterre-like interlaced design of quatrefoils about a central crucifix, floral slips to the spine.

She also suggests that this design was perhaps prompted by the kind of parterre, or ornamental garden, the Princess was likely to have seen through her window at a country house such as Hatfield.

Davenport goes on to describe another book cover embroidered by the Princess Elizabeth, that for the collection of prayers composed by Katherine Parr, copied by Elizabeth, and presented to Henry VIII in December 1545. Of both books, he writes, 'the technique, as well as the design are peculiar for the time in which they were done' (p. 35). The peculiarity he notes is that when books were sent out to professional embroiderers for binding, the work was generally done 'in rich velvet . . . instead of a very elementary braid work' (p. 36). These books, however, are bound in linen or canvas, a simplicity that supports the idea that they are the work of the Princess Elizabeth's own hand, rather than of a professional embroiderer.

Men were often professional embroiderers, particularly those working as court embroiderers, but domestic embroidery was usually done by women. Embroidery, as sixteenth-century conduct books agree, is a craft that all girls of good family learned. After surveying such treatises, the twentieth-century art historian Roszika Parker notes that embroidery 'was taught in such a way as to inculcate obedience and patience during long hours spent sitting still, head bowed over an increasingly technically complex, demanding art'.[23] Parker's analysis of domestic embroidery suggests the sort of cultural attitudes to which Elizabeth Tudor's embroidered book cover would appeal (pp. 75, 64):

> [I]n the Renaissance, . . . embroidery was considered as both defence and evidence of chaste femininity. . . . No other activity so successfully promoted the qualities that Renaissance man, anxious to define sex difference, wanted in a wife. Embroidery combined the humility of needlework with rich stitchery. It connoted opulence and obedience. It ensured that women spent long hours at home, retired in private, yet it made a public statement about the household's position and economic standing.

Thus, the embroidered book cover that Princess Elizabeth had prepared carried two sorts of message. One was the cultural association of which Parker speaks, linking embroidery with a chaste and feminine maiden, head bowed and eyes lowered to her work, as she created an object of ornamental richness. The other sort of message is that provided by the cover design: at its centre are the initials KP, suggesting the embroiderer's affiliation with a powerful woman, Katherine Parr. Yet the initials, like sixteenth-century women's power, are contained. The KP is placed within a cross, suggesting piety, that is itself further contained by strap work. The strap work includes entwined knots, a traditional symbol of virginity. In the corners, Princess Elizabeth has embroidered pansies, traditional symbols of love and thought.[24]

As a synecdoche for a marriageable girl, *The Glass of the Sinful Soul* is highly effective. Whoever wins the hand of the princess will win a chaste maiden, suggested both by the careful embroidery and the toning down of Marguerite de Navarre's ardent language. The subject matter and the dedicatory letter both testify to her piety and humility, even though the italic hand and rich materials promise fashion and wealth. The choice of a French Catholic text may hint that the Princess Elizabeth could be contented in the foreign household of a French or even Spanish prince, while the references to Queen Katherine Parr promise that prince will gain a powerful English ally. The care and elegance of the handiwork suggests good health, thorough education, and attention to an attractive appearance.

This analysis depends, of course, on the existence of marriage negotiations that might use such a synecdoche in the period between late 1544, when the preparation of the first gift must have been planned, through January 1546, when she presented her other gift books to Katherine Parr and Henry VIII. If no marriage prospect were in view for the Princess Elizabeth, then the book is not likely to have been prepared as a potential lure for a suitor. As it happens, however, such negotiations did take place. Not one but three potential husbands were proposed for Elizabeth during the crucial time frame.

During that time period, Henry VIII was conducting negotiations with several monarchs—François I of France, Christian III of Denmark, and Charles V of the Holy Roman Empire—as he struggled to commence, conclude, and carry on several wars. In 1544 William Paget reported Cardinal Jean Du Bellay's remark that 'he [*i.e.*, the Cardinal] had talked at Boulloyn of a marriage of your [*i.e.*, King Henry's] younger daughter . . . to some prince of France . . . .' (L&P, 21 October 1544). As Prescott points out, Du Bellay claimed that he, Marguerite de Navarre, and Madame d'Étampes 'formed an English party at the Valois court', so his proposal that Elizabeth be married to a French prince would not have been dismissed. Hearing the Cardinal's proposal, Henry VIII (or one of his counselors) may have suggested that a translation of Marguerite's text, prettily presented, would make a useful task for the princess. Were the marriage negotiation to fall apart, no harm would be done by having the princess demonstrate her education and affection; were a negotiation to go forward, the book could prove useful in presenting the princess and flattering a powerful ally in France.

The French were not the only nation interested in allying themselves with the English royal family. In addition to 'some prince' suggested by the French, Henry's representatives reported a second candidate to wed Elizabeth. Unlike the Roman Catholic French, the Danes were ruled by a firmly Protestant king, Christian III. In late January 1545, Henry VIII and his Privy Council sent a proposal via William Paget that either Elizabeth or Mary might marry the king of Denmark's brother, the Duke of Holst (L&P 26 January 1545). Clearly something led to these marriage negotiations. Perhaps some event in the Princess Elizabeth's life drew attention to her marriageable status. The nearness in time of this Danish proposal to that of Cardinal Du Bellay may suggest that Henry VIII's government, abruptly realizing that his daughters were potentially valuable as marriage prospects, began to seek a second offer for them. More likely, it did not take Du Bellay's suggestion to draw that possibility to anyone's attention. Both the French and the Danish negotiations resulted from the Henrician government's desire to settle Mary and Elizabeth Tudor advantageously.

Henry's instructions to his representatives make it clear that he would be willing to have either daughter marry. Given that information, it is interesting to note the letter of 20 September 1544 that Katherine Parr wrote to Mary Tudor. In it the Queen urged her stepdaughter to publish under her own name her translation of Erasmus's *Paraphrase of the Gospel of St. John*. (Although Mary had begun the task, she abandoned it, and it was finally completed by Dr Francis Mallett and published in January 1548 as part of a larger project.)[25] Clearly as the English court thought about marriage plans for both of the princesses, both were urged to produce material examples of their piety and learning.

In the case of Mary Tudor, the translation project seems to have been balked by the princess's refusal to cooperate, but Elizabeth Tudor, a more biddable child, continued to produce translations for her family. The Catholic eroticism of Marguerite de Navarre's *Miroir de l'âme pecheresse* would be unsuitable for the potential Danish match, given King Christian III's firm Protestantism. It is interesting that late in 1545 Elizabeth did another gift translation of Calvin's *Institution Chrétienne* for Katherine Parr's 1546 New Year's gift. This manuscript would have been altogether suitable to show a Protestant prince, although the

Danish match may not have been its object. The English and Danes discussed the possible marriage at some length, for several references to marriage with the Danish Duke are mentioned in government documents, but these negotiations seem to have fallen into abeyance by the summer of 1545 (L&P 10 June 1545), probably before Elizabeth began her work on the Calvin text.

Soon after the Danish negotiations began to lag, a third prospect, more glittering than the others, came into view. Charles V and Henry VIII were struggling to conclude a peace treaty, and in October 1545 part of that process involved attempts to link the two rulers through marriage. On a number of occasions the representatives of the Emperor and of the English king discussed marrying Henry's first daughter, Mary Tudor, to the Emperor himself; marrying Prince Edward to the Emperor's daughter Mary; and marrying Henry's second daughter, Elizabeth, to Charles V's son, Philip of Spain. Thus firmly tied, the two royal families could then join forces to dominate Europe. At first things went well; the Emperor's negotiator Eustace Chapuys assured Paget that 'th'Emperor's lips water at my Lady Mary' (L&P 10 November 1545). A later report about the Spanish negotiator Cardinal Granvelle shows his enthusiasm for the matches:

> Grandvela, joining his hands together, casting himself back and lifting up eyes, said, *Est il possible?* with a marvellous fashion of rejoice, and . . . he thanked God of it; and then told how he himself suggested it to the Emperor, who liked it, and then he praised the young ladies, and spoke of the importance of this amity for the quiet of Christendom . . . (L&P 30 November 1545)

In this negotiation, as in the others, a pretty book of translations could have been a useful tool had the parties been able to agree on terms. The negotiations coincided with the preparation of Princess Elizabeth's third gift book, this time Katherine Parr's *Prayers, or Meditations* written out for Henry VIII, also in an embroidered cover. But for a third time within a year, no agreement was reached. When Henry's representatives pressed the Spanish about concluding the arrangements, it all came apart. So far as the Princess Elizabeth was concerned, '*qualitas* alone dissuades them': she was not good enough to marry Philip of Spain.

Because all these marriage negotiations failed, Henry VIII's government never needed a synecdochic gift to seal the bargain for Elizabeth's hand. If I am correct, however, in seeing these early works by Elizabeth Tudor as tools to be used in the diplomatic negotiations attendant on marrying Princess Elizabeth, that is not to say that the works are in any way inauthentic or diminished. Clearly they speak to a twentieth-century reader, as they once could have to a sixteenth-century prince, of an educated and intelligent young woman. The achievement of this manuscript is not simply in its text, however, but in the production and the presentation of that text. Reading the material object is far more revealing than analyzing an eleven-year-old's translation. But the twentieth-century is so accustomed to imagining Elizabeth as the independent virgin queen that it requires an effort to consider her as an obedient child-bride.

NOTES

1 The title Elizabeth wrote down in her manuscript is *THE glasse of the synnefull soule*; her work is also called *The Mirror of the Sinful Soul*. All quotations are taken from the manuscript, Bodleian Library ms Cherry 36. I am grateful to Dr Bruce Barker-Benfield and the staff of the Bodleian Library for helping me in my inspection of the manuscript. A facsimile and transcription of the manuscript may be found in Marc Shell, *Elizabeth's Glass* (Lincoln, Nebraska, 1993) and in Percy Ames, *The Mirror of the Sinful Soul* (London, 1897). The best treatment of the material book is the essay by Margaret H. Swain, 'A New Year's Gift from the Princess Elizabeth', *The Connoisseur*, August 1973, pp. 258–66.

2 Anne Lake Prescott, 'The Pearl of the Valois and Elizabeth I: Marguerite de Navarre's *Miroir* and Tudor England', *Silent But for the Word*, ed. Margaret Hannay (Kent, Ohio, 1985), p. 69.

3 J. E. Neale, *Queen Elizabeth I* (London, 1934), p. 15.

4 Janel Mueller discusses Parr's religious convictions in 'A Tudor Queen Finds Voice: Katherine Parr's Lamentation of a Sinner', *The Historical Renaissance*, ed. Heather Dubrow and Richard Strier (Chicago, 1988), pp. 15–47; and 'Devotion as Difference: Intertextuality in Queen Katherine Parr's Prayers or Meditations (1545)', *Huntington Library Quarterly*, 53 (1990), 171–97.

5 Elizabeth was not herself imprisoned in the Tower of London until her sister's reign, but her mother Anne Boleyn and cousin Catherine Howard had both been held there before their executions.

6 Elizabeth's manuscript of *The Glass of the Sinful Soul* is dedicated on 'the last day of the yeare of our Lord God 1544' so it is a New Year's Gift for 1545. The manuscript for Parr's prayers has a dedication to Henry VIII dated 20 December 1545 so it was a New Year's gift for 1546; it is the British Library, Royal ms 7 D. X. The complementary 1546 gift to Parr, the Calvin translation, is dated 'ce penultime jour de l'an 1545'; it is at the Scottish Record Office, RH 13/78. The final gift translation is the Ochino sermon, *De Christo Sermo*, for Edward VI that Elizabeth prepared in 1547; it is Bodleian ms Bodl. 6. In 'A New Year's Gift from the Princess Elizabeth', *The Connoisseur*, August 1973, pp. 258–66, Margaret Swain suggests that other such gift books may have existed, as many as six for Katherine and Henry.

7 She left Katherine Parr's household because of increasing attention from Parr's new husband Thomas Seymour in the summer of 1547. Early in that year, Bernardino Ochino had entered England as Cranmer's guest: W. K. Jordan, *Edward VI*, 2 vols (Cambridge, Mass., 1968), I, 192–3, 372–3. Thus her gift makes perfect sense,

appealing as it does to her brother's taste for Protestantism by making use of an author of particular interest. Such a gift might help her should anyone cast aspersions on her character.

8 Martin A. S. Hume, *The Courtships of Queen Elizabeth: A History of the Various Negotiations for Her Marriage* (London, 1896), pp. 6–7; Frank A. Mumby, *The Girlhood of Queen Elizabeth* (London, 1909), pp. 15–18; *CSP Venetian*, entries for 17 March 1535 and December 1535. For the rumours, *CSP Venetian*, 17 March 1540 and 30 October 1542 concern 'the daughter of Henry VIII', who is said to be about to marry a Frenchman (1540) or Charles V (1542). Thus these rumours may pertain to Mary, and the second one probably does. The final rumour seems more well founded; *CSP Spain*, 8 July 1542.

9 Susan Doran's *Monarchy and Matrimony: The Courtships of Elizabeth I* (London, 1996), p. 30.

10 Victor von Klarwill, *Queen Elizabeth and Some Foreigners* (London, 1928), p. 44.

11 Roy Strong, *Gloriana: The Portraits of Queen Elizabeth I* (New York, 1987), p. 22.

12 The portrait may have been painted about the same time that Elizabeth sent her brother the translation of Ochino. It is often reproduced; Elizabeth Pomeroy gives a detailed analysis in *Reading the Portraits of Queen Elizabeth I* (Hamden, Conn., 1989), pp. 4–6. Another analysis that emphasizes the Protestant elements is by John King, *Tudor Royal Iconography* (Princeton, 1989), p. 211. As Ames points out, the painter is unknown, although the work is in the style of Holbein (*Mirror*, pp. 7–9).

13 *Letters and Papers, Foreign and Domestic, of the Reign of Henry VIII, 1509–1547*, ed. James Gairdner and R. H. Brodie, 22 vols. (London, 1862–1932), late January 1545. Hereafter cited as L&P, references are by date.

14 If Princess Elizabeth chose the source text, it is surely worth noting that Elizabeth's mother, Anne Boleyn, had once been in Marguerite's service. But it seems most unlikely that an eleven-year-old, however precocious, would choose the text she would translate.

15 Gary Ferguson, *Mirroring Belief: Marguerite de Navarre's Devotional Poetry* (Edinburgh, 1992), p. 27. In *The Grammar of Silence* (Washington, 1986), Robert Cottrell approaches the *Miroir* very differently from Ferguson, using Lacan's ideas to read the poem's iconicity. He too, however, is struck by the work's doubleness, paradox, and ambiguity.

16 For a discussion of the incident, two essays in Hannay's *Silent But for the Word* are relevant: Elaine V. Beilin, 'Anne Askew's Self-Portrait in the *Examinations*', pp. 77–91, and John N. King, 'Patronage and Piety: The Influence of Catherine Parr', pp. 43–60. See also the essays by Mueller, cited above.

17 Alfred Fairbank, 'Introduction,' in *Renaissance Handwriting*, ed. Fairbank and Berthold Wolpe (London, 1960), p. 32. I am grateful to Laetitia Yeandle for her advice on my analysis of the handwriting of the manuscript.

18 For Belmain's instruction, see Berthold Wolpe, ibid., pp. 66–67. The French psalter poem is reproduced in J. H. Plumb, *Royal Heritage* (London, 1977), p. 75.

19 Jonathan Goldberg, 'Hamlet's Hand,' *Shakespeare Quarterly*, 39 (1988), p. 324; see also Goldberg's *Writing Matter* (Stanford, CA., 1990).

20 Hilary Jenkinson, *The Later Court Hands* (New York, 1927), p. 63.

21 Roger Ascham, *The Scholemaster*, ed. Edward Arber (Birmingham, 1870), p. 67; my emphasis. Belmain was the princess's tutor when she prepared the manuscript, but William Grindall succeeded him in 1544, dying of the plague in 1548. After Grindall's death Ascham became tutor. Fairbanks relates an anecdote that indicates the importance Ascham placed upon handwriting: '. . . before [Ascham] was

appointed Elizabeth's tutor he sent a silver pen to Mrs. Ashley, her governess, as a token and offered to mend Elizabeth's silver pen' (*Renaissance Handwriting*, p. 33).

22 Cyril Davenport, *English Embroidered Bookbindings* (London, 1899), pp. 32–33.

23 Rozsika Parker, *The Subversive Stitch* (New York, 1989), p. 83.

24 I am grateful to Eugene Hill of Mount Holyoke College for the observation about the knots. A common sixteenth-century association for pansies was with love, thanks in part to the alternate names, 'heart's ease' and 'love in idleness', but the pun on 'pensee' meant that pansies are also associated with thoughts: Esther Singleton, *The Shakespearean Garden* (New York, 1931), pp. 200–3.

25 Betty Travitsky, *The Paradise of Women* (New York, 1989), pp. 78, 274.

Dame Flora's Blossoms:
Esther Inglis's Flower-Illustrated Manuscripts

Anneke Tjan-Bakker

'I have presumit to present you with a few blossoms I have effected of Dame Flora, houping the variety of writing containing a good sujet and diversitie of flowers therin shall give you sum delectation and the rather because it is a woman's work'. So writes the calligrapher Esther Inglis (1571–1624) in her manuscript dedicated to Thomas Wotton (1587–1630) in 1606. Using the Dame Flora metaphor, she refers both to the anthological nature of her work and to the flower illustrations that accompany it. This style, the combination of 'flowers of verse' with colourful flower illustrations, was a style she used for a relatively short time only and it was the most prolific period of her career. A list of the sixteen flower manuscripts, which were all produced in 1606 and 1607, is included as an appendix at the end of the article. By mainly concentrating on the illustrative aspect of these manuscripts, I will try to answer why one particular pattern dominated her texts during this period and why she was so prolific. At the same time I hope to show how appropriate the Dame Flora metaphor was for this particular type of work.

In order to contrast her work of the 'flower period' with her earlier work, we need to establish the characteristics of the style she used before. Esther Inglis had probably started her calligraphic career already quite young as a writing mistress in the French school which her parents ran in Edinburgh.[1] A number of her early manuscripts have the nature of a copy book—books with specimens of various styles of writing that were used to teach writing. After her marriage, in or around 1596, to Bartholomew Kello she seems to have worked for her husband as a scribe. According to David Laing, Kello had received a learned education, probably at St Andrews, and appears to have obtained occasional employment in ecclesiastical matters,[2] but at the time of his marriage, however, he was a clerk for foreign correspondence at the court of James VI. This meant that he was expected to provide all kind

of documents, such as passports, testimonials and letters of recommendation, 'to be grantit and direct be our Souverane Lord to forrayne
Princes, Personnages, Estaitis and Nationis.' These writings were to be
put 'in cumlie and decent maner of lettir and forme be the maist
exquisit & perfyte wreater within this Realme.'[3] Although she is not
mentioned by name, Laing is convinced that this referred to Esther
Inglis.

Yet, at the same time that she produced these official documents,
Esther Inglis also used her writing skills to produce a number of gift
books. For not only was Kello in charge of producing all kind of documents, he was also regularly sent abroad to deliver them. On these mis-
sions he took the opportunity to present the 'forrayne Princes' and
'Personnages' with one of his wife's manuscripts, in the hope to receive
a monetary reward in return. This probably was a welcome addition to
Kello's income, for the financial position of Esther Inglis and her husband was never very bright.[4] Some of the dedicatees of this period were
Queen Elizabeth, Prince Maurice of Nassau, the Earl of Essex, and
Anthony Bacon (1599), the Vicomte de Rohan (1600 and 1601), and the
Vicomtesse de Rohan and Catherine de Bourbon (1601). Most of these
manuscripts have a rather sober and unadorned black-and-white style.
The prose texts are usually introduced through impressive pen drawings
on the title-page. These are, however, not Esther Inglis's own creation,
for she copied them from existing models.[5] Each page of text has an
ornamental border, at first painstakingly drawn and stippled by hand,
but later replaced by etched borders. The manuscripts were so meticulously executed that they give the impression of being printed works.
They were, however, highly unique and personalized works of art.

A major change in their circumstances took place when James VI
became King of England in 1603 and the court left Edinburgh in order
to resettle in London. Since their livelihood depended on the court,
Kello and his wife must have followed the King to London, as so many
Scots did. Their entry in the *album amicorum* of a fellow Scot called
George Craig[6] shows them to be in London in August 1604. It is difficult to tell if there was work for them in the early years in England, for
there are no manuscripts for 1603 and 1604. On the one hand, a lot of
the missions Kello had been sent on had involved the secret diplomacy
concerning the succession to the throne of England and this was no
longer necessary now. On the other hand, it has been suggested that
these were golden times for the Scots who came down. Immediately
after his succession James had showered offices, titles, land and money
on his favourites. Cecil admitted that 'the king hath given away very
much . . . his three first years were his Christmas.'[7] England seemed a

source of inexhaustible wealth to the Scots and, as Akrigg states, 'James's Scots must have felt that the Golden Age had indeed returned.'[8] Yet many others who had come to London for a career after James's accession to the English throne were disappointed and promptly left again.

Perhaps Kello and his wife had hoped to resume their teamship as clerk and scribe working for the court when they arrived in London, but given the fact that James had inherited from Queen Elizabeth a well-run court, this may nog have been so easy. They did not leave England, however, which could mean that there actually was work for them, but it could just as well mean that they were hanging on, hoping for some kind of preferment for Kello as a reward for services rendered to the King in the past. I am inclined to think the latter, for when Esther Inglis started to produce manuscripts again in 1605, she did so in her own right. Her husband no longer formed the *trait-d'union* between her and the dedicatees of the manuscripts as had been the case in Scotland.

The first manuscript Esther Inglis presented in England was dedicated to Susanna Herbert (1587–1629), a person she did not know, in February 1605. For this she had used leaves with unfinished verses and decorative alphabets that she had already produced in the period before her marriage, when she was still a writing mistress. The booklet was obviously put together to demonstrate her skill as a calligrapher. In the dedication she writes:

> The Bee draweth noght (MOST NOBLE AND VERTUOUS LADIE) hwny [honey] from the fragrant herbis of the garding for hir self: no more have I payned myself mony yearis to burie the talent God hes geven me in oblivion. And therfore albeit I be a stranger and no way knowen to your L[adyship] yitt have I tane the boldnes to present you with thir few flouris that I have collected of Dame FLORAS blossomes: Trusting your L. will accept heirof als kindlie as from my heart I have done it, and in humilitie offers the same to your L. and the rather becaus it is the work of a woman of one, desyrous to serve and honour your Ladyship, in any thinge it shall please your L. to command. Gif heirefter I may understand this litill thing to be agreable to you, truelie I shal accompt my selfe the more fortunat to have the favourable acceptance of one of the most renowned Ladies of this Isle in godlines and verteu. Not myndit to werie your L. with forder Epistle, I pray God blis and preserve your L., and your noble husband in long life, good health and prosperitie.[9]

We see that Esther Inglis presents her talents to Susanna Herbert, who had only just recently become Lady Herbert. This was just about a month earlier, on 27 December 1604, when she had married Philip Herbert, afterwards Earl of Montgomery (1584–1649). She may, therefore, still have been in the process of setting up her own household. By making clever use of the parable of the talents, which tells of the good servant who used his talents wisely and who was, therefore, well rewarded by his lord, Esther Inglis subtly points out that she is not only hoping for a possible position in Lady Herbert's household, but that she is hoping to be rewarded just for this manuscript as well.

A reward for a gift book could vary from a few shillings to a few pounds. We do not know if she received a reward or if her hopes for commissions from Susanna Herbert materialized, but we do know that by the end of 1605 Esther Inglis was approaching more potential patrons. The world of patronage was a precarious one. Competition was fierce and the demands on patronage were often too heavy to be met.[10] Sometimes gifts were accepted without the hoped-for financial reward. In one of his satires, Joseph Hall (1574–1656) complained that '. . . grand *Maecenas* casts a glavering [flattering] eye, On the cold present of a Poesie: And least he might more frankly take than give, Gropes for a french crowne in his emptie sleeve.'[11] The noblemen and gentry who took their patronal obligations seriously were not very numerous and not always very wealthy either. Jacobean patronage was marked by great uncertainty and patronage seekers often had to apply to many patrons more or less simultaneously.[12] This is exactly what we see Esther Inglis doing.

In January 1606 three people received a New Year's gift book from her: Robert Sidney (1563–1626), the Countess of Bedford (1581–1627) and Lady Erskine of Dirletoun (?–1621). Like Lady Herbert, they were all three strangers to Esther Inglis. This time, however, she had switched to a new style, for her books are now smaller and oblong in size[13] and each page of text has been illustrated with a colourful flower or a small bird. Her title-pages have flower borders, reminiscent of the borders found in the Ghent-Bruges style of illuminated manuscripts that was so popular from 1475–1550 (PLATE 1), but the oblong size Esther Inglis used is exceptional, as it is never found in medieval manuscripts. It has been estimated that over a thousand manuscripts in the Ghent-Bruges style still exist today. They made ideal precious gifts.[14] Apart from the *Discours de la Foy*, dedicated to Queen Elizabeth on 1 January 1591, Esther Inglis had not worked the New Year's gift market before. The New Year's gift had been a long established tradition, which meant that the giver usually received a gift in return.

In all three of these New Year's gift books, she used selections from the Book of Proverbs, four or five lines on each page only, which she did

PLATE I. *Title page of Esther Inglis's* Cinquante Octonaires sur la va vanite *[sic]* et inconstance du monde, *1607: Windsor Castle, The Royal Collection (Original page 120 × 155mm). Reproduced by permission of Her Majesty the Queen.*

not hesitate to break off in the middle of a sentence. Just as with the manuscript dedicated to Susanna Herbert, these texts were meant to demonstrate her skill as a calligrapher. Each page displays a different style of handwriting, but unlike the manuscript for Lady Herbert there is no accompanying alphabet. Instead, on top of each page there is a colourful flower, bird or butterfly in the style of the Ghent-Bruges illuminations. The limning, or the illumination of a manuscript, was new for Esther Inglis. Although 'to limn' can simply mean 'to represent in drawing or painting' and in a very limited sense 'to paint a miniature portrait', Esther Inglis used in in the old meaning of 'to illuminate', as her French dedication to the Countess of Bedford points out—'escrit et illuminé par moy'.

In Scotland she had included meticulously drawn title-pages and yet she referred to her work as 'escrit par', 'escrites en diverse sortes de lettres par' or simply 'de la main de'. The fact that now she also stressed the decorative element of her work, indicates that she had come into contact with a different style of document. Roy Strong describes limning as an art form peculiarly expressive of Protestant England, its heyday finishing around 1620.[15] Two of the most important limners at the English court were Nicholas Hilliard (1574–1619) and Isaac Oliver (1560?–1617). After 1603, Hilliard remained limner to King James, whereas Oliver became the official miniaturist of Queen Anne in 1605. Later he also became limner to Prince Henry. Both Hilliard and Oliver also contributed to the occasional illuminated royal manuscript and it may well have been the case that Esther Inglis became familiar with the new colourful style of decorating documents through Hilliard, Oliver or their workshops. A number of the people she approached during this period indicate a connection with the Court of Queen Anne and that of Prince Henry,[16] which until 1610, when he became Prince of Wales, operated very much under his mother's influence. It is quite possible, therefore, that she became acquainted with Oliver, a fellow Huguenot, who also worked for both Queen and Prince. When she produced the *Cinquante Octonaires sur la Vanité et Inconstance du Monde* as a New Year's gift for Prince Henry in 1607, she used prints by Hans Vredeman de Vries for the decorations of arms and armour of Octonaires 1–5.[17] A few year later these prints were also used by Oliver to decorate the Letters Patent of the creation of Prince Henry as Prince of Wales.[18] Henry's love for the martial arts was widely known.

Allthough the production of Books of Hours in the Ghent-Bruges style was over by the 1550s, flower borders continued to be popular in documents produced for the court in England. Hilliard, for instance, still used flowers in the border of his illumination in the 'Liber Ceruleus' of the Order of the Garter in 1603. Letters patent, indentures, treaties, and the official books of the Order of the Garter were already being decorated in the Ghent-Bruges style in the early 16th century, often with the inclusion of a royal portrait. The flowers in the title-pages of Esther Inglis's manuscripts for 1606–1607 and those at the top of the other pages of the three New Year's gifts for 1606, all closely resemble the flowers one finds in Books of Hours or in Missals containing musical scores of the late fifteenth or early sixteenth centuries. She must have copied them, for as Scott-Elliot and Yeo have established, Esther Inglis was not an inventive draughtswoman.[19] Where she found her examples, however, is difficult to determine. Did she copy directly from a Book of Hours? Were there perhaps still fifteenth-century model books in circulation that she could have used?[20] Or did loose leaves of Books of Hours circulate to be used as examples?[21]

In July 1606 Queen Anne's brother, King Christian of Denmark, came to England for a state visit. With him came his Chancellor, Christianus Friis (1556–1616), who was famous for his generosity. For him Esther Inglis prepared another flower illustrated manuscript. She had ample time, for, as she states in her dedication to him, the arrival of the King had been talked about for the previous five months. She adds that he has been 'tant recommandee de tous pour vostre vertu et grand sage, ayant maintes fois en escosse, oye parler de vostre tresillustre nom.' This manuscript bears the date 29 July 1606, which was the day of 'Great Brytaine's kind Welcome to her dear Brethren the Danes'[22]—the perfect day to present Friis with a gift book.

On the whole, the decorations in this manuscript are similar to the ones in the three 1606 New Year's gifts, with the exception of two. Unlike the other flowers, which suggest a 'medieval' source, these two are contemporary. Esther Inglis had taken them from a florilegium,[23] called *Florae Deae* (*c.*1590)[24] (PLATES 2 and 3). This series of twelve engravings of flowers also includes some insects, a lizard, a mouse, two birds and two frogs. Curiously, she would use the two frogs as an illustration to octo xx[25] in her *Octonaries upon the Vanitie and Inconstancie of the World* (1607). The series must have been very popular. Some of its flowers, for instance, can be traced in a window of painted glass at Lydiard Park in

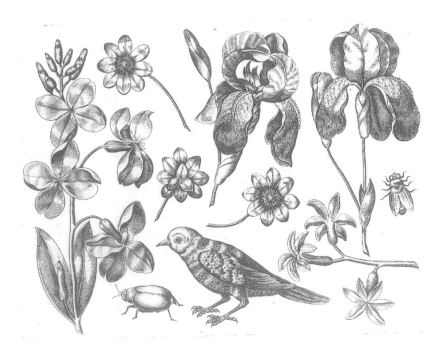

PLATE 2. *Folio 3 of* Florae Deae, *Anonymous, c.1600: Private collection (Original page 129 × 176mm). Reproduced by permission.*

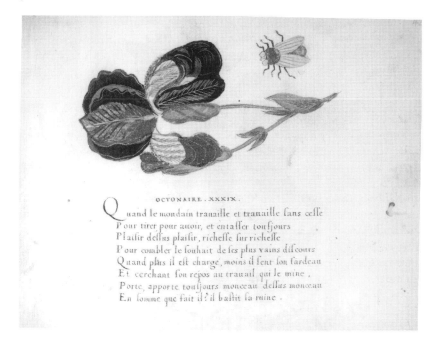

OCTONAIRE . XXXIX .

Quand le mondain tranaille et tranaille fans ceſſe
Pour tirer pour auoir, et entaſſer touſjours
Plaiſir deſſus plaiſir, richeſſe ſur richeſſe
Pour combler le ſouhait de ſes plus vains diſcours
Quand plus il eſt charge, moins il ſent ſon fardeau
Et cerchant ſon repos au trauail qui le mine ,
Porte, apporte touſjours monceau deſſus monceau
En ſomme que fait il? il baſtit ſa ruine .

PLATE 3. *Octonaire 39 of Esther Inglis's* Cinquante Octonaires sur la va vanite *[sic]* et inconstance du monde, *1607: Windsor Castle, The Royal Collection (Original page 120 × 155mm). Reproduced by permission of Her Majesty the Queen.*

Wiltshire, painted by Abraham van Linge in about 1629.[26] Others can be found in the borders of a number of watercolour drawings with panoramic views of Belgian cities from 1608–1609 by Adrien de Montigny (d.1615).[27]

Another gift book, which had cost Esther Inglis considerable time to prepare in 1606, is the *Argumenta in Librum Psalmorum*, dedicated to Sir Thomas Egerton, Lord Ellesmere (1540?–1617). Egerton had been Lord Keeper under Queen Elizabeth and had been reappointed to this position by King James in April 1603. On 19 July 1603 James created him Baron Ellesmere and on the 24th made him Lord Chancellor. The manuscript which Esther Inglis dedicated to him consists of 101 leaves and is the most voluminous she produced. This was a gift of the highest quality she could produce and it was probably intended to help her husband's career. As Lord Keeper, Egerton had the right to present all the benefices belonging to the Crown.

The dedication, in which Esther Inglis states that he will receive the manuscript from her husband's hands, is followed by 42 lines of groveling Latin verse by Bartholomew Kello to Egerton. Kello calls him 'Solamen miseris' [solace for the wretched] and adds that it is to Egerton only that he turns for help: 'Te solum appello: expertus succedere fauste Auspicijs (foelix) cuncta peracta tuis' (It is to you only that I appeal, knowing that all things under your favour end happily and prosperously). After the appropriate words of praise to his Maecenas Kello concludes with a plea: 'Ergo fave audenti, spirantem dirige: inermem Facta conaturum fortia tolle mana. Emergam angusto (Mecoenas) carcere, vestro Praesidio ut campo liberiore fruar' (Therefore, favour your servant and give his life direction. Accept the helpless man who wants to perform great deeds. I will climb out of my narrow dungeon, and under your protection, mecoenas, graze in the free field). It is not clear whether the manuscript was presented to the Lord Chancellor in 1606 or 1607. The title states 'Exarata Londini, 1606', but the self-portrait that is included in the manuscript bears the date 1607. Whether it was the result of his plea or not, on 21 December 1607 Bartholomew Kello was collated to the Rectory of Willingale Spain in Essex, one of the livings in the Crown's possession.[28]

Many decorations in the Egerton manuscript are still of the 'medieval' type, but now there are more flowers from contemporary sources. Eighteen of the flowers were taken from the *Florae Deae* set of engravings, and fourteen others were copied from a set of prints called *Fiori Naturali per Ricami d'ogni sorte* (*c.*1600) (PLATES 4 and 5). The *Fiori Naturali* set is extremely rare; the only known copy is in the Pierpont Morgan Library.[29] The rarity is perhaps due to the fact that these prints were meant to be used as examples, in this case *per ricami d'ogni sorte* (for all kind of embroidery). They were usually sold as loose leaves, which then served as patterns for embroiderers, but also for painters, decorators, goldsmiths, sculptors, and so on. Often the design was copied by means of 'pouncing'—pricking through the outline of the required motif, then dusting charcoal through the holes, to produce a copy on the piece to be decorated. This was the technique which Esther Inglis used as well. First of all, the flowers she copied are the exact same size as those in the source they were taken from, which is the reason why they often appear out of scale with the text. But secondly, although this was not really visible on the relevant page of the manuscript, when I looked as a print-out from a microfilm of the page, it unexpectedly showed the pinpricks around one of the flowers in the *Octonaries upon the Vanitie and Inconstancie of the World* of December 1607. This method of copying meant, however, that the originals were likely to be short-lived.

PLATE 4. *Folio 6 of* Fiori Naturali, *Anonymous, c.1600: New York, Pierpont Morgan Library, PML 37979 (Original size 153 × 110mm). Reproduced by permission of the Pierpont Morgan Library.*

PLATE 5. *Octonarie 1 of Esther Inglis's* Octonaries upon the Vanitie and Inconstancie of the World, *1600: Washington, D.C., Folger Shakespeare Library, MS V.a. 91 (Original page 113 × 161mm). Reproduced by permission of the Folger Shakespeare Library.*

After a certain amount of usage they became worn out and were simply thrown away.

It seems that Esther Inglis did not add the flower illustrations until after she had written the texts. At least, this is what she did for the *Octonaries* and with this text it got her into problems. When I compared all six flower illustrated copies of the *Octonaries* (Nos. 1, 8, 9, 11, 15 and 16 of the Appendix) with the originals by Antoine de la Roche Chandieu (1543–1591)[30] her numbering did not always correspond with Chandieu's. When writing the text she had reserved space at the top of the page for the illustration. Together with the illustration she introduced the numbers of the octonaries, but for some reason (perhaps something as arbitrary as a gust of wind or the children knocking them off the table) their order got mixed up before they were illustrated and thus numbered. It seems she did not have the originals at hand to check the correct order.[31] Later, in her unillustrated copies of the *Octonaires* in French, she reverted to the correct numbering of them.

The year 1606 was Esther Inglis's most productive year as far as gift
books are concerned. Not only did she produce the ones that bear the
date 1606, but she also prepared six more as New Year's gifts for 1607.
In these manuscripts she predominantly used the *Florae Deae* and the
Fiori Naturali flowers. To reinforce her status as a calligrapher, she had
included in the three New Year's gifts dated 1606 the device of two
crossed gold quill pens within a wreath surmounted by a gold and jew-
elled crown, with the motto NIL PENNA SED USUS. This was a
favourite symbol of calligraphers, which she had probably copied from
Jacob Houthusius ('Antverpianus'), *Exemplaria sive formulae scripturae orna-*
toris xxxvi (1591). Not only was it a favourite symbol, it was a prestigious
one as well. Both the 'Golden Pen of Twentie Pounds' and the 'Prix de
la Plume Couronnée' were first prizes that could be won in handwriting
competitions that existed both in England and abroad. The device is
repeated in most of her flower manuscripts, sometimes without a motto
and sometimes with the motto VIVE LA PLUME (PLATE 6). Since
it only occurs in the manuscripts from this period, it is tempting to

PLATE 6. *Folio 54 of Esther Inglis's* Cinquante Octonaires sur la va vanite
[sic] et inconstance du monde, *1607: Windsor Castle, The Royal Collection*
(Original page 120 × 155mm). Reproduced by permission of Her Majesty the Queen.

speculate if Esther Inglis had participated in a calligraphic contest in 1605 and won. Verses included in the last flower manuscript of 1607, the one dedicated to William Jefferay, do call her the 'only Paragon and matchles Mistress of the golden Pen'. Scott-Elliot and Yeo are convinced this is standard praise only, but it could explain her large production of a particular style of manuscript as a way to make capital out of winning such a prize. Her fame of being the 'Mistress of the golden Pen' would only last until the next contest and she would, therefore, have to make the most of it as quickly as she could.

It is clear that, although Esther Inglis may not have been an inventive draughtswoman, she was anxious to present herself as a highly skilled one—one who is not only worth employing, but also whose work is worth collecting, as she makes clear in her dedication of the flower manuscript dated 26 January 1607, to William Douglas, the Earl of Morton. She states: 'That one unknown to your Lo[rdship] has emboldned hir selfe to present you with a few grapes of hir collection, I hope your Lo: shal not altogether mislyk therof. Therfore sen I hard of your cumming to this countrie, I have bene exercised in perfyting this little book dedicated to your Lo: Beseeching you accept of it and the rather becaus it is a womans work. Thus assuring thir blossomes I have collected of Dame Flora shall have sum hid corner in your Lo: cabinet, I pray God (most noble Lord) to have you allways in his keeping.'

She hopes he will have a place for this gift in his 'cabinet'. This shows that she saw her work as a collector's item, as indeed it still is today. Part of the essential apparatus of the nobleman, or the learned gentleman, was a cabinet of curiosities. In a work called *Gesta Grayorum*[32] we find it included in the 'four principal Works and Monuments of your self': first, 'The collecting of a most perfec and general Library'; next, 'A spacious, wonderful Garden'; but third 'A goodly huge Cabinet, wherein whatsoever the Hand of Man by exquisite Art or Engine, hath made rare in Stuff, Form, or Motion, whatsoever Singularity, Chance and the Shuffle of things hath produced . . .'[33] It is not in Morton's 'library' that Esher Inglis hopes her work will find a place, but in his 'cabinet'.[34]

After the manuscript to Morton in January 1607 there follows only one other flower manuscript. This is *Octonaries upon the Vanitie and Inconstancie of the World*, dated 23 December 1607 and dedicated to her 'freinde and landlord' William Jefferay. Since there is almost a whole year between the Morton manuscript and this one, we can actually say that the production of Esther Inglis's flower manuscripts stopped after January 1607. Everything points to the fact that during 1606 and 1607 she was trying to make ends meet. With her large production of manuscripts she tried to generate both work and money. If, for example, she got £5 each for the six New Year's gifts and the manuscript to the Earl of Morton in 1607,[35] then she would have had £35 for the whole year. 'M^{ris} Prymrose nurse to the Prince' received £30 as a yearly salary. Together with some commissioned work this would probably have been enough for her family, which consisted of four children by now, to survive until Kello was inducted Rector of Willingale Spain on 21 December 1607. The last flower manuscript from this period is signed from 'Mortelaik' [Mortlake], a village within walking distance from Richmond Palace, Prince Henry's main seat. The date, 23 December, is probably the date that Esther Inglis left Mortlake to move to Essex to join her husband in his new rectorship. Since it is dedicated to her 'freinde and landlord', this last manuscript may even have been a going-away present and a way to pay the rent at the same time.

What I have tried to establish so far is that Esther Inglis's large production of flower manuscripts was galvanized by pressing financial needs. She was trying to find patronage and the new style she used was to demonstrate her skill as a calligrapher. After 1607 her production of manuscripts decreased dramatically. With the exception of a few title pages, the colourful decorations disappeared and her gifts became really small in size—some of them not much larger than a matchbox—although she had occasionaly used this size before. After 1608, she used one, or at most two, styles of script for the text of the work only. There could be several reasons why she produced the flower illustrations only in 1606/1607. Perhaps she miscalculated their attraction as curiosities, perhaps their style had become outmoded, or perhaps they were simply too labour intensive to be worth producing over and over again. Moreover, if she only had one set of each florilegium, the technique of pouncing meant that she was limited in the number of times that the flowers could be copied.

Another reason for not returning to this style may have been that she had found some continued patronage, possibly at Prince Henry's court. In early biographies Esther Inglis is said to have been nurse to Prince Henry and although this has been refuted by Scott-Elliot and Yeo, it seems at least to suggest a known connection to Prince Henry's court. Perhaps together with her husband's stipend at Willingale Spain it offered them enough stability financially not to have to work the market again. Kello kept his living until the end of 1614. During the seven years that her husband held the benefice, Esther Inglis produced only eight manuscripts that we know of, five of which are dedicated either to Prince Henry or to Sir David Murray (1567–1629), the Prince's Gentleman of the Bedchamber. The fact that she rarely approached other patrons seems to reinforce the argument that she had found some kind of prolonged patronage in his household, at least until the Prince's death in 1612, and had, therefore, no further need to advertise her calligraphic skills.

The fact that she only produced the flower illustrations in 1606/1607 seems to be contradicted by two manuscripts that have been included in the Appendix below: Nos. 1 and 16. The first bears the date 1600 and the second 1609. They are each a copy of the *Octonaries upon the Vanitie and Inconstancie of the World*, the one dated 1609 with the English text only and the one dated 1600 with both the original French text and the English translation. In both these manuscripts she mainly used the flowers from the two florilegia as her illustrations. If we are right in our speculations about the limitations of the technique of pouncing, both manuscripts must have been produced by her in 1606/1607. So why are they dated 1600 and 1609 respectively?

Unlike her other flower manuscripts, these two contain writing mistakes. Originally, they were both dated 1600, but in 1600 she was still in Scotland, producing a different type of manuscript and styling herself Esther Anglois, fille Françoise.[36] The two manuscripts simply do not fit in with her other work from 1600. For No. 16 she changed 1600 into 1609 and dedicated it to Lord Petre. Perhaps she decided to use this manuscript after all because, apart from the date, it contained only one other writing error, which she corrected by pasting over it a slip of paper with the correct text.

No. 1, however, contains a large number of writing errors in the French text. Most of these mistakes were too serious to be corrected. In octo 16, for instance, she used the first two lines of the next octo by mistake. The English text has the correct translation. She wrote 'Le Mondain se nourrit tousjours De l'espoir de ses vains discours', whereas her English text reads 'The wordling [*sic*] still desyres, and ever feares withall A contraire martyredome, his hart doth doubly gall', which is the correct translation of the first two lines she should have written: 'Le Mondain craint tousjours et tousjours il desire, Doublement tourmenté d'un contraire martyre.' Mistakes of this nature occur more often.[37] We see that Esther Inglis must have been word-blind with regard to the translation of 'mondain'. Only once or twice does she write the correct translation 'worldling', in all other cases she uses 'wordling'. Since she never used this manuscript as a gift book, she may not have felt it necessary to correct the 1600 date.

Finally, what can we say about Esther Inglis's use of flowers in general? First and foremost she used them to produce attractive manuscripts—

the kind of manuscript that would generate money and work. Her technique of copying the flowers from the florilegia after she had written the texts got her into some trouble with the numbering of Chandieu's *Octonaires*, but this was obviously never considered too serious a mistake. She still turned them into gift books, with the exception of one, which actually contained too large a number of writing errors to be corrected.

The attractive quality of the manuscripts, however, may not have been the only reason why Esther Inglis turned to flower illustrations. We see that in many of her dedications she stressed the fact that it is 'a woman's work'. It shows that she was aware of the special position of a woman in what was predominently a man's world. As a woman she was limited in her choice of texts and we see that she concentrated on biblical or devotional texts. Jonathan Goldberg says about this: 'Inglis transcribes just the sorts of text that Vives thought appropriate for a woman; she is a copyist of religious texts.'[38] Is this also true for her illustrations? Are these also prudent, chaste and devotional enough to be a 'woman's work'? In the medieval Books of Hours, the flowers were initially connected with Marian symbolism. The white lily represented her purity, the violet and the strawberry her humility, the carnation Christ's suffering, the marigold obedience, and so on. Soon, however, the decorative purpose outweighed the symbolic purpose, especially in the Ghent-Bruges style books. Besides, as a Huguenot Esther Inglis is not likely to have reverted to Catholic religious symbolism.

On the other hand, she must have been aware that flower symbolism existed. In the only independent portrait of her, made in 1595, the year before she got married, we see a small 'knot' of flowers in the top lefthand corner (PLATE 7). Two joined sprigs, of what could be lavender, form the basis for a knot with a carnation and woodbine. The carnation appeared frequently on engagement portraits as a symbol of love and chastity, the woodbine appears less frequently, but is used, nevertheless, in paintings as a symbol of faithfulness. As a climber it needs support to grow. There is no evidence that she had this type of symbolism in mind, however, when she used flowers to illustrate her manuscripts.

Is it possible that she may have had a more general symbolism in mind? In many 17th-century paintings flowers were often used as a *vanitas* symbol, an image of the transience of life. Certainly, when they occur as illustrations with the *Octonaries upon the Vanitie and Inconstancie of the World*, one is inclined to think that Esther Inglis included her flowers for this reason:

PLATE 7. *Portrait of Esther Inglis, Anonymous, 1595: Edinburgh, Scottish National Portrait Gallery (Original size 726 × 632mm). Reproduced by permission of the Scottish National Portrait Gallery.*

The world a gardine is: The floures her pleasures are:
Of faire and fragrant ones, it hath exceeding plainty
The pale-hewde Flowre de Luce, The Rose so sweet and dainty,
All sortee of Gillifloure, whose fyne parfume be rare,
And there the Soussy doth beyond his fellows thryve,
The Vyolet is there, and there the Pansye groce;
But Death the winter is, that straight away doth dryve
The Luce with all the reste; The Gillifloure and Rose.

(octo 34)

As this octonarie shows she was aware of flowers as a *vanitas* symbol, but I do not think this was uppermost on her mind when she chose to illustrate her texts with flowers, for she used flowers to illustrate all her other texts as well in this period. Moreover, she also included small animals and insects.

The answer probably lies in a prefatory sonnet by Jacques le Moyne de Morgues (*c.*1533–1588), also a Huguenot who lived in London, to one of his studies of plants:

Discordant harmony and balanced movement,
Winter and Summer, Autumn, reborn Spring,
Renewing her sweet scents and colouring,
Join in the praise of God's unfailing judgment.

This loving God gives every argument
To look for zeal from each created thing,
To bless His Name eternally and sing
All He has made in earth and firmament.

Above all He made man with head held high
To watch each morning as new light arrives
And decorates earth's breast with varied flowers.

There is no fruit, or grain, or grub, or fly
That does not preach one God, the least flower gives
Pledge of a Spring with everlasting colours.

Iaques le Moinne, dit de Morgues. Peintre.[39]
1585

Plants and animals convey the abundance of God's creation, which compels wonder and admiration. The belief that God was manifest in the most insignificant creature was widespread. Seen in this light, it becomes clear how appropriate the Dame Flora metaphor, which Esther Inglis used for both her verses and her illustrations, actually was.

APPENDIX

Esther Inglis's flower-illustrated manuscripts

1. *Octonaries upon the Vanitie and Inconstancie of the World. Writin by Esther Inglis, the first of Ianuar 1600.* [Washington, D.C., Folger Shakespeare Library, MS V.a. 91]

2. *A New Yeers Guift for the Right Honorable and Vertuous Lord my Lord Sidnay of the hand writing and limning of mee Esther Inglis the first of Ianuar, 1606.* [University of Texas at Austin, The Carl H. Pforzheimer Library, MS 40]

3. *Une Estreine pour tresillustre et vertueuse Dame la Contesse de Bedford, escrit et illuminé par moy Esther Inglis ce 1 de Janvier, 1606.* [Private collection]

4. *A New Yeeres Guift for the Right Honorable and Vertuous Lady the Lady of Arskene of Dirltoun. Of the hand writting and limning of mee Esther Inglish, the 1. of Iannuar, 1606.* [Chicago, Newberry Library, Wing MS-ZW 645.K29]

5. *Tetrasticha selecta historiae Geneseos, Estherae Inglis manu exaratae. Londini 1606.* (Dedicated to Christianus Frisen, 29 July 1606.) [Berlin, Staatsbibliothek, MS Lat.oct.14]

6. *Argumenta in Librum Psalmorum Davidis Estherae Inglis Manu Exarata Londini 1606.* (Dedicated to Lord Chancelor Ellesmere.) [Cambridge, Massachusetts, Harvard University, Houghton Library, MS Typ 212]

7. *Argumenta in Librum Geneseos Esthere Inglis manu exarata Londini 1606.* (Dedicated to Thomas Wotton.) [Private collection]

8. *Cinquante Octonaires sur la va vanite* [sic] *et inconstance du monde. Dediez a monseigneur le Prince, pour ses estrennes, de l'an, 1607. Escrit et illuminé par moy Esther Inglis.* [Windsor Castle, Royal Library]

9. *Cinquant* [sic] *Octonaires sur la vanité et inconstance du monde, dediez a tresillustre seigneur le conte de Shrewsbury, pour ses estrennes l'an 1607.* [Edinburgh, National Library of Scotland, MS 25240]

10. *Argumenta singulorum capitum Eccles: per tetrasticha manu Estherae Inglis exarata strenae nomine egregio et dignissimo adolescentulo, M. Thomae Pukering oblata 1607.* [New York, Pierpont Morgan Library, MA 2149]

11. *Cinquante Octonaires sur la vanité et inconstance du monde, dediez, a tresillustre et puissant seigneur Lodowic Duc de Lenox &c: pour ses estrennes Escrit et illumine par Esther Inglis 1607.* [Edinburgh, Scottish Record Office, GD 18/4508]

12. *Les Quatrains du Sieur de Pybrac dediez a tresillustre et tresnoble Seigneur, monseigneur le Conte de Salisberrie, pour ses estrennes, de l'an 1607 Escrit et*

illuminé par moi Esther Inglis. [Edinburgh, University Library, MS La.III.439]

13. *Les Quatrains du Sr. de Pybrac dediez a tresnoble et treshonorable Seigneur, Monseigneur de Hayes, pour ses estrennes 1607 Escrit et illumine, par moy Esther Inglis.* [Chicago, Newberry Library, Wing MS-ZW 645.K292]

14. *Argumenta in singulorum, capitum Evangelii Matthaei Apostoli, per tetrasticha manu Estherae Inglis exarata Londini xxvi Ianuarii, 1607.* (Dedicated to William Douglas, Earl of Morton.) [Private collection]

15. *Octonaries upon the Vanitie and Inconstancie of the World, writin and limd be me, Esther Inglis the xxiii, Decemb: 1607.* (Dedicated to William Jefferay.) [Washington, D.C., Folger Shakespeare Library, MS V.a. 92]

16. *Octonaries upon the Vanitie and Inconstancie of the World. Writin and limd be Esther Inglis the first of Ianuar, 1609.* (Dedicated to Lord Petre.) [New York Public Library, Spencer Collection, French MS 14]

NOTES

In writing this article I have received a gread deal of help and encouragement from Dr Peter Beal. I am also grateful to Professor Bart Westerweel (Leiden University) for commenting on an earlier draft. Thanks for their helpful advice are also due to Professor Paul Hoftijzer (University of Amsterdam), Anthony Wells-Cole (Temple Newsam House), Georgianna Ziegler (Folger Shakespeare Library), Elspeth Yeo and A.H. Scott-Elliot.

1 A full description of Esther Inglis's life and career can be found in A.H. Scott-Elliot and Elspeth Yeo, 'Calligraphic Manuscripts of Esther Inglis (1571–1624): A Catalogue', *Papers of the Bibliographical Society of America*, 84 (1990), 11–86; henceforth referred to as 'Catalogue'.

    Scott-Elliot and Yeo recorded 55 manuscripts. Yet, after their seemingly definitive catalogue, already four other works by Esther Inglis have come to light: (1) *Quatrains du Sieur de Pybrac gentilhomme François, Escrit En diverse sortes de lettres; Par Esther Anglois Françoise, A Lislebourg ce 30 Dec. 1600*, dedicated to Henri, Vicomte de Rohan (private collection); (2) *Cinquant Octonaires sur la vanité et inconstance du monde, dediez a tresillustre seigneur le conte de Shrewsbury, pour ses estrennes l'an 1607*, (National Library of Scotland, MS 25240; (3) *Quatrains de Sieur de Pybrac, 1616*, dedicated to Robert Boyd of Trochrig (National Trust for Scotland, Culzean Castle); and (4) *Les Cinquante Octonaires sur la Vanité et Inconstance du Monde escrits par Esther Inglis a Lislebourg Iuil. 1616*, dedicated to 'Madamoiselle de Trochrig espouse de monsieur Robert Boyd' (National Trust for Scotland, Culzean Castle).

2 David Laing, 'Notes relating to Mrs Esther (Langlois or) Inglis, the celebrated calligraphist, etc.', *Proceedings of the Society of Antiquaries of Scotland*, 6 (1865), 287.

3 The warrant is reproduced in the article by David Laing, but it is now lost.

4 'Catalogue', 14.

5 See 'Catalogue', 17. Illustrations of this type of work can be found in 'Catalogue', Plates 9–17.

6 Edinburgh University Library, MS La.III.525, ff. 7 and 8. The *Album* spans the years 1602–1605.

7 Quoted by David Thomas in 'Financial and Administrative Developments,' in *Before the English Civil War. Essays on Early Stuart Politics and Government*, ed. Howard Tomlinson (London, 1983), p. 105. Thomas also states that 'during the first four years of his reign, [James] distributed £68,000 in gifts, £30,000 in pensions and £174,000 in debts owed to the crown. By 1610 his annual expenditure on fees and annuities to royal servants and courtiers was £80,000. This was £50,000 a year more than Elizabeth had spent.'

8 G.P.V. Akrigg, *Jacobean Pageant or The Court of King James I* (London, 1962), p. 49. He also recounts the story of Sir Roger Aston, the King's Master Falconer, who, when asked how he did after his arrival in England, confided, 'Even my Lords, like a poore man wandring above forty yeares in a Wilderness, and barren Soyle, and now arrived at the Land of Promise.'

9 Harvard University, Houghton Library, MS Typ. 428.1

10 See Phoebe Sheavyn, *The Literary Profession in the Elizabethan Age* (New York, 1967), chapter 1: 'Authors and Patrons'.

11 Joseph Hall, *Virgidemiarum*; quoted in Sheavyn, p. 8.

12 See Linda Levy Peck, *Court Patronage and Corruption in Early Stuart England* (London, 1990; rpt. 1993), p. 22.

13 The manuscript dedicated to Susanna Herbert measures 150 × 200mm. The Scottish manuscripts for 1599 and 1601, with the exception of two, measure 185 × 130mm. on average, whereas the flower-illustrated ones are on average 100 × 135mm.

14 See *Flemish Illuminated Manuscripts 1475–1550*, ed. Maurits Smeyers and Jan Van der Stock (Ghent, 1996).

15 Roy Strong, *Artists of the Tudor Court* (London, 1983), p. 9.

16 Of Queen Anne's favourites she approached Susanna Herbert, Robert Sidney and the Countess of Bedford. Sidney was Queen Anne's Lord High Chamberlain and Surveyor General—the man responsible for the entertainments, plays and other festivities at Anne's court—and Lucy Harington, Countess of Bedford, was the Queen's closest and most influential friend. Susanna Herbert was Susanna de Vere, the third daughter of Edward de Vere, Earl of Oxford. In May 1603 she had turned sixteen and had been included among the Queen's ladies, probably through the influence of her uncle Robert Cecil, Earl of Salisbury (1563?–1612). She soon became one of Queen Anne's favourites and appeared in many of the Queen's court masques. Cecil, who in October 1603 had been appointed Lord High Steward to Queen Anne, was also one of the dedicatees of this period. As far as Prince Henry's court is concerned, she dedicated a manuscript to him and to two of his companions: Thomas Puckering (1592–1636) and Thomas Wotton (1587–1630).

17 *Panoplia seu armamentarium ac ornamenta*, by Hans Vredeman de Vries, was published by Gerard de Jode in Antwerp in 1572.

18 Oliver depended heavily on continental prints. See Jill Finsten, *Isaac Oliver: Art at the Courts of Elizabeth I and James I* (New York & London, 1981).

19 'Catalogue', 17.

20 Celia Fisher in her dissertation at the Courtauld Institute of Art—*The Development of Flower Borders in Ghent-Bruges Manuscripts 1470–1490* (London, 1996)—is convinced that sketchbooks of plant studies, to be used as guides or examples by the illuminator producing a Book of Hours, existed, but none of these model books is known to have survived.

21 The way that the antiquary and scholar Sir Robert Cotton (1571–1631) bound some of the manuscripts which he collected seems to point to the fact that loose leaves were in circulation. For instance, he used a fifteenth-century illuminated flower border and initial as frontispiece to BL Cotton MS Nero A.ii. To this page, which must have been taken from a medieval Book of Hours, he added his own text and his coat of arms. He went even further in BL Cotton MS Galba A. xviii, where the vellum title page is a floral border taken from a Book of Hours, with the middle part cut out, pasted around another image that was cut out and pasted on. The collection that follows is totally unconnected with the flower-border page.

22 See J.B. Nichols, *Progresses of King James I* (London, 1828), II, 53–54. The King of Denmark had arrived on 18 July 1606, 'After many reports and long expecting'.

23 *Florilegia* in the sense of 'a book consisting largely or entirely of pictures of flowers' were very popular in the 17th century. They were an extension of the herbals, the botanical books, that flourished during the mid-16th century, in particular in the Low Countries and Germany. These books, however, depicted the plant, gave its name and described its practical use. The *florilegia*, or flower books, depicted flowers only and usually no longer served a botanical purpose. Their purpose was to be used in the decorative arts. The engravers of the *florilegia* often copied extensively from the older herbals, as well as from each other. A large number of the flowers which Adriaen Collaert (1560–1618) used in his *Florilegium* (*c*.1590), for instance, can be traced to the herbals of Rembertus Dodoneaus, Matthias Lobelius, and Carolus Clusius, published by Christophe Plantin (*c*.1520–1589) in Antwerp. Similarly, many of the flowers used in the *Florae Deae* set can be traced to the *Altera Pars Horti Floridi*, by Chrispyn de Passe the Elder (1565–1637). Although it is usually bound together with the *Hortus Floridus* (1614) by his son Crispyn de Passe the Younger (1593-after 1670), it had been published separately at an earlier date as well, without a title page or texts.

24 The title-page of the set is captioned: *FLORAE DEAE Inter patrios & exoticos flores sedentis artificiosa delineatio variorum florum subsequente efigiae*, with verses in Latin below. Possibly the earliest set is in the collection of the Kunstbibliothek in Berlin. It is dated *c*.1590 and states 'Sadler Excud.' If the date is correct, this could have been either Johannes Sadeler (Brussels *c*.1550–Venice 1600) or his brother Raphael Sadeler (Antwerp 1561–Munich 1632), both of whom signed their engravings 'Sadler'. The second generation of Sadelers always included the middle *e* in their name. The Sadeler family played a prominent role in the Antwerp school of engraving. At the end of the 16th century whole families, such as de Passe, Wierix, de Jode, Collaert and Galle, were involved in print-making. Occasionally the *Florae Deae* set has been attributed to Justus Sadeler (Antwerp 1583–Leiden 1620), the son of Johannes Sadeler. Considering the fact that he was only seven in 1590, he is not very likely to have been the engraver. Sam Segal, in his *Flowers and Nature, Netherlandish Flower Painting of Four Centuries* (The Hague, 1990), attributes the set to Adriaen Collaert, on the basis that it is sometimes found together with Collaert's *Florilegium*.

25 Esther Inglis is not very consistent in the way she refers to the verses. Sometimes she calls them 'octonaires', or 'octonaries' in English, and sometimes she uses the abbreviated form 'octo'. When referring to her rendering of the verses, I will follow her denomination of them.

26 See Michael Archer, *The Painted Glass of Lydiard Tregoze* (Swindon, [1975?]). I am grateful to Anthony Wells-Cole for bringing this to my attention.

27 The set in the Print Room of the Royal Library Albert I in Brussels (F26714–26745) consists of 32 drawings. In five of them the flowers can be traced to the *Florae Deae* prints.

28 On the other hand, it may not have been through Egerton at all that Kello got the living. He could also have gotten it through Sir David Murray, Prince Henry's Gentleman of the Bedchamber. On 1 January 1608, several days after Kello's appointment in Willingale Spain, Esther Inglis dedicated to Murray 'A Treatise of Preparation to the Holy Supper . . . Translated out of French in Inglishe . . . by Bartholomew Kello . . .' There was not really any need for Kello to translate the 'Treatise', because it had already appeared in print in English as early as 1578. It may, therefore, have been a sign of Esther Inglis and her husband's gratitude, the more so since the dedication includes a long passage on the value of a beautiful soul, such as Murray's.

29 Pierpont Morgan Library, New York, PML 37979. Most of its flowers are direct copies—in mirror image—from Adriaen Collaert's *Florilegium*, which was published in Antwerp around 1590. The interesting question is how this florilegium came to be copied in Italy. One possibility is that this was done by either Johannes (1550–1600) or Justus Sadeler (1583–1620), father and son, who lived in Venice from the mid 1590s. Justus, who spent most of his life in Venice, was an important figure in the artistic relationship between northern and southern Europe between 1600 and 1620. In *Les Graveurs des écoles du Nord à Venise (1582–1620), les Sadeler, entremise et entreprise* (3 vols., Paris, 1987), 30, Ph. Sénéchal states that 'Artistically, Justus did not attempt to follow new trends, either Italian or Flemish: many of the originals he copied dated back to 1580. *Naturalia* after Adriaen Collaert were apparently popular . . . It made better commercial sense to copy works that were already successful throughout Europe . . . than to commission drawings or engravings from artists of his generation.'

30 The first integral publication of the *Octonaires sur la Vanité et Inconstance du Monde* by Antoine de la Roche Chandieu was in 1583 by Guillaume Laimarie in Geneva under the title: *MEDITATIONS Sur le Psalme XXXII. Traduictes de Latin en François, & revuës par l'auteur mesme, Avec une preface à ceux qui se sont despartis de l'Eglise reformee. Ont esté aussi adjoustez cinquante octonaires sur la vanité du monde. Par A. Zamariel. Avec privilege. Par G. Laimarie. M.D.LXXXIII.* Zamariel was one of Chandieu's pseudonyms.

The *Octonaires* were very popular and appeared in numerous anthologies, such as *Cantiques du Sieur de Maisonfleur* (Paris, 1586) and *Cantiques du Sieur de Valagre et du Sieur de Maisonfleur* (Paris, 1587). Esther Inglis could have used any of these, but she probably used the first integral publication of 1583. There are a number of important differences in spelling between the several publications of the *Octonaires*. Certain spellings in French which only occur in the 1583 edition also occur in Esther Inglis's manuscripts. Chandieu must have written his verses much earlier than 1583, for some twenty of his *Octonaires* had already appeared in a manuscript dated 1576 and twenty-six *Octonaires* by Chandieu were set to music in 1581 by Paschal de L'Estocart, to be followed in 1606 by Claude Le Jeune, who set twenty-nine *Octonaires* by Chandieu to music: see Françoise Bonali-Fiquet, *Antoine de Chandieu. Octonaires sur la Vanité et Inconstance du Monde* (Geneva, 1979).

31 Humfrey Lownes, the printer who printed Josuah Sylvester's translation of Chandieu's *Octonaires*, probably did not have Chandieu's originals at hand either. He must have gotten hold of them after Sylvester's death, for they were published in 1620, two years after Sylvester had died. Scott-Elliot and Yeo state that no printed translation into English exists of the *Octonaires*, but this is not true. Lownes published them in *Du Bartas his Divine Weekes and Workes with a Compleate Collection of all the other . . . Workes Translated and Written by . . . Josuah Sylvester Gent.* under the title 'Perspective Spectacles of Special Use, to discern the Worlds Vanitie, Levitie & Brevitie'. Lownes

probably did not know that they were translations of the *Octonaires* by Chandieu or he would have given them their proper title. The verses are in the correct order, however, and much better translations into English than Esther Inglis's. Of course, Esther Inglis was not a poet. Her translations stick closely to the French, for example, when there is an alexandrine in French, she will use an alexandrine in English. Sylvester uses the iambic pentameter throughout for his translations.

32 The *Gesta Grayorum: or, the History of the Prince of Purpoole, Anno Domini, 1594* did not find its way into print until 1688. This account of the Christmas revels at Gray's Inn in 1594–5 includes six speeches by councillors, which have been attributed to Francis Bacon. The quotation is from the speech by the second councillor, the one 'advising the Study of Philosophy'.

33 *Gesta Grayorum 1688*, Malone Society Reprints (1914), pp. 34–35.

34 Peter Beal pointed out to me that a previously unknown manuscript by Esther Inglis which he discovered in 1994 was indeed lying in an elaborate, lacquered 17th-century cabinet, one which had belonged to Sir William Temple (1628–99). This manuscript of the *Quatrains du Sieur de Pybrac*, dedicated to Henri, Vicomte de Rohan and dated 30 December 1600, was sold at Sotheby's on 13 December 1994, lot 21.

35 This is a reasonable amount to assume. A few years later, on 20 April 1609, Prince Henry's Privy Purse Accounts record a payment of £5 'To Mrs Kello for geving a booke of armes to his highness' (PRO E. 101/433/8).

36 It seems that at first Esther Inglis styled herself Langlois or Anglois, which was her father's last name, and that she changed to the Scottish version Inglis (pronounced 'Ingls') after 1602. However, in the dedicatory Latin verses by Andrew Melville, included in the portraits for 1599 and 1601, she is already referred to as 'Estherae Inglis'. Puzzling enough, in the same verses for the portrait in 1602 she is called 'Estherae Anglam'.

37 Another example occurs in octo 23, where the original line 3 reads: 'Pourqouy, povres Mondains, faictes-vous la guerre' and line 5: 'Pourqouy, povres Mondains, prenez-vous tant de peine', but Esther Inglis mixes them up, writing line 5 where line 3 should have been and vice versa. Her English translation follows the correct French text: 'Why do yee all the frame of heav'n and earth desioint Wordlings [*sic*], with endless warrs, who most of earth may have? Why (wordlings) [*sic*] do yee still perplex your selfs with paine'.

38 Jonathan Goldberg, *Writing Matter: From the Hands of the English Renaissance* (Stanford, 1990), p. 147. Goldberg quotes Jean Luis Vives, who wrote: 'when she shall learn to write, let not her examples be void verses, nor wanton or trifling songs, but some sad sentences prudent and chaste, taken out of holy scripture, or the sayings of philosophers, which by often writing she may fasten better her memory' [*Instruction of a Christian Woman* (1592), p. 55].

39 The original French text can be found in *Le Moyne's Botanical Watercolours* (San Francisco, 1990). The sonnet was translated by R.N. Currey.

Hand–Ma[i]de Books:
The Manuscripts of Esther Inglis, Early-Modern Precursors of the Artists' Book

Georgianna Ziegler

One imagines that William Blake would have loved computers; that he would have been the Peter Greenaway of his age, not content to experiment with calligraphy and image on the page, but to make the book come alive. His Urizen/Jehovah figure would push out of moving storm clouds in the frontispiece to *Europe*, with lightening flashing as he spreads his geometric calipers. Like Prospero's *Primer of the Small Stars* in Greenaway's film, the 'pages [would] twinkle with travelling planets, flashing meteors and spinning comets'.[1]

In our time, Greenaway's has been one of the most imaginative minds to combine the beauty of old scripts, engravings, woodcuts, bindings and rich colours from the early modern book with the third–dimensional capacity of movement allowed by film and computer technology. Outside of Greenaway, however, most interaction of books and computers thus far has focused on two techniques. On the one hand, effort has been made to scan texts and images *from* books, or photographs *of* books, and to place these images on the computer screen, either as small exhibitions or as samples of works in order to make 'rare' materials more widely accessible. On the other hand, projects are underway to encode texts so that they will be fully searchable for the computer researcher. Both of these endeavours are quite laudable, and a few of them that encourage simultaneous viewing of several different versions of a text, sometimes with sound attached, are beginning to stretch the boundaries of 'book' as a concept. But by and large, what we have seen so far are attempts to replicate the BOOK on the SCREEN. Thus, in spite of our prophesying the demise of the book, we are busily using our new technology to preserve it in a different format. We are not, then, very different from our ancestors in the fifteenth century, who at the dawn of printing attempted to recreate the familiar forms of the manuscript codex.

Fortunately, there have always been innovators; indeed, the printed book itself was an innovation over the laboriously hand-created manuscript. The best innovators adapt and combine techniques from different technologies to create new objects that make us look again, with a difference. I began with Blake because his innovations in combining drawing, printing, and engraving brought new life to the printed book, rolling off presses in ever greater numbers by the end of the eighteenth century. Blake made people look again at what they might have begun to take for granted, and his work has been considered a precursor to the modern artists' book.[2] It might be argued, however, that to begin with Blake is already too late. The anonymous artist who in 1499 Milan broke the flat surface of the page to suggest the text printed on a curtain, from behind which we can just see the feet and robes of monks about to walk through into 'our' space, was already using handpainting to give a three–dimensionality to the printed page.[3]

If this artist were working today, he would likely be making 'artists' books', defined by Johanna Drucker as 'a work by an artist self-conscious about book form, rather than merely a highly artistic book'.[4] The growth in popularity of this genre also belies our insistence on the death of the book. These works begin with the received notion of the form of a book, and then stretch its boundaries, experimenting with typography and illustration, breaking through the physical shape of page and binding, to create a work of art focused on a theme. As it happens, many artists' books are created by women who find that the medium allows them a flexible way of exploring personal feelings and concerns. Again we can find a precursor, much earlier than the eighteenth century, in the calligrapher Esther Inglis.

More attention has been paid recently to this talented Scotswoman of Huguenot ancestry who made a number of gift books for Queen Elizabeth, King James, the princes Henry and Charles, and members of the court. The few known facts about her life are to be found in the essays by George Ballard, David Laing, and Dorothy Judd Jackson, and in the near-comprehensive bibliography of her works by A.H. Scott-Elliot and Elspeth Yeo.[5] Her parents fled from France as Protestant refugees around 1569. Nicholas Langlois, her father, became Master of the French School in Edinburgh with a stipend from James VI, while her mother, Marie Pressot, practiced as a skilled calligrapher.[6] In another essay I have shown that Inglis and her husband Bernard Kello were active supporters of the Protestant cause and that many of her books were strategically-placed gifts to members of the Protestant circles around Elizabeth and James.[7]

Over fifty-five manuscript books by Inglis have been identified. Most were presentation copies of Protestant religious texts: the Psalms from the Geneva Bible and other versions; verses from Proverbs and Ecclesiastes, and the moralistic *Quatrains* of Guy de Faur, Sieur de Pybrac, and *Octonaires* of Antoine de la Roche Chandieu, two prominent French sixteenth-century religious writers. Following a common practice, Inglis made multiple copies of the same work with different dedications for gifts, thus turning the book into a 'work of art'.[8] The recycling of already-printed texts back into manuscript form was not unusual at the time, as has been well documented by Henry Woudhuysen.[9] It is one aspect of Inglis's work that parallels the practice among many current book artists, who use already-known and published texts as a take-off point for their own creativity. A recent work by Stephanie Later, for example, called *Song of Songs* reproduces parts of the Biblical text calligraphically on pages decorated with small illuminations and vine scrolls, in an exquisite binding that replicates medieval carved ivory. This artist book was part of an exhibition of the works of ninety women artists called 'Women of the Book: Jewish Artists, Jewish Themes', where the term 'book' refers to the created object, to the Bible, and to Jews themselves, 'the People of the Book'. Samples from the exhibition are now mounted on a computer web site.[10] The sense of a strong religious identity shaping the work of these contemporary women also provided much of the inspiration for Esther Inglis, who might herself be called a 'woman of the book', given the central importance of the newly-vernacularized Bible to the early Protestants. As Margaret Ezell has pointed out, seventeenth-century women in particular distributed a good deal of religious writing—their own and others'—though manuscript publication.[11]

The act of writing itself had once been considered talismanic. Thus Wolfgang Fugger, in the dedication of his handwriting manual (1553) recounts the story of a teacher who went to the King of Egypt and told him that 'by artifice that which is said or thought could be drawn in a manner which would enable another man's understanding, opinion, mood and sense to be affected thereby'.[12] The King of Egypt was not impressed, but this quality of wonder attached to writing reasserted itself in the early days of the printed book as an affirmation of the importance of hand creation. 'No print can quite compare with the work of the living hand', wrote Juan de Yciar in his handwriting manual, appropriately entitled *The Subtle Art* (*Arte Subtilissima*), 1550.[13] These same qualities—the inspired nature of handwriting and its concomitant influence on those who read it—are reflected in the dedicatory matter to the books made by Esther Inglis. In one of the Latin poems praising

Inglis's talent, John Johnston writes that 'Nature would grieve that she had been surpassed by mortal hand, were it not that she knew that these rare gifts came from great God'. In another, Andrew Melville writes:

> One hand, emulous of nature, expresses a thousand figures, animating feeble signs with painted figures, creating . . . signs that are redolent of heaven. The elaborate edge of the page surrounds these signs. It's a wonderful work, but more wonderful is the hand.[14]

Inglis herself recognizes the handmade quality of her work as a divine gift, but also as something that will give it value for the receiver. On her title-pages and in her dedications she constantly reiterates that the book was 'escrit de ma main,' 'fait de ma main,' 'escrit et trace par ma plume et pinceau'. In many of her self-portraits she presents herself standing behind a table, usually with a pen in her hand, and some combination of inkwell, book, paper, musical score and instrument in front of her.[15] On the paper or open book is often written: 'De l'Eternel le bien, de Moi le mal ou rien', reiterating the Protestant notion that all good gifts come from God and that we are worthy only through God. In her dedication of a collection of the Psalms of David for Prince Maurice of Nassau (1599), Inglis points to the 'many sorts of characters' in which it is written, intending that the variety of writing should delight the eye while the spirit of the recipient will be raised toward 'le grand Createur'.

It has long been known that a person's handwriting—his or her 'hand'—reveals something of that person's individuality. John Bulwer, the author of the *Chirologia/Chironomia* (1644), called the hand '"the *Spokesman* of the body" . . . second only to the tongue'. Michael Neill, after quoting Bulwer, goes on to say, 'The hand writes the self [and] also speaks it'. The hand is the 'symbolic guarantor of individual difference, privacy, and possession against the mechanical usurpations of print'. 'The very act of writing indeed may seem to involve an uncanny mimesis; for . . . scripture routinely represents "the hand of God" as the instrument of divine power . . .'.[16] As an artist, therefore, Inglis is a lesser god, a handmaid of the Lord, as she styles herself, creating handmade books that contain the mark of her own identity as well as the word of God through her.

In addition to the talismanic quality of handwriting, however, there were also practical and commercial associations. In his detailed study of manuscript culture during the Tudor/Stuart period, Henry Woudhuysen notes that 'even after the advent of printing, the traditional skills which the scribes of medieval manuscripts . . . had so laboriously acquired could still find an appreciative market'.[17] He gives as an example the career of Peter Bales, whose writing skills led him to be an expert witness in court cases and work for Sir Francis Walsingham, while like Inglis creating beautiful manuscripts for wealthy patrons, including most likely Queen Elizabeth.[18] Bales and his fellow poet and scribe, John Davies of Hereford, also served as tutors to Prince Henry, and Davies tutored Henry's friend Thomas Puckering, as well as a number of other courtiers. I mention this connection because Inglis worked in the same circle, dedicating several of her manuscripts to the Prince and to Thomas Puckering. These young men were obviously taught to appreciate such high-quality work by learning the rudiments of handwriting themselves.

In creating her books, as we noted, Inglis recycles already-printed texts back into manuscript form, but she makes them her own by selecting the style and what Don McKenzie has called 'the material forms of books, the non-verbal elements of the typographic notations within them, the very disposition of space itself'.[19] Earlier in her career, Inglis drew inspiration primarily from the designs of printed books, copying in meticulous detail engraved title borders, printers' ornaments, and historiated initials. Later she turned to colour and the reproduction of the kinds of flowers, fruits, or small animals that appear so often in the borders of Flemish manuscripts. Finally, late in her career, she turned back again to the printed book, creating several masterpieces including a reproduction of fifty-one of the *Emblemes ou devises chrestiennes* by Georgette de Montenay for Prince Charles. Here I want to focus on two of these manuscript books that use elements from printed books to see how Inglis incorporates a variety of 'material forms' into designs of her own.

Two of the most beautiful books from her early period are the *C.L. Psaumes de David*, dedicated to Prince Maurice of Nassau in 1599 (Washington, D.C., Folger Shakespeare Library MS V.a.93), and *Le Livre de l'Ecclesiaste*, dedicated to the Vicomtesse de Rohan in 1601 (New York Public Library, Spencer Coll. Fr. MS 8). Both combine elements from a variety of sources, not all of which have been identified, but which work together to create books with the character of the recipient in mind. The title-page of the book for Prince Maurice reproduces an unidentified printed border of a four-columned arch. At the centre of the pediment rest a corslet of armour, shield, and weapons, appropriate for the Prince who spent so much of his time in the field fighting for the Protestant cause in the Netherlands. These are flanked by allegorical male and female figures, each holding palm fronds, that appear on several of the other title-pages.[20] The columns beneath are wound with laurel; this plant and the palm branches denote victory for the cause so dear to Inglis, her family, and the Prince.

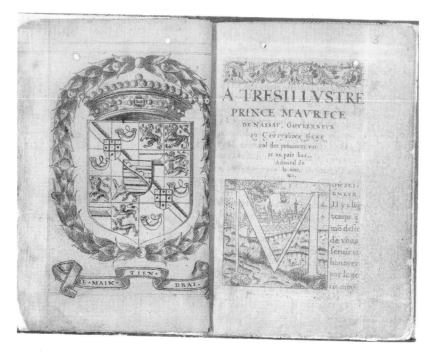

PLATE I. *Esther Inglis's Dedication to Prince Maurice of Nassau in her manuscript of* C.L. Psaumes de David, *1599: Washington, D.C., Folger Shakespeare Library MS V. a. 93, pp. 2-3 (Original size of each page 95 × 65mm.) Reproduced by permission of the Folger Shakespeare Library.*

    The first opening of the book reveals a splendid double-page design (PLATE I). On the left, the large coat-of-arms of Nassau is topped with a crown, the whole surrounded by a laurel wreath This decorative leaf motif is carried over to the top of the facing page in the stylized vegetation of the border ornament. The triangles and squares of the Nassau arms are then echoed by the triangular shape of the lettering at the head of the dedication, the square of the historiated M with text beneath, and the strong left diagonal line of the M that mirrors the diagonal bar of the facing arms. Inglis uses these and other decorative motifs throughout the volume to create a sense of unity in multeity. The Psalms in French prose are written in sixteen different styles of handwriting (*Catalogue*, 36), but all are unified by ornamental tail-pieces and by the red-lined border around the text. The last page of Psalms again brings the text into a modified triangle, echoing the first page of dedication, and this is followed by the design of a leek, tied with a ribbon bearing the word VIRESCIT (from the motto of Philip, Count of Nassau), within a wreath of leaves, topped by a crown; the whole mirroring the opening arms of Nassau. This same motif of leek in a laurel wreath with a crown appears also embroidered on the front and back velvet covers of the book, along with a leafy design that appears as well in the decorated gauffering of the book's edges.[21]

The binding would be brought to the attention of any person handling the book, as he or she would be required to turn the book sideways with the open edge towards themselves in order to read the two texts that follow the Psalms. The first is a four-line poem in French that I have identified as coming from the 1584 edition of Georgette de Montenay's *Emblematum*.[22] Its message is appropriate to the book's recipient, for the poem uses military imagery to emphasize that one's safety rests in the Lord: 'I am safer in the midst of distress than any warrior in a city or fortress. In all assaults I rest in God'. Still holding the book sideways, the viewer turns the page and sees in the next opening an emblem at the top with its Latin verse below (PLATE 2). I have identified the source as Boissard's *Emblemes Latins*, printed in Metz in 1588 with engravings by Theodor de Bry, and French interpretations by Pierre Joly Messin (PLATE 3). The emblem chosen by Inglis shows a large open book resting on a table with legs carved in female forms, standing over an open grave. In the background is a large obelisk and a burning wall. A quill pen hovers over the page, writing a Latin motto. The gist of the emblem is the sentiment expressed in Shakespeare's sonnets, that the written word outlives men and marble monuments. In the final 'Prieure a Dieu' that ends the volume, Inglis says that she has 'perfected' this book through the grace of God, a sentiment similar to that which appears on the open book in her self-portrait, included early in this volume, after the dedication to Prince Maurice.

The whole volume thus concludes with a cluster of motifs that echo the opening. The city or fortress from de Montenay's emblem is depicted in the burning wall of Boissard's emblem and in the background of the historiated M that opens the dedication. It signifies the earthly destruction in which Prince Maurice is engaged in order to bring about spiritual victory, the triumph of the word of God in the Protestant cause. The defeat of death by the word as shown in Boissard's emblem and in the final prayer is thus implicated in the purpose and creation of this book itself, written by the quill pen that appears in Boissard's emblem, in Inglis's self-portrait, and in the hands of the allegorical male and female figures on the title-page.

Not all of Inglis's manuscripts are so tightly structured, melding design, purpose, and text into a creative object that ties together

PLATE 2. *A double-page opening in Esther Inglis's manuscript of* C.L. Psaumes de David *written for Prince Maurice of Nassau, 1599: Washington, D.C., Folger Shakespeare Library* MS V. a. 93, ff. 190v–191r *(Original size of each page 65 × 95mm.) Reproduced by permission of the Folger Shakespeare Library.*

external and internal format, image and meaning. The best ones, however, such as French MS 8 from the Spencer Collection at the New York Public Library (PLATE 4), astound by the bravura of their reproduction of engraved and printed design by hand. Though Inglis uses the obsequious self-effacement that was expected of artists, writers, and women in particular, she is always aware of her own talent and of the pleasure it must afford the recipient.[23] The double text of French MS 8, including versions of *Ecclesiastes* and *The Song of Songs*, is dedicated to Catherine de Parthenay, Vicomtesse de Rohan. Inglis offers the fruits of her pen to this Protestant, highly-cultured woman, with the variety of hands that she says she has drawn in more diverse ways than anyone else of that

EMBLEMATA.   41

Ad Hugonem Babelum Hippolytanum.

34.   Viue ut viuas.

ΚΑΛΩC ΑΚΟΥΕΙΝ Η ΠΛΟΥΤΕΙΝ ΘΕΛΕ
ΚΑΙ ΖΗΤΕΙ CΕΑΥΤΩ ΔΟΞΑΝ
ΕΓΚΑΤΑΛΙΠΕΙΝ

Non omnis vivit, vitâ qui spirat in istâ;
Sed qui post fati funera vivit adhuc:
Et cui posteritas famæ præconia servat
Æternum is, calamo vindice, nomen habet.

F

PLATE 3. *A page in Jean Jacques Boissard's* Emblemes Latins *(Metz, 1588) used as a source by Esther Inglis: Washington, D.C., Folger Shakespeare Library P.N 6349 B6 F51 Cage, p. 41 (Original size 180 × 136mm.) Reproduced by permission of the Folger Shakespeare Library.*

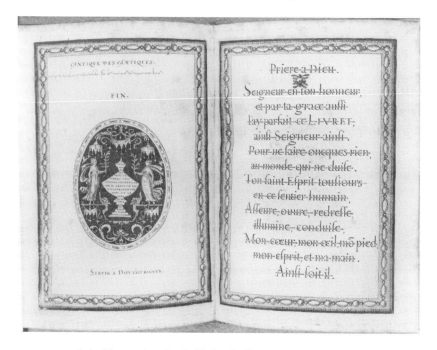

PLATE 4. *A double-page opening in Esther Inglis's manuscript of* Le Cantique du Roy Salomon, *1601: New York Public Library, Spencer Collection Fr. MS 8, ff. 24v–25r (Original size of each page 174 × 136mm.) Reproduced by permission of the Spencer Collection, The New York Public Library, Astor, Lenox and Tilden Foundations.*

time. If the impression left by the total design and binding of the Folger Psalm manuscript is emblematic, this manuscript suggests a jewel box or *wunderkabinet.*

Covered by the original lacy gilt-tooled red morocco binding by Clovis Eve, it opens to reveal a title-page of masks, flowers, butterflies and birds, topped by a putto, that Inglis adapted from a border in Clement Perret's handwriting manual of 1569, as she did the second title-page to *The Song of Songs* with its birds, goats, masks, charming dogs and butterflies.[24] Each page of text is set within an etched border of balls and beads on a stippled background, so that looking through the manuscript is rather like opening drawer after drawer of a private cabinet to see the treasures hidden in each. Inglis thought of her work within such a context, for she suggests to the Vicomtesse that the book might 'obtain a place in some retired corner of your cabinet'. Indeed, the book as or within a box or cabinet is an object created by some modern artists who are seeking to expand the concept of book as holder or container. Stephanie Later's *Song of Songs*, for example, fits within a box decorated with a vine design that echoes that on the page, while Ellen Wallenstein-Sea creates a book *as* a box; entitled *Auschwitz Box*, it shows a Jew imprisoned behind chickenwire, literally 'boxed in'. Inglis, a product of her time, is not yet as self-consciously inventive about the physical shape of the book; she has not literally designed her book as a small *wunderkabinet*. Nevertheless, her imaginative use of variety in framing and marking to enhance the text, and her stated placement of the book within a cabinet, make her a direct precursor of these sister artists.

As with a *wunderkabinet*, part of the fun in this manuscript comes through recognition. The careful viewer will notice elements of the title-page designs that reappear as ornamental headers and footers to the sections of the text: the parrot-like birds on the dedication page, on page 20, and with Andrew Melville's dedication to the Vicomtesse in part 2; single flowers on the pages with Melville's poem to Inglis, her poem to the Reader, and several pages in *The Song of Songs*; two masks and a flower at the end of *Ecclesiastes*. The lacy quality of design is emphasized by the repeated bands of vegetative scrollwork combining leaves, strawberries, pinks, and other flowers, a laciness that is reinforced by some of the handwriting styles, so that parts of the manuscript look like needlework. This is particularly true of Chapters IX through XII of *Ecclesiastes* and of the last opening in *The Song of Songs* (PLATE 4). Here the facing pages take on the quality of a sampler; the lettering on the right looks literally stitched to the page, while the oval on the left, showing two female figures and designs from nature on either side of an urn with text from Psalm 117 replicates the kind of white-on-black work done on seventeenth-century samplers.[25]

As Peter Beal has noted, 'Esther Inglis's calligraphic skills are basically an extension in the field of manuscripts of the traditional feminine handicraft of needlework, the aesthetic of which is to some extent reflected in the decorative patterns, borders, and layout she employs in her copying . . . as well as in the heavily embroidered bindings she sometimes supplies'.[26] Inglis was by no means the only practitioner of this style. A less 'professional' but nevertheless interesting example is found in a manuscript copy of the Book of Common Prayer, dating from 1576, made for Robert Heasse, curate of St Botolph without Aldgate (Folger MS V.a.174). On many of the pages, the text is framed by borders of repeated designs, flowers, cross-hatchings, featherstitchings, or, as on folio 19, the design of a ribbon pulled through featherstitching.[27] The reciprocal relationships among needlework, handwriting, and printed books are complex and deserve further investigation. One thinks, for example, of religious and moralistic texts as well as emblematic and other images drawn from books that occur in samplers and embroidered work; or of embroidered bindings on printed or manuscript books; or of embroidered texts with hidden messages meant to be 'read', as with some of the handiwork of Mary Queen of Scots.[28] Several scholars have recently begun to study this reciprocity between private and public, needlework and print. Lisa Klein writes that 'women were adept at using their status as handmaids, together with the signifying potential of their hand-made embroideries, in ways that were empowering as well as expressive', while in her survey of needlework by sixteenth-century political women as well as seventeenth-century commoners, Susan Frye suggests that 'they took seriously the masculinist association of the needle with the tongue, but instead of letting the needle silence them, they used it as their instrument of communication'. The pro-Protestant political intent of much of Inglis's work admits her to this category.[29]

Although it would be simplistic to state that all of Inglis's books are gendered in design for the recipient, it does seem that such is the case with these two. The Folger manuscript with its geometric patterns and military motif was obviously suited to Prince Maurice of Nassau as Protestant warrior, while the Spencer manuscript, basing its designs on drolleries and the natural world and replicating needlework, is an object for a lady's cabinet.

In a recent essay, Roger Chartier reflects on the interactions between printed and electronic texts. One of the advantages of the latter, he observes, is that they allow the reader to insert him or herself into the text, to become 'an actor of multivocal composition', modifying, reassembling and creating new texts. By the sixteenth century, printers had taken over the marking of texts with their layout, ornaments, headings, glosses, etc., leaving the reader, as Chartier puts it, to 'insinuate his or her own writing in the virgin spaces of the book'.[30] While this evolution in the reader's position vis à vis the printed text is generally true, I would like to complicate the issue by suggesting that artists' books have already allowed such interventions over the centuries. What are formally called artists' books today rely on the (dis)-placement of familiar book structures and formats to create highly individualized objects that invite readers and viewers to find the unexpected in the anticipated. But such playing with text and its modes of embodiment is not new. In the seventeenth century an imaginative reader, Esther Inglis, was already interacting creatively with printed books, manipulating and adapting not only the material form and design, but the very texts themselves, cutting, combining, replacing to make remarkable books of her own.

NOTES

1 Peter Greenaway, *Prospero's Books: A Film of Shakespeare's The Tempest* (New York, 1991), pp. 17, 20.

2 Johanna Drucker in *The Century of Artists' Books* (New York, 1995) discusses Blake and Morris as artists with 'distinctive visions of the book as a form which could function as a force for spiritual and social transformation', p. 22.

3 New York, Pierpont Morgan Library, M.434, f. 1r: 'Lodovico Sforza, Duke of Milan, making donations to the monks of S. Maria delle Grazie'.

4 Drucker, p. 21. Elsewhere, Johanna Drucker has described her own work as dedicated 'to the power of visual material form to proliferate meaning within a semantic field through visual structure', a theoretical way of describing the impact of artists' books from any century. See ' "Through Light and the Alphabet": An Interview with Johanna Drucker by Matthew G. Kirschenbaum, University of Virginia, 1997' (www.iath.virginia.edu/pmc/text-only/issue.597/kirschenbaum.597).

5 George Ballard, *Memoirs of several ladies of Great Britain*, ed. Ruth Perry (Detroit, 1985; orig. pub. Oxford, 1752); David Laing, 'Notes relating to Mrs. Esther Inglis', *Proceedings of the Society of Antiquaries of Scotland*, 6 (1865–66), 284–309; Dorothy Judd Jackson, *Esther Inglis, Calligrapher* (New York, 1937); A.H. Scott-Elliot and Elspeth Yeo, 'Calligraphic Manuscripts of Esther Inglis (1571–1624): A Catalogue', *The Papers of the Bibliographical Society of America*, 84 (1990), 10–86 (noted hereafter as *Catalogue*). At least three other Inglis manuscripts have surfaced since the *Catalogue*. In 1993 the National Library of Scotland purchased a manuscript of the *Octonaries* dedicated to the Earl of Shrewsbury (1607); the Sotheby's sale of 13 December 1994, lot 21 offered another manuscript of the *Quatrains*, dedicated to the Duc de Rohan (1600); and in 1995, Thomas Lange reported 'A rediscovered Esther Inglis calligraphic manuscript in the Huntington Library', *PBSA*, 89 (1995), 339–42, corresponding to the 'untraced' emblematical drawing of Mary, Queen of Scots (*Catalogue*, no. 52). See also Kim Walker, *Women Writers of the English Renaissance* (New York, 1996), pp. 147–51.

6 In his article on female calligraphers, Robert Williams writes that judging 'from the single surviving example of her writing in the Newberry Library, Chicago . . . it is hard to deny that Marie Presot [mother of Esther Inglis] ranks among the leading scribes of her time'. She was a master of the French and Italian hands, may have known the French calligrapher Jean de Beauchesne personally, and probably taught in her husband's school in Edinburgh, as there are payments recorded to both husband and wife by the city: 'A Moon to Their Sun: Writing Mistresses of the Sixteenth and Seventeenth Centuries', *Fine Print*, 11 (1985), 90.

7 Georgianna Ziegler, ' "More Than Feminine Boldness": The Gift books of Esther Inglis', in Mary Burke, *et al*. (ed.), *Women, Writing, and the Reproduction of Culture in Tudor and Stuart Britain* (forthcoming Syracuse UP, 1999).

8 H.R. Woudhuysen, *Sir Philip Sidney and the Circulation of Manuscripts 1580–1640* (Oxford, 1996), p. 98. Woudhuysen says that these books were 'created finally for beauty rather than for use'. Based on the evidence in Inglis's dedications, however, it appears that she expected her recipients to profit from the religious content as well as from the visual beauty of her works. On the distribution of multiple copies to different patrons, see also Harold Love, *The Culture and Commerce of Texts* (Amherst, 1998), pp. 59–61.

9 Woudhuysen, *Sidney*, chapters 2, 3.

10 www.colophon.com/gallery/womenofthebook

11 Margaret J. M. Ezell, *The Patriarch's Wife* (Chapel Hill, 1987), pp. 65–69.

12 Wolfgang Fugger, *Handwriting Manual . . . 1553*, trans. Frederick Plaat (London, 1960), p. [7].

13 Juan de Yciar, *A Facsimile of the 1550 edition of Arte Subtilissima*, trans. Evelyn Shuckburgh (London, 1960), p. 8.

14 Inglis includes copies of these Latin poems in a number of her manuscripts. I am indebted to Professor James Binns of the University of York for his translations.

15 Inglis was obviously influenced in her self-presentation by the portrait of Georgette de Montenay that appears in the 1584 edition of her *Emblematum Christianorum*, a book that Inglis drew upon for a later manuscript which she presented to Prince Charles in 1624 (British Library, Royal MS 17 D.XVI). The inclusion of a musical instrument in a female self-portrait was a topos found among early women artists, beginning with Sophonisba Anguissola in 1561. Frances Borzello in *Seeing Ourselves: Women's Self-Portraits* (New York, 1998), pp. 46–47, places Inglis in this context. Susan Frye discusses the self-portraiture of Inglis with 'its emblems of intellectual and physical cross-dressing', in 'Esther Inglis and Early Seventeenth Century Print Conventions of Authorship', an unpublished paper which she kindly shared with me.

16 Michael Neill, ' "Amphitheaters in the Body": Playing with Hands on the Shakespearean Stage', *Shakespeare Survey*, 48 (1995), 28, 30. On early handwriting and Esther Inglis see also Jonathan Goldberg, *Writing Matter* (Stanford, 1990), pp. 146–53, and more generally, Goldberg's *Desiring Women Writing* (Stanford, 1997).

17 Woudhuysen, *Sidney*, p. 29.

18 Based on the evidence in some of her dedications and in letters of her husband, Bartholomew Kello, there is no doubt that Inglis's work had a religious/political side as well. See Ziegler in Burke, forthcoming. Woudhuysen believes that Bales made 'the beautiful manuscript of Sir Henry Knyvett's *The defence of the realme*, dedicated to Queen Elizabeth in 1596' (p. 36). Inglis must have known that such gifts were acceptable to the Queen when she dedicated two of her own manuscripts to Elizabeth in 1591 and 1599. Woudhuysen mentions other manuscripts made for the Queen by William Teshe, John Davies, Jean de Beauchesne, Petruccio Ubaldini, and Henry Howard, Earl of Northampton (Woudhuysen, pp. 31–32, 37, 40, 41, 100). Beauchesne, like Inglis, belonged to the Huguenot circle. Elizabeth herself, of course, knew some of the skills required to make presentation manuscripts with embroidered bindings, as witnessed by the volumes she prepared as a girl for her stepmother Katherine Parr and her father Henry VIII. See M.H. Swaim, 'A New Year's Gift from the Princess Elizabeth', *The Connoisseur* (August 1973), 258–66; and Marc Shell, *Elizabeth's Glass* (Lincoln, Nebraska, 1993).

19 D. F. McKenzie, 'The Book as an Expressive Form', in *Bibliography and the Sociology of Texts* (London, 1986), p. 8. Johanna Drucker distinguishes the 'marked text' as one which shows the intervention of the printer who orders and hierarchizes a text through his use of type sizes, formats, ornaments, etc. See Kirschenbaum, *Interview*.

20 These figures appear also on the top of the arch in the title-page to Jean Boissard, *Emblemes Latins* (Metz, 1588), the source for the emblem at the end of Inglis's book (see below).

21 The identification of the motto and the description of an earlier state of the binding may be found in *Catalogue*, 37. The manuscript as it now exists is very fragile; the velvet binding has faded to brown and much of the original colouring and embroidery are only faintly visible. Inglis used the leek design in at least one other manuscript, Oxford, Christ Church MS 180; Scott-Elliot and Yeo have identified it as the printer's

rebus used by Girolamo Porro who published *De gli Automati* (Venice, 1589). Inglis reproduced the architectural frame from this title-page in the Christ Church manuscript and two others (see *Catalogue* p. 33).

22 Although it was not until 1624 that Inglis offered her reproduction of much of de Montenay's book to Prince Charles, she obviously knew it at a much earlier date, as her use of this poem indicates. It is also evident that Inglis patterned her self-portrait after that of de Montenay.

23 Inglis frequently refers to herself in her dedications as transcending the usual shamefastness or timidity of women. Her marked sense of self-worth and pride in her work was certainly encouraged by the support of her father and the male humanist scholars who wrote in praise of her talents, and of her husband with whom she worked.

24 *Catalogue*, p. 46.

25 For cut-work samplers, where the white design could be brought forth by being placed on a dark background, see Rozsika Parker, *The Subversive Stitch* (London, 1986), figs. 51, 52. The topos of women by an urn or funerary monument is common in later samplers from the eighteenth and nineteenth centuries.

26 Peter Beal, *In Praise of Scribes* (Oxford, 1998), p. 14, n. 65.

27 I am indebted to Laetitia Yeandle, Curator of Manuscripts at the Folger Library, for pointing out this example.

28 On the cryptic embroidery of Mary Queen of Scots, see Margaret Swain, *The Needlework of Mary Queen of Scots* (Carlton, Bedford, 1986), chapter 9. See also Jayne Elizabeth Lewis, *Mary Queen of Scots: Romance and Nation* (London and New York, 1998), pp. 66–67.

29 Lisa M. Klein, 'Your Humble Handmaid: Elizabethan Gifts of Needlework', *Renaissance Quarterly*, 50 (1997), 462. Susan Frye, 'Sewing Connections: Elizabeth Tudor, Mary Stuart, Elizabeth Talbot, and Seventeenth-Century Anonymous Needleworkers', in Susan Frye and Karen Robertson (eds), *Maids and Mistresses, Cousins and Queens: Women's Alliances in Early Modern England* (Oxford, 1999), p. 166. See also an important study, 'The Needle and the Pen: Embroidery and the Appropriation of Printed Texts', by Ann Rosalind Jones, forthcoming in Jones and Peter Stallybrass, *Renaissance Clothing and the Materials of Memory* (Cambridge, 1999). I am grateful to Ann Jones for a preview of this chapter.

30 Roger Chartier, 'Representations of the Written Word', *Forms and Meanings* (Philadelphia, 1995), p. 20.

Two Unpublished Letters by Mary Herbert, Countess of Pembroke

Steven W. May

During her lifetime the Countess of Pembroke's reputation for patronage exceeded even her reputation as a poet or author of any kind. The two letters transcribed below from the Thynne Papers at Longleat House illustrate this major component of her reputation as they augment the collection of twenty letters included in the recently published Clarendon Press edition of *The Collected Works of Mary Sidney Herbert, Countess of Pembroke*.[1]

None of Pembroke's letters in this edition concerns literary patronage, and only two of the letters portray the Countess writing as a patron on behalf of others. In Manuscript Letter II (p. 286), dated from Wilton 9 September 1591, she recommends an unnamed midwife to her sister-in-law, Lady Barbara Sidney, Sir Robert's wife. Manuscript Letter IV (p. 287), dated from Wilton 1 June 1596, urges Dr Julius Caesar, Master of the Court of Requests, to continue his favour toward one of Mary's unnamed female servants who pursued a 'long and troublesome sute' in the court. The remaining letters concern for the most part Lady Pembroke's efforts to promote suits of her own or to thank others for favours to her and her family.[2] Both letters from the Longleat archive, however, show the Countess actively involved in her role as patron, writing for favours on behalf of social inferiors.

The letters are addressed to her Wiltshire neighbour John Thynne (Sir John from 1603), who, upon his father's death in 1580, had inherited Longleat, the house and manor some twenty-odd miles northwest of the Pembroke seat at Wilton. Unlike the Countess, Thynne was not a particularly accomplished nor highly-regarded figure among his peers in the politically active class. His father's efforts to complete the building of Longleat House all but came to a halt during his son's quarter century of ownership. Although he served as sheriff of Wiltshire in 1593–94, his service on the commission of the peace for Somerset and Gloucestershire had terminated by 1587. As early as 1589 he was under investigation by the Privy Council with regard to his feud with the Queen's Esquire for the Body, Sir James Mervyn, and Thynne was eventually deprived of his office as Steward of the Royal Manors in Wiltshire.[3] Given his reputation and background, Lady Pembroke's warm and playful letter to her neighbour in 1595 (PLATE 1) comes as something of a surprise:

I thanke yow, good servaunt, for ye care yow had to redress the wrong offered to Ales Blage: I pray yow continue yor favour to her, and suffer not ye wrong shee hath receaved to goe vnpunished. Yow shall therin doe that, wch I shall take very kindly. And so I bid yow farewell. At wilton this .1. of October. 1595.

Yo^r M^{rs} & assured
frend
M. Pembroke[4]

Only the letter's subscription and signature are holograph. The irregular, cursive italic hand of the text argues a non-professional scribe or one very much off duty in the penning of this document. Mary's stance as the mistress in a courtly love relationship with her 'servaunt' Thynne extends to the letter's endorsement; it is written in the same scribal hand as the main text and reads, 'To my good servant Iohn Thinne esquier'. Clearly she and Thynne were well-enough acquainted to engage in what was for late Elizabethan times a rather old-fashioned courtly love flirtation. But who was the Alice Blage whom Thynne had protected, and what qualified him to offer her further protection?

The most likely identification would seem to be Alice the wife of Thomas Blague (Blage), royal chaplain and parson of Great Braxted, Essex. Blague served as one of the Queen's chaplain's from at least 1582, and probably as early as 1580 when Elizabeth presented him to the living at Ewelme, Oxfordshire. As chaplain in ordinary, however, Blague was increasingly in attendance at court and non-resident at his several livings which were increased with the deanery of Rochester in 1592 and another parsonage in 1599. Blague's last service to the Queen was his appearance as chaplain at her funeral, but he continued to prosper under James. He was appointed to the Commission for Ecclesiastical Causes at Canterbury in 1603 and granted the rectory of Bangor in 1604.[5] Thus, it would not be surprising if Lady Pembroke had met the wife of so highly favoured a clergyman at court, or that Alice had appealed to Mary for help in facing the unnamed opponent who had wronged her. In 1613, the recently widowed Alice vigorously defended her interests when she filed suit in the Court of Requests against one Richard Draper whom, she alleged, had violated a rental contract with her late husband.[6]

PLATE 1. *Letter by the Countess of Pembroke, in the hand of an amanuensis with her autograph subscription and signature, to John Thynne, 1 October 1595: Longleat House, Thynne Papers, vol. VI, fol. 311r. (Original size 289 × 205mm.) Reproduced by permission of the Most Honourable the Marquess of Bath.*

During the mid-1590s, however, I have discovered no such court case involving Alice or Thomas Blague in Requests, Star Chamber, or Chancery, and there is further reason to doubt that this royal chaplain's wife is the Alice Blage referred to in the Countess's letter to Thynne. First, it is curious that Alice's persecution seems not to affect her husband. Second, the wife of a royal chaplain or, indeed, of any beneficed clergyman, held sufficient social status to merit the honorific title, Mrs (mistress). By naming her plain 'Ales Blage', the Countess suggests either that Alice is so familiar a personal acquaintance of both herself and Thynne that she can dispense with the title of respect, or that Alice Blage is a woman of the underclass.[7] It is, furthermore, difficult to posit what current influence at court Thynne could have mustered to defend the wife of a royal chaplain, least of all during the autumn of 1595. At the very time of Mary's letter, Thynne's treatment of another woman was under close and unsympathetic scrutiny by the Privy Council. In a stern letter of 19 November 1595, the Council accused him of seizing the farm and goods in Wiltshire of 'one Christian Daniel, a very poor widdow . . . whilest shee lay imprizoned heer in London at your suit'.[8] Thynne was ordered to restore the widow's farm and goods or justify his actions before the Council. Ironically then, just as the Countess was praising Thynne for his protection of Alice Blage and encouraging his continued support of her cause, he was under orders from the central government to redress his injustice to a poor widow in his own neighbourhood. The Daniel case suggests that it was in local affairs, not London, that Thynne exercised the most influence, presumably at meetings of the Wiltshire assizes or quarter sessions court. Mary's letter implies, moreover, that it is within Thynne's power to see that Alice's persecutor does not 'goe vnpunished'. Lady Pembroke's protégée Alice Blage was in all likelihood a plaintiff to the Wiltshire judiciary. If so, the Countess might well have struck a familiar, playful tone in writing to Thynne the better to cajole a man whose willingness to persecute at least one woman of the underclass was becoming known even to the Privy Council in London. If Alice was, however, the same servant on whose behalf Mary wrote to Sir Julius Caesar the following June, no record of that case seems to have survived among Court of Requests documents. The ironic certainty remains that Thynne had helped Alice at about the same time that he was victimizing widow Daniel.

In her second letter to Thynne some eight years later the Countess is both more formal and more insistent. The shift in tone reflects alterations in her social status coupled with several setbacks that she endured in the spring and summer of 1603. She had suffered her first demotion early in 1601 with the death of her husband Henry, second Earl of

Pembroke. Mary was now the dowager Countess of Pembroke, still a
woman of high social rank and prestige but with less wealth and influence than she had commanded when she wrote Thynne in 1595. In 1603
her status was further diminished by the death of Queen Elizabeth, who
had held the Countess in consistently high esteem. Mary never attained
to a similarly high regard with either King James or Queen Anne, and
while her eldest son William, now Earl of Pembroke, was highly
favoured by the King, Pembroke remained at odds with his mother during the early years of the reign.[9] Mary's rapport with the recently
knighted Sir John Thynne had no doubt suffered as well from her late
husband's complaint to Lord Burghley in 1598 that Thynne had lodged
harrassing lawsuits against some of the Earl's tenants.[10]

These straitened circumstances are reflected in the endorsement of
Mary's letter of 27 September 1603 (PLATE 2); it is entirely formulaic
without any touch of the courtly flirtation in which the earlier letter was
couched:

> To the right worshipfull and my verie good freind Sr Iohn Thinne
> knight give theis.
>
> I haue ben moved on the behalf of Iames Sympson to entreat your
> favo^r that yow will respite him as your tenant in Channon rowe, the
> extremitie of the time, together wth the procurem^t of one Catesby draw-
> ing him thither, and for that the same Catesbie is since dead I ernestlie
> entreate yow to respite the said Sympson my freind vntill yow shall haue
> necessary vse thereof yo^{r}self; yow shall finde him verie carefull to content
> yow in his profession whose sufficiencie vpon small tryall will witnes his
> deserts, his honest care of performance to any reasonable condicion
> causeth me the more ernestlie to write vnto yow for him, wch if yow shall
> graunte I shall rest thanckfull for the same thus presuming of yor accept-
> ance I haue given the said partie assurance thereof. I wish yow all con-
> tent & bid yow farewell. Greenew^{ch} this 27 of September. 1603.
>
> > Yor. verie loving freind
> > M. Pembroke
>
> > In graunting my request herein
> > y^u may doo me a spesiall kindnes
> > for that he hath worke of myne in
> > his hands of no small importance:
> > the safty whereof will make me
> > acknowlidg my selfe beholding & no
> > less thankefull vnto y^u.[11]

This letter's scribal main text, in a regular, rounded, mixed secretary-
italic cursive, contrasts with the casual and irregular hand of the 1595

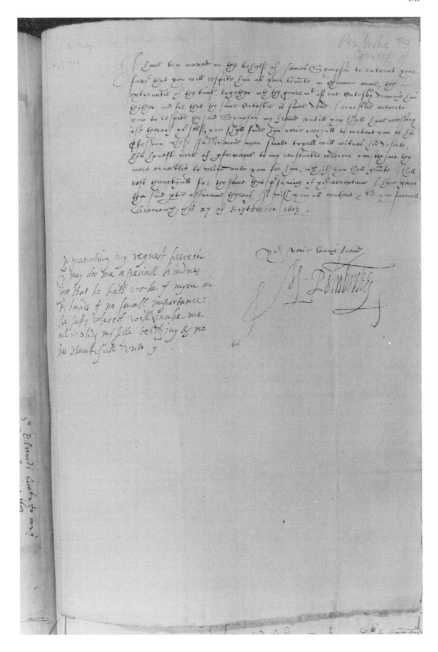

PLATE 2. *Letter by the Countess of Pembroke, in the hand of an amanuensis with her autograph signature and postscript, to John Thynne, 27 September 1603: Longleat House, Thynne Papers, vol. VII, fol. 280r. (Original size 315 × 197mm.) Reproduced by permission of the Most Honourable the Marquess of Bath.*

letter. Mary's signature is followed by her holograph postscript with its further exhortation on Simpson's behalf.

Simpson not only had the Countess's work 'in his hands', but her allusion to his sufficiency 'in his profession' coupled with his lack of a title in her references to him mark Simpson as a craftsman of some sort rather than a gentleman. Lady Pembroke's letter suggests that Catesby had arranged for Sympson to occupy Thynne's house in Westminster. This was probably the Thomas Catesby, of St Andrew's, Holborn, whose will was recorded in 1603.[12] Afterward, Sir John apparently planned to evict Sympson who then asked the Countess to intervene with Thynne for a continuation of his tenancy. The Westminster address was a highly desirable one for Sympson for several reasons. Stow describes Cannon Row in Westminster as a fashionable neighbourhood populated by 'diuers Noblemen and Gentlemen' including 'Iohn Thine Esquier'.[13] Thynne was residing there early in 1601 at the time of the Essex rebellion when he wrote excitedly to his wife, 'Good Pug, . . . presently the Court was guarded, all men commanded to horse . . . and I was commanded to attend Her Majesty's person at the lobby door where I waited till three of the clock the next night. . . . From my house in Cannon Row.'[14] Thynne had good reason, however, not to occupy the house during September of 1603. Lady Pembroke's letter mentions 'the extremitie of the time', undoubtedly the plague epidemic that was claiming more than 2000 victims per week in London during most of September.[15] Westminster was far from being a safe refuge from the disease although it was considered safer than the city proper.

Mary had indeed critical work in hand in 1603, which explains why she risked her life by remaining in the London area that September. She had come up to London from Cardiff in April to take part in Queen Elizabeth's funeral. The timing of this journey was unfortunate, for city officials were then at work to abrogate the Pembrokes' legal rights pertaining to the castle and town of Cardiff.[16] Her steward, Hugh Davyd, had followed after the Countess bringing with him her 'money, plate and jewels'. Davyd was ambushed on the road, however, and robbed of this treasure, suffering head wounds from which he died in mid-July. Earlier that month, Lady Pembroke resided in or near Windsor where her son, William, was installed Knight of the Garter on 2 July. She remained in the London area in part to prosecute one Edmund Mathew, whom she accused of inciting the attack on her steward.[17] Between 4 July and 6 September she wrote four increasingly urgent letters to Sir Julius Caesar, Master of Requests, imploring him to bring her case against Mathew to the King's attention.

Even if Mary still retained access to Baynard's Castle, the Pembroke residence in the city, she declined to stay there as the plague's virulence increased. Instead, she had found lodgings in Greenwich by the date of her last letter to Caesar on September 6. Although Margaret Hannay states that the Countess resided there at Queen Anne's court (p. 187), the court had departed for Windsor where Anne at last joined it in the course of her progress from Scotland.[18] Greenwich Palace had no doubt been closed in June, leaving Lady Pembroke to find other lodgings in the area from which she likewise subscribed her letter to Thynne. Mary was further distracted that summer by the arrest in mid-July of Sir Walter Ralegh who was subsequently convicted of high treason. Dudley Carleton confided 'a pretty secret' to John Chamberlain, 'that the lady of Pembroke hath written to her son Philip and charged him of all her blessings to employ his credit and his friends and all he can do for Raleigh's pardon.'[19] But it was in the context of prosecuting Mathew that, a few weeks after her last appeal to Caesar, Lady Pembroke wrote to Sir John Thynne on Sympson's behalf. What kind of skilled craftsman might she have wished to maintain in Westminster under these circumstances? By late September she probably realized that she lacked the access at court to command royal intervention in her case against Mathew. Her only alternative was to enter the matter into litigation. To this end she pleaded with Caesar to send her the original copy of an examination in the case that he had taken at Windsor (Manuscript Letters XIII and XIV). She may have planned as well to sue the rebellious officials of Cardiff, a case that she entered in Star Chamber 1 December 1604. About a year later, she filed suit against Edmund Mathew in the same court.[20] At some point, perhaps as early as September 1603, Lady Pembroke needed the services of a capable scrivener to prepare and copy all the documents pertaining to these multiple lawsuits. A formal petition to King James on Ralegh's behalf would also have required drafting by a professional scrivener. Perhaps Sympson was the man and, accordingly, someone 'whose sufficiencie vpon small tryall' Sir John Thynne might put to the test in managing his own legal affairs.

The Countess of Pembroke typifies most other aristocratic patrons of Renaissance English authors in that we have very little independent evidence to substantiate the formulaic expressions of gratitude in her clients' dedicatory epistles. In his dedication of 'The Ruines of Time', for example, Spenser thanked Lady Pembroke 'To whome I acknowledge my selfe bounden, by manie singular fauours and great graces'. Similarly, in a dedication to the Countess in 1601 Nicholas Breton pledged 'the duty of my heart's seruice, in al humble thankfulnesse for your bountifull vndeserued goodnesse'.[21] What favours, graces, and goodness, we may legitimately ask? The biographical record does not even establish that Mary so much as met Spenser or Breton in person. Accordingly, her letters on behalf of Sympson and Blage are instructive because they concretely demonstrate her readiness to use her influence on behalf of social inferiors. She may well have elicited dedicatory epistles from such protégés as Spenser and Breton with epistles of her own on their behalf such as those she addressed to Thynne in 1595 and 1603.

NOTES

1 Ed. Margaret P. Hannay, Noel J. Kinnamon, and Michael G. Brennan, 2 vols (Oxford, 1998). The edition of Thynne Papers VI, f. 311, and VII, f. 280, is published by permission of the Marquess of Bath, Longleat House, Warminster, Wiltshire.

2 Although some letters express mixed motives, in Manuscript Letters 3, 11, 12, 13, 14, 15, and 16, Mary requests favours of others, while she thanks her correspondents for favours in letters 5, 6, 7, 9, 10, and Printed Letters 1–2. The intent of Manuscript Letters 1 and 8 and Printed Letters 3 and 4 might best be summarized as merely informative or serving to clarify and defend the interests of the Pembroke family.

3 David Burnett, *Longleat The Story of an English Country House* (London, 1978), pp. 45–46; *The House of Commons, 1558–1603*, ed. P. W. Hasler (London, 1981), Vol. III, 504–6.

4 Longleat House, Thynne Papers, vol. VI, f. 311.

5 *DNB*; PRO SP 12/273/42 records Blage's presentation to the parsonage of Earde, Canterbury; for his appointment to the Ecclesiastical Commission see HMC *Salisbury*, XV (1930), 224. The funeral accounts are in PRO LC 2/4 (4), f. 54.

6 PRO REQ 2 412/17, where Alice identifies herself as the widow of 'Thomas Blague . . . Chaplen and Parson of Greate Braxted in the county of Essex deceased'.

7 Alice, the widow of Humphrey Goslinge, married Ralph Blage of London, gentleman, 28 July 1587, but, again, if this is the Alice Blage on whose behalf Lady Pembroke wrote to Thynne, she too, as a gentleman's wife, should have been termed Mrs Alice: Joseph Lemuel Chester, *Allegations for Marriage Licences Issued by the Bishop of London, 1520 to 1610*, Harleian Society Publications, XXV (1887), 162.

8 *Acts of the Privy Council of England*, ed. John Roche Dasent (London, 1907), XXV, 79.

9 Margaret P. Hannay, *Philip's Phoenix Mary Sidney, Countess of Pembroke* (Oxford, 1990), p. 184.

10 Pembroke to Sir Robert Cecil, 18 June 1598, complaining about 'Mr. Thyn, my neighbour': HMC *Salisbury*, VIII (1899), 219–20.

11 Longleat House, Thynne Papers, vol. VII, f. 280.

12 *Index of Wills Proved in the Prerogative Court of Canterbury, 1584–1604*, ed. Edward Alexander Fry (London, 1901), 73 Bolein, p. 82.

13 John Stow, *The Survey of London*, ed. Charles Kingsford (London, 1908), II, 102.

14 Alison D. Wall (ed.), 'Two Elizabethan Women: Correspondence of Joan and Maria Thynne 1575–1611', *Wiltshire Record Society* vol. XXXVIII (1983), pp. 17–18.

15 Leeds Barroll, *Politics, Plague, and Shakespeare's Theater* (Ithaca, 1991), p. 223.

16 Hannay, pp. 180–1.

17 Hannay, p. 181.

18 Anne can be traced with King James at Hampton Court on 20 July (*Calendar of State Papers . . . Venice*, ed. Horatio F. Brown [London, 1900], X, 72), on a separate progress in Oxfordshire in August and September, rejoining the King at Woodstock 8–20 September, and thereafter traveling with him to Winchester for the winter: E. K. Chambers, *The Elizabethan Stage* (Oxford, 1961), IV, 117; HMC *Salisbury*, XV (1930), 243.

19 *Dudley Carleton to John Chamberlain 1603–1624, Jacobean Letters*, ed. Maurice Lee, Jr. (New Brunswick, 1972), pp. 44–45, letter of 27 November 1603.

20 Hannay, pp. 180–1.

21 'The Ruins' is the first poem in Spenser's *Complaints* volume (1591): *The Works of Edmund Spenser A Variorum Edition* (Baltimore, 1966), VIII, 36. Breton, 'A Diuine Poeme . . . The Rauisht Soule, and the Blessed Weeper' in *The Works in Verse and Prose of Nicholas Breton*, ed. Alexander B. Grosart (1879; rpt. New York, 1966), I, 4.

Elizabeth Ashburnham Richardson's 'motherlie endeauors' in Manuscript

Victoria E. Burke

'[T]he matter is but devotions or prayers, which surely concernes and belongs to women, as well as to the best learned men.'

Elizabeth Richardson, *A Ladies Legacie to her Daughters*, sig. A2^r.

Elizabeth Richardson's work was formerly thought to consist of one printed volume of 1645, *A Ladies Legacie to her Daughters. In three Books. Composed of Prayers and Meditations, fitted for severall times, and upon severall occasions. As also severall Prayers for each day in the Weeke.* The recent discovery of two manuscripts, however, offers a more complete picture of Richardson's writing practice. These manuscripts demonstrate how one woman treated both her manuscript and printed texts: as sites for continual revision. *A Ladies Legacie* is composed primarily of prayers and meditations, one of the more common forms of writing by women in the early modern period. In the Second Lamp of his *Monument of Matrones* (1582), Thomas Bentley printed the prayers of Katherine Parr, Lady Jane Grey, Elizabeth Tyrwhit, Lady Frances Abergavenny, as well as those translated by Dorcas Martin.[1] Extant manuscript collections of prayers and meditations include the prayers and Biblical quotations compiled by Elizabeth Hastings, Countess of Huntingdon, 1633, four copies of which are in the Huntington Library, San Marino (MSS EL 6871, HM 15369, HA Literature 1(6), HA Religious 2(8)), the meditations and scriptural notes of her daughter-in-law Lucy (Huntington Library, MSS HA Personal 18(1) and HA Religious 3(16)), and the meditations of Lady Mary Carey of the 1650s (Oxford, Bodleian Library, MS Rawl. D. 1308). Richardson also had precedents in the mother's advice writing tradition, such as the frequently reprinted *Mothers Legacie to her unborn Childe* of Elizabeth Jocelin (1624), and *The Mothers Blessing* of Dorothy Leigh (1616), as well as Elizabeth Grymestone's *Miscelanea, Meditations, Memoratives* (1604), Elizabeth Clinton's *The Countess of Lincolnes Nurserie* (1622), and M.R.'s *The Mothers Counsell, or, Live within*

Compasse (1624).[2] Anne, Lady Halkett's advice to her children exists in manuscript and printed form: the earliest work is 'The Mothers Will to her vnborne child beeing writt [att Pitfirane] when I was with Child of my deare Betty 1656,' which is followed by 'a thanksgiueing affter my deliuerance outt of Childbed' (Edinburgh, National Library of Scotland MS 6489, pp. 198–259), while the second is addressed to her growing son, 'To My Son Robert Halkett [oct 20 1670],' and headed 'Ins:[tructions] to my Son' on most versos (National Library of Scotland MS 6492, pp. 244–308). Halkett's *Instructions for Youth . . . For the Use of those young Noblemen and Gentlemen, whose Education was committed to her Care* was published in 1701, two years after her death, at the instigation of her minister Samuel Cooper.

Unlike most other mothers' legacies, Richardson's advice writing was not published after her death: it was printed in 1645 when she was still very much alive, sending presentation copies of the volume to family members and annotating its errors.[3] Though she announces her text as a legacy, it was printed in her lifetime, unlike Jocelin's, Grymestone's, and Halkett's works. Addressed to her four adult daughters and her two daughters-in-law, the volume comprises three books. The first was written at her relation the Duke of Buckingham's house in Chelsea in 1625 (his mother was Richardson's cousin), the second at her own house in Barking, Essex, in 1635, just after the death of her second husband, Sir Thomas Richardson, and the third at an unspecified time. But Richardson's mother's advice writing began much earlier (earlier than other known writing of this kind, with the exception of Grymestone); a manuscript in Washington, D.C., Folger Shakespeare Library MS V.a.511, dated 1606, contains prayers and meditations on topics similar to those published in 1645, but none of these seems to be a direct source for the printed work. The Folger manuscript also contains a précis of and meditation on Mary Sidney, Countess of Pembroke's translation of Philippe de Mornay's *A Discourse of Life and Death* (discussed by Margaret Hannay in her article). The East Sussex Record Office at Lewes, on the other hand, holds a manuscript (ASH 3501) which is closely related to the first book of the printed edition, dated 1626 but given in 1635 to Richardson's eldest daughter, Elizabeth. Both of these manuscripts give a fuller picture of Richardson's writing, of her sources (particularly, that of another woman writer), and of her attitudes to print and manuscript.[4] The two extant manuscripts of Richardson's work indicate her continual revision of her writing, in the form of marginal notes, alterations, and additions. Her revisions continue in extant printed copies of her work; even two apparent presentation copies refuse to be fixed in any final state. For Richardson, alterations were not relegated to private notes, but appear in the most apparently 'final' form of her text.[5]

Elizabeth Richardson was the eldest daughter of Sir Thomas Beaumont and Catherine Farnham of Stoughton in Leicestershire. Her first husband was John Ashburnham, whom she married on 27 November 1594, and by whom she had ten children, six of them surviving to adulthood. Knighted on 14 March 1604, her profligate husband died imprisoned for debt in the Fleet on 29 June 1620. Her four surviving daughters, to whom she addressed her prayers in 1625, were Elizabeth (d. 1644), Frances (b. 1599), Anne (d. 1628), and Katherine (b. 1614). Elizabeth married Sir Frederick Cornwallis about 1630; Frances married Frederick Turville; Anne married Sir Edward Dering as his second wife on 1 January 1625; and Katherine married John Sherlock on 14 July 1634. Richardson's two sons, John (1603–71) and William (d. 1679) had illustrious careers at court; their wives are addressed in the introductory epistle of the 1645 printed volume. John's first wife, one of Richardson's dedicatees, was Frances Holland (1613–49) and his second was Elizabeth Kenn, the Dowager Lady Poulett (1593–1663); William married Jane, widow of James Ley, Earl of Marlborough (d. 1671 or 1672). Richardson's other children lived just a few days or months: John (1596), Anne (1597) and Edward (1606), while Mary lived to be 19 years of age (1600–19). She married her second husband (as his second wife), Sir Thomas Richardson (1569–1635), on 14 December 1626, and was created Baroness of Cramond on 29 February 1628 through his influence, which apparently elicited 'many gibes and pasquinades . . . for the amusement of Westminster Hall.' A letter to the Duke of Buckingham of August 1627 indicates that she enjoyed the society of his wife, as well as Lady Carlisle, and the Queen; she also waited on the Queen of Bohemia in The Hague that year. On 9 September 1629 she was granted an annual pension of £300 for the duration of her life. She died at Covent Garden, and was buried with her first husband on 3 April 1651 at St Andrew's, Holborn.[6] In both manuscripts she uses the name Ashburnham, even though by 1635, the date of the East Sussex Record Office manuscript, she had been widowed by her second husband. In the printed edition she uses both names: Ashburnham in the epistles before Book One and Richardson in Book Two, as well as on the title page of the volume. It is not surprising that she would use the name she shares with her children in the manuscripts since they are the dedicatees of these works.

The Folger manuscript, MS V.a.511, is a quarto whose cover measures 200 by 158mm., and whose pages measure 198 by 155mm. Of the 86 folios, Richardson's meditations, prayers, and treatise appear on the first five leaves and the last 23 (*i.e.* ff. 1v–5r, and 64v–86v). The rest of the folios are blank except for one page dated 6 February 1699, headed, 'An acc.ᵗ of what plate is put into a grate flat box Couered wᵗʰ. Red Lether./.' and four leaves which contain an early eighteenth-century list of books (ff. 54–57, rectos only) and sums totaling £112 in a different hand (f. 57v). She heads her work 'Instructions for my children, or any other Christian, Directing to the performance of our duties, towards God and Man;—drawne out of yᵉ holy Scripture.' Four projected sections are listed:

i. Precepts for a ciuill and christian life, in behaviour, worde, & deed.
2. The vertues & vices, wᵗʰ yⁱʳ rewards & punishments, contayned in Gods law, or yᵉ ten comaundements.
3. An instruction for prayer ~~meditations vpon~~ *præ*cepts or ['precepts or' in different pen] sentences of Scripture, & tuelue Prayers.
4. A Treatise, concerning Life, and Death.

Although only parts three and four are actually included (ff. 64v–86v), additional material appears on earlier pages, which could be considered part of the first section. Below the table of contents is a paragraph on how parents should teach their children God's word with Biblical sources in the margin. Folio 2 (PLATE I) contains 'Of the intent and effect of this booke' which reads very much like a preface to a printed work— perhaps even the inclusion of it shows how closely print and manuscript were linked in Richardson's mind, or perhaps it shows that she did intend it for print. She describes the manuscript as 'A Booke of Precepts, Instructions, and Prayers, wᶜʰ I haue written, and for the most part collected, ~~all~~ out of yᵉ holie scriptures, for the direction of my children,' but she raises the possibility of having other readers, asking that if any other should chance to see her 'motherlie endeauors' to excuse her since no profound knowledge is expected from her sex. Though she is indicating the possibility of a wider audience for her work, she at the same time exaggerates the modesty topos in the revisions of her manuscript. In this case, however, she has substituted the phrase 'motherlie endeauors' for 'poore labors' in the epistle. This is a significant emendation, which genders her efforts and places them in an established tradition of mother's advice writing.

The following two pages contain headings only, in the form of further projected dedications, and then appears a paragraph consisting of 'Certaine Sentences, worthie often to be remembred,' and beneath it, 'A godlie and fruitfull meditation' (f. 3v). The latter comprises three lists, grouped on the left hand side of the page, urging the reader to remember three things past (the evil we have done, the good we have not done, the time we have lost), to consider three things present (the shortness of

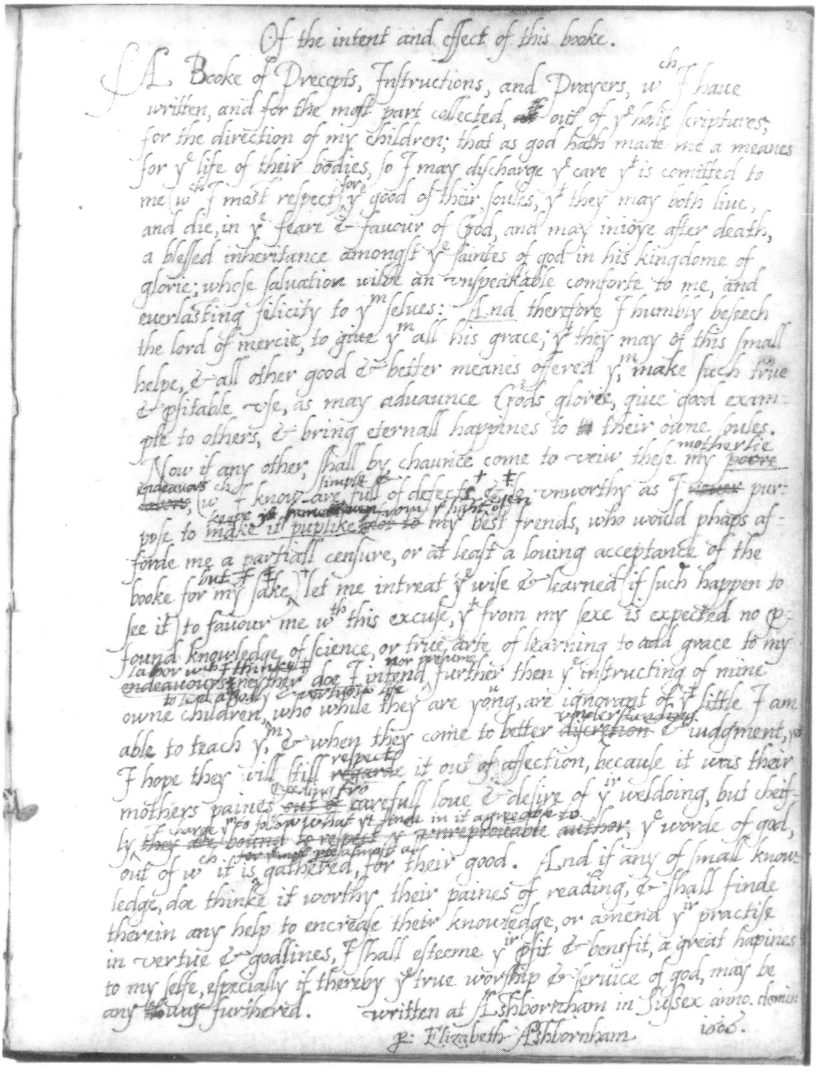

PLATE 1. *Epistle in the Folger Manuscript of Elizabeth Ashburnham Richardson's prayers and meditations: Washington, D.C., Folger Shakespeare Library MS V.a.511, f. 2r (Original size 198 × 155mm.) Reproduced by permission of the Folger Shakespeare Library.*

life, the swift passing of time, how hard it is to be saved), and to foresee
three things to come (death most certain, god's judgment most severe,
hell's pains most intolerable). A short prose meditation on these exhor-
tations faces it on the right hand side of the page. Another striking visual
pattern appears on fol. 4; under the heading, 'Vse time well, for it tari-
eth,' are six sentences with the last word or two underneath each. These
terminal words form their own admonition: 'none/ good/ of men,/ as
thy selfe/ knoweth/ y^t readeth it.'

These word games are followed by a series of meditations, addressed
to the reader and with marginal scriptural references, followed by
prayers, addressed to God. The first is a meditation on the profit of wisdom and holy knowledge, followed by a prayer for knowledge and
understanding before reading or study. This pattern, of meditation followed by prayer, is followed in the final section of the manuscript, but
with 58 folios between them (which include the material by later hands).
The third section begins with a brief meditation on how prayer and
thanksgiving are the most acceptable sacrifice we can give to God,
which leads into 'The duties concerning Prayer' also titled in a different
pen 'An instruction for prayer.' Then follow twelve sets of meditations
followed by prayers, numbered as such, and listed in the index at the
back of the volume. The topics are as follows: a preface to prayer,
prayers on faith, repentance and humility, confession of sins, the church
and temporal blessings, sickness, thanksgiving for benefits, affliction,
thanksgiving for deliverance, a prayer for the morning, a prayer for
night, and a conclusion for any prayer. Though Richardson often meditates on the same scriptural passages, none of this early material seems
to have been a direct source for the later printed volume. The overall
impression is that this is an independent, though incomplete, and much
earlier attempt at a formula she was to refine in the next forty years.

The material characteristics of the Folger manuscript can give us further insight into the status of Richardson's writing. The limp vellum
binding is single ruled in gilt, with gold-tooled initials E A on either side
of a central quatrefoil design; a rectangular panel encloses the centrepiece, with four floral patterns pointing towards the corners of the cover.
Holes at the top and bottom of the fore-edge indicate where ties held the
covers together. This manuscript was probably acquired as a pre-bound
blank book, which is suggested by the number of blank leaves and stubs.
In spite of the elaborate binding, it is not a polished or finished work.
Richardson has copiously emended and corrected the text, and has written only two of the four sections announced on the title page.

Richardson's hand is a clear, non-cursive italic. Her minuscule *e*'s are
distinctive, with a nearly vertical stroke joining the curve of the body of

the letter. Many minims, particularly on *n*, *m*, and *i*, begin and end with a slight hook, and many of the descenders are hooked horizontally to the left, and on occasions slightly clubbed. She uses punctuation regularly, superscripted abbreviations, and occasional ligatures. She has written from fol. 1v to the middle of 4r (just the title), from 64v to 71v and 86r–v. A second hand has completed the prayers from 4r to 5r, and from 71v to 85v, and Richardson often corrects the second hand's work. The second hand may have been that of a servant or household steward, but probably not a daughter, since the eldest could not have been more than ten years of age in 1606. Her preface, 'Of the intent and effect of this booke' (f. 2r) is subscribed 'written at Ashbornham in Sussex anno domin p*er*. Elizabeth Ashbornham 1606.' The watermark in the paper (an eagle with a crozier on its breast and three circles beneath it) dates it to 1595–96,[7] suggesting that Richardson may have owned the blank book for a few years before deciding to write her mother's legacy in it. The types of additions she has made to the second hand are significant: she has added entire lines of text and new titles, altered words throughout the prayers and meditations, and added numbering to the prayers. She has gone back to what she has written in her own hand, and altered that as well.

MS V.a.511 was acquired by the Folger in 1969 from Hammond booksellers. How it passed from Richardson to the writer of the 1699 inventory to the early- to mid-eighteenth-century person who has written the list of books is uncertain. If it remained in the Ashburnham family it had left their possession by the mid-nineteenth century. A few pencil notes suggest the codes of a bookseller, but it is not clear who that might have been. The manuscript was evidently not something preserved as a treasured heirloom by later generations: the book purchaser who recorded part of his library in its pages saw the manuscript as a useful pocket-sized repository for his own notes. The list of books records this later owner's taste in literature, which included the classics (Virgil, Plutarch, Euripides, Lucian, Martial, Aristotle, Xenophon), topical pamphlets such as *The speech of James Earl of Derwentwater: who was beheaded on Tower-Hill for high treason against His Majesty King George, February the 24th, 1715/16*, and religious writing, such as William Sherlock's *A discourse concerning the divine providence* (1694), Robert South's sermons, and John Norris's *Letters concerning the love of god* (1695). This compiler shared Richardson's interest in prayer, owning works such as the nonconformist minister Matthew Henry's *A Method for prayer* of 1710. This manuscript was a source of blank paper for its later users; in spite of its elaborate binding it was put to practical use, and acknowledging this later use is a vital part of understanding its function as a material object at different points in its history.

In contrast to the Folger manuscript, which was at least begun in 1606, if not completed by that date, the East Sussex Record Office manuscript of Richardson's work (ASH 3501) is dated 1635. The volume comprises 35 leaves, nineteen of which contain the Richardson prayers at the beginning of the volume. They are followed by ten blank leaves, then two with eighteenth-century financial receipts, and four more blanks. As the title page indicates (PLATE 2), the work which follows was written earlier, and the dedicatee had already lost one copy of it:

1635. A Rememberance for my foure Daughters./ Elizabeth. Frances. Anne. & Katherine. This to my most deere, and entirely beloued Daughter, as she well deserueth. Elizabeth Ashbornham. From yor affectionate Mother. E.A: with my blessing, & prayers, for your present, & future happines. Which for my sake, accept, esteeme, and ymploye, though in it selfe vnworthy. Peruse, Ponder, and Practise./ Sweet Besse, (as you loue me) keep this, though you lost y^e first. Eliza: Cramond 1635./

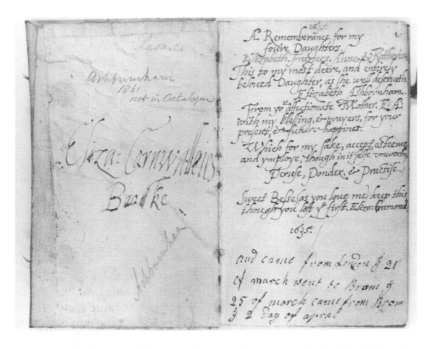

PLATE 2. *Title-page of the East Sussex Manuscript of Elizabeth Ashburnham Richardson's prayers and meditations: Lewes, East Sussex Record Office ASH 3501, front pastedown and f. 1r (Original size of each page 140 × 90mm.) Reproduced by permission of the Ashburnham Estate and the East Sussex County Archivist.*

The first volume to which Richardson refers is the first third of the printed version, dated 1625 in its printed form (*see* sig. A2v–A4r) and dated in this manuscript 1626. Another possible way of reading 'ye first' is in apposition with 'Eliza: Cramond,' so that it refers not to a book, but to Richardson herself. Other mother's legacies are depicted as substitute mothers which will provide instruction once their author is dead (for example, Thomas Goad calls Jocelin's book a 'mother in instruction').[8] A different, probably professional, hand has written the introductory epistle in the manuscript, headed, 'ffrom Chelsy in August. 1626. A letter to my foure Daughters. Elizabeth, ffrances, Anne, & Katherine Ashbornhame' (ff. 2r–4r), which matches the printed version's in nearly every instance, with only a few variants. For example, one full sentence appears in the printed version but not in the manuscript;[9] but more commonly the differences are of a few words. In two cases the manuscript is more belittling of her efforts: her 'motherly remembrance' of the printed version is a 'small token & Motherly remembrance' in the manuscript, and her 'labour' is her 'little labour' in the manuscript (sig. A3r and f. 2v). Perhaps when her work reached print she removed those qualifications in order to appear more authoritative.

After the epistle to her daughters a dedication specifically to her eldest daughter appears within the postscript, in which she hopes that the daily use of this volume will help to effect her salvation. What follows the epistle are twelve items: one meditation (which addresses God in the third person, and contains marginal Biblical references), six prayers, another meditation, and four more prayers. These have all been numbered, but not sequentially, suggesting that the manuscript is not finished, even though it is ostensibly designed to be a presentation copy. Four of the numbers have been crossed out and other numbers put in their places.[10] All of the items in the manuscript correspond to prayers or meditations in the printed version, and often longer entries in the manuscript have been divided into two or more in the printed volume. The printed version was later greatly expanded, for the final seven items in the printed version have no correspondence in the manuscript. A note in the printed text before the twenty-first prayer makes that clear: 'Here is one Prayer more which I joyne to these, because it concerned one of my daughters, to whom this Booke belonged, though it was lately penned upon a very strange accident' (sig. C7v). This must refer to Elizabeth Cornwallis, who is the subject of the next prayer. It indicates that she initially dedicated this book of prayers to her eldest daughter and that she continued to add to her work. With the exception of the second prayer in *A Ladies Legacie to her Daughters* (a paragraph headed, 'A

Prayer to the Holy Ghost') all of the items up to sig. CIV, number 15 (which include two unnumbered meditations) appear in the manuscript volume, though in a different order.[11] Prayers 16 to 22 were added later, possibly after 1635, when this manuscript was ostensibly presented to her daughter.

Again, physically the manuscript announces itself as a presentation copy, but it contains elements which contradict that claim. There are three hands in the manuscript: Richardson's, a professional hand, and a less polished hand. Richardson has written the title-page, she has signed the epistle, and she has added interlinear corrections throughout the manuscript (including the postscript of the dedicatory epistle). The second hand has transcribed the epistle, which it has dated 1626, and has specified the date of composition of the prayers as 1625. The third hand (PLATE 3), which occurs in the rest of manuscript, is more puzzling. Conceivably it is a very rough form of Richardson's hand, given a few tiny similarities (for example, in the *cl*, *ch*, *st*, and *sh* ligatures). But more

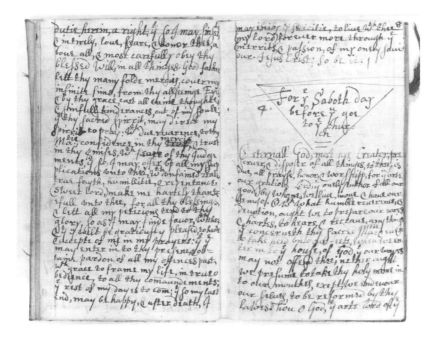

PLATE 3. *Two pages of prayers in the East Sussex Manuscript of Elizabeth Ashburnham Richardson's prayers and meditations: Lewes, East Sussex Record Office ASH 3501, ff. 7v–8r (Original size of each page 140 × 90mm.) Reproduced by permission of the Ashburnham Estate and the East Sussex County Archivist.*

commonly the differences are striking: the *e*'s in this section are always capitals, while Richardson's are always minuscule; the ascenders and descenders are angled very differently from Richardson's curved horizontal manner. But the question remains: why should Richardson have made such a rough copy of her prayers? Was it a task for a daughter to transcribe her mother's work? Perhaps it fell to Elizabeth Cornwallis, since she lost the first copy she was given. The lack of proper order of the prayers, the additions in Richardson's hand and the irregularity of the main hand belie the idea that this is a presentation copy. Other aspects, however, fit: the volume is a small octavo (measurements of the cover are 142 × 96mm. and of the pages are 140 × 90mm., though fol. 30 is cropped along the fore-edge, so its width is approximately 75mm.), bound in limp vellum with the remains of green ties at its fore-edge. Unlike the Folger manuscript, there is here no gilt ornamentation, either on the cover or on the edges of the pages. The scribes were probably writing in a pre-bound book, given that one stub appears at the beginning of the manuscript, and two appear after fol. 19, the end of the Richardson section. Was there more material which was torn out?

The manuscript was first owned by Richardson's eldest daughter, who has signed the front pastedown: 'Eliza: Cornwalleies Boocke'. Someone from the Cornwallis household probably wrote the note which appears at the bottom of the title-page: 'and came from London ye 21 of march went to Brom ye 25 of march came from Brom ye 2 day of apral.' Brom must refer to Brome, Suffolk, where Sir Frederick Cornwallis held his main estate, and where Elizabeth and their descendants lived. On 15 July 1766 the manuscript seems to have been owned by a John Walsh who has signed a receipt for an indenture of £100 (f. 30). The money is owed to Mr Richard Wesmacott and witnessed by Richard Bower and James Jinnold. On fols. 30v and 31r are versions of parts of the same receipt, so Walsh was probably practising writing it several times in this manuscript, which he treated as a source for blank paper. Pencil notations by what must have been a nineteenth-century bookseller appear on the pastedowns, but they are not the same as those in the Folger manuscript. That hand has written 'Ashburnham 1861 not in Catalogue' which indicates that the manuscript does not appear in the three-volume *Catalogue of the Manuscripts at Ashburnham Place*, published in 1861. But the manuscript has been written into the 1853 catalogue in pencil on an interleaved blank page (East Sussex Record Office, ASH 4329), and so it was presumably acquired (if not rediscovered) by the Ashburnham family sometime after 1853. The most likely purchaser of the volume was the fourth Earl, Bertram (1797–1878), an avid bibliophile, whose collection of printed books and manuscripts was

dispersed by the fifth Earl, also called Bertram (1840–1913).[12] This manuscript did not apparently remain in the family in which it originated;
it took a nineteenth-century descendant to reacquire it.

Most printed mother's advice works take the form of direct advice to
children about how to live a Christian life, while Richardson's works are
primarily prayers which can be said by the reader. They are practical
volumes in that they are to be repeated, instead of portions of advice to
be internalized. The first, fragmentary, section of the Folger manuscript
contains some explicit sections of advice, but mostly in spiritual terms.
An exception is 'Certaine Sentences, worthie often to be remembred'
(f. 3v) which includes statements on remembering the end of what you
take in hand, on doing good, and on not meddling in other people's
affairs. Her paragraph on teaching children (f. 1v) is drawn largely from
Biblical sources, and is addressed to other parents of children who
might be reading this. A wider audience than her children is suggested
here, and in the phrase 'or any other Christian' of her title.

Richardson's manuscript writings have the air of being unfinished
documents, with which she was never fully satisfied. Her editing and
altering of her text seems to have been a continuous process, no matter
how apparently 'fixed' that text was, even in print. She prepared a presentation copy for her brother Sir Henry Beaumont, now in the
Bodleian Library (Vet. A.3 f. 132), which contains autograph changes
and additions throughout, including, 'These should haue Joyned to y^e
weekly exercise (sig. H2v). She has also revised the first page of the epistle, adding the dates when the volume was written and printed, as well
as altering the title (PLATE 4), and has added 'Prayers for each day of y^e
weeke' as a title to sig. D3r, plus a concluding sentence to 'An
Exhortation': 'Before y^u prayest p^{re}pare thy selfe, and tempt not God'
(PLATE 5). A holograph manuscript epistle which appears in the
Houghton Library copy of the printed volume at Harvard University
(*EC C8495 645I) is a dedication to her grandson, Sir Edward Dering,
of Katherine Philips's circle. In it she writes that she has corrected some
errors (including emending the title to *A Mother's Legacie to Her Six
Daughters*, as she had done in the copy for her brother), and urges him
to do the same: 'But indeed it is so falsly Printed, as wthout it be corrected, you will meet w^t many absurdities, w^c by some may be imputed
vnto me, though not by you; therefore I haue a little helped ye most
faulty places, desiring you to do ye like by this, in ye other 2. bookes.'[13]
Perhaps Dering had a manuscript copy of the texts, from which he was
to correct the faulty printed version.[14] But given how unstable the two
extant manuscript texts are, perhaps there was never any one version
which was deemed perfect by Richardson. Before the discovery of the

PLATE 4. *First page of the Epistle in* A Ladies Legacie to her Daughters *with the author's autograph revisions: Oxford, Bodleian Library Vet. A3. f. 132, sig. A1ʳ (Original size 144 × 94mm.) Reproduced by permission of the Bodleian Library.*

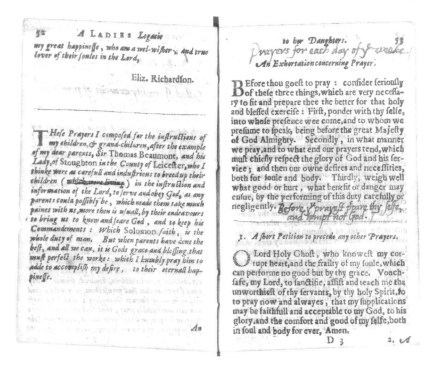

PLATE 5. *Pages 52 and 53 of* A Ladies Legacie to her Daughters *with autograph additions by the author: Oxford, Bodleian Library Vet. A3. f. 132, sigs D2ᵛ–D3ʳ (Original size of each page 144 × 94mm.) Reproduced by permission of the Bodleian Library.*

Folger and East Sussex Record Office manuscripts, the full extent of this revising sensibility was not apparent. These manuscripts indicate that Richardson's mother's advice writing spanned forty years, and that it predates most other examples of the genre. They also demonstrate that even presentation copies of Richardson's 'motherlie endeauors' were never considered by their author to be completed documents.

NOTES

1 *The Second Lampe of Virginitie: Conteining diuers godlie Meditations, and Christian Praiers made by sundrie vertuous Queenes, and other deuout and godlie women in our time* in Thomas Bentley, *The Monument of Matrones: conteining seuen seuerall Lamps of Virginitie, or distinct treatises* ([London], 1582), sig. L2ᵛ–X4ᵛ.

2 These are discussed in Elaine V. Beilin, *Redeeming Eve: Women Writers of the English Renaissance* (Princeton, 1987), pp. 266–85. Sylvia Brown's article in this journal analyses the differences between Elizabeth Jocelin's manuscript and printed works. Brown's forthcoming edition of the works of Jocelin, Leigh, and Richardson is to be published by Sutton.

3 Charlotte F. Otten (ed.), *English Women's Voices 1540–1700* (Miami, 1992), p. 302, includes a facsimile of Richardson's manuscript dedicatory epistle to her grandson (Harvard University, Houghton Library, *EC C8495 6451), discussed below. The Bodleian Library's copy of the printed volume (Vet A.3 f.132), discussed below, is a presentation copy for her brother Sir Henry Beaumont (the initials H B appear on the upper and lower covers in gilt) and contain many revisions in the author's hand. This copy also ends with two signatures not in the Thomason Tracts copy in the British Library (E.1165[4]). These leaves contain: 'My owne Prayer in Meeter, or to be sung as a Hymne,' 'Other short Verses to the like purpose,' and a prose meditation on how to order one's soul and body to be acceptable to God.

4 I would like to thank Laetitia Yeandle of the Folger Shakespeare Library and Christopher Whittick of the East Sussex Record Office for bringing these manuscripts to my attention; Sylvia Brown for identifying Elizabeth Richardson as the same person as the author of *A Ladies Legacie*; and Peter Beal for comments on both of these manuscripts.

5 For discussions of the malleability of manuscript and print see Max W. Thomas, 'Reading and Writing the Renaissance Commonplace Book: A Question of Authorship?', *Cardozo Arts and Entertainment Law Journal*, 10 (1992), 665–79, rpt. in Martha Woodmansee and Peter Jaszi (eds.), *The Construction of Authorship* (Durham, NC, 1994), pp. 401–15; and Arthur F. Marotti, 'Malleable and Fixed Texts: Manuscript and Printed Miscellanies and the Transmission of Lyric Poetry in the English Renaissance', *New Ways of Looking at Old Texts: Papers of the Renaissance English Text Society, 1985–1991*, ed. W. Speed Hill (Binghamton, NY, 1993), pp. 159–73.

6 For biographical information see *The Visitations of the County of Sussex, Made and taken in the years 1530 By Thomas Benolte, Clarenceux King of Arms; And 1634 By John Philipot, Somerset Herald*, ed. W. Bruce Bannerman, Harleian Society 53 (London, 1950), pp. 16–18; East Sussex Record Office, Ashburnham Parish Registers, PAR 233/1/1/1, and early twentieth-century pedigree by Lady Catherine Ashburnham, ASH 116; George Edward Cokayne, *The Complete Peerage*, III (London, 1910), pp. 488–91 and 453; E.K. Elliott (ed.), *Leicestershire Parish Registers. Marriages.*, X (London, 1913), p. 110; William A. Shaw, *The Knights of England*, II (London, 1906), p. 129; G.E.C, *Complete Baronetage*, II (Gloucester, 1983; first pub. 1900–09 in 6 vols.), pp. 6–7; *The Visitation of the County of Leicester in the Year 1619*, ed. John Fetherston, Harleian Society 2 (London, 1870), pp. 60–61 and 169–72; *Dictionary of National Biography*, I (Oxford, 1917), pp. 635–6; XVI (Oxford, 1917), pp. 1133–4; John Campbell, *The Lives of the Chief Justices of England*, 3rd. edn., II (London, 1874), p. 15; *Calendar of State Papers, Domestic . . . 1627–8* (London, 1858), p. 326; *Acts of the Privy Council of England. 1627 September–1628 June* (London, 1940), p. 5; Guildhall Library, St Andrew's, Holborn parish registers; will proved 7 April 1651, Public Record Office, PROB 11/216/63.

7 C. M. Briquet, *Les Filigranes . . . a facsimile of the 1907 edition*, ed. Allan Stevenson, I (Amsterdam, 1968), No. 1370.

8 I am grateful to Sylvia Brown for this suggestion.

9 'Neither hath the Lord withdrawn his favour so from us as to leave us utterly desolate to despair, but hath graciously raised us comfort by honourable friends to be

carefull and deare parents unto us, whom God preserve and shew mercy to them and theirs, as they have done to us' (sig. A3ʳ).

10 Items 7, 5, 6, and 3, were first numbered 3, 13, 7, and 9, respectively.

11 The order of the prayers and meditations in the manuscript is as follows: 1, 2, 4, 7, 5, 6, 8, 9, 10, 3, 11, and 12. These correspond with the following in the printed version: [i], 1 and 3, 5 and 6, 4, 8 and 9, 10 and 11, 13, the unnumbered meditation between 13 and 14, 14, 7, 15, and 12.

12 Francis R. Steer, *The Ashburnham Archives: A Catalogue* (Lewes, 1958), pp. xv–xvi.

13 Otten, p. 302.

14 No material by Richardson, in print or manuscript, is listed in the catalogue for the Dering sale at Puttick and Simpson's on 8 June 1858.

Elizabeth Ashburnham Richardson's Meditation on the Countess of Pembroke's *Discourse*

Margaret P. Hannay

Included in a manuscript of prayers begun by Elizabeth Ashburnham [later Richardson] in 1606 (Folger MS V.a.511, described by Victoria Burke above) is 'A discourse of ye teadiousnes of life and profitt of death'. This is a précis of and meditation on the Countess of Pembroke's *A Discourse of Life and Death* (1592), her translation of the *Excellent discours de la vie et de la mort* (1576) by Philippe de Mornay, seigneur du Plessis-Marly, a Huguenot soldier and statesman who was a friend and ally of Pembroke's famous brother Sir Philip Sidney. The meditation appears to have been composed, or supervised, by Richardson.[1] Although it is transcribed in a second hand, it has corrections in Richardson's own hand. It is included in Richardson's autograph four-part table of contents at the beginning of the miscellany under the listing '4. A Treatise, concerning Life, and Death' (f. 1^v). At the conclusion of the miscellany it is listed again in an autograph table of contents: 'The fourth part; is a Treatise ~~concerning~~ declaring the troble of life, and profit of death. Finis. Elizabeth: Ashbornham' (f. 86v). The 'discourse' is congruent with Richardson's printed prayers, in tone (particularly the consciousness of sin), in style (as in the frequent doublets), and in phrasing (for instance, life as the 'vale of . . . misery', Satan's 'malice and subtiltye', herself as but 'dust and ashes').

'A discourse' is particularly interesting as a rare example of an early modern woman's reflection on printed work by another woman. It is also important in the reception history of the works of the Countess of Pembroke. *Antonius*, her translation of Robert Garnier's drama *Marc Antoine*, was widely influential, but *A Discourse of Life and Death* printed with it in 1592 was infrequently mentioned by her contemporaries, even though it was separately reprinted three times (1600, 1606, and 1608) and reissued once (1607).[2] A handwritten copy, anonymously transcribed inaccurately from the 1592 edition, was discovered at the British

Library by Hilton Kelliher and J. K. Moore.[3] A 1600 printed copy in
private hands was also customized early in the seventeenth century—by
inserting circular emblems at front and back, adding marginal quotations from Seneca, Ecclesiastes, and the Psalms, and transcribing poems
(including 'Like as the damask rose') on the end papers. *A Discourse of Life
and Death* was evidently seen as a useful meditation to be shaped to the
reader's own need.

Mornay's doctrinal works were highly regarded in Protestant circles
and were translated into English, Italian, Dutch, and 'every language',
as his wife Charlotte Arbaleste reported.[4] The *Excellent discours de la vie et
de la mort* was written at her request, she says, and it is dedicated to
Mornay's sister 'Madamoiselle du Plessis'. A female audience might
therefore be anticipated; nevertheless, the reader is constructed as an
educated, upper-class man ('mon ami') active in public service.[5]
Mornay alters the *ars moriendi* tradition by focusing more on living well
than on making a good death; he first discusses life in some 600 lines
and then death in less than 300 lines. After an opening poetic meditation on our fear of death (lines 1–46), he discusses the trials of this life
through the Senecan ages of man, treating infancy (47–57), childhood
(58–73), youth (74–129), manhood or 'perfit age' (130–604), and old age
(605–46), pausing to sum up the nature of our lives (647–75), before the
concluding section on the benefits of death (676–962).[6] Drawing on
both classical and biblical sources, Mornay baptizes the ideas of the
Stoics, particularly as transmitted by Seneca, emphasizing the virtuous
life that is based on reason rather than on emotion so that the person
remains unmoved by the vagaries of Fortune. To this Stoic ideal
Mornay adds thoughts from the Book of Ecclesiastes, attributed to
Solomon in the early modern period, and from Christian doctrine.[7]

Richardson's meditation is entitled, with heavy deletions, 'A ~~treti~~ discourse of ~~life~~ yᵉ teadiousnes of life and profitt of death' (f. 84). The correction of the title from what is apparently intended as 'treatise', as listed
in the contents, to 'discourse' suggests that Richardson was working
with the Countess of Pembroke's translation before her; the 'teadiousnes' of life and 'profitt' of death are added as editorial comment.[8]
The original title may mean that the transcriber knew, or knew of, the
*Six Excellent Treatises of Life and Death, Collected (and published in French) by
Philip Mornay, Sieur du Plessis: And now (first) Translated in to English* (1607)
bound with copies of the 1607 and 1608 editions of *A Discourse of Life and
Death.*[9] The treatises, originally published in French with Mornay's
Excellens Traitez et Discours de la Vie et de la Mort (1581), were 'Plato's
Axiochus'; Cicero's discourse on death; selections from Seneca's work,
particularly from the *Epistulae morales*, 'De consolatione ad Polybium',

and 'De Providentia'; St. Cyprian's sermon in time of plague; and St. Ambrose's treatise 'touching the benefit and happinesse of Death'. To these were added 'Certain places of Scripture, Prayers and Meditations, concerning Life and Death', a compilation of consolatory scriptural passages followed by meditations on them. The Richardson manuscript does not seem indebted to any of those six treatises, despite the original title 'Treatise'. She adds none of the classical material and only one scriptural passage that appears in the *Six Excellent Treatises*, a frequently-quoted passage from Job 1: 21 also used by Cyprian ('wee brought nothinge into ye world, and yt is certaine y^t wee shall carrie nothinge out, naked wee came, and soe wee must retorn'). The scriptural passages of consolation that form the sixth treatise are notably lacking in Richardson's manuscript. Thus 'A discourse' is probably based on the 1592 edition of *A Discourse of Life and Death*, which did not include the *Treatises*. Further evidence for her use of this first edition is provided in the spelling. Inconsistency is the most notable characteristic of Richardson's spelling in both her own hand and in the scribal hand; 'A discourse' wavers between 'y^{ir}' and 'their', for example, 'y^m' and 'them', and the suffix 'ie' or 'y'. Nevertheless, 'A discourse' clearly uses some older spellings that match the 1592 edition rather than the more modern spellings of those words in 1600 and subsequent editions. Like the 1592, it uses the suffixes 'eth', 'nes', and 'lie' frequently; and it also uses such spellings as 'happie', 'seperate', 'trauaile', and 'wee'.[10] Richardson does not appear to have consulted the earlier English translation by Edward Aggas, *The Defence of Death* (1577), or Mornay's own Latin sources. The only obvious correspondence with the original French edition is that she concludes the text with 'Amen', unlike Aggas and Pembroke; this need not prove direct reliance on Mornay, however, since she concludes her prayers with 'Amen' or, more rarely, its equivalent 'So be it'.

The Countess of Pembroke follows Mornay closely in both content and form, although she makes some subtle changes in wording and emphasis in her translation.[11] In contrast, Richardson's 'discourse' exemplifies the scribal tradition of reading as rewriting. In reducing the thirty-one pages of the printed edition to four handwritten leaves, she provides her own paragraphs of introduction and conclusion, summarizes Pembroke's translation, and meditates on it. Richardson reflects class and gender issues by omitting the lengthy section on the courtier's ambition, and by adding comments on female experience of arranged marriage and of childrearing. She alters the Christian/Senecan tone of the *Discourse* by omitting most classical references, exempla, and poetic metaphors, and by adding scriptural quotations with emphasis on sin

and judgment. Her repeated replacement of classical allusions by scriptural quotation raises the question of whether she is ignorant of the classics or whether she, like Elizabeth Jocelin, is deliberately turning from
classical to scriptural authority. Jocelin, who had been taught by her
learned grandfather, Dr William Chaderton, Bishop of Lincoln, was
praised for setting aside her classical knowledge in writing for her child:
'In the whole course of her pen, I observe her piety and humility: these
lines scarce shewing one sparke of her secular learning: this her candle
being rather lighted from the lamp of the Sanctuary'.[12] Richardson
may have lacked Elizabeth Jocelin's learning, or she may have similarly
sought to light her candle only 'from the lamp of the Sanctuary'. In
either case, her omissions and additions seem to be quite deliberate,
simplifying the rhetoric and emphasizing Christian piety.[13]

The body of her 'discourse' follows *A Discourse of Life and Death* in
structure and quotes extensively from it; approximately one fifth of the
total is direct quotation, sometimes reproducing sequential passages
and sometimes bringing together phrases widely separated in
Pembroke. The introduction and conclusion are the most independent
sections. She supplies the opening rhetorical question, including the
word play on 'senceles and sensually affected', a prose style consistent
with Pembroke's. Richardson adds references to mermaids and sirens,
and three brief metaphors—the meadow full of serpents, the garden full
of poison flowers, and the fountain of vanity.[14] This is surprising,
because she normally omits the poetic metaphors characteristic of both
Mornay and Pembroke. For example, Pembroke says that our passing
from one age to another is but passing from 'evill to evill' like 'one wave
driving on an other, untill we be arrived at the Haven of death'
(669–71). Richardson renders it, 'nowe shall wee haue newe assaults and
combats, fallinge but from one mischiefe to another, like waues of ye sea
driuinge eache other, thus chaunginge but neuer endinge our miseries'.
There is no haven here. She generally seems uncomfortable with
metaphors, believing that they need explanation. To clarify the reference to our life as 'a sea open to all windes' (11), for example, she adds
a phrase to make it the 'sea of woes'. She simply omits most metaphors,
such as children who dislike medicine, or people who fear having teeth
pulled or being bled by the surgeon. She also omits references to New
World exploration, children's games, lion keepers, clothing, mountain-
climbing, creditors, and even the plague.

All of the exempla that make *A Discourse* so vivid are removed. To
illustrate the choice between reason and passion, Mornay uses
Hercules, for example; to illustrate the internal war he uses Sinon and
the Trojan horse; and to establish the miseries caused by high place, he

uses a series of historical figures, including Dionysius II of Syracuse, Augustus, Tiberius, Pyrrhus, and Alexander, as well as the Holy Roman Emperor Charles the fifth, who had abdicated and had taken refuge in a monastery. All of these classical and historical references are omitted. Richardson does not refer to Penelope's web, a metaphor embellished by Pembroke, nor to the ass carrying the statue of Isis, nor to the image of Hecate that frightened children, nor to the Cimmerians who live 'in perpetuall night' (347–48). Richardson not only removes the classical references, but also much condenses the section on scholarship, omitting Mornay's reference to scholars of various disciplines (arithmetic, geometry, music, astrology, philosophy, history, medicine and theology), giving instead a single sentence to the search for 'knowledge, wisedome, and learninge'. She eliminates the allusion to the famous maxim 'Know thyself', inscribed on the Temple of Apollo at Delphi and mentioned in Plato's *Protagoras*. Pembroke translates, 'The Philosopher discourseth of the nature of all other things: and knowes not himselfe' (577–78), which Richardson renders with a reference to I Cor. 8: 1, 'knowledge in many puffeth y^m vp, y^t in knowinge muche they forgett ^{ymselues}'.[15] She appears more comfortable with biblical citations than classical allusions. Yet she also omits biblical exempla, such as Lot's experiences in Sodom, the temptation of Christ, and the Israelites who missed the 'garlike and onions of *Egipt*' (539).

Despite these reductions, the most notable quality of the prose is its wordiness in the constant, almost obsessive, use of doublets—more than 60 doublets in four pages. This appears an exaggeration of Pembroke's style and is closer to that of Aggas, but her doublets do not seem derived from his. Some doublets are directly quoted from Pembroke, such as 'sence nor apprehension' (54) or 'well and happilie' (57), though Pembroke frequently replaces Mornay's doublets with a single term.[16] Richardson characteristically adds doublets. For example, the sentence 'We enter it [life] in teares, we passe it in sweate, we ende it in sorow' (47–48) is expanded to 'Wee all enter this life in cryinge and teares, wee passe ^{it} wth cares and paines, and end it in sorrowe and feare'. She also adds heavy alliteration, as in 'a false fable finelie and cunninglie framed'; Pembroke frequently alliterates doublets in her translation, but uses such extended alliteration in her poetry more than in her prose.[17]

Richardson's meditation is more biblical than Senecan—and more pessimistic than either tradition. She adds scriptural quotations, including 'for all y^t will liue godlie, must suffer persecucion' (II Tim. 3: 12) and 'who soe will followe christ, must take vp a crosse' (Matt. 16: 24) and 'couetousnes is ye roote of all euill' (I Tim. 6: 10). Her choice of biblical passages is much less cheerful than Mornay's. For example, both quote

Ecclesiastes 1: 14 on 'vanity' and 'vexacion', and each adds an additional quotation from Ecclesiastes. Mornay chooses (Ecc. 7: 1), 'Better, saith *Salomon*, is the day of death, then the day of birth', to which he adds the Christian application: 'and why? because it is not to us a last day, but the dawning of an everlasting day' (761–64). Richardson chooses (Ecc. 12: 1): 'remember o^r Creatour in ye tyme of youth, before ye euill daies comme, and ye yeares approche wherein we shall saie, wee haue noe pleasure in y^m'. Despite the tone of world-weariness, she herself was comparatively young when she compiled this manuscript.

Richardson's theology here and in her prayers seems much more centered on sin than Mornay's. She expands warnings about the world, the flesh, and the devil. Whereas Mornay mentions the pain of death that frightens us, saying that it is only during life that we feel pain, she alters the phrase to say that it is sin rather than death that causes pain— sin and the 'horrour of ye seuere Iudgment'. She concisely summarizes Mornay's concluding arguments (671–914) with her statement that, 'Nowe is there noe hopefull comfort for ye end and release of all these miseries, and ye beginnynge of neuer endinge happines, but death onely, y^n wch nothinge is more assured, thoughe ye tyme thereof be most vncertaine vnto vs; for as soone as wee are borne, wee beginne to drawe to our end, ye encrease of o^r dayes, beinge ye decrease of o^r liues, and once to dye well, wee had neede to dye daylie in o^{r}selues, and to ye world'. Yet her conclusion replaces Mornay's poetic praise for death and for the eternal life to come with a meditation on age, bodily corruption, and God's judgment—old age as 'deth yn life', our bodies as the 'heires of serpents, and foode of wormes', and our fear of the 'day of wrath'. Mornay's conclusion reaches a poetic crescendo, presenting death as the 'entraunce of the porte where wee shall ride in safetie from all windes' (689–90) and the 'place of all joyes' (889), to the point that he feels it necessary to caution the reader not to hasten the day of death. Richardson ends by adapting a biblical promise in a single clause: 'but to those y^t liue godlie, death is an aduantage for all thinges are theirs, and they Christs, wth whome they shall liue for euer: amen'. This is the only real promise of transcendence she includes.

More striking than her alterations in theological emphasis are the alterations that she makes to personalize the text, to make it fit her gender, social situation, and experience. Like Pembroke in her rendering of the Psalms, Richardson frequently removes masculine pronouns by changing to first person plural, second person, or third person plural, anticipating modern efforts to use non-sexist language.[18] The alterations are the more remarkable because she addresses the manuscript to children and all other Christians—not only to her daughters, like her printed work.

In the meditation on the ages of man that forms the body of the text, she presents both infancy and old age from a caregiver's perspective. Pembroke had altered the verb describing a baby's lack of mobility from the inability to 'move' to the inability 'to support himselfe', suggesting 'the point of view of the mother instead of the child', as Diane Bornstein observes.[19] Richardson adds specific details, noting that the infant is 'wrapped in swadlinge clothes' and 'nourished by ye care and trouble of others'. She gives a similar description of old age: 'wee are comme backe to infancie . . . beinge wearysome to our selues, and noisome to others'. The caregiver is the one who might find the aged 'noisome'. Richardson also emphasizes the difficulties of teaching adolescents, when she says that they are 'hardlie brought vnto anie thinge y^t is good, but by ye labour and diligence of their frinds, and wth greate repininge and discontent in y^m selues'. She replaces Pembroke's lively depiction of the temptations of youth with a scriptural quotation and commonplaces on the world, the flesh, and the devil. Whereas Pembroke translates Mornay accurately in depicting a young man's own passion that 'entertains him with a thousand delights' and presents him with 'a thousand worldly pleasures' (76–78), Richardson externalizes the temptation. The world, she says, 'entertaines, wth a thowsand delightes, to perswade vs to vanitie'. When she moves the discussion of retirement from the world into this section on youth, instead of its more traditional placement with manhood or 'perfit age', she may, perhaps, reflect a young woman's enforced seclusion on her husband's estate.

Most significantly, in her description of the age that brings freedom from teachers and parents, when youths are finally freed from 'their subieccion to others', she adds a parenthetic statement on the contrast for young women: 'unles yt be some vnfortunate women, y^t are remoued from ye slauerye of their youthes gouernours, to comme vnder ye tyrannie of an vndiscreete husband, wch bondage sildome doth release duringe their liues'. It is a grim view of marriage, evidently derived from her own marriage to Sir John Ashburnham.

More than a third of Mornay's essay is devoted to the traditional temptations of 'perfit age', avarice (143–214) and ambition (215–557). For his anticipated aristocratic male reader, the dangers of avarice or ambition are all too present. Pembroke translates faithfully, retaining this perspective of the courtier, familiar to her from her own residence at court and from the experience of her male relatives. Richardson drastically condenses the section on the dangers of avarice to just ten lines, with the emphasis altered from the pursuit of wealth to the dangers of covetousness and the need to be content; writing in a period of poverty, caused by the poor business decisions of a profligate husband, she is not concerned about the dangers of wealth. Similarly, she gives just thirteen lines to ambition, which was not a significant temptation for someone of her gender and social position. She thereby omits the memorable comparison of the fetters of the prisoner to the chains of office (303–11).

In this 'discourse' itself there is no direct reference to her own situation, but in the manuscript she includes a prayer that God will give her husband 'a discreate and carefull minde, in disposinge of his estate, y^t in all things he may take y^e best and fittest course for o^r good y^t by thy blessinge wee maie haue happie and prosperous succes, $\mathord{\leftrightsquigarrow}$ in all that he vndertakes, soe as wee may liue in quiet and contentm^t, and may be able in a competent sort, to prouide for all y^t depende vppon vs' (f. 73). Her difficulty in being obedient to such a man is reflected in a superscribed reminder to herself that she has added to a prayer later, in a different pen. She first prays that 'I may carefullye perfome my dutie towardes thee, instructe in my children in thy trueth knowledge and feare' (ff. 73v–74). Later she inserts above the line in the middle of the sentence, 'please & content my husband'. Her husband's extravagances caused hardship to his children. In her dedicatory 'Letter to my foure Daughters', dated 1625, she says 'though I am so vnhappy as to be left destitute, not able to raise you portions of wealth' yet she hopes by her writing to add to 'the portion of Grace' that God will give to her daughters.[20] She says that her gift of her writings as a legacy to her daughters in lieu of money is valuable because of the spiritual advice they contain, yet that gift also reveals a high valuation of her own words, despite her habitual use of the modesty topos. Her position as a mother gave her authority to speak.

Richardson's manuscript 'A discourse of ye teadiousnes of life and profitt of death' thus demonstrates the reading process of an intelligent woman schooled in the scriptures who reads, reflects on, and reshapes the Countess of Pembroke's *A Discourse of Life and Death* in a way that she finds meaningful for her own situation. Print did not entirely stabilize the text for her. Rather, her reading became rewriting, as she entered into the text to mould it to her own needs. Her meditation is thus in many ways freer and therefore more original (though far less learned and poetic) than the work on which it is based, the Countess of Pembroke's translation of Mornay's *Excellent discours de la vie et de la mort*. Choosing a plain style shorn of exempla and classical allusion, Richardson reshapes *A Discourse* into aphorisms suitable for the 'Instructions for my children, or any other Christian' promised by her title.

APPENDIX

'A ~~treti~~ discourse of ~~life~~ ye teadiousnes of life and profitt of death' from Elizabeth Ashburnham, 'Instructions for my children, or any other Christian' (Washington, D.C., Folger Shakespeare Library MS V.a.511, ff. 84–85v)[21]

Howe commeth yt to passe, y^t mankinde onelie (amongest all other creatures) beinge endued wth reason, should aboue all other liuinge thinges, be most senceles and sensually affected, in desiringe and endeuouringe wth all their power, the longe continuance of this present life (ye vale of all mischiefe and miserie,) and soe much feare and hate ye approche of death, wch is ye beginninge of all true & euerlasting happines. O howe <u>doe they</u> ^{many} bend their eares ^{vn}to ye Siren songe, and listen to ye pleasant voice of ye Mermaide, till they sinke in ye gulphe; vnhappie wretches bewitched wth ye deceaueable traines and shewes of this vaine world, which if it be rightlie considered wth incorrupt eyes, is but a bottomeles pitt of errors, a markett of deceipte, a prison of darkenes, a continuall tempest of sondry stormes and troubles, a sea of woes open to all windes; wherein wee are tossed and continually tormented; sometime wthin, sometime wthout; a barren land wherein noe good thinge is attained but by greate labour and care, a greene and plesant meadowe full of serpentes, readie to stinge all y^t seeke to take repast therein; a gallant and beautifull garden, but ye flowers thereof are full of poison, a fountaine of vanitie, a false fable finelie and cunninglie framed, a springe of Idle thoughtes, a delightfull dreame wherein wee see nothinge but deceite, to conclude wth ^{wise} Salomon vanitye of vanities all is but vanitie, and vexacion of spiritt; wherein noe good is to be found, nor anie euill wantinge, our purpose is restles our hope frustrate our securitye wthout safetie, our intent failinge of the euente, our trauailes wthout end; all wee enioye is but abuse, and neuer doe wee attaine to true content in anie state or age, Nowe all will graunt y^t life in yt selfe is not simple good, but to liue well and happielie, is that wch euerie one aymeth at; yet if wee take a viewe of ye whole course of our liues, wee shall hardlie finde one, y^t can or will confesse to haue attained therevnto. Wee all enter this life in cryinge and teares, wee passe ^{it} wth cares and paines, and end it in sorrowe and feare; all men both highe and lowe, haue one manner of comminge into life, and shall haue a like goinge out: Euery one cometh from him y^t was first made of y^e dust of y^e ground, and falleth to y^e earth (wch is of like nature) wth lamentacion; wrapped in swadlinge clothes, nourished by y^e care and trouble of

PLATE 1. *The first page of the 'Discourse' in the Folger MS of Elizabeth Ashburnham Richardson's prayers and meditations: Washington, D.C., Folger Shakespeare Library MS V.a. 511, f. 84r. (Original size 198 × 155mm.) Reproduced by permission of the Folger Shakespeare Library.*

others, beinge le^{a}ste able of all creatures to helpe and supporte y^{m}selues; and onelie more happie in this age then afterwardes, in that they haue noe sense nor apprehension of their ~~most~~ ^{owne} vnhappienes. But ^{when} they growe to youth (wch is ye death of infancie) whereto ^{are} they ~~are~~ inclined, ^{or} how like they to spend ye time [end of f. 84; no catch phrase] but in follye or mischiefe; beinge hardlie brought vnto anie thinge y^t is good, but by ye labour and diligence of their frindes, and wth greate repininge and discontent in y^{m}selues. Come wee to ye next age soe muche desired and longed for of all, which freeth y^m from their subieccion to others, and bringeth ye hoped libertye, w^{h}erein they shalbe, at their ^{owne} gouerment and disposition (vnles yt be some vnfortunate women, y^t are remoued from ye slauerye of their youthes gouernours, to comme vnder ye tyrannie of an vndiscreete husband, wch bondage sildome doth release duringe their liues) but who soe enioyeth this wished freedome, to take a course of life to their <u>owne</u> ^{best} likinge, haue yt a doubtfull choise, whether to take ye waie of vertue, or of vice, to haue reason, or passion for y^{ir} guide, and fewe are they wch by ye especiall grace of god, chuse y^e <u>best</u> ~~right~~ waie. And in seekinge after virtue, wee can expect but future, <u>and</u> ^{not} present happines, for all y^t will liue godlie, must suffer persecucion, and who soe will followe christ, must take vp a crosse, for ye life of a christian is a continuall warefare, hauinge three most dangerous and deadlie enemies; ye deuill, ye world, and ye fleshe, wth whome wee can take noe truce; y^t olde serpent and destroier of mankinde, his malice and subtiltye, his snares and baites, daylie laide to endanger our soules is well knowne; ye other two beinge but his companions and instruments, to worke our vtter destruccion. The world entertaines wth a thowsand delightes, to perswade vs to vanitie, the fleshe euer, lusteth and rebelleth against ye spirit, to leade vs captiue slaues to sin and all vngodlienes; wee cannot finde a place in ye world to retyre our selues, where ye world will not finde vs; wee may seeke to auoide ye infeccion and contagion of others wickednes, and yet still be full of corrupt affeccions in our selues, while wee liue; Let vs chaunge companie, house, country, and all els, wee shall still finde euill and vnquietnes, till wee be seperate from o^r selues by death. Nowe if wee will let ye raines loose to o^r vnrulie passion, and suffer o^r selues to be allured by ye deceiptfull enticements thereof, and runne headlonge into all vice and sensuallitye, hopinge thereby to tast and enioye all ye pleasures and commodityes, of this vile world, or ye licentious fleshe, promiseth to their louers in this life. These seeminge pleasures may more truelie be called displeasures, hauinge not soe muche sweetenes as bitternes in y^m, gotten wth paine and perill, spent and past in a moment, and followed wth a longe and heauie remorse of conscience, like sweete meates y^t

turne into Choller; none soe pleasant to ye mouth, but leaues an vnsauory after taste, nor anie soe moderate, but hath his corasiue and carries his punishment in yt selfe, and ye best and happiest euent, is grieuous repentance; and yet wee passe ouer an infinite number of inconueniences and dangers, y^t this ill guided age throwes them into; this is ye age y^t children ^{soe} earnestlie desire, and ye wisest olde folkes ofte tymes muche lament. Next followeth y^t wch is called perfect age, wherein euery one seeketh to be accounted wise and discreet, and by [catch phrase at end of f. 84v is 'their'] their good carriage, to purchase credit and estimacion in ye world, and rest to y^{m}selues in future time; and indeede in this age are they able more perfectlie to discerne ye imperfeccions of humane nature, wch ye simplicitye of childhood, and lightnes of youth, could not discouer; but nowe shall wee haue newe assaults and combats, fallinge but from one mischiefe to another, like waues of ye sea driuinge eache other, thus chaunginge but neuer endinge our miseries. Then sues to y^m for entertainement, couetousnes, pride, ambition, enuie, vaine glorie and ye like; howe manie for lucre sake aduenture ye losse of their liues, both temporall and eternall, thinkinge there is noe other good to mortall men, but in gettinge mortall possessions, and w^{hen} they haue y^m, seldome vse y^m, heapinge vp riches and cannot tell who shall enioye y^m, settinge all their harte and hope vppon a vile excrement of ye earthe, of wch the more they drinke, ye more thirstye, beinge neuer satisfied nor content, attayninge them for ye most parte, wth greate paines and wearines of ye body, and doth possesse y^m wth noe lesse feare and trouble of minde: whereas yf wee obteine thinges necessarye att gods handes, we ought to be satisfied, for wee brought nothinge into ye world, and yt is certaine y^t wee shall carrie nothinge out, naked wee came, and soe wee must retorne; for couetousnes is y^e roote of all euill and y^e corrupcions of their hoordinges, shall but serue to witnes against y^m in y^e day of wrath. Pride and ambition is hatefull both to god and man, and enuie fretteth y$^{[e]}$ harte, and drieth vp y^e bones, beinge continually vexed, eyther att their owne harmes or at others good, still discontented y^t they are not equall wth y^e highest, and neuer are thankefull y^t there are thowsands vnder y^m; and what ys that vaine honour wee soe greedelie hunt for, but a smoke and a blast of winde, wch when ye sunne of fortune goes downe vppon vs, it is quite gone, and ye place thereof cannot be founde; what doth pride profitt vs, or what good doth ye pompe of riches bringe vs, all those thinges are passed awaie like a shadowe, or a shippe y^t goeth ouer ye waues of ye sea, ye trace and path whereof cannot be seene; why is earthe and ashes proude, seeinge when they dye, they are but ye heires of serpents, and foode of wormes; what haue wee y^t wee haue not receaued from god, and what honour can wee haue of our selues, if others will not yeelde yt vnto vs; but ye glory and honour wee aspire to, att ye best, is but vaine, and all y^t auarice can obteine but grosse and base, for wch wee must suffer muche ill, to gett y^t wch is ill; only are they happie who in minde liue content, and they most vnhappie, whome all they can haue cannot content. Nowe some fewe of ye wisest spend muche of this age in seekinge for knowledge, wisedome, and learninge, wch indeede is ye best bestowed tyme of all other, but these cannot be gotten w^thowt greate and painefull labour and diligence, and endles trauaile of ye minde, for ye more wee knowe, ye more wee desire to knowe, the fuller ye minde is, ye emptier yt findes it selfe, and who soe encreaseth knowledge [catch phrase at end of f. 85 is 'encreaseth'] encreaseth sorrowe in seeinge his owne ignorance; for ye most wee knowe, is to finde y^t we knowe nothinge, and our best perfeccion, is to iudge truelie of our owne imperfeccions, yet knowledge in many puffeth y^m vp, y^t in knowinge muche they forgett ^ymselues soe turninge ye righte and beast vse of our liues to their owne hurte. Then commeth old age wch is but ye post and messenger before death, and may fitter be called deth y^n life, wherein all ye sences growe weake and oft fayle, except ye sense of paine, repayinge ye riott of youth, wth many infirmityes, and findinge a bitter after tast in minde or body, and oft in both of ye former euilles in all ye ages past, and as by death wee retorne againe to ye earth, from whence wee came, soe in this age wee are comme backe to infancie, wch was ye first steppe we set on earth, beinge wearysome to our selues, and noisome to others; therefor Solomon wisheth vs to remember o^r Creatour in ye tyme of youth, before ye euill daies comme, and ye yeares approche wherein we shall saie, wee haue noe pleasure in y^m, o^r dayes are then but sorrowes, beinge tyred wth ye perpetuall taske this life tyes vs to, wherein when wee haue done o^r best, we must beginne againe, passinge from one euill to an other, grieuinge in ye remembrance of y^t is past, doubtfull in ye expectacion of what is to comme, and takinge noe content in ye present tyme. Nowe is there noe hopefull comfort for ye end and release of all these miseries, and ye beginnynge of neuer endinge happines, but death onely, y^n wch nothinge is more assured, thoughe ye tyme thereof be most vncertaine vnto vs; for as soone as wee are borne, wee beginne to drawe to our end, ye encrease of o^r dayes, beinge ye decrease of o^r liues, and once to dye well, wee had neede to dye daylie in o^rselues, and to ye world; all fleshe waxeth olde as a garment, and this is ye condicion of all times, they must dye ye death; as ye greene leaues on a tree, some fall and some growe, soe is ye generacion of fleshe and blood, one cometh to an end and another is borne, for all corruptible thinges shall fayle, and ye number of ᵒᵘʳ dayes are but fewe and euill; euen a spann longe, and there is an appointed tyme to man vppon earth, wᶜʰ wee shall not passe; our life is but a vapour yᵗ appeareth for a little while, and afterwards vanisheth awaie; yf we attaine vnto seauenty yeares it is muche, and yet our strength is bu[t] labour and sorrowe; great trauell is created for all men, and a heauie yoake for yᵉ children of Adam, from yᵉ daie they comme from their mothers wombe, till they retorne to yᵉ mother of all things, both he yᵗ sitteth on yᵉ glorious throne, and he yᵗ is beneath in dust and ashes, all must retorne to yᵉ earthe from whence they camme for man is not Lord ouer yᵉ spiritt to reteyne yᵉ same neither can deliuer him-selfe in yᵉ day of death. But thoughe death can be auoided by none, yet it is causeleslye feared by all, partly by oʳ weake nature, shunninge yᵉ paine, yᵗ lyfe at partinge, ᵒʳ ʳᵃᵗʰᵉʳ ˢⁱⁿ not death laieth vppon vs, but chiefe-lie by yᵉ memory of an euill passed life, and yᵉ horrou[r] of yᵉ seuere Iudgment presentlye to followe; but to those yᵗ liue godlie, death is an aduantage for all thinges are theirs, and they Christs, wᵗʰ whome they shall liue for euer: amen.

NOTES

1 I am grateful to Laetitia Yeandle, Noel Kinnamon, Michael Brennan, and Mark Bland for their helpful comments on this manuscript.

2 See 'Origins, Early Reception, and Influence', *The Collected Works of Mary Sidney Herbert, Countess of Pembroke*, ed. Margaret P. Hannay, Noel J. Kinnamon, and Michael G. Brennan (Oxford, 1998), vol. I, pp. 33–45. On women writers' familiar-ity with the works of Pembroke and her niece Lady Mary Wroth in the late seven-teenth and early eighteenth centuries, see Carol Barash, *English Women's Poetry, 1649–1714: Politics, Community, and Linguistic Authority* (Oxford, 1996), pp. 16–17.

3 Sloane MS 1032, ff. 1–28; *Collected Works*, vol. I, p. 314.

4 *Mémoires de Charlotte Arbaleste*, trans. by Lucy Crump, *A Huguenot Family in the XVI Century: The Memoirs of Philippe de Mornay, Sieur du Plessis Marly, Written by his Wife* (London, 1926), p. 170.

5 Philippe de Mornay, *Excellent discours de la vie et de la mort* (1576), sig. B8ᵛ.

6 Line numbers here and throughout refer to Pembroke's translation, *A Discourse of Life and Death* (1592), in *Collected Works*, vol. I, pp. 229–54.

7 See '*Discourse*: Literary Context' in *Collected Works*, vol. I, pp. 208–20.

8 Smaller changes also indicate that Richardson was correcting 'A discourse' with Pembroke's *Discourse* before her, such as the addition of 'soe' to children 'earnestlie desire', corresponding to Pembroke, line 129.

9 The anonymous English translation of the *Treatises* was evidently undertaken by someone other than Pembroke, as evidenced by the note of 'The Translator to the Reader', 'Here knowe, that the first Discourse, mentioned in the ['French Authors'] Advertisement ensuing, is none of these six here set down; but another precedent to these, and formerly translated by the Countesse of Pembroke': *Six Excellent Treatises of Life and Death, Collected (and published in French) by Philip Mornay, Sieur du Plessis: And now (first) Translated in to English* (London, 1607), sig. A2ᵛ.

10 Diane Bornstein (ed.), *The Countess of Pembroke's Translation of Philippe de Mornay's Discourse of Life and Death* (Detroit, Michigan, 1983), p. 21. I am indebted to Noel Kinnamon's extensive collation of spelling variants in editions of *A Discourse of Life and Death*.

11 On Pembroke's translation, see Paul Joseph Jackson, 'An Elizabethan Translator: The Countess of Pembroke with Particular Attention to her *Discourse of Life and Death*' (unpublished doctoral thesis for the University of Washington, 1940); Bornstein, *The Countess of Pembroke's Translation*, pp. 1–21 and 73–97; and '*Discourse* : Fidelity to Originals' in *Collected Works*, vol. I, pp. 220–8.

12 'The Approbation' in Elizabeth Jocelin, *The Mother's Legacie, To her unborne Childe* (London, 1624), sig. A2ᵛ.

13 On the malleability of manuscript texts, see Arthur Marotti, *Manuscript, Print, and the English Renaissance Lyric* (Ithaca, NY, 1995), pp. 135–208. Harold Love discusses the editorial role of the scribe in *Scribal Publication in Seventeenth-Century England* (Oxford, 1993), pp. 119–22.

14 Several of these images were also used by Alice Sutcliffe, *Meditations of Mans Mortalitie* (London 1634; facsimile ed. Patrick Cullen, in *The Early Modern Englishwoman*, vol. VII, Aldersgate 1996), as Sylvia Brown has noted (private correspondence). See particularly references to sirens and mermaids (28, 82, 162, 193), the body as dung or as the food of worms (89, 149, 159), and the world as a fountain of cares (81). Like Richardson, Sutcliffe stresses sin and judgment, and quotes Ecclesiastes 12: 1. Sutcliffe is unlikely to have read Richardson's manuscript, however; both appear to be using widely-circulated metaphors.

15 The descriptive phrase 'puffed up' also appears in Pembroke's section on ambition (line 273).

16 Bornstein, *The Countess of Pembroke's Translation*, 18; *Collected Works*, vol. I, p. 63.

17 Cf. Richardson's later printed prayers, as in the description of 'this miserable, mutable, and mortall life', Elizabeth Richardson, *A Ladies Legacie to her Daughters* (London, 1645), sig. G8ᵛ.

18 On gender issues in Pembroke's *Psalmes* and dedicatory poems, see Beth Wynne Fisken, 'Mary Sidney's *Psalmes*: Education and Wisdom', in *Silent But for the Word: Tudor Women as Patrons, Translators, and Writers of Religious Works*, ed. Margaret P. Hannay (Kent, Ohio, 1985), pp. 166–83; and ' "To the Angell spirit . . .": Mary Sidney's Entry into the "World of Words" ', in *The Renaissance Englishwoman in Print: Counterbalancing the Canon*, ed. Anne M. Haselkorn and Betty S. Travitsky (Amherst, Massachusetts, 1990), pp. 263–75; Gary Waller, 'The Countess of Pembroke and Gendered Reading', in *The Renaissance Englishwoman in Print*, pp. 327–45; Wendy Wall, *The Imprint of Gender: Authorship and Publication in the English Renaissance* (Ithaca, NY, 1993), pp. 310–19; Louise Schleiner, *Tudor and Stuart Women Writers* (Bloomington, Indiana, 1994), pp. 52–81; Margaret P. Hannay, ' "House-confined maids": The Presentation of Woman's Role in the *Psalmes* of the Countess of Pembroke', *English Literary Renaissance*, 24 (1994), pp. 44–71.

19 Bornstein, *The Countess of Pembroke's Translation*, p. 76.

20 Richardson, *A Ladies Legacie*, sig. A2. Her second marriage, to Sir Thomas Richardson, seems to have been far happier, as evidenced by her 1634 note on her sorrow at his death, sig. D2.

21 In this transcription the diacritical marks in words ending in 'con' have been rendered as 'cion'; the diacritics over the nasals *m* and *n* have been rendered by doubling. The right margins are justified with a varying design of line fillers, not reproduced here.

The Approbation of
Elizabeth Jocelin

Sylvia Brown

In January 1624, a chaplain to the Archbishop of Canterbury named Thomas Goad licensed a book for publication, authorizing its entry in the Stationer's Register as 'The mothers legacye to her unborne Child, by ELLEN. JOSLIN'. Licensing was one of the jobs of an archbishop's chaplain, and Goad licensed a range of books in the 1620s, including George Sandys' *Metamorphoses* and Lady Mary Wroth's *Urania*, but concentrating especially on anti-Catholic and anti-Arminian tracts.[1] Goad, however, went further than usual with this piece of maternal writing. He oversaw its publication and wrote an introductory preface which he called 'The Approbation', providing some biographical details as well as praising the virtue of the author. He appears also to have changed her text.

We know about and can analyse Goad's changes because of a London, British Library manuscript signed 'Eliza Joscelin' (Add. MS 27467). It is substantially the text which Goad published, but with suggestive differences. Several pieces of evidence indicate that Add. MS 27467 is Elizabeth Jocelin's own autograph fair copy. Firstly, it is written in a careful italic of the kind most often taught to women. There are indications that it is a copy: corrections in the manuscript show, for instance, where the copyist's eye has skipped, or where words have been copied twice. Most telling of all, however, are the revisions evident in the manuscript. These are precisely the kind of revisions an author (rather than an amanuensis) would make. Some do not change the sense substantially, but betray an authorial sensitivity to word choice: 'accuse', for instance, is changed to 'condem' (fol. 26v). Other revisions—which will be discussed below—change the direction of thought completely and in that way also show an author at work. Significant revisions were sometimes inserted after the fair copy was made; for example, inserted above a crossed-out word, with a sharper pen and darker ink. But they were also sometimes made in the process of writing, suggesting that the copyist was also the author.[2]

The corrections and revisions made in the British Library manuscript are, almost without exception, reproduced in Goad's edition of 1624, *The Mothers Legacie, To her vnborne Childe*. The two minor exceptions revert to earlier versions of the manuscript clearly visible under the strike-outs, suggesting that the manuscript was Goad's copytext.[3] Goad's changes to it are generally additions. He is less likely to replace or cut Jocelin's words, but when he does so, the changes are significant.

If the British Library manuscript is—as I take it to be—Elizabeth Jocelin's original version of the legacy, then it provides unusually explicit evidence for a condition of early modern women's writing which we have come to assume, but which we are rarely able to demonstrate so fully: the editorial interference with women's writing which made it into print with the help of men, the silencing of women's words.[4] A comparison of the British Library manuscript with the printed version allows us to see precisely what Goad chose to excise or modify: knowing what was consigned to silence, as well as what was given qualified approval to circulate more publically, can give us a better sense of the cultural processes underlying the construction and approbation of the woman writer in the period. The manuscript itself, moreover, can tell us something about the woman writer's self-construction and self-silencing as well, for the drift of Goad's changes is anticipated in some of the manuscript's corrections. Thus, if Goad's editorial interference is a particularly clear illustration of what has been termed the male 'gatekeeping' of women's writing, Jocelin's self-editing uncomfortably reminds us of the extent to which women participated in their own social control.[5]

Nonetheless, Jocelin's revisions also demonstrate the care with which she chose her words and defined her religious and her writing identities. In this private, domestic manuscript, she engaged with issues and controversies extending beyond what we have traditionally understood as the private sphere. Jocelin's text may also help us to modify and expand what we take to be the 'private' writing of early modern women and to revalue texts which are devotional, domestic, or written primarily for familial or for manuscript circulation.

1. *Biographies and Provenance*

Elizabeth Jocelin is not the first author of a mother's legacy, but her work is arguably the genre's most poignant example.[6] Sometime during her first pregnancy, between January and early October 1622, Jocelin set herself the task of writing a 'letter' ['1r'] of religious admonition to her unborn child which 'might serue for a foundation to better learning' (fol. 2r). In the prefatory epistle to her husband Taurell (PLATE 1),

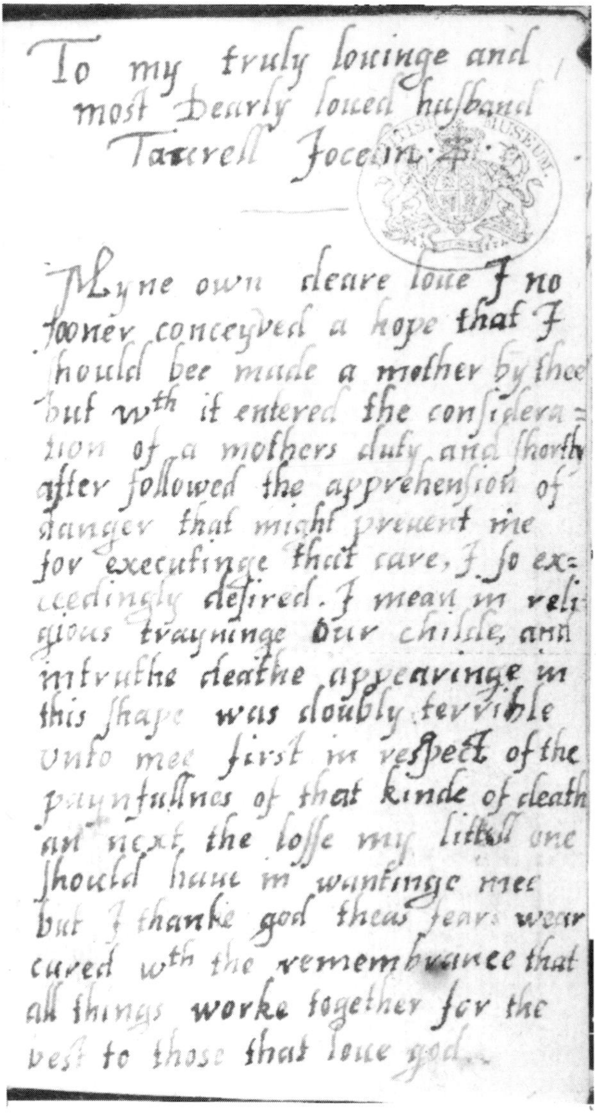

PLATE 1. *Opening of the dedicatory epistle to Taurell Jocelin in Elizabeth Jocelin's* The Mothers Legacie: *London, British Library Additional* MS *27467, fol.* 1r *(Original size 121 × 71mm.)*

Elizabeth Jocelin recounts the 'motherly zeale' (fol. IV) as well as the fear which prompted her to write:

> Myne own deare loue I no sooner conceyved a hope that I should bee made a mother by thee but wth it entered the consideration of a mothers duty and shortly after followed the apprehension of danger that might preuent me for [*sic*] executinge that care, I so exceedingly desired. I mean in religious trayninge our childe, and in truthe deathe appearinge in this shape was doubly terrible vnto mee first in respect of the payn-fullnes of that kinde of death an[d] next the losse my littell one should haue in wantinge mee (fol. 1r).

Jocelin's words and her fear were sadly prophetic. She did in fact suffer the painful death she had imagined, dying of fever nine days after the birth of her daughter Theodora on 12 October 1622. She was just twenty-seven.[7]

Goad's 'Approbation', which prefaces his version of Jocelin's legacy, gives an intimate, if highly conventionalized, glimpse of Jocelin's childbed—and deathbed. After blessing her newly baptized child and giving thanks that she had lived to see it a Christian, Jocelin calls for a winding sheet to be laid upon her, which, as Goad approvingly notes, she ordered as soon as she 'felt her selfe quicke with childe'. Then, 'giu-ing a comfortable testimony of her godly resolution, she ended her prayers, speech, and life together' (sigs. a5^r–a6^r). Except for the striking and morbid detail of the shroud, Goad's narration of Jocelin's death could come straight from any of a number of seventeenth-century deathbed narrations or funeral sermons for women; and, as often with those conventional genres, the exemplary death sets up the posthumous publication of devout 'remains'.[8] Goad, a well-known writer of manu-script verses himself, notes among Jocelin's remains poetry which is 'ingenious, but chaste and modest, like the Author'; also 'some imper-fect notes' resulting from her studies of Divinity; but is concerned prin-cipally with, and only publishes, 'this small Treatise found in her Deske vnfinished' (sigs. a3^v, a4^r).

Goad is not specific about how precisely the manuscript treatise came into his hands. His own words in the 'Approbation' suggest that he came to edit Jocelin's work in the course of licensing it for publication, but he also claims to have known Jocelin personally. He writes,

> I willingly not onely subscribed my *Approbat* for the registering the *Will* among the most publique Monuments, (the rather worthy, because pro-ceeding from the weaker sex) but also, as bound to do right vnto knowne vertue, vndertooke the care of the publication thereof, my selfe hauing

heretofore bin no stranger to the Testators education and eminent vertues (sigs. A4^v–a1^r).

Again, Goad filters the facts through the conventional terms of religious praise. But we might inquire further into what is particular about Goad's approbation as well as what is conventional. Why might this particular man have been interested in Jocelin's work? How and when might he have known her? What possible agendas could underlie both his approbation of Elizabeth Jocelin and his changes to her text?

One might begin to answer these questions by looking more closely at Goad himself. Thomas Fuller wrote of him that he 'had a commanding presence, an uncontrolable spirit, impatient to be opposed, and loving to steere the discourse (being a good Pilot to that purpose) of all the Company he came in'.[9] During the early 1620s, the period of his encounter with Jocelin's text, Goad was acting principally as domestic chaplain to George Abbot, Archbishop of Canterbury. He was probably living for the most part at Lambeth Palace, not yet having taken up permanent residence in Hadleigh in Suffolk, where he had been made rector by Abbot in 1618. As chaplain, Goad occupied himself with confuting Jesuits and licensing and writing books against Arminius. In 1619, three years before Elizabeth Jocelin's death, he replaced Joseph Hall as a delegate to the Synod of Dort, an international Calvinist meeting which condemned the doctrines of the Dutch Arminians.[10] In other words, Goad enthusiastically promoted the orthodox Calvinist position held by Abbot.[11]

But although we might therefore attach the label of 'enthusiastic Calvinist' to Goad, we can only do so with qualifications. He himself certainly bridled at the insulting label of 'Puritan'. It was common for anti-Arminian works to be condemned as such in the 1620s, but Goad and his fellow defenders of orthodox Calvinism in a work of 1626 reject the insult, defying any reader who 'hath viewed this table [comparing Arminianism with the old heresy of Pelagianism], [to] cast a scorne upon it, as composed by some gloating Puritane'.[12] In 1636, when corresponding with Matthew Wren, who was then Bishop of Norwich and a furious enforcer of conformity, Goad conveys his distaste for nonconformity and for those who defect '*in tribum puritannicum*'.[13] William Laud had become Archbishop of Canterbury upon Abbot's death in 1633, and now that the ecclesiastical hierarchy (consisting of men whom Goad would once have denounced as Arminians) actively encouraged the suppression of Puritanism, Goad was happy to go along with the establishment line. What is perhaps most important to remember about Goad is that, as in Fuller's description, he liked authority. He was a career cleric, high up in the hierarchy: he was not only chaplain to the Archbishop and rector of Hadleigh, but the holder of a number of other livings and a prebendary of Winchester Cathedral as well. In 1633, he was made Dean of Bocking.[14] He had an investment in the authority of the established Church of England to regulate religious belief and worship, and he was interested in protecting that investment. Indeed, a number of changes to Jocelin's text suggest a desire to protect just such an interest.

Jocelin herself was born into the ecclesiastical establishment: she was the only grandchild of William Chaderton, Master of Queen's College and Professor of Divinity in Cambridge, and subsequently Bishop of Chester and then Lincoln.[15] Jocelin's parents separated and her mother died at an early age, so she was raised and educated in her grandfather's household—probably at his house at Southoe when he was Bishop of Lincoln.[16] It is possible that Goad may have known Elizabeth Brooke (as she was then) during her time in the bishop's house, as he declares himself 'no stranger' to her education. On the other hand, he is most explicit about her adult studies. Even after her marriage (besides 'the domestique cares pertaining to a wife'), Goad notes that she employed herself in the study of morality and history—helped by her knowledge of foreign languages—and exercised her 'taste and faculty in Poetry'. Unsurprisingly, he is particularly approving of her ability to memorise 'above 40. lines in English or Latine' on first hearing and to carry away an entire sermon, as well as the fact that her last years were 'addicted to no other studies than Diuinity' (sigs. a3^r–a4^r).

Like the preacher of an edifying funeral sermon, Goad here attempts to shape our responses to Jocelin's life: we are both to admire and emulate her godly example. His shaping of her text, by excisions and alterations, is an extension of his preacherly purpose. In my examination of his textual shaping in the next section, I want to suggest that Goad's preacherly purpose had a more worldly or political bent, following the establishment line he himself defended under both Abbot and Laud, and that he appropriates Jocelin's text to this purpose. In other words, his alterations to the writing of a recently deceased young mother belong to the same religious and political agenda as, for example, his licensing and writing of anti-Catholic and anti-Arminian tracts.

This suggests that Goad found in Jocelin's text what he considered to be inconsistent with strict religious orthodoxy. Are there details in Jocelin's own particular history which suggest any inclination towards unorthodoxy?

Goad sees in Jocelin's desire to urge her unborn child—if a son—to become a minister both her 'zealous affection to the holy Ministry' and 'the lineaments of her owne parentage'. Jocelin has inherited her own legacy from Bishop Chaderton: one which ultimately descends to the male heirs, as Goad hastens (somewhat unnecessarily) to point out, for her child is dedicated to the ministry only 'if by sex capable' (sig. a1ʳ). Concern for the state of the ministry was also one of the more typical preoccupations of the Puritan tribe which Goad despised, and Jocelin introduces the topic with characteristic Puritan rhetoric.[17] It may be significant, then, that Goad gives Jocelin's concern a pedigree which is at once safely orthodox and safely familial and domestic, deflecting readers away from the possibility of radical or political interpretations of Jocelin's 'zealous affection'. For Jocelin undertakes, among other things, to pass to a child of either sex *knowledge* of what it is to be one of the 'true laboringe ministers' (fol. 8v). Not only is a concern for the idleness of the ministry typical of those who wanted the Reformation in England to be more thorough. Jocelin's imparting of the knowledge of the true minister is itself an enactment of Christian ministry. She, and the written advice which substitutes for her after her death, becomes a channel for Christian grace and vocation. Thus, while both Jocelin and Goad (at least in the early 1620s) were committed to a Calvinist Protestantism, Jocelin's style of religious commitment is perhaps the more zealous, the more godly, and so the more potentially unorthodox—and for Goad, perhaps too much so for a *woman*.

Finally, Jocelin's other family connections may suggest Puritan possibilities. By the 1620s Elizabeth Jocelin's husband Taurell held the manor at Oakington, four miles north-west of Cambridge, which, later in the century, was infamous for nonconformism.[18] The Tanner manuscripts also include a letter, dated 22 July 1643, from 'Torrell Jocelyn' to the Speaker of the House of Commons, William Lenthall. In it, Jocelin requests reinforcements and ammunition to help defend the Isle of Ely for the Parliamentary side.[19] Supporting Parliament does not mean that Taurell Jocelin was necessarily a Puritan, either in the 1640s or the 1620s, but it is possible that the household of Elizabeth Jocelin's married life was more actively, even politically, Puritan then the household in which she spent her girlhood.

It is impossible to do more than speculate on such circumstantial evidence. The words of Jocelin's manuscript itself, however, have more interpretive potential. Not only are her concerns typical of the godly, but she chooses to express them with carefully chosen words which held special resonance for the godly. In the next section I shall argue that Goad recognized the radically reformative potential of some of those words, and by analysing his changes, try to arrive at a nuanced picture of both his and Jocelin's positions within the spectrum of English Protestantism.

2. *Goad's Gatekeeping*

The evidence of Goad's changes allows us to modify the model of the male gatekeeping of female texts, for it seems that Goad was motivated as much by his religious and political investments as by gender ideology. Goad's approbation of Jocelin rested as much on his cooling of her 'hot Protestantism' as on his representation of her life and writings as 'chaste and modest'.[20] Indeed, later in this essay I shall argue that his moderation of the political potential of her religious advice is completely bound up with his project of presenting her as a modestly domestic female author acceptable for publication.

Patrick Collinson has argued that Puritanism in pre-Revolutionary England was not simply about the reformation of church government (or indeed of civil government), but was a more broadly based movement arising out of an intensification of common Protestant concerns, such as with the priority of Scripture over tradition, the importance of preaching and catechizing, and the necessity of keeping the Sabbath. Jocelin's legacy participates in the culture of intense Protestantism, both by including its typical anxieties (about the religious education of children and the need for more 'true laboringe ministers') and by using recognizably godly language (writing of 'motherly zeale' for instance).[21]

Goad clearly found some of Jocelin's godly rhetoric too intense. In the dedicatory epistle to her husband, Jocelin discusses the way her child should be brought up, should she die. She writes: 'I pray thee bee carefull when it is young first to prouide it a religious nurse no matter for her complexion' (fol. 2r–v). Jocelin's request echoes the preoccupation of Puritan sermons and treatises on household government with servants, particularly those who care for children, as potentially corrupting because unsound in doctrine and ungodly in behaviour.[22] Goad, however, chooses to weaken Jocelin's godly exhortation by leaving out religion altogether, changing it to: 'O make choise, not so much for her complexion, as for her milde and honest disposition' (sig. B4r).

Goad also tones down Jocelin's sabbatarianism. In the body of her treatise, Jocelin writes to her unborn child at length and with passion about the necessity of keeping the Sabbath. She begins:

> Remember that thou keep holy the Sabathe day this duty so often and earnestly comanded by god himselfe so strictly obserued by the Jews (whoo that day might kindell noe fire nor vse any labor insomuch that the L: [*i.e.* Lord] whoo is the god <of> mercy himselfe comanded the man that gathered sticks on that day to be stoned): and a long time after zealously kept by the christians (fol. 34v).

cf. H.S.

Jocelin chooses to begin her exhortation with the strictest kind of sab-bath-keeping: the law of the Old Testament Jews which prescribed the death penalty for as small a violation as gathering kindling on the Sabbath. This strictness may have seemed to Goad too much like the rigidity and judaizing of which Puritans were often accused, for he cuts virtually all of Jocelin's opening passage and substitutes a much more conformist definition of 'the Lords Day' as a commemoration of the Resurrection institutionalized 'by the Church'. Goad also removes some of the indignation from Jocelin's voice as she complains about widespread laxity. '[W]ee keep noe sabboath . . .', she writes. Of those who will bridle their desires to sanctify that day, 'truly thear are so few that it is hard to instance one' (fol. 34v). Goad changes this to 'too many keepe no Sabbath' and leaves out Jocelin's reiteration of the complaint, 'truly thear are so few' (sigs. F2ᵛ–F3ʳ). Here, Goad's changes represent more than minor differences of religious sensibility. Rather, they repre-sent different understandings about the relationship of Old Testament practices to seventeenth-century Christianity as well as different politi-cal understandings about the need for religious reform—disjunctions which reproduce conflicts between conforming Protestants happy with the status quo and those more Puritan members of the English Church who want to push the Reformation further.

Goad also changes Jocelin's glosses on the meaning of two of the Commandments, and again these changes register not only differences in their theological understanding of sin but also differences in their understanding of social relations. Jocelin discusses how breaking the lead commandment of each table necessarily involves breaking all the other commandments of that table.[23] Thus, idolatry inevitably leads to bowing down to images, abusing God's name, and profaning the Sabbath. Analogously, the first commandment of the second table to honour parents, if broken, leads to murder and adultery. To demon-strate this (not obvious) point, Jocelin writes,

> and what difference shall I say thear is between a disobedient childe and an adullterer the one forsakes the wife of his bosom the other forsakes the holy spirit the sweet guide of his soule (fol. 39r).

Goad's version is completely different. The adulterer 'forsakes her by whom he giueth being vnto others' while the disobedient child 'despiseth those from whom hee had his owne being' (sigs. Fııʳ–v). Goad's version characterizes these sins as violations of relationships between clear superiors and subordinates, moreover describing the relationships in a way which seems to deny substantial being to the subordinates. Wives and children are passive vessels or recipients; only those who head households, husbands and parents, are able to *give* being actively through or to them. For Jocelin, on the other hand, adultery and disobedience to parents both represent the betrayal of relationships which are more affective than hierarchical. Jocelin's understanding of how these sins work is much more creative than Goad's, and much more radical in its implications. Her chiastic structure leads the reader to draw a parallel between 'the wife of his bosom' and 'the holy spirit the sweet guide of his soule' with suggestive implications for both marriage and the workings of the Holy Spirit. The believer's relationship with the latter takes on the erotic intimacy of marriage, while marriage becomes a spiritual relationship, in which the wife acts like the Holy Spirit as the 'sweet guide' of her husband's soul—an image which redounds on Jocelin herself, particularly on the childrearing advice she gives her husband Taurell in the epistle addressed to him.

Goad's changes suggest that he found Jocelin's understanding of the commandments unacceptable, even potentially dangerous. Knowing what religious, political, and social turmoil was yet to come in seventeenth-century England, we can see in Jocelin's words, however moderate, a familial relationship with the sectarian women threatening patriarchal hierarchies by arguing for spiritual equality and even superiority, or with female Quaker authors listening to the intimate whisperings of the Inner Light.[24] But Goad would not have needed the advantage of historical hindsight to recognize the Puritan potential for overturning hierarchies. The hierarchy of priest over believer had been subjected to zealous Protestant challenge since the authorization of an English Bible which every believer could read for him or herself.[25] That Jocelin decided to write a treatise of religious advice to her child suggests that she shared the general godly concern to expand the spiritual responsibilities of the laity; indeed, the very rationale of the treatise is the instruction of her child, son or daughter, in how to practise these responsibilities in daily life. While I do not think that Goad had any quarrel with the layman, and even the laywoman, taking part in the care of his or her own spiritual welfare, I think he was worried about the zeal of the laity encroaching on priestly privilege—particularly if it was a woman trespassing on his territory. Again, this worry is demonstrated in the modifications to Jocelin's text.

For instance, where Jocelin writes,

Marke I pray thee theas followinge rules for orderinge thy ~~thoughts~~ <life> spend the day as I instruct thee and god will blesse thee and all thy good endeuors (fol. 13r)

Goad cuts 'spend the day as I instruct thee' (sigs. C7^{r-v}). Although godly manuals written by irreproachable mainstream Puritans such as William Gouge encouraged mothers in their role of religious instructors to their children, Goad's cut seems to mark an unease about sharing the job of spiritual direction.[26] Elsewhere, to Jocelin's exhortation, 'at no time mayntaine arguments agaynst the truthe' (fol. 27r), he adds, 'especially in sacred or morall matter' (sig. E3^r). And to the advice to 'meddle not wth othe[r] mens occasions but whear maies[t] doo good' (fol. 44r), Goad continues, 'and hast a calling to it' (sig. G8^r).[27] His revisions could be made purely out of professional self-interest—as when he drops from Jocelin's description of 'true laboringe ministers' (fol. 8v–9r) the detail that they labour 'wthout ceasing'.[28] Nonetheless, the changes are signs of significant lexical and ecclesiastical differences between hotter and cooler Protestants: with the former entertaining a more vigorous notion of 'ministry' and a less restricted definition of 'calling', as we shall see below.

Where Jocelin is too zealously godly, she also threatens the chaste modesty which makes her acceptable to Goad as a female author. So, although I have been arguing in this section that Goad's changes to her text had to do with religious cooling and moderation—with making her less distinctively one of the godly in her language and concerns, and so less of a threat to the Calvinist but still conformist Church of the early 1620s and to the authority of its clergy—each of the changes also modifies her identity as a woman writer, lessening the challenge she presents to established roles for women, making her *less* of a teacher and preacher.

3. *On Education*

Thus, Goad's changes make the printed version of the legacy less godly, less religiously radical, at the same time as they make Jocelin a less outspoken, more modest female writer. Goad's approbation of Elizabeth Jocelin is therefore a complex process in which religious, political, and gender ideologies inextricably work together. The process is further complicated by Jocelin herself, for in her own writing, and particularly in her revisions, she anticipates some of Goad's moderating moves.

In her account of *The Mothers Legacie*, Elaine Beilin points out Jocelin's ambivalence about the godly imperative which impels her to enlarge the female sphere and write for the sake of her child's salvation. (She goes so far as to characterize this imperative as a 'vocation for public preaching' which bursts through female 'doubts and self-deprecation'.[29]) Beilin sees more ambivalence in the initial letter to Taurell Jocelin, where Elizabeth Jocelin is justifying herself as a writing woman, than in the text of the legacy itself, where she speaks as a teacher. There, Beilin writes, she 'retires safely behind conventional doctrine'.[30]

This assessment of Jocelin's treatise as 'conventional' is shared by other critics.[31] For their evidence, however, these critics have been relying on Goad's version which, as we have seen, tends to remove what could be construed as excessively godly or excessively outspoken. The ambivalence which Beilin has detected, and which problematizes any simple characterization of Jocelin as 'conventional' or 'radical', is toned down in the printed legacy: by Goad's emendations, but also by the simple fact that Jocelin's revisions are not reproduced in print. Her changes to her own manuscript—the traces of internal debate and multiple positions—provide the clearest evidence of all for Jocelin's ambivalence towards what is 'conventional'.

In this section I shall argue that Jocelin's manuscript sustains a higher level of ambivalence and problematizes conventions of female education and vocation more than the edited version, which has been the only version discussed by critics. Moreover, Jocelin's ambivalence centers not only on sexual identity, but also on a carefully delineated religious identity.[32] Jocelin's revisions, like Goad's emendations, are motivated by a tangle of religious and gender ideology.

Some of Jocelin's revisions can be taken to illustrate the difficulty women writers of the period had in representing their own learning and eloquence. Jocelin intensifies, for instance, a conventional expression of hope that her legacy will not be unprofitable: 'I hope it will not be ˄ <alltogether> vnprofitable'.[33] She also crosses out the word 'eloquence', with its Ciceronian connotations of effective public rhetoric, replacing it with 'skill to write' (PLATE 2):

> if I had ~~eloquence~~ <skill to write> I would write all I apprehend of the happy estate of true laboringe ministers, but I may playnly say that of all men they are the most truly happy they are familiar wᵗʰ god they labor in his vineyard [6 blank folios . . . fol. 9r] wᵗʰ out ceasing and they are so beloued of him that he giues them abundance of knowledge Oh be one of them let not the scorn of euill men hinder thee (fol. 8v–9r).

The first line is already conditional, so it seems as if even a hypothetical claim to eloquence may be too bold a line to take.[34] But Jocelin's subject is significant here: she is about to write of the state of the ministry which was, as has been discussed, a contentious contemporary issue and the target of a number of Goad's changes. Jocelin's retreat from eloquence here suggests that she was perfectly aware of the importance of her topic: the six blank pages she leaves in the midst of the passage could

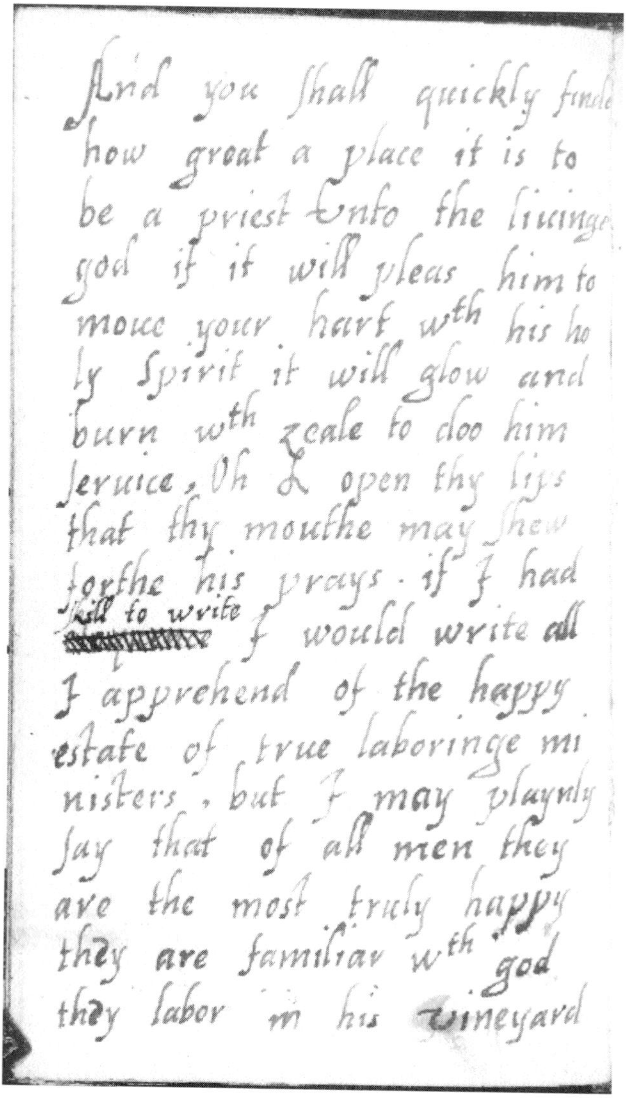

And you shall quickly finde
how great a place it is to
be a priest Unto the liuinge
god if it will pleas him to
moue your hart wth his ho
ly Spirit it will glow and
burn wth zeale to doo him
seruice, Oh & open thy lips
that thy mouthe may shew
forthe his prays. if J had
~skill to write~ f would write all
~XXXXXXXXX~ J would write all
J apprehend of the happy
estate of true laboringe mi
nisters, but J may playnly
say that of all men they
are the most truly happy
they are familiar wth god
they labor in his vineyard

PLATE 2. *Page in Elizabeth Jocelin's* The Mothers Legacie *showing revision:
London, British Library Additional* MS *27467, fol. 8v (Original size 121 × 71mm.)*

be for later considered thoughts on a subject to which she was never able to return.[35]

Yet this does not mean that Jocelin is silenced. She goes on to extol the 'happy estate of true laboringe ministers' and, significantly, does so 'playnly'. Her retreat from eloquence may in fact be a conscious gesture against the excesses of rhetoric, like that made by Puritan preachers such as Thomas Gataker, Laurence Chaderton, and William Perkins.[36] On this reading, Jocelin's emphasis on Puritan plain speech aligns her with the godly ministry and against ungodly scorners. Thus, the modesty which Goad praises in the 'Approbation'—he writes that her legacy scarcely shows 'one sparke of the elementary fire of her secular learning' (sig. a2ᵛ)—is anticipated by Jocelin herself. And it is not merely a modesty appropriate to women, but to all plain-speaking godly people, given the revaluation of divine over merely human learning.[37]

Yet the ambivalence which Jocelin's readers note in passages discussing women's education reflects Jocelin's attraction to learning beyond merely 'learninge the Bible' and her desire to reconcile such learning with female virtue:

> *education*
> If it bee a daughter . . . I desire her bringinge vp may bee learninge the
> Bible as my sisters doo. good huswifery, writing, and good work other
> learninge a woman needs not though I admire it in those whom god
> hathe blesst wᵗʰ discretion yet I desire it not much in my own hauinge
> seen that somtimes women haue greater portions of learninge then wis-
> dom wᶜʰ is of no better vse to them then A Maynsayle to fly boat wᶜʰ runs
> it ~~vnd~~ vnder water, but wheare learning and wisdom meet in a vertuous
> disposed woman she is the fittest closet for all good ₍ₐ₎ <nes> she is like a
> well ballaced ship that may bear all her sayle she is; indeed I should but
> shame my selfe if I should go about to prays her more (fol. 2v–3r).[38]

Except for small changes, Goad left this passage intact. Yet Jocelin's position on female learning is anything but straightforward here. Like a zigzagging sailboat herself, she changes tack no fewer than four times: 'though . . . yet . . . but . . . indeed'. She is conventionally worried about whether the learned woman can be virtuous, but she also participates in a more general anxiety about the possibility of reconciling religious virtue (or wisdom) with secular learning that is not necessarily gender specific. At the same time, she comes very close to associating learning in a woman with God's blessing ('I admire [learning] in those whom god hathe blesst wᵗʰ discretion'), and her modesty at the end of the passage is tantalizingly open to interpretation. It may represent Jocelin's confusion on the subject or anxiety that she does not measure up to her own character of the discreet learned woman, but it could also be read as a self-conscious, even a proud worry that the reader may think that she is writing about *herself*.[39]

Revisions in the manuscript confirm that she is of two minds on the topic of female learning, as she continues on the subject of a daughter's education:

> howsoeuer thou disposest of her educatyon I pray thee labor by all means
> to teache her ~~truly though~~ true humilitie though I as much desire it may
> bee <as> humble if it bee a son as a daughter (fol. 3v).

She revises in the process of writing, not in afterthought, changing the more open-ended exhortation to her husband to teach a daughter 'truly' to 'teache her true humilitie' (PLATE 3). Even so, 'true humilitie' could be glossed by Jocelin's own text as that discretion which would enable a daughter to balance secular learning with religious virtue. Jocelin herself refuses to resolve her ambivalent position in the epistle to Taurell Jocelin, for her final thought on a daughter's education is to leave the matter to him:

> I will leaue it to thy will If thou desirest a learned daughter I pray god
> giue her a wise and religious hart that she may vse it to his glory thy com-
> fort and her own Saluatyon (fol. 3v).

This is undeniably a gesture of wifely deference; on the other hand, it does not foreclose other possibilities. In fact, later in the legacy, Jocelin includes learning among the characteristic qualities of the virtuous woman. Whereas the worldly woman is commended only for her clothes, the truly virtuous woman is praised because she is 'wise or learned or religious' (fol. 20v). Significantly, she has gone too far here for Goad, who changes this passage to 'wise or honest, or religious' (sig. D6ᵛ).

So, the combination of wisdom, learning, and religion in a woman *was* imaginable for Jocelin. Her ambivalence, indeed, comes from her ability to imagine roles and vocations for women beyond the conventional norms she herself recognizes and which are enforced by Goad, and again it is within the terms of her more godly style of religion that she pushes the boundaries of convention. Reading within these terms allows us to arrive at a somewhat modified understanding of Jocelin's 'distinctions between the sexes', which even those critics who emphasize Jocelin's ambivalence see as clear and absolute. Beilin, for example, sees Jocelin bestowing on her son a vocation of leadership, while the daughter's way will be to

> follow the examples of virtuous and religious women like Anne,
> Elizabeth, Esther, and Susanna, all of whom are seen in the light of their

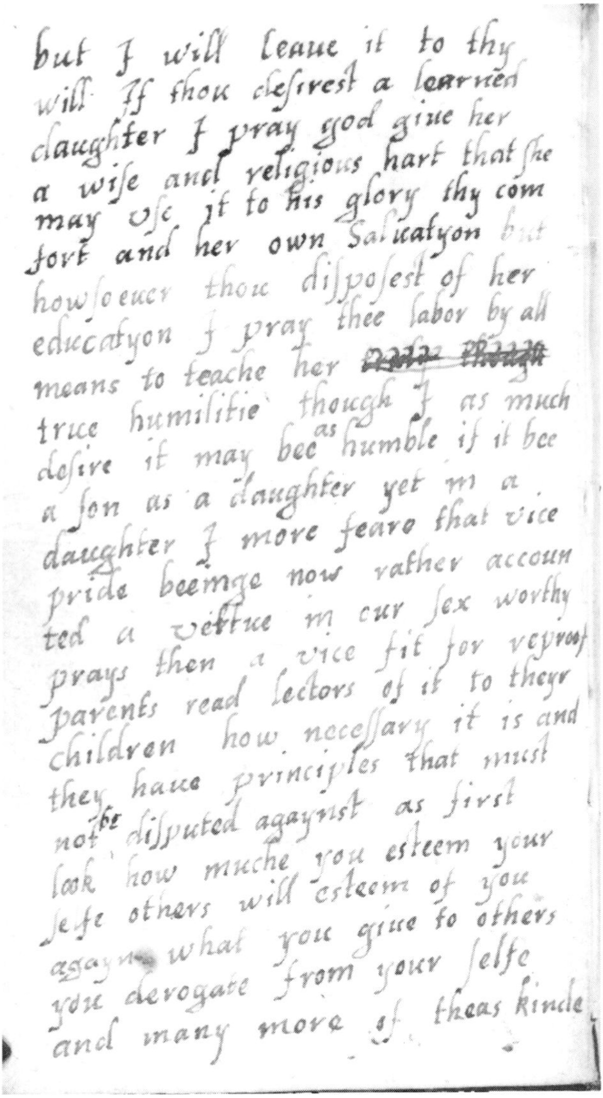

but I will leaue it to thy
will If thou desirest a learned
daughter I pray god giue her
a wise and religious hart that she
may use it to his glory thy com
fort and her own Saluatyon but
howsoeuer thou disposest of her
educatyon I pray thee labor by all
means to teache her ~~pride though~~
true humilitie though I as much
desire it may bee as humble if it bee
a son as a daughter yet in a
daughter I more feare that vice
pride beeinge now rather accoun
ted a vertue in our sex worthy
prays then a vice fit for reproof
parents read lectors of it to theyr
children how necessary it is and
they haue principles that must
not be disputed agaynst as first
look how muche you esteem your
selfe others will esteem of you
agayne what you giue to others
you derogate from your selfe
and many more of theas kinde

PLATE 3. *Page in Elizabeth Jocelin's* The Mothers Legacie *showing revision of part of the epistle to Taurell Jocelin: London, British Library Additional* MS *27467, fol. 3v (Original size 121 × 71mm.)*

feminine virtues of service and chastity. Even Esther appears primarily as 'religious', having taught her maids to fast and pray.[40]

Leaving aside the question of whether godly men might not also have been urged to 'follow' Christian examples, Jocelin's examples do leave a daughter considerable scope for emulative leadership.[41] Susanna, whose story Jocelin hopes 'the strictest will allow for a worthy example' (fol. 21r), is the heroine of an addition to the apocryphal Book of Daniel. She maintains her innocence against the false accusations of the elders of Judah (who have unsuccessfully tried to seduce her by threatening her reputation) and is vindicated by God's intervention through the prophet Daniel. In the seventeenth century, Susanna's story was sometimes used as a parable against corrupt religious or political leaders— notably by Susanna Parr in her 1659 self-vindication, *Susanna's Apology Against the Elders*, written to defend herself against the Independent minister Lewis Stuckley, who had expelled her from his congregation. Although Jocelin is not using the story in this oppositional way here, she is citing the example of a woman whose virtue was not merely a private matter, but had public, reformative effects. And even in following 'religious Ester whoo taught her mayds to fast and pray', a daughter will be doing a very similar spiritual and social job to the hoped-for ministry of the son: teaching her flock what is necessary for salvation (fol. 21r). And Esther's piety, too, had public, reformative consequences: she is praying and fasting with her maids in preparation for an audience with the king, whom she will petition on behalf of her people (Esther 4:16).

Jocelin left expanded spiritual possibilities for a daughter. Goad, I believe, recognized this and revised accordingly. Jocelin counsels her child—son or daughter—to shun the ungodly practice of swearing oaths:

> allways keep a watche before thine own lips and remember that thou needest not swear if thou doest not accustom thy selfe to ly for if thou vsest to tell truthes thy word will be as current as thy oathe I hope thy callinge if god haue made thee man will bee of authority to reproue this vice in others and not to delight in it thy selfe (fol. 31v).

Here Jocelin adds to the picture of what sort of minister she wishes her son to be: clearly one of the godly sort, for whom the commandment against taking the name of the Lord in vain had literal force. But like a son, a daughter will also have a 'callinge', which she must not dishonour by swearing. Jocelin continues:

> if thou beest a daughter thou hast a callinge to wch thou must not dishonor thou art a christian and christ comands thou shouldst not swear at

all. Mat.5.3,4 beside thou art a mayd and such ought thy modesty to be
that thou shouldst scars speak but when thou answerest thou that art
young speak if need bee and yet scarsely when thou art twise Asked
Eccle: 32 8 (fol. 31v).

If the daughter does not have the formal authority to reprove vices in
others, and if her sex together with her youth urge silence on her more
than speech, the positive emphasis on her vocation or calling in this passage—'thou hast a callinge'—nonetheless counterbalances her mother's
more restrictive advice. The word 'calling' is itself weighty, particularly
in the godly lexicon. Behind it lies the potent assertion of the priesthood
of all believers: used by some Protestants to argue not only for a more
'democratic' distribution of spiritual responsibility between clergy and
laity, but also for at least a spiritual equality between women and men,
resulting in some gains in religious authority for women.[42]
    Goad rearranges this passage to place the emphasis on the daughter's
silence rather than on the responsibilities or privileges of her Christian
calling: 'If thou beest a Daughter, remember thou art a Maid, and such
ought thy modesty to bee, that thou shouldst scarce speak, but when
thou answerest' (sig. E10ʳ). In Goad's version, it is not the daughter,
specifically, who has a calling corresponding to that of the minister-son.
Instead, after the emphasis on the daughter's silence, the passage
returns to the most general sense of calling, applicable to both sexes:
'Whatsoeuer thou be, thou hast a calling . . . thou art a Christian' (sig.
E10ʳ). Goad's subtle rearrangement here is of a piece with his other
changes protecting clerical monopolies. Here though, he is neutralizing
a possible threat to gender as well as religious hierarchies, for the
woman who sees her own calling as a close counterpart to the ordained
minister's is a threat to both. Goad's emendation is itself evidence for
the radical potential of asserting that women have spiritual callings
which allow them to act, in effect if not *in officio*, as ministers of Christ.
    Jocelin's ambivalence about taking up the positions of author,
teacher, and preacher is dramatised by the double-writing of her revisions. But far from resolving her ambivalence in 'conventional religious
teachings', we can see in Jocelin's text, and especially in her manuscript,
her exploration of the possibility of an expanded education and vocation for her daughter. And while we may argue that it is largely Goad
who resolves her ambiguities into convention, his position is more complicated than that of a general spokesman for orthodoxy. Goad backed
his own local religious and political orthodoxy: an establishment
Calvinist Protestantism which aimed to promote the sort of godly discipline which Jocelin's life and writing exemplified, but which also sought

to contain the radical potential inherent in godly Puritanism and above all to protect its own hieratic authority. Hence, Goad's interest in publishing Jocelin, and his need to change and control her.

Moreover, what constituted 'conventional religious teaching' was itself being contested in England as Jocelin was writing and Goad was editing. These historical contests—between 'hot' and 'cold' Protestants, between Calvinists and Arminians—have sometimes been obscured by another, more contemporary contest: the contest between feminism and the enduring conventions of patriarchy which have limited women's expression and self-realization. Feminist critics have tended to range 'religion' with those shackles which women must shake off before they can become true authors, ready to enter a canon of women's literary history.[43] Within this analysis, which continues as one influential paradigm for the study of early women writers, 'religion' remains an under-explored term. The religious culture in which these writers were immersed, from which and for which the majority of them wrote, was not a monolith, however, and women were not necessarily striving to crawl out from under its oppressive weight. On the contrary, religion constituted a rich and diverse cultural field, constantly changing and reconfiguring its terms, teeming with subtly differentiated dialects and styles, and full of possibilities for good and ill, emancipation and oppression. Thus, some of what has been dismissed as 'religious' in Jocelin's text, and so conforming to convention and restricting self-expression, could be re-interpreted as self-definition and finely tuned positioning within a historically specific religious culture.

4. Conclusion: Private or Public?

One would very much like to know how Theodora read her mother's written legacy. If she read the manuscript now in the British Library, she would have known the unedited version. She would also have had before her the manuscript revisions—which leave the strike-throughs perfectly legible—and so might have reconstructed some of her mother's ambivalences about women's education.

Unfortunately, there is no evidence that Theodora seized on the possibilities of her mother's legacy and became a particularly learned or even a particularly godly woman herself. We do know that she remained Taurell Jocelin's only child and was therefore, like her mother, a considerable heiress. In 1643, she married Samuel Fortrey, an entrepreneur involved with the draining of the Cambridgeshire fens, who became by 1663 'one of the Gentlemen of his Majesties most Honourable Privy Chamber' and the author of a pamphlet which argued that strict uniformity in religion was best for the generation of trade and wealth.[44] Theodora and Samuel had three sons (Samuel, William, and James) and four daughters (Mary, Trevor, Elizabeth, and Catherine). None of Jocelin's grandsons became ministers.[45]

But must we then conclude that Jocelin's legacy did not do what she intended it to do, that it was ineffectual in private and only redeemed by the fortunate accident of publication? Although the effects of Jocelin's treatise on her own family are perhaps something we can never know, we *can* rethink the labelling of her manuscript as a purely private production intended only for her unborn child. The received wisdom that women and their writing (particularly if in manuscript) were restricted to and limited by a clearly defined private sphere in the early modern period is increasingly being challenged by scholars.[46] And there are indications that Jocelin at least imagined her work reaching a wider audience—perhaps through printing, as happened, perhaps through the circulation of her manuscript beyond her immediate family. '[N]eyther the true knowledge of mine own weaknes', she writes, 'nor the fear this may com to the worlds ey and bringe scorn vppon my graue can stay my hand from expressinge how much I couet thy saluation' (fol. 11r). Even the ostensibly 'private' reason for which she undertakes the writing of the legacy—her child's 'religious trayninge', her concern for its salvation—takes Jocelin into the wider community of the godly by addressing that community's typical concerns and promoting its particular programme: Sabbath-keeping, the importance of a labouring ministry, the necessity of keeping godly servants, strict abstinence from oaths, and taking one's Christian calling seriously whether one is a man or a woman. It is precisely these excursions from purely domestic concerns that Jocelin's editor most often censors as he supervises her posthumous appearance before 'the worlds ey'.

Goad's editorial agenda can in fact be reconceptualized as the reinforcement of the private status of both Jocelin and her text. His narration of the 'birth' of the treatise in the 'Approbation' describes Jocelin engaged in conversation so private and secret as to be solipsistic, enclosed within the most private of female domestic spaces, the 'Closet':

> And about that time, vndauntedly looking death in the face, priuatly in her Closet betweene God and her, she wrote these pious Meditations; whereof her selfe strangely speaketh to her owne bowels in this manner, *It may seeme strange to thee to receiue these lines from a mother, that died when thou wert borne* (sigs. a5^{r–v}).

Goad's revelation of the secret, his opening of the scene in the closet, gives him cultural capital as the 'discoverer' of female virtue and writing, at the same time as it invests Jocelin's text itself with the authority and the sincerity of secrecy.[47]

Goad draws a clear boundary around Jocelin and her legacy, containing both within an inviolably private domestic space while, at the same time, paradoxically drawing attention to the violation of the boundary through publication. For instance, he expresses (rather unconvincing) surprise that the printer has styled Jocelin's prefatory letter to her husband an 'Epistle Dedicatory' (sig. a2ᵛ). This is, in fact, a perfectly just running title for Jocelin's epistle, but Goad's astonishment has an ulterior motive. Here again he is reinforcing the private status of Jocelin's text by implying that it is prefaced by a private letter from a wife to her husband: not a formal literary epistle and not really the sort of thing a printer normally handles.[48]

Finally, to give one last example from his emendations, Goad changes Jocelin's justification for writing—'I considered it was to my own not to the world' (fol. 2r)—to 'I considered it was to my owne, and in priuate sort' (sig. B3ʳ). The use of the word 'priuate' here delineates the nature and intention of Jocelin's writing for Goad and for the readers of his edition, but it also substitutes for another important term in the godly lexicon, 'the world'. In saying that she is *not* writing 'to the world', Jocelin is making the godly distinction between what is and what is not of the world, between the carnal and spiritual, between the unregenerate darkness and the few lights which illumine it.[49] For the godly and for Jocelin, writing out of a separation from the world has moral and spiritual authority. Goad's revision, however, makes this religiously inflected reading less possible.

Goad completes Jocelin's domestication. By returning to Jocelin's own words and revisions, it is possible to see the ways in which her domestic treatise reaches beyond the household and beyond the roles conventionally assigned to women and to the laity, as well as to see evidence that at least one of her early readers judged that she pushed these boundaries a bit too far. But it is also possible for us to use Jocelin's 'private' manuscript in a reassessment of domesticity itself. For Puritans before 1640, the household was the focus for edification: not only in the sense of religious instruction, but more importantly, in the sense of proselytizing, of 'building up' the godly. Through its participation in the project of edification, Jocelin's text, even as a family manuscript, has a social life which cannot be dismissed merely as 'private'. In the terminology of the godly, Jocelin's text was designed to be 'effectual', to effect conversion.

In a sense, Goad's appropriation is a tribute to just this quality of Jocelin's legacy: he wanted to own its effectiveness for himself and for

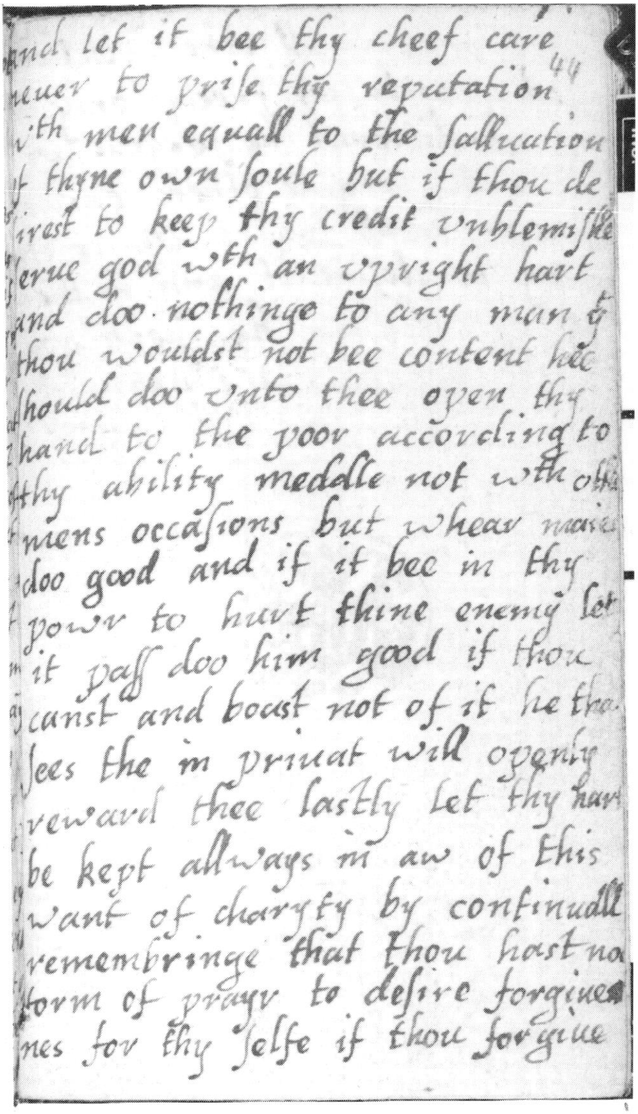

and let it bee thy cheef care
neuer to prise thy reputation 44
with men equall to the saluation
of thyne own soule but if thou de
irest to keep thy credit vnblemishe
serue god with an vpright hart
and doo nothinge to any man t
thou wouldst not bee content hee
should doo vnto thee open thy
hand to the poor according to
thy ability meddle not with othe
mens occasions but wheaur maui
doo good and if it bee in thy
powr to hurt thine enemy let
it pass doo him good if thou
canst and boast not of it he the.
sees the in priuat will openly
reward thee lastly let thy har
be kept allways in aw of this
want of charyty by continuall
remembringe that thou hast no
form of prayr to desire forgiue
nes for thy selfe if thou forgiue

PLATES 4 and 5. *Final pages of Elizabeth Jocelin's* The Mothers Legacie*:
London, British Library Additional* MS *27467, fol. 44r–v (Original size of each page 121
× 71mm.).*

not others all other petitions
god grants vs freely only th[is]
is conditionall he forgiue vs
as wee forgiue others our
sauior hathe taught vs no oth[er]
way to desire it and in the
18 of Mathew he shows god
will no otherwise grant it

12 JY 66

the religious establishment which he supported and which supported him. And Goad is not the last. An edition printed at Oxford in 1684 replaced Jocelin's recommendation of the prayers of the Puritan preacher Henry Smith with a directive to use the Book of Common Prayer, while nineteenth-century editors indignantly restored Smith and reappropriated Jocelin for Victorian godliness and sentimentality.[50]

These later editions all started with Goad's version of course. We may at last hear Jocelin speak for herself—and it is not a simple, nor an altogether humble, nor an entirely maternal voice that we hear.

APPENDIX I

Jocelin's Manuscript

Jocelin's manuscript is British Library Additional MS 27467, for which the catalogue entry reads 'THE Mother's Legacy to her unborn child, by Eliza Joscelin, wife of Taurell Joscelin. *Autograph*. See Sloane MS 4378. Paper; early XVIIth cent. Duodecimo'. (Sloane MS 4378 is a copy in several hands of the printed edition of Jocelin's legacy, including Goad's printed 'Approbation'.)

The manuscript has been rebound in royal blue velvet, probably by a nineteenth-century private collector (see below). Its pages have been trimmed (to measurements of 121 × 71mm.) and gilded. Small leather rectangles with gilt lettering were appliquéd to the spine after its acquisition by the British Library and read: 'E. JOCELINE. * THE * MOTHER's * LEGACY * TO HER * UNBORN * CHILD. * BRIT. MUS. * ADDITIONAL * 27, 467'.

Blank unnumbered folios and written numbered folios occur in the following order: 2 blanks; fols. 1–6 (dedicatory epistle to Taurell Joscelin); 3 blanks (perhaps left for another epistle to the unborn child?); fols. 7–8; 6 blanks (in midst of the passage on the ministry); fols. 9–44; 5 blanks. In addition, two extra leaves were added both at the beginning and at the end when the MS was rebound in the nineteenth century.

On the verso of the first added leaf, in the top right-hand corner, appears the stamp of 'B.M.PICKERING'. On the second blank folio, a note in ink reads: 'transferred from Dept: of Printed Books 6 Oct. 1866'. Folio 44v has been stamped '12 JY 66'.

I have been unable to trace the complete provenance of Jocelin's manuscript, but the stamps and the note above are traces of its history immediately before acquisition by the British Museum around or before July 1866. The manuscript was acquired with three other printed books, all editions of Jocelin's legacy of roughly duodecimo size, now catalogued with the British Library shelfmarks C.37.c.49/50/51 respectively, and each of which is also stamped with the date '12 JY 66'. These are enclosed in a box, with room enough to spare for a fourth book just the size of Jocelin's bound autograph. The box also has an inside pocket which contains a cutting from a sale catalogue (not as yet identified) advertising the 'four copies of this very interesting work' as Lot 47: a

copy of the third impression printed by John Haviland for Hanna
Barret in 1625, the 1684 edition printed at the Theater in Oxford, the
1853 Edinburgh edition with a biographical and historical introduction
by Dr Lee, and the autograph. The last is clearly the star of Lot 47 and
is described thus:

> JOSCELIN (ELIZA) TO MY TRULY LOVINGE AND MOST DEARLY LOVED HUSBAND
> TAURELL JOCELIN (with the Mothers Legacie to her unborne Childe)
> THE ORIGINAL MANUSCRIPT, in blue velvet, g.e.
> For a new edition this Manuscript ought to be carefully consulted, as it
> furnishes a superior punctuation and a few various readings.

This description has been annotated with a note, 'Transferred to the
MSS. Dep^t. 6 Oct. 1866. WBR', so this was clearly the sale at which the
British Library bought the manuscript. The cutting also notes the box:
'a brown morocco box, lettered like a book, by F. Bedford, in the pocket
of which are autograph notes from J. Gutch, B. M. Pickering, and
F. Bedford respecting the MS. and binding'.

The notes also are still in the pocket, each addressed to 'The Rev'd
C. H. Crawford'. Charles Henry Gregan Craufurd was a well-known
book collector. (A catalogue of February 1854 describes a sale of a selection of his 'exceedingly choice, rare, and valuable books' by Sotheby &
Wilkinson.) He was also a clergyman and had published a reprint of
Jocelin's legacy (the 1684 edition) as an addendum to a collection of his
sermons in 1840.

Evidently Craufurd remained very interested in Jocelin's work and
assembled the collection later acquired by the British Museum. The letter to Craufurd from John Matthew Gutch, another well-known book
collector, seems to be dated 22 March '57 (although the 5 appears to be
a 6, which is impossible as the note is also stamped '12 JY 66' and Gutch
died in 1861). It shows that Craufurd was then negotiating for a printed
copy which Gutch owned and which Pickering had for sale (probably
the 1625 edition if Craufurd had used his own 1684 edition for the
reprint appended to his sermons in 1840). The letter from Francis
Bedford, dated 25 April 60, concerns the repair and binding of a 'black
& grubby' printed edition: certainly the 1625, which is bound in black
morocco covered with very fine blind tooling and bears the stamp
'BOUND BY F. BEDFORD'. Its pages are still somewhat darkened. The final
letter, from the bookseller Basil Montagu Pickering, has unfortunately
been cropped and so is not dated. It concerns the autograph, which
Pickering has for sale and is offering to Craufurd:

> there can be not the slightest doubt that it is the original as there are
> words run through in this & written over & the corrected words are those

used in [the] printed edition at Edinburgh all in [her?] hand but if you
do not care for it I dare say I shall sell it directly I only mentioned it thinking you would like it the price is 10/10/. it is prettily written & is in capital order

Once Craufurd had his little collection together, he was evidently
pleased enough with it to make sure all the copies were in good order
and expensively bound, and to have Bedford make the handsome box
as well as repairing and binding the 1625 edition. One wonders why he
parted with it. He lived until 1876, so a posthumous sale is not a possible explanation.

APPENDIX II

Select Collations

Below I transcribe some of Jocelin's revisions as well as select passages
where Jocelin's and Goad's texts differ materially. The selection has
been made with a view towards supporting the issues raised in this
essay. The complete text of Jocelin's manuscript, together with textual
notes detailing Goad's revisions, can be found in Sylvia Brown (ed.),
*Women's Writing in Stuart England: The Mothers' Legacies of Dorothy Leigh,
Elizabeth Joscelin, and Elizabeth Richardson* (Stroud, 1999).

Transcriptions from Jocelin's manuscript come first, cited by folio
numbers; those from the edition of 1624 (printed by John Haviland, for
William Barret) come second, cited by signatures. Extrapolations or editorial material are enclosed in square brackets. Omissions are indicated
by three dots. Angle brackets < > indicate an insertion above the line.
Additions which have been careted in are indicated by a caret ˄.

fol. 1v] it came into my minde that deathe ~~would~~ <might> depriue me of time
    If I should neglect the present

sig. B2ᵛ] it came into my mind that death might depriue me of time if I should
    neglect the present

fol. 2r] agayn I considered it was to my own not to the world and my loue to
    my own might excuse my errors

[sigs. B3ʳ⁻ᵛ] Againe, I considered it was to my owne, and in priuate sort, and
    my loue to my owne might excuse my errours

fol. 2r–v] when ~~he or she~~ <it> shall fayle in duty to god or to the world do not
    let thy fondenes winke at such folly but seuerally correct it: and that thy troble

may be littel when it coms to years I pray thee bee carefull when it is young
first to prouide it a religious nurse no matter for her complexion

[sigs. B4^{r-v}] when it shal faile in duty to God, or to the world, let not thy indul-
gence winke at such folly, but seuerely correct it: and that thy trouble may
bee little when it comes to yeeres, take the more care when it is young. First,
in prouiding it a nurse: O make choise, not so much for her complexion, as
for her milde and honest disposition

fol. 3v] howsoeuer thou disposest of her educatyon I pray thee labor by all
means to teache her ~~truly though~~ true humilitie

[sigs. B6^{v}–B7^{r}] howsoeuer thou disposest of her education, I pray thee labour
by all meanes to teach her true humility

fol. 6r] I send it only to the eys of a most louing housband and a childe
exceedingely beloued to whom I hope it will not be $_{\land}$ <alltogether> vnprofitable

sig. B11^{r}] I send it only to the eies of a most louing Husband, and of a childe
exceedingly beloued, to whom I hope it wil not be altogether vnprofitable

fol. 8r] fortefy your selfe wth remembringe of how great worthe the ~~saluation~~
<wining> of one soule is in gods sight

sig. C2^{r}] fortifie your selfe with remembring of how great worth the winning of
one soule is in Gods sight

fol. 8v–9r] if I had ~~eloquence~~ <skill to write> I would write all I apprehend of
the happy estate of true laboringe ministers, but I may playnly say that of all
men they are the most truly happy they are familiar wth god they labor in
his vineyard [six blanks] wth out ceasing

[sigs. C2^{r-v}] If I had skill to write, I would write all I apprehend of the happy
estate of true labouring Ministers: but I may plainly say that of all men they
by their calling are the most truly happy; they are familiar with God, they
labour in his Vineyard

fol. 13r] Marke I pray thee theas followinge rules for orderinge thy ~~thoughts~~
<life> spend the day as I instruct thee and god will blesse thee and all thy
good endeuors

[sigs. C7^{r-v}] marke I pray thee these following rules for ordering thy life, and
God will blesse thee and all thy good endeuours

fol. 14v] hee would tear your body and drag your soule too hell while you
sle<e>p~~t~~e.

sig. C9^{v}] he would teare your body and drag your soule to hell while you
slept

fol. 20v–21r] you will hear a well drest woman (for that is ye stile of honor) more
comended then a wise or learned or religious woman

sig. D6^{r-v}] you will heare a well drest woman, (for that is the stile of honour) more commended, than a wise or honest, or religious woman

fol. 24r] a set form of prayr is most necessary, my reaso[n] is that your seruants beeinge vsed to it are allways ready to go alonge wth you word for word as you pray and continuance makes them to vnderstand euery word wch must needs cause greater deuotion

[sigs. D10^{v}–D11^{r}] a set forme of prayer is most necessary: my reason is, that your seruants being vsed to it, are alwaies ready to goe along with you in their hearts, word for word, as you pray, and continuance makes them to vnderstand euery word, which must needs cause greater deuotion, and giue more life to the prayers

fol. 27r] at no time mayntaine arguments agaynst the truthe for it is hard to do it wthout offendinge the god of truthe,

sig. E3^{r}] At no time maintaine arguments against the truth, especially in sacred or morall matter: for it is hard to doe it, without offending the God of truth

fol. 27v–28r] yet my fear thou shouldst know the way and ~~yet~~ go aside

sig. E4^{v}] But my feare thou shouldest know the way, and yet goe aside

fol. 28v–29r] dou[bt] not, he that depriued thee of thy hope to try thee: will (If thou bear it well) ~~reward~~ <giue> thee [corrected from 'thy'] as great or a greater blessinge then thou hopedst for

sig. E6^{r}] doubt not hee that depriued thee of thy hope to try thee, will (if thou beare it well) giue thee as great or a greater blessing then thou hopest for

fol. 31v] if thou beest a daughter thou hast a callinge to wch thou must not dishonor thou art a christian and christ comands thou shouldst not swear at all. Mat.5.3 4 [*corrected from '3'*] beside thou art a mayd and such ought thy modesty to be that thou shouldst scars speak but when thou answerest

sig. E10^{r}] If thou beest a Daughter, remember thou art a Maid, and such ought thy modesty to bee, that thou shouldst scarce speak, but when thou answerest: thou art young, speake if need be, and yet scarcely when thou art twice asked, *Eccles.* 32. 8. Whatsoeuer thou be, thou hast a calling, which thou must not dishonour: thou art a Christian, and Christ commands thou shalt not sweare at all, *Mat.* 5. 34.

fol. 34v] Remember that thou keep holy the Sabathe day this duty so often and earnestly comanded by god himselfe so strictly obserued by the Jews (whoo that day might kindell noe fire nor vse any labor insomuch that the L: [*i.e.* Lord] whoo is the god <of> mercy himselfe comanded the man that gathered sticks on that day to be stoned): and a long time after zealously kept by the christians sig. F2^v] Remember that thou keep holy the Sabbath day. This duty so often and earnestly commanded by GOD himselfe in the old Testament, so confirmed to vs in the new, by the Resurrection of our Sauiour, in memory whereof it is called the Lords day and perpetually celebrated by the Church

fol. 35v] how canst thou bee so deuoyd of grace as not to obey so iust a master so mercifull a father so gracious a teacher
sig. F4^v] how canst thou be so deuoid of grace, nay of reason, as not to obey so iust a Master? so mercifull a Father? so gracious a Teacher?

fol. 36r] thearfore for christs sake be watchefull that the diuell deceyue you not nor non of his ministers draw thee away from this days duty
[sigs. F5^{r–v}] Therefore for Christs sake be watchfull that the Deuill deceiue you not, nor none of his instruments draw thee away from this daies duty

fol. 37r] though thou hearest a minister preache as thou thinkest weakly yet giue him thine attention and spend not the time in readinge or any other meditations, and thou shalt finde that he will deliuer somethinge profitable to thy soule
[sigs. F8^{r–v}] though perhaps thou hearest a Minister preach, as thou thinkest, weakly, yet giue him thine attention, and thou shalt finde that hee will deliuer something profitable to thy soule

fol. 39r] what difference shall I say thear is between a disobedient childe and an adullterer the one forsakes the wife of his bosom the other forsakes the holy spirit the sweet guide of his soule
[sigs. F11^{r–v}] what difference, shall I say, is there betweene a disobedient childe, and an adulterer? the one forsakes her by whom he giueth being vnto others, the other despiseth those from whom hee had his owne being

fol. 39v] willt not thou bee ready to excuse thy selfe by throwinge calumnious aspertyons on thy parents
[sigs. F11^v–F12^r] Wilt not thou be ready to excuse thy vnnaturall obstinacy, by throwing calumnious aspersions on thy parents

fol. 42r] read the 13 of the first to the corinths thear St Paul shows that all vertues are of no force wthout this loue.
sig. G4^v] reade the 13. of the first to the *Corinthians*; there Saint *Paul* shewes that without charitie euen spirituall graces are of no worth

fol. 44r] meddle not wth othe[r] mens occasions but whear maies[t] doo good
sig. G8^r] meddle not with other mens occasions, but where thou maist doe good, and hast a calling to it

fol. 44r–v] thou hast no form of prayr to desire forgiuenes for thy selfe if thou forgiue not others all other petitions god grants vs freely only this is conditionall

sig. G8ᵛ] thou hast of thy Sauiour no other forme of praier to desire forgiue-
ness for thy selfe, than that wherin thou couenantest to forgiue others. All
the other petitions we present vnto God absolutely: onely this is conditionall

NOTES

1 The precise date for Jocelin's entry is 12 January 1623/4. Edward Arber, *A Transcript
of the Registers of the Company of Stationers of London; 1554–1640 A.D.* (London, 1877), IV,
p. 72 and *passim* for Goad's other licensings. W. W. Greg's *Licensers for the Press, &c.
to 1640* (Oxford Bibliographical Society, 1962), N.S. X, pp. 37–38, lists some of
Goad's most 'literary' licensings, but does not include Lady Mary Wroth's controversial *Urania*, which Goad licensed on 13 July 1621, and which Wroth later
requested be withdrawn from circulation. See also note 10 below.

2 Peter Beal has pointed out to me one feature of Add. MS 27467 which could suggest
that it was copied by someone other than the author. On fol. 7r, the latter half of the
word 'happy' has been filled in with darker ink, as if a copyist could not initially read
the word and came back to it later. The bracket after 'happy' could conceivably be
for the purpose of drawing the scribe's attention to the word. Another explanation,
however, is that the copyist retraced faint letters here: this is clearly the case at several other points in the manuscript. The bracket, moreover, can more obviously be
understood as corresponding to another, ten words earlier, enclosing the parenthet-
ical clause, '(hauinge found that the true cause; was to make thee happy)'. All other
uses of brackets in the manuscript clearly mark parenthetic clauses, phrases, or inter-
jections. I believe that there are more indications that it is an authorial manuscript
than the contrary, although a definite specimen of Elizabeth Jocelin's hand (which
I have not been able to find) would be the ideal confirmation. See also B. M.
Pickering's letter quoted in Appendix I above. Hereafter Jocelin's manuscript will be
cited in the body of the essay by folio.

3 See Appendix II above, fol. 14v and 27v–28r. It is possible that a scribe copying
Jocelin's manuscript for Goad introduced the changes found in the printed version.
Goad's introductory 'Approbation', however, is evidently the work of someone who
loved 'to steere the discourse' (Thomas Fuller's characterization of Goad) and who
was evidently interested in appropriating Jocelin. This, together with the consistent
character of the changes (protecting clerical privilege, for instance), make a better
case for Goad's intervention than for that of an hypothetical scribe.

4 See the opening, for instance, of Gary Waller's essay, 'Struggling into Discourse: The
Emergence of Renaissance Women's Writing', in *Silent But for the Word: Tudor Women
as Patrons, Translators, and Writers of Religious Works* (Kent, Ohio, 1985). Margaret Ezell,
however, in *Writing Women's Literary History* (Baltimore,1993), Chap. 2, suggests that
we not accept too completely the myth of silence for pre-1700 women writers, as
propagated by Woolf's 'Judith Shakespeare'. Jocelin's legacy went through at least
eight editions in the seventeenth century. We need not assume, moreover, that
because she initially chose to write and transmit her legacy as a manuscript that she
was therefore 'silent'. Ezell urges us not to diminish manuscript writing and reading
to the detriment of a truly inclusive women's literary history (pp. 53–54).

5 *A Biographical Dictionary of English Women Writers 1580–1720*, ed. Maureen Bell *et al.*
(London, 1990), p. 281, explains the term 'gatekeeping': 'Women's texts "helped"
into print by men reveal the marks of male control, and the existence of such control needs to be taken into account when we read them.' Jocelin's self-corrections,

on the other hand, dramatise the workings of the 'wider social conventions and pressures which made women reluctant to expose themselves as "fools in print" '.

6 Her most immediate predecessor, and perhaps her model, is Dorothy Leigh whose legacy *The Mothers Blessing* was first printed in 1616. Kristen Poole suggests a possible family connection between the two in ' "The fittest closet for all goodness": Authorial strategies of Jacobean Mothers' Manuals', *Studies in English Literature*, 1 (1995), 83–85. But see the introductions to Leigh and Jocelin in Sylvia Brown (ed.), *Women's Writing in Stuart England* (Stroud,1999), for problems with this hypothesis.

7 These details are given in Goad's 'Approbation', in Elizabeth Jocelin, *The Mothers Legacie, To her Vnborne Childe* [ed. Thomas Goad] (London, 1624), sigs. a4ᵛ–a5ᵛ [STC 14624]. Hereafter, Goad's edition will be cited in the body of the essay by signature. BL Add. MS 5849 gives Goad's account some corroboration. In 'Particular Extracts from the Register of Hokinton' [*i.e.* Oakington], the date of Elizabeth Jocelin's burial is given as 26 October 1622.

8 For instance, 'Mrs. Elizabeth Moores Evidences for Heaven Collected by her self' appended to a series of sermons by Edmund Calamy, the first of which was preached at Moore's funeral. For Calamy's description of 'the *blessed end* shee made', see *The Godly Mans Ark* (1658), pp. 230–2. On Peter Ley's funeral sermon on Jane Ratcliffe (printed 1640), which contained edited selections from Ratcliffe's voluminous commentaries on Scripture, see Peter Lake, 'Feminine Piety and Personal Potency: The "Emancipation" of Mrs Jane Ratcliffe', *The Seventeenth Century*, 2 (1987), 143–65. John Donne supplies a celebrated analogue for Jocelin's 'morbid' gesture. Isaak Walton tells the story of Donne modelling for his funerary monument tied up in a shroud, with his eyes closed, standing on an urn. Donne kept the resulting picture (from which his marble monument was carved) beside his bed, where it 'became his hourly object till his death': *The Compleat Walton* (Nonesuch Press, 1929), p. 263. As with Jocelin, the story is meant to show a religious preparedness for death.

9 *Worthies of England* (1662), 'Cambridgeshire', p. 159.

10 Nicholas Tyacke refutes the rumour that Goad went over to the Arminians at Dort in *Anti-Calvinists: The Rise of English Arminianism, c.1590–1640* (Cambridge, 1987), pp. 99–100. Both Goad and his fellow archepiscopal chaplain Daniel Featley disputed with Jesuits and were present at conferences with the Jesuit John Fisher in the early 1620s. See *The Romish Fisher Caught and Held in His Owne Net* (1624), cited in Anthony Milton, *Catholic and Reformed: The Roman and Protestant Churches in English Protestant Thought, 1600–1640* (Cambridge, 1995), p. 46. Goad and Featley also worked together in producing anti-Catholic and anti-Arminian tracts as well as licensing them— often reciprocally. Goad, for instance, 'edited' *The Fryers Chronicle*, a collection of scurrilous stories about monks and nuns, and Featley licensed it on 20 September 1622: Arber, IV, 43. Tyacke notes Goad's industry in the 1620s in both writing and licensing books against the Arminians (p. 99).

11 Abbot nominated Goad to replace Hall (who had fallen ill) at Dort. He certainly would not have done so if he had not been confident that Goad would represent his own position. Abbot's *DNB* entry details his uncompromising adherence to Calvinism and opposition to the Arminian party, even as the latter was gaining the ascendancy in the 1620s: 'He had inherited from his parents a strong affection for the reformed faith'. His fortunes definitively turned on the accession of Charles I, and he was stripped of all effectual archepiscopal power in 1627.

12 'To the Reader', *Pelagius Redivivus* (1626), sig. A3ᵛ. According to William Prynne, Goad wrote this work with Featley (Tyacke, p. 99, n. 55). They are presumably the 'two English Divines' who the prefatory epistle states first composed it in Latin

(sig. A2^r). On the use of 'Puritan' as an ill-defined and all-purpose insult, see Christopher Hill, 'The Definition of a Puritan', *Society and Puritanism in Pre-Revolutionary England* (London, 1964), pp. 1–4. In the present essay, I use the adjectives 'Puritan' or 'godly' to describe the religious culture of a body of Protestants united and identifiable by their desire for further 'reform from within the Church, as contrasted with separatists on the one hand, and those who were satisfied with the established discipline on the other'. Puritanism was characterized by a recognizable agenda: contemporaries often mentioned Sabbatarianism, hostility to popery and oaths, reproving 'the vanity of the time', or merely zeal in religion (Hill, pp. 4–6 and *passim*). These enthusiastic Protestants themselves used the terms 'Puritan' and 'godly' (preferring the latter, but also accepting the former insult with pride) to mark their difference from the worldly majority. In *The Elizabethan Puritan Movement* (Oxford, 1967), Patrick Collinson remarks that the distinction between Puritans and 'merely formal Protestants' was 'as much sociological as theological' (p. 26).

13 Oxford, Bodleian Library, MS Tanner 68, fol. 45. See Kevin Sharpe, *The Personal Rule of Charles I* (New Haven, 1992) on Matthew Wren's campaign for conformity, pp. 369 ff.

14 *DNB*. Thomas Fuller, *The Church History of Britain*, ed. J. S. Brewer (Oxford, 1845), V, 468.

15 Not to be confused with the famous Cambridge Puritan Laurence Chaderton, who inspired 1640s Presbyterians. William Chaderton, like Goad, was a defender of establishment Protestantism. Chaderton famously opposed the Presbyterian Thomas Cartwright on the question of reforming church government, delivering the Lady Margaret lectures in Cartwright's place when he was deprived of that Professorship and ejected from Cambridge University. Throughout his career, Chaderton was a strict enforcer of conformity. See his *DNB* entry.

16 Chaderton died in 1608, however, when Jocelin was twelve. Perhaps her acute consciousness of death came from her early experiences. Goad smooths over the parental separation: 'I view the deepe impression, long since, when shee was not above six yeeres old, made in her minde by the last words of her owne Mother, charging her vpon her blessing to shew all obedience and reuerence to her Father (Sir *Richard Brooke*) and to her reuerend Grandfather' (sigs. a2^{r-v}). In his *Historical Antiquities* (1673), II, 327, Sir Peter Leycester wrote that 'through some dislike after Marriage, Sir *Richard* and . . . his Wife lived asunder'. Leycester also gives the information that Elizabeth 'had all her Mothers Lands'. She was a considerable heiress.

17 For instance, she begins her long passage on the happy estate of 'true laboringe ministers': 'it is true that this age houlds it [*i.e.* the ministry] a most contemptible office fit only for poor mens children younger brothers and such as haue no other means to liue, but for gods sake be not discouraged wth theas vayn speeches but fortefy your selfe wth remembringe of how great worthe the ~~saluation~~ <wining> of one soule is in gods sight' (fol. 8r): see Appendix II above. Dorothy Leigh also encourages her sons to become ministers and writes extensively on the ministry, and with particular anger on the subject of the idle non-preaching clergy or 'dumb dogs' (see *The Mothers Blessing*, pp. 238–9). In pre-revolutionary England, preaching became, in Hill's words, 'a puritan shibboleth' (p. 17). See also Hill's chapter on 'The Preaching of the Word' (pp. 16–58) as well as 'The role and status of ministers' in John Morgan, *Godly Learning: Puritan Attitudes towards Reason, Learning, and Education, 1560–1640* (Cambridge, 1986), especially p. 85.

18 *A History of Cambridgeshire and The Isle of Ely; The Victoria History of the Counties of England* (Oxford, 1989), vol. IX. Like Chaderton (and Goad), Taurell was a Cambridge man,

matriculating as a fellow-commoner from Jesus College in 1606. He was admitted
to Lincoln's Inn in 1608. His odd Christian name comes from his paternal grandmother, Anne Torrell: *The Visitations of Essex* (1612), Harleian Society, XIII (1878),
226–30. An episcopal visitation of Oakington in 1685 notes it as being infected by
persistent dissent, 'the most Scandalous and worst in the Diocese'; quoted in John
Twigg, *The University of Cambridge and the English Revolution 1625–1688* (Cambridge,
1990), p. 261. The transcript of 'Extracts from the Register of Hokinton' in BL Add.
MS 5849 notes increasing numbers of burials from 1678 in the *'Peice of Ground* purchased by the *Schismaticks'* (fol. 93v).

19 Bodleian, MS Tanner 62, fol. 181.

20 Percival Wiburn declares that the 'hotter sort of protestants are called puritans' in *A
Checke or Reproofe of M. Howlet's Vntimely Schreeching* (1581), cited in Collinson, *The
Elizabethan Puritan Movement*, p. 27.

21 Collinson writes, for instance, the 'puritans were not a sect on their own but a presence within the Church, believing what other Protestants believed, but more
intensely': 'The Jacobean Religious Settlement: The Hampton Court Conference'
in *Before the English Civil War*, ed. Howard Tomlinson (London, 1983), p. 29. In *English
Reformations: Religion, Politics, and Society under the Tudors* (Oxford, 1993), Christopher
Haigh also characterizes the godly ministers of Elizabeth's reign as demanding a
more 'intense' kind of Protestantism from their people—requiring not only 'sermon-
going, home catechizing, and Bible-reading' but genuine conviction and authentic
spiritual experience: see Chapter 16, 'Evangelists in Action', especially p. 282. One
way of producing intensity and conviction was to intensify common Protestant discourse, creating a distinctively godly language which was capable of expressing zeal
for further reformation as well as outrage at continuing abuses.

22 On servants as potential contaminants of a godly household, see Dorothy Leigh: 'It
is not for you, by any meanes, to keep any vngodly, profane, or wicked person in
your house; for they bring a curse vpon the place wherein they are' (*The Mothers
Blessing*, p. 59). William Gouge, in *Of Domesticall Duties* (1622), writes, 'one scabbed
sheepe is enough to infect a whole flocke' (p. 649). Jocelin is thinking in particular of
a wetnurse for her motherless child. In *The Countesse of Lincolnes Nurserie* (Oxford, 1622)
Elizabeth Clinton urges her readers to breastfeed their own children, with the strong
suggestion that a child, 'perhaps one of Gods very elect', literally sucks true religion
from its mother's breast: 'food of syncere milke, even from Gods immediate providence' (sig. D1ʳ). See Dorothy McLaren, 'Marital Fertility and Lactation 1570–1720'
in *Women in English Society 1500–1800*, ed. Mary Prior (London, 1985), p. 29, for a late-
sixteenth-century example of the suckling of sick adults and of the belief that a
woman's milk was affected by her character. When Dr John Caius in his last illness
suckled a 'froward' woman, he became 'peevish and so full of frets'; but when he
sucked 'another of contrary disposition', he was 'quiet and well'.

23 See J. Sears McGee, *The Godly Man in Stuart England: Anglicans, Puritans and the Two
Tables, 1620–1670* (New Haven, 1976) on the importance of 'table-thinking' as a way
of interpreting moral law.

24 See Phyllis Mack, *Visionary Women: Ecstatic Prophecy in Seventeenth-Century England*
(Berkeley, California, 1992).

25 Rosemary O'Day in *The English Clergy: The Emergence and Consolidation of a Profession
1558–1642* (Leicester, 1979) identifies a broad trend towards laicization in the Church
in the eighty years before the English Revolution: cited in Morgan, p. 79.

26 See Gouge, p. 546, *'Of mothers peculiar care in nurturing young children.'* Goad may also
have wanted to prevent the reader thinking that God's blessing is a consequence of

spending the day as Jocelin instructs, which would virtually be the <u>Arminian heresy of believing that God's grace can be earned</u>. See note 32 below for Jocelin's similarly careful Calvinism.

27 Goad evidently means a ministerial calling here. Compare my discussion of the daughter's calling in the section 'On Education'.

28 Sig. C2ᵛ. Jocelin's autograph, however, leaves six blank pages between 'they labor in his vineyard' and the continuation of the sentence, 'wᵗʰ out ceasing'. (See Appendix II above.) So either Goad, or perhaps a scribe making a copy for the licensor from Jocelin's manuscript, may have found the six blanks distracting enough to make a slip here.

29 *Redeeming Eve: Women Writers of the English Renaissance* (Princeton, 1987), p. 267. For Beilin's discussion of Jocelin's ambivalence 'about herself as a scholar and writer', see pp. 273–4.

30 Beilin, p. 275.

31 Patricia Crawford, for instance, writes somewhat dismissively of five mothers' legacies (including Jocelin's) published chiefly before the Civil War: 'Their advice was conventional': 'Women's Published Writings 1600–1700', in *Women in English Society 1500–1800* (London, 1985), p. 222. Poole emphasizes Jocelin's passivity and orthodoxy compared with Dorothy Leigh. And Mary Ellen Lamb points to Jocelin's obsessive anxiety about learned women in 'The Cooke Sisters: Attitudes toward Learned Women in the Renaissance', in *Silent But for the Word*, pp. 114–15. She understands Jocelin to be asking 'that her child, if a daughter, be denied the opportunity she herself had experienced' (p. 114). My interpretation of Jocelin's advice to her daughter, however, <u>does not read the prohibition as this clear-cut</u>.

32 Beilin writes that Jocelin 'refers specifically to her sex as the source of her self-doubt' (p. 272). Some of Jocelin's <u>corrections, however, suggest her anxiety to keep as close as possible to orthodox Calvinism</u>. Jocelin urges a son to remember 'how great worthe the ~~saluation~~ <wining> of one soule is in gods sight' (fol. 8r). Salvation, strictly speaking, is not up to the minister but to a predestinarian God, who shows mercy on the elect notwithstanding any desert on their part. Thus, Jocelin urges her child to bear suffering and God will '~~reward~~ giue thee as great or a greater blessinge then thou hopedst for' (fol. 29ʳ). Both of these revisions show Jocelin <u>making the effort to be scrupulously Calvinis</u>t. The Goad of the early 1620s would have approved.

33 Fol. 6r. It could also be argued, however, that the addition of 'alltogether' moderates the negative force of 'vnprofitable': the modified sentence actually sounds less harsh than the original.

34 The revision appears to have been made later, after consideration, in darker ink and with a sharper pen.

35 Goad writes that she left her treatise unfinished, 'by reason either of some troubles befalling her about a moneth before her end, or of preuention by mis-reckoning the time of her going with this her first (now also last) Childe' (sig. a4r). In some editions of the legacy (for instance, the second impression of 1624 and the edition printed in 1632), the text ends with the words '*Sine fine finis*'.

36 Morgan, pp. 128, 132–7.

37 For reformed Protestant wariness of 'merely human' learning, see 'The Dangers of Learning', in Morgan, pp. 62–78. On Puritan plain style see pp. 128–30.

38 The 'sisters' are Jocelin's step-sisters, daughters of her father's second wife whom she calls her 'mother Brooke' in the same passage (fol. 3r). After the death of Elizabeth's mother, Sir Richard married Katharine, daughter of Sir Henry Nevill of Billingsbere in Berkshire, by whom he had five sons and three daughters: Mary,

Anne, and Dorothy (Leycester, p. 327). Goad's major change to this passage actually
seems to make Jocelin's female curriculum *less* conventional: he changes 'good work'
to 'good workes' (sig. B5ᵛ). In the singular, 'work' usually meant 'needlework', a conventional female occupation.

39 On Jocelin's extraordinary learning, see the introduction to her legacy in Brown
    (ed.), *Women's Writing in Stuart England*.

40 Beilin, p. 275: the 'distinctions between the sexes, already so clear in the dedication,
    are reflected in Jocelin's instructions for a son as opposed to a daughter'.

41 Susan Amussen's study of women's wills suggests that women more often assumed
    that their daughters were competent and capable of transacting business than did
    men, more often naming daughters as executors, for instance. Amussen suggests that,
    in this way, women offered a 'subtle critique of the patriarchal assumptions of the
    period by giving more authority and power to their daughters than their husbands
    did': *An Ordered Society: Gender and Class in Early Modern England* (Oxford, 1988), p. 92.

42 See 'Male and Female Power: Visionary Women and the Social Order' and
    'Talking Back: Women as Prophets during the Civil War and Interregnum,
    1640–1655' in Mack, *Visionary Women*; also Ezell's chapter on the important role of
    women in the early history of Quakerism and the accompanying proliferation of
    texts by Quaker women: 'Writings by Early Quaker Women' in *Writing Women's
    Literary History*. Crawford, in 'Women's Published Writings 1600–1700', notes that
    religious writing was the most important area of publication for seventeenth-century
    women' (p. 221 and Appendix 2, Table 7.3). Assessing social rather than literary
    gains for women through religion remains problematic, however. Collinson's essay,
    '"Not Sexual in the Ordinary Sense": Women, Men and Religious Transactions',
    in *Elizabethan Essays* (1994), pp. 119–150, discusses the paradox of women's centrality
    to early modern religion, especially Protestant religion, without the necessary con-
    sequence of emancipation. Puritanism in particular, although it did not diminish
    patriarchal authority in the long run, did provide opportunities for subtle subversion
    (p. 131).

43 This is clearly the assumption of Marilyn Williamson in *Raising their Voices: British
    Women Writers, 1650–1750* (Detroit, 1990) who accordingly sees women's 'genuine lit-
    erary output' beginning in 1640 (p. 16). She is very up-front, however, about her
    omission of women's religious writing: 'I admit that in seventeenth-century England,
    religious values are social and political, but the issues are so complex that they would
    have required another framework besides that of gender ideology, which I have
    used' (p. 10). Beilin's book *Redeeming Eve*, on the other hand, can be seen as a redemp-
    tion of early religious writers (like Jocelin) for a female literary canon. But Beilin's
    authors seem trapped by a paradox: they redeem virtue but are bound within its lim-
    itations; virtue allows them to express themselves but limits their expression. Ezell's
    central argument in *Writing Women's Literary History* is applicable here: the model by
    which early modern women writers have been assessed for success has been inap-
    propriately imported from the nineteenth and twentieth centuries. The anachronis-
    tic model declares that women become 'real' authors only when they become
    professionals writing for money and for publication in a print culture and when they
    participate in modern (and particularly modern feminist) anger and alienation. With
    this model in the ascendancy, 'pious, docile' women are naturally dismissed.

44 *Englands Interest and Improvement* (1663), pp. 6–11. Fortrey clearly had the years of civil
    war and the Interregnum in mind while writing his pamphlet. He argued that even
    small differences in religion should not be tolerated, as the zeal of religion will make
    small things seem great (p. 10). In 1651, he was himself a Commissioner appointed

by Parliament to raise punitive assessments in Cambridgeshire: BL Add ms 5805, fol. 54v. See also 'Samuel Fortrey', *DNB*, and *History of Cambridgeshire and The Isle of Ely*.

45 *The Genealogist* (1879), vol. III, 298.

46 Patricia Crawford argues against the idea of women's relegation to a private domestic sphere isolated from the public arena in 'Public Duty, Conscience, and Women in Early Modern England', in *Public Duty and Private Conscience in Seventeenth-Century England: Essays Presented to G. E. Aylmer*, ed. John Morrill, Paul Slack and Daniel Woolf (Oxford, 1993), pp. 57–76. Poole's article summarizes some recent reappraisals of a strict separation of public and private spheres (corresponding to male and female) in the early modern period (pp. 70–71).

47 Private thoughts are sincere thoughts. Cf. Leigh on private prayer: 'This is certain, that there are none godly, but those that pray priuately and truely to God according to his word . . . . the wicked can heare the word, reade, come into publike assemblies of prayer: the hypocrite will talke of faith, as if he had come presently from heauen; but to goe into a priuate place, and lay open his heart before God, confesse his own imperfections, and pray that hee may not be an hypocrite, hee is farre inough from it' (*The Mothers Blessing*, pp. 111–12). And Jocelin herself advises doing good to an enemy and not boasting of it: 'he tha[t] sees the[e] in priuat will openly reward thee' (fol. 44r).

48 But see Ezell on epistles as more than a private genre in her discussion of their use as a favoured Quaker form: *Writing Women's Literary History*, pp. 141–5.

49 The godly were the few who stood apart from the worldly majority, and various metaphors were used to signify their separation: lights in the darkness, the salt of the earth, the leaven in the lump. Jocelin addresses her child as one of the lights: 'eschue euill: for thear is not the least sin thou canst doo but the enemis of truthe <will> be glad to say 'loe this is one of them that professes god in his mouthe but see what his life is; thearfore a great care ought a christian to haue especially those whome god has set as lights in his churche' (fols. 28r–v)

50 The imprint of the 1684 publication of *The Mothers Legacy to her Vnborn Child* offers a tantalizing possibility regarding Theodora Jocelin's reading of her mother's text. It was printed at Oxford, 'at the Theater for the satisfaction of the *Person* of *Quality* herein concerned'. Who does the legacy concern if not the 'unborn child' herself, Theodora? Her own inheritance as well as her marriage would certainly have qualified her as a 'person of quality'. It would be ironic if a conformist edition sponsored by Theodora continued the work of neutralizing her mother's potentially disruptive godliness. The 'Church of England' bias of the 1684 edition was indignantly exposed and rectified by Dr Robert Lee, a Scotch Presbyterian minister and professor in his biographical and historical introduction to an edition of 1853 printed in Edinburgh (see Appendix I above). Randall Davidson, Bishop of Rochester and subsequently Archbishop of Canterbury, read Add. ms 27467 in the British Museum and thought he could see physical distress and approaching death in the handwriting towards the end. He wrote that he was moved to tears in his introduction to a reprint of the sixth edition of Jocelin's legacy, *The Mother's Legacy to her Unborn Child By Elizabeth Jocelin Anno 1622* (London, 1894), p. vi.

'Monument of an Endless affection': Folger MS V.b.198 and Lady Anne Southwell

Jean Klene

Although Washington D.C. Folger MS V.b.198 began life as an account book for military matters, it became a text which shows an intriguing domestic collaboration between Lady Anne Southwell (1573–1636) and her second husband, Captain Henry Sibthorpe (?–1650s).[1] Conventionally, we refer to commonplace books as if they were the product of a single writer, most often a gentleman compiler, although in fact many show multiple generations of ownership and use. What is notable about the Southwell-Sibthorpe volume is the way the pages of the text suggest a lively domestic and textual collaboration.

This article brings together and expands some of the preliminary assertions about the manuscript's multiple voices contained in the 'Textual Notes and Commentary' of the 1997 diplomatic edition.[2] In addition, it will explore some of the parallel features between Folger MS V.b.198 and Southwell's other manuscript, London, British Library Lansdowne MS 740 (hereafter cited as L740). These texts permit us to expand our sense of early modern literary and domestic life in several ways. First, they enlarge our impressions of 'seventeenth-century domestic life [and] our image of "the patriarch's wife"' as part of a reassessment of our understanding of the models of patriarchal authority in early modern society.[3] Looking at the framing commentary and emendations of Sibthorpe as well as Lady Southwell's verses, especially those which cry out in anger against profligate men, reveals a woman whose husband declares her to be the epitome of the 'good wife' even while her clear, strong voice challenges the notion that the early modern wife was always a passive partner—chaste, silent, and obedient. Second, when the texts of the wife and husband are read in connection with each other rather than in isolation, the mingled lines of Southwell and Sibthorpe bound together in this volume invite us to reconsider our sense of women's participation in literary culture and of patriarchal response to it.

THE MANUSCRIPT

Seventy-four leaves from different paper stocks make up the Folger manuscript (see Appendix below). It was apparently the result of Captain Sibthorpe's and Lady Southwell's attempts to gather her compositions and favoured selections into an existing volume or gathering of leaves, five of which had been used in 1587 and 1588 by John Sibthorpe for recording receipts of payments to soldiers. The separation of those leaves, fols 5v, 6r–v, 62, 63 and 64, suggests that they were already bound at the time Lady Southwell acquired them. The volume was tightly bound, making it now impossible safely to identify conjugate leaves.

Various scribes did the writing for Lady Southwell, but the most important one for this study is her second husband, Captain Henry Sibthorpe. His handwriting, based on a study of two signed pages (see PLATES 3 and 4 below), appears in a number of places,[4] some of which will be discussed hereafter.

Like the commonplace books compiled by many at the time, the volume contains a wide variety of entries: apothegms, poems, letters, inventories, selections from bestiaries, scriptural commentary, an excerpt from Augustine's *City of God*, a booklist and household and financial records. The framing leaves begin with the date, 'December 2 1626', when the volume became a place to record 'The works of the Lady Ann Southwell' (see PLATE 1). She included her own compositions and a few by others—some favourites and some for her own use in composing, like the formulaic, 'Like to a lamp wherein the light is dead' (fol. 9v), which served as a pattern for embellishing her own elegies. One for Lady Ridgeway and another for Frances Howard, the Countess of Somerset (fols 21 & 23), show how she incorporated some of the similes. On fol. 5, in her own angular hand (see PLATE 2 for a characteristic example of her ungainly hand on another page), she begins to write the list of Aristotle's *predicabiles* and *praedicamenta* (the 'common places' heading sections of most continental commonplace books, according to Ann Moss[5]). Excerpts from Gesner's translations of Topsell's works, *The History of Four-Footed Beasts* (London, 1607) and *The History of Serpents* (London, 1608), begin with Southwell's explanation: 'I, having surveyed the book, have for my own memory set down some particulars that I best affect' (fol. 68). Her choice of apothegms not only includes conventionally wise ones by 'Bishop [John] King' (1559?–1621) and the martyrologist John Foxe (1516–87), but also some witty ones, like 'A Glutton digs his own grave with his own teeth'.

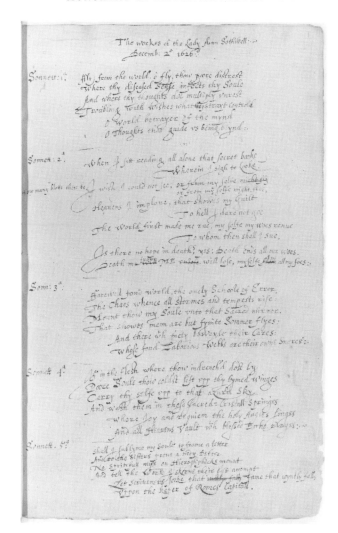

PLATE 1. *The first page of* The workes of the Lady Ann Sothwell *in the hand of an amanuensis: Washington, D.C., Folger Shakespeare Library* MS *V.b.198, fol. 1r. (Original size 335 × 213mm.) Reproduced by permission of the Folger Shakespeare Library.*

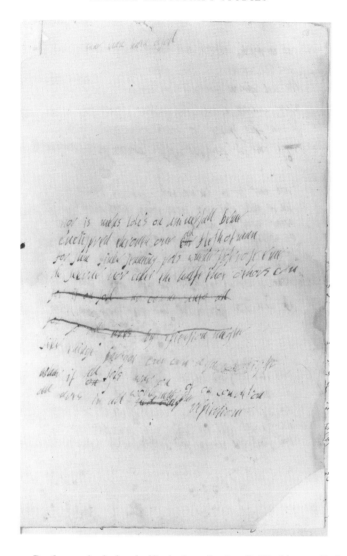

PLATE 2. *Draft poem in the hand of Lady Anne Southwell: Washington, D.C., Folger Shakespeare Library MS V.b.198, fol. 58r. (Original page size 320 × 209mm. at the top and 203mm. at the bottom.) Reproduced by permission of the Folger Shakespeare Library.*

BIOGRAPHY AND POETRY

Different works in the volume show various aspects of Lady Southwell's life. First, Sibthorpe provides and signs historical data and also shows his admiration and love for his deceased wife on the last two signed leaves. Other pages suggest concerns that one or both may have had for others, like the demoted deputy Falkland (fol. 4), the deceased Lady Ridgeway (fol. 21) and Robert Johnson (fol. 72), the widowed Elizabeth (Stuart) of Bohemia (fol. 22), and the curate Roger Cocks (fol. 21). Entries like the booklist (fols 64v–66) show the reading interests of the two, and inventories for moving household items from 'Clerkenwell to Acton' in 1631 (fols 59, 60v, and 61) supply more biographical details. Entries probably added after Southwell's death suggest that the widower continued to treasure the volume and tried to make the 'monument' more complete—at least for himself and perhaps a few friends. Given the deletions, ink blots, and indecipherable writing of some leaves, it is unlikely that the volume would have been intended for presentation to anyone.

Because her main concerns seem to have been focused on an intelligent search for God, Southwell would probably have been pleased with Sibthorpe's statement that she was a 'Nurse of religion [and] learning's better part', but not surprised. At the end of the Lansdowne poems, he had already said, 'her chiefest study is / to know God . . . , herself, and that which good is' (L740, fol. 167v). Although almost every line of the drafts which she wrote in her own hand wrestles with questions of God, herself and the good (fols 44v–46r & 57r–58v), her compositions radically differ from pious meditations in the vivid way that she often dramatizes the search. Some lines are indeed prosaic, but in her best ones, she seems sufficiently at home with theology and the Scriptures as to domesticate 'Paul in the stocks' and the cowardly 'Belial's brats . . . crawl[ing] under the bed' in a thunder storm (L740, Precept 4, stanza 42). As fascinating as medieval devils, the antics of weak human beings fill her meditations. The one against stealing, for example, reads as if it were titled, 'Stealing, the Leveler', in that the sin, like Death, levels kings and clowns. Southwell often noted that questions of justice affect all.

From the last leaves we also learn that Lady Southwell was the 'Eldest daughter of Sir Thomas Harris of Cornworthy in the County of Devon, Knight and Sergeant at Law.' She was 'married first to Sir Thomas Southwell of Spixworth in the County of Norfolk, Knight', and the two were sent as planters to Ireland, at Castle Poulnelong seven miles up the

Bandon River from Kinsale.[6] Although living in a lonely spot away from her native land, she had many interests, judging from the topics in her compositions and the people to and about whom she wrote. In October 1623, for example, she wrote to Sir Richard Boyle, Earl of Cork, to ask for the land rights of Sir Richard Edgecombe, a 'constant friend' of her deceased father. She was adamant in her request but face-tious in discussing it: 'But if you will neither do me good in this respect, nor tell me why, I must be forc'd to put up a petition against you to the Countess, who by this time, I hope, is strong enough to put you ten thousand pound in debt by the birth of another son or daughter.' Since the Countess had already delivered twelve children, this was no idle threat.[7] Her ability to banter with a powerful politician was remarkable, especially for a woman in 1623.

The lady had been born Anne Harris, the first child of Elizabeth (Pomeroy) and Thomas Harris, a Member of Parliament and friend of a neighbouring landowner, Sir Walter Ralegh. Given their friendship and the habits of those involved in manuscript culture, it is no surprise that a poem usually ascribed to Ralegh, 'The Lie', was included in the commonplace book.[8] The cynical mood of the poem often arises in her own poems, especially when she discusses the 'peacocks' at court.

Anne's first marriage, which took place on 24 June 1594, had been to Thomas Southwell, son of Richard Southwell and nephew of the poet and Jesuit martyr Robert Southwell.[9] The groom was evidently the man of her father's choice, judging from what she says in the poem against 'Adultery': maidens are bound unto their father's will and there-fore they should pray for his 'care and skill / to choose for them a wise and honest mate' (fol. 51v, lines 260–1). As an M.P., her father may have met some of the Southwells in London or while working on parliamen-tary committees in 1586–87 for Norfolk elections.[10] The groom belonged to a prominent family with both courtly and literary connec-tions. Various Southwells had been politically active (and in and out of favour) since the early sixteenth century. Thomas's mother, Alice (Cornwallis), may have introduced her daughter-in-law to the writer William Cornwallis, friend of John Donne.

Although Lady Southwell may have enjoyed the circle into which the first marriage gave her limited entry, nothing in the manuscript identi-fies a happy memory from their thirty-two years together. Some of the poems must have been written during the time of the first marriage, as, for example, the one to Bishop Adams (fol. 18) in neighbouring Limerick. He died in March 1625/6,[11] and her first husband in June of 1626. Furthermore, when a speaker talks about the King—with his 'books, his works, [and] his piety'—'that governs Britain now' (fol. 42v, lines 333 & 327), this also seems to date the composition before or during 1625, when James I, well known for his books and especially his *Demonology*,[12] died. The lines were taken out of the poem when it was expanded. Although the works may have been originally intended to honour James, 'the king's Majesty' at which they were finally aimed was probably Charles I.

After her first husband's death, Lady Southwell was 'married to Henry Sibthorpe, Sergeant Major and Privy Councilor of the Province of Munster in the kingdom of Ireland, with whom she lived ten years' (fol. 74). Judging from Sibthorpe's assertion on the last leaf that the two had lived happily together for ten years until her death in 1636, the volume might have been a gift to his wife—or at any rate acquired—around the time of their marriage. While the funeral baked meats from Sir Thomas's burial in June 1626[13] may not have furnished forth the second marriage tables, Henry and Anne probably did marry by the date on the first leaf: 2 December 1626 (see PLATE I above), since he writes that they had been married ten years. Henry may have been the son of John Sibthorpe, who had been at the battle of Ostend[14] and recorded payments to militia men in 1587–88.

Some of the strong opinions expressed in Southwell's compositions, especially those about the conduct of unfaithful men, may have festered over many years. Poems like 'Anger', 'Nature, Mistress of affection', 'Thou shalt not commit Adultery', 'Come forth foul Monster [Envy]' and 'Anger, what art thou' express a deep bitterness. The violent dialogues on envy and anger, for example, answer a question with a bludgeoning short answer, like 'A flame of hell', 'The Heart of fools', 'Damnation', 'Madness itself', or 'Hell and despair' (fol. 9). In another poem, 'Nature, Mistress of affection', she is quite clear about his abuse: 'thy hate, like hell fire, doth burn, / and at all my best acts spurn'. Moreover, her resentment against husbands who deny wives their 'due' appears in both 'Nature' and 'Adultery', defying the docile and overly modest stereotype of the early modern wife. In the satiric 'Blessed Life', her complaints are even revised to be gender-specific. After ranting about men who live 'by Senses sports', she concludes:

> Voluptuous men are neither good nor Wise,
> Nor never shall a blessed life comprise.

(fol. 8v)

The noun 'minds' was changed to 'men' by a carefully drawn *e* written boldly over the original *y* (of 'mynds') and the deletion of the *ds*.

In the meditation against 'Adultery' she concludes a passage in the words of St Paul, 'Then think whatever seeming face we [women] carry, / 'tis better die a virgin than to marry' (fol. 48, lines 41–42). Her advice cleverly applies at least the beginning of Paul's recommendation to both sexes that 'it is better to marry than to burn' (1 Cor. 7:9).[15] Because she deleted the bellicose 'we hold your sex our soul and body's foe', and in her own hand wrote the more politically astute Pauline line about what was 'better', she was shrewdly triumphing. Many would have hesitated to challenge what, at least at first, sounded like Paul's recommendation.

In her meditation against adultery, she could hardly have been more vehement in her condemnations of profligate men than in saying:

> But let us draw this twofold monster's face,
> this double-damning vile Hermaphrodite,
> whose fellowship doth fly from state of grace,
> and when their cankred sores, are brought to light,
> the surgeon Christ the med'cine must apply,
> whose balsom live; forsake and die.
>
> (fol. 47v, lines 13–18)

Nevertheless, she concludes both 'Nature' and 'Adultery' with lines of resignation to the domestic martyrdom such men 'of nought' condemn their wives to[16] and finally accepts the indifference against which she had railed. She can also scold women about their 'follies' (fol. 51). After all, both 'turned fools in Paradise', but her lines much more often complain about wayward men.

In contrast to her invective against men, her husband offers praise of her as the good wife. Sibthorpe effusively inscribes her wifely virtues on folios 73 and 74 (PLATES 3 and 4). He defers to the local curate by putting Roger Cocks's encomia first. The clergyman declares himself 'a true lover / and admirer of her virtues' (fol. 73). Perhaps the captain also felt that the curate's praise gave his own more validity. Cocks's lines speak allegorically of the lady's superiority. They begin calmly, punning on her name and dramatizing her allegorical role, as a 'Well' nourishing 'the lower plains' until Death and Time '(like envious Philistines)' try to 'stop the current' but are defeated by 'Victorious fame.' Fame then 'strikes a flame / Out of her Ashes', which, like a phoenix, burns 'so bright / That it may give the world perpetual light'. Sibthorpe includes none of Cocks's hyperbolic but not very personal lines in the final inscription.

After the near-apocalyptic applications by Cocks, Sibthorpe praises his wife in double columns, in a cramped handwriting that seems to be done in haste—by contrast to the more careful calligraphy of the final leaf. His tribute to Lady Southwell's accomplishment as a good wife is centered prominently:

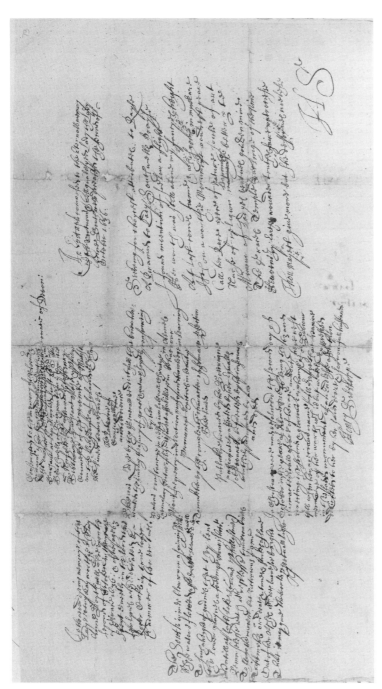

PLATE 3. *Encomia on Lady Anne Southwell by Roger Cocks and Henry Sibthorpe in the hand of Henry Sibthorpe: Washington, D.C., Folger Shakespeare Library MS V.b.198, fol. 74r. (Original page size 354 × 210mm. with an insert of 200 × 368mm.) Reproduced by permission of the Folger Shakespeare Library.*

> The Pattern of
> conjugal love
> and obedience.

On folio 74 (PLATE 4), the three lines are set out as a single line, but attention is called to the line by the white space above and below. The hyperbole on both leaves about Southwell's excellence as a wife, however, makes one wonder whether this aspect of her life had been questioned and whether Sibthorpe was perhaps protesting too much. The speaker of her poem, 'O how happy were I, dearest, / if thou were as thou appearest', chastizes a husband, but admits to unspecified 'faults' of her own, punning on herself as a Queen and a 'queane' (or impudent woman).[17] She says that her faults are his 'Addition' (fol. 9v). We can only wonder what they were.

The modest Sibthorpe begins by citing the authority 'of all that knew her' and then lists aspects which would have flattered any housewife. She was

> reputed the living treasury of grace and nature Jointly conspiring,
> by her
> Zealous constancy in religion, liberal charity in Alms,
> Exemplary Virtue in life, discreet affability in behaviour,
> Pious frequency in devotion, profound knowledge in learning, [and]
> Permanent Exactness in beauty,
> To make her up the complete character of female perfection.

Peculiar to Lady Southwell may be the phrase 'profound knowledge in learning' and the way that Sibthorpe centers some lines for emphasis. Nevertheless, the long lines were divided in half and arranged to form the more succinct and visual pillar of praise on folio 74.

On both of the last two leaves, the captain registers pride in his wife by writing that she was 'Publicly honoured by her sovereign'. *How* she was honoured, the records have yet to reveal, unless Sibthorpe was referring to the 'Queen's letters', which her first husband had insisted were the instigation for her trip to Berwick to welcome Queen Anne. Thomas was writing to Cecil in 1603 to clear his name and that of his wife.[18] If she was at court at any time, no record of it has yet emerged.

Testimony to some of the respect Lady Southwell enjoyed in 1636—from others as well as from her husband—has endured. First, she was buried in the chancel of the parish church, an honour in itself. Over the years, her poetic accomplishments have been mentioned by a few historians, like George Ballard in 1775 and Alexander B. Grosart in 1886. Although the burial plaque is gone, a larger one containing the 'wife's

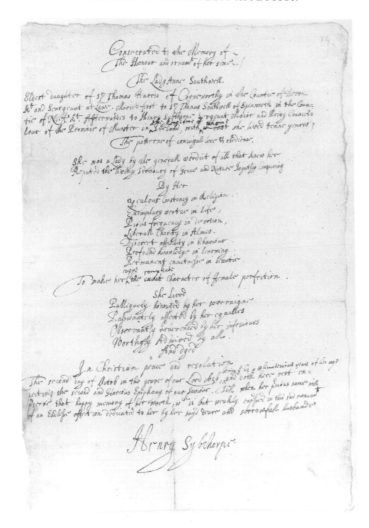

PLATE 4. *Memorial tribute to Lady Anne Southwell in the hand of Henry Sibthorpe: Washington, D.C., Folger Shakespeare Library* MS V.b.198, *fol. 74r. (Original page size 335 × 210mm. with an insert of 270 × 188mm.) Reproduced by permission of the Folger Shakespeare Library.*

inscription' from folio 74 still hangs on the back wall of Saint Mary's in Acton.[19]

The church stands not far from the couple's home. Receipts on folios 71 and 72v tell the story of their renting 'tenaments' from the court lutenist Robert Johnson and his wife Ann. Lady Southwell and Captain Sibthorpe may have enjoyed a social life in Acton which included evenings of literature and music, judging from the interactions the manuscript shows among Lady Southwell, her landlord Robert Johnson, and the curate Roger Cocks. Victoria Burke has wisely speculated that Cocks is the 'noble neighbor' addressed on folio 26.[20] The quality of Lady Southwell's 'apparel' (listed on fol. 61) suggests some wealth and the possibility of social gatherings. Her dresses were made of satin, velvet and taffeta; even petticoats were often 'trimmed with gold', embroidered and lined with taffeta. In her scarlet cloak and hood, 'laced with silver', no one would have mistaken her for a Puritan.

With Robert Johnson as a central figure, the Acton group probably sang the 'sonnets' which appear on the first folio. They also appear— with a few variations—in several early modern songbooks.[21] She probably played the 'virginals' or spinet, which had been part of her household goods, moved on 25 June 1631 from Clerkenwell to Acton (fol. 61, line 21). Her knowledge of music theory is illustrated in places like her 'Letter to Doctor Adams' (fol. 18, line 17) and stanzas 11 and 12 of Precept 3 (L740). Her friendship with Johnson is also suggested when, in a short eulogy on him (fol. 72), she expresses an intimate knowledge of the last moments before his death. Her friendship with Roger Cocks, the 'Minister at Acton' and author, is suggested by the praises mentioned above that he sings for her, as well as by the poem she wrote celebrating the publication of his 'book of the birth of Christ' (fol. 21). She also included in her eulogy for Johnson the main points of Cocks's homily at the musician's funeral (fol. 72). His explication of lines from Matthew 11: 16–7 appears on folio 66v.

Sibthorpe's encomia on Lady Southwell conclude with a prose statement that she died the 'second day of October in the year of our Lord 1636, being the 63rd and Climaterical year of her age'. Expressions of love and admiration similar to those discussed above are also found in the poem at the end of the two meditations composed by his wife and inserted into the Lansdowne manuscript. In this text, his use of the present tense throughout the poem expresses an active love and admiration for his wife during her lifetime, just as the eulogy after her death shows his sense of bereavement. He insists that many an admirable quality 'lives in her behavior' and encourages other women to follow her example, mainly for their own peace of mind (L740, fol. 167v).

The Lansdowne manuscript expands meditations from the Folger document on commandments three ('Thou shalt not take the name of the Lord thy God in vain') and four ('Remember the Sabboth day to keep it holy'). Rhymed couplets above the two precepts dedicate the meditations 'to the king's most excellent Majesty', whichever king that may have been. The main scribe seems to be Samuel Rowson, who also wrote much of the Folger volume, but many emendations and marginalia seem to be in Sibthorpe's easily legible hand. Lady Southwell's hand never appears here.

COLLABORATION ON THE MANUSCRIPT

While we cannot be sure how much Sibthorpe added after his wife's death, about his collaboration there can be no doubt. The most playful example of their interaction appears on fol. 49, which shows her simultaneously obeying and defying his instructions. When he complains in the margin about her using the rhyme 'wife / life too oft', she seems to accept his criticism by changing, in her easily recognizable hand, a sufficient amount of lines 71 and 72 so as to replace the objectionable nouns with 'duty' and 'beauty'. The implication in the strong masculine rhyme that a 'wife' could be one's 'life' is replaced with the less threatening feminine rhyme, 'duty / beauty'. Deconstructing the apparent obeisance of the altered lines, however, Southwell uses the new rhyme even more often than the deleted ones. No second objection appears. Did he not notice, or did he approve of the new rhyme? Apparently, she knew how to keep peace, too.

Folio 4 also involves both husband and wife. Lady Southwell composed a letter to console the demoted deputy, Sir Henry Cary, Viscount Falkland (fol. 4). Because of his own 'goodness', she insists that he must be at peace and begs him to ignore the fickleness of Fortune. His demotion was 'rather a loss to the nation than to' Falkland. Sibthorpe's hand adds a note under the letter, explaining that the above is a 'copy of a letter written by the Lady Anne Southwell, to the Lord deputy Falkland of Ireland'. When Sibthorpe says 'written', he means 'composed', for Southwell's handwriting (witness PLATE 2 above) must have been enigmatic even to her contemporaries. Although she can write legibly, as she does on fol. 40, lines 165–70, she usually formed many letters with the same basic downstroke, with only slight variations, omitted silent letters, and spelled phonetically. She had probably composed the letter as a return for the kindness the Viscount had shown Sibthorpe in petitioning Charles I in a letter of 4 October 1627. Falkland had testified that Sibthorpe 'had a company in the Cadiz expedition, and kept it for nearly two years in Ireland, till it was delivered to Sir Ralph Bingley for the expedition to France'. Reporting that other people had been promoted over Sibthorpe's head, Falkland had asked that the captain 'be allowed the command of one of the substitute companies sent over' to Ireland.[22]

The letter may have been inserted by both husband and wife, or Sibthorpe alone may have pasted it onto the leaf after his wife's death and added the note. Perhaps he wanted to underscore her prestige through the importance of the addressee and the voice of authority with which she spoke to him. Her belief in returning a favour done for her husband Captain Henry seems clear also. So too is her difference from the 'silent' and reserved model female. As in the letter to the Earl of Cork mentioned above, she spoke up when good reasons warranted it.

A third place involving both husband and wife, albeit in a different way, is on the leaves containing a list of his and her books (fols 64v–66r). Because the heading, 'A List of my Books', refers to only one person, it was probably written by the Captain after his wife's death. Some of the volumes had no doubt been part of the three 'Trunks of books' (fol. 60v, lines 9 and 14) listed in the 'Inventory of the Lady Anne Southwell's goods sent from her dwelling at Clerkenwell to her house at Acton' (fol. 59).

At first, the 'my' of the heading seems to refer to the Lady, because most of the titles seem like those she would have owned. They cover topics she cared passionately about, such as poetry (by Donne, Spenser and Ariosto) and theology ('Calvin's Institutions' and his 'Sermons upon Job', Hooker's 'Ecclesiastical Polity' and 'Lectures' by 'Doctor [John] King', the 'Bishop Kinge' whose apothegm she had included on fol. 69r. He was also father of the Henry King (1592–1669), two of whose poems she had had copied into the volume on fols 21v and 24r). Her frequent mockery of Roman Catholicism suggests that she would have been very interested in what probably was Henry's book: 'Sir Christopher Sibthorpe's book against Popery' (item 22). All of the theology books could have been Sibthorpe's, or items shared by both; but he never echoes, quotes or refers to them, as she often does. Given her father's smooth incorporation of Scripture in making his parliamentary arguments,[23] her reading of theology had probably been encouraged at an early age.

Other books owned by Captain Henry were probably those like 'Machiavelli's Art of war' (item 24), 'The Art of Riding' (item 32), and 'Blundevil's Horsemanship' (item 33). Books with publication dates after 1636, like 'The Martyrdom of King Charles' (item 92), were also evidently the captain's.[24] A few changes in the hand, the ink and the width of the pen, as at item 77 until the end, suggest that the widower wrote the booklist in different styles at different times over a long period. The flamboyance of the writing, with sweeping strokes in many capitals and often in descenders, may even suggest how proud he was of the books.

Another place in the volume where Sibthorpe's hand seems to appear is in the short poem, 'All married men' (fol. 16). As he begins to write, he seems to be hesitating by putting carefully placed periods between each word. These are not the scattered dots of a pen which frequently appear in a manuscript. Nor are they the extension of a letter, for after the word 'married', the *d* ends in an ascender above the bowl of the letter; and after 'desire', another period is under the raised loop of the secretary *e*, not to the right of the concluding stroke. Why the periods are included is unclear, but the writer could conceivably have been unsure about including a poem beginning with criticism of husbands.[25] Line 2 is not what a woman was expected to write about 'married men':

> All.married.men.desire.to.have good wives,
> but.few.give good example.by their lives.

When domestic comedy emerges in lines three and four, no more periods appear between the words: 'They are our head; they would have us their heels. / This makes the good wife kick; the good man reels'. Turning next to Genesis, the speaker begins the well-known creation story:

> When God brought Eve to Adam for a bride,
> the text says she was taen* from out man's side,   *taken

At first, the speaker seems about to invoke the familiar superiority topos, arguing Eve's superior creation because she was taken from Adam's flesh, over his creation from muddy clay.[26] Instead, a different idea, familiar to the imaginations of theologians and artists since the Middle Ages, follows:

> A symbol of that side, whose sacred blood
> flowed for his spouse, the Church's saving good.
>
> (lines 7–8)

Illustrations like those in *The Rohan Book of Hours*[27] depict the analogy of Christ giving birth to his spouse (a small woman as the Church), just as Adam gives birth to Eve. In conclusion, the speaker despairs over a man's understanding of such love, and the poem ends in wry wit:

> This is a mystery, perhaps too deep
> for blockish Adam that was fallen asleep.
>
> (lines 9–10)

Although problems about the poem dissolve in good humour, the motif of Christ's love for his spouse (lines 7–8) projects the basis of Southwell's subversive theory about marriage.

In other compositions, she explicitly recommends the Pauline analogy: 'Husbands, love your wives, even as Christ also loved the church, and gave himself for it' (Ephesians 5:25). As she says in 'Adultery', if husbands do not follow Christ's example in loving their spouses, then wives need not obey them:

> Then see this copy of a loving head,
> and if His fair example thou neglect,
> we cannot think our bonds are forfeited,
> though we your yoke and fellowship reject.
>
> (fol. 50, lines 155–8)

She reaches her conclusion, 'Who lives in spirit is dead unto the law; / the flesh and spirit never Jointly draw' (lines 159–60) in an echo of Paul's exhortation to the Galations about the supremacy of the spirit (chapters 4–5). In Romans 5:18, he has the same message: 'If you be led by the spirit, you are not under the law'. While Southwell's role models, the cunning Jael and Judith (L740, Precept 4, stanza 24), use a nail and a sword to conquer the enemy, she wields an intellectual weapon in her search of theological literature for answers to major problems.

Another way that Sibthorpe collaborates on the Folger volume is in adding the headings above some poems. Often in an inadequate space, explanatory titles have been inserted above and to the right. It is possible that a few were added immediately after the poem itself was written, yet unlikely that many were. More space would have been left, had scribes begun to realize the necessity for it. For some titles, there are indications that the date must have been a later one. Folio 21, for example, clearly in Sibthorpe's hand, shows a title running to the right and below, with letters that, after a large and clear 'An Epitaph', are smaller, crowded into an inadequate space until the right edge of the paper: 'upon Cassandra MacWilliams, wife to Sir Thomas Ridgeway, Earl of Londonderry, by the Lady A. S.'. Having written two other compositions to Lady Ridgeway and the moving elegy below, 'Now let my pen be choked with gall', Lady Southwell would not have given Cecily's name as 'Cassandra'. Hence it seems doubtful that she was present when the heading was completed. On folio 21v, Sibthorpe may have been remembering the circumstances surrounding the poem's being copied into the book: 'An Elegy Written by Mr. Barnard, brother to Mistress Jernegan, / that died at / Acton'. He may not have known that 'Mr. Barnard' had copied a poem composed by Henry King: 'The Exequy', or perhaps he considered that the use of the composition was more important than the author and title. Two headings are similarly inscribed above the psalm being sent to the Earl of Castlehaven, one on the left (with a vertical line separating it from the verse) and the other on the top, extending to the right (resulting in an indecipherable last name on the cropped page: 'Written by the lady A[nne] B——————') and finishing in the line below (fol. 7).[28] With the explanatory headings, Sibthorpe has considerably improved the volume by giving a more complete picture of Lady Southwell and her society.

To say that the captain continued to work on the volume as a memorial does not mean that he intended it for publication or for any kind of presentation copy. Many leaves were hardly presentable. Her indecipherable drafts, for example, could puzzle a reader in any era. Other leaves, like those containing the long meditations, have words that have been deleted but not replaced, stanza numbers that have been changed many times but are still out of order, blank lines in a stanza which was never finished, alternative readings of some phrases, ink blots and a few indecipherable scratches. At one point, she aptly refers to her poetry as 'these blotted lines' (fol. 19v).

Some of the deletions in both manuscripts are puzzling in that either husband or wife may have made them. Where no correction or evidence of her hand appears, it may be that, after her death, Sibthorpe decided for political reasons to delete certain lines. In the poem exploring her 'Grandam's cause', for example, someone deleted lines describing the Edenic hermaphrodite:

God called them Adam both, and did unite
Gen. 5:2   both male and female one hermaphrodite,
And being one there's none must dare to sever
without a curse, what God hath joined together.

(fol. 26v, lines 25–28)

The scriptural source shows Southwell's awareness of the contradictory stories in Genesis. Her hand does not appear anywhere on the yellowed leaf, tipped into the volume, but her feminist ideas do. Here she cautions against the 'wilfull heresy / In thinking females have so little wit / as but to serve men they are only fit'. A fearful Sibthorpe may have been concerned about the negative associations of the word 'hermaphrodite' and hence deleted the lines, or Southwell herself may have reconsidered them. By contrast, the phrase, 'double damning vile Hermaphrodite' on folio 47v remains untouched in its setting of the 'twofold monster's face'. Perhaps the condemnation provided an acceptable context.

The Lansdowne meditations also have a few puzzling deletions, apparently for political reasons, like the revised stanza referring to Jael and Judith as those whom God enabled as He will also 'enable' Lady Southwell and anyone else who calls on Him. Such enabling threatens important men. A deletion in the Lansdowne manuscript, six stanzas about a sect, the 'family called love', was restored by a *stet* and a sentence (suggesting that the meditations were to be recopied): 'These verses & those that follow, though crossed out, are fit to stand' (fol. 165). She had written that this sect was more scandalous even 'than the popish bulls or Roman sword' (fol. 165r–v). Did Sibthorpe feel that Charles I would agree?

CONCLUSION

Other manuscripts have shown writers eulogizing their spouses, but few the working relationship between a husband and wife in the way that Folger MS V.b.198 does. In the mutual endeavour of Lady Anne Southwell and Captain Henry Sibthorpe, the volume became an uncommon commonplace book. Within the patriarchy of their society, the two worked together in the 'sympathy' modeled by Christ and his Church (L740, Precept 4, stanza 9). Their interaction does not deny the system Southwell herself acknowledges, but rather expands our notion of that society.

Many questions remain about the manuscript and the marriages of Lady Southwell, but a few things are evident in the volume. An intelligent, well read, creative and witty writer, Lady Southwell used St Paul to prescribe a husband's conduct towards his wife. By her logic, wives could be free from marriage bonds with uncaring spouses. Her second husband, Captain Henry Sibthorpe, explicitly encouraged her work, even though he sometimes seemed fearful of the strong statements she had made. He served as a scribe for her, a mentor of her poetic skills, and a co-compiler, after her death as well as before. Early modern society may have felt that the woman should be chaste, silent and obedient to her husband, but Lady Anne Southwell shows us a respected woman who could be highly outspoken and independent, a negotiator with an advisor (as she shows in changing an objectionable rhyme) and a demanding petitioner to the powerful (like Sir Richard Boyle, the Earl of Cork, and Sir Henry Cary, the Viscount Falkland).

Although she presumably enjoyed her relationship with her second husband, she was keenly aware of the patriarchal system of the larger society. 'Dare you but write,' she says, 'you are Minerva's bird, the owl at which these bats and crows must wonder'. She knows that others will 'criticize upon the smallest word— / this wanteth number, case, that tense and gender'. But criticism never stops her, even when her native land lays 'an envious stepdame's hand' on her. Why, she does not say. Instead, she practices the guile of her politically astute role models, Abigail, Rahab, Jael and Judith, in proposing practical solutions when critics persist: 'then must you frame a pitiful epistle / to pray him be a rose was born a thistle' (L740, Precept 4, stanza 74). She knows what success sometimes requires. Ideas about early modern women need to be expanded to include her, one not only strong enough to cope with patriarchy but also witty enough to disarm the irritation men might feel about her feminist ideas. The incongruity of juxtaposing legal, ecclesiastical and every-day language could prompt amusement if not acceptance. Some readers might even recognize the 'willful heresy' of 'thinking females have so little wit / as but to serve men they are only fit'.

APPENDIX

The Folger folio volume measures 355 by 235 mm. in its nineteenth-century cover, a deep red Russia leather[29] with letters in gilt on the spine, saying, 'Lady Southwell's Works 1626'. The marbled end-papers and two flyleaves at either end were probably added at the same time when the exposed edges of the leaves were gilt. The watermarks in the volume are predominantly those of Nicholas Le Be, similar to Briquet 8080, predating 1600. Only the last two leaves, containing what Sibthorpe labels the 'wifes inscription' (fol. 74v), have watermarks dating from the early seventeenth-century,[30] suggesting that these were the last two folios added to the volume. The leaves within the volume usually measure 335 by 210mm.

The Lansdowne volume is a quarto of 173 leaves, which Hilton Kelliher discovered was once among the collections of the Yorkshire antiquary Ralph Thoresby (1658–1725). The leaves measure approximately 204 by 155mm.[31] and have been tipped onto guards in the volume. They usually have the popular pot watermark with the initials 'BR' on the front, similar to Briquet 12704. Other works appearing in the seven different sections (with pages of slightly differing lengths) include poems by John Donne (fols 57–137v) and 'The Wife' by Sir

Thomas Overbury (fols 75–79v). Prose works by Donne and Anne Southwell also appeared in the popular Overbury book, *A wife now The Widdow of Sir Thomas Overburye* (London, 1614; STC 18904).[32]

NOTES

1 According to what her second husband, Captain Henry Sibthorpe, says on fol. 74 (PLATE 4).

   Tracing the provenance of the manuscript begins with the purchase by Sir Thomas Phillipps (1792–1872) from Thomas Thorpe (catalogue for 1836, n. 1032). Bertram Dobell purchased it as Phillipps MS 8581 at a sale at Sotheby's, London, 15 June 1908, lot 699. In 1927 Henry Clay Folger, founder of the Folger Shakespeare Library, purchased it from P. J. and A. E. Dobell, shortly after the publication of their Catalogue of Poetical Manuscripts, which described it as 'a volume of Papers in various hands, containing a number of Poems by Lady Ann Southwell and a few by other writers'.

2 Recently edited by Jean Klene as *The Southwell-Sibthorpe Commonplace Book: Folger MS V.b.198* (Tempe, Arizona, 1997), and henceforth cited as Klene. Although Klene is a diplomatic edition, reproducing the idiosyncracies of the manuscript as carefully as possible, in the present article the spelling has been modernized and contractions silently expanded; capitalization is retained—with occasional capitals added when necessary—and punctuation has been added.

3 Ezell, *The Patriarch's Wife: Literary Evidence and the History of the Family* (Chapel Hill & London, 1987), p. 2. See also Ezell, 'Elizabeth Delaval's Spiritual Heroine: Thoughts on Redefining Manuscript Texts by Early Women Writers', *English Manuscript Studies 1100–1700*, 3 (1992), 216–37.

4 I am indebted to Laetitia Yeandle, Curator of Manuscripts at the Folger Shakespeare Library, for help in identifying the scribes and in rechecking the measurements of the folios reproduced here.

5 *Printed Commonplace Books and the Structuring of Renaissance Thought* (Oxford, 1996), p. 144 *et passim*.

6 John Lodge, *The Peerage of Ireland* (London, 1754), p. 228, note e.

7 The Lismore Papers at Chatsworth, England, vol. 14, fol. 160. She sent a similar petition to Sir Thomas Browne (not the famous writer). For the Earl of Cork's family, see Nicholas Canny, *The Upstart Earl: A Study of the Social and Mental World of Richard Boyle First Earl of Cork 1566–1643* (Cambridge, 1982), p. 88.

8 Agnes Latham says that lines 31–34, 37–40, and 43–46 are 'peculiar to Lady Anne Southwell' (*The Poems of Sir Walter Ralegh* [London, 1929], p. 158), but some of the variations (31–34 and 37–40) also appear in copies of the poem reproduced in *The First and Second Dalhousie Manuscripts, Poems and Prose by John Donne and Others A Facsimile Edition*, ed. Ernest W. Sullivan, II (Columbia, 1988), pp. 110 and 181. Michael Rudick's forthcoming edition of Ralegh's works may tell us more about 'The Lie'.

9 I am indebted to M. J. Swarbrick, chief archivist, City of Westminster, for a photocopy of the church records. For the pedigree, I am indebted to the late Gordon Southwell, who shared with me his copy of Francis Steer, *Woodrising Church, Norfolk: Notes on the Southwell and other families connected with the parish* (The Diocese of Norwich, 1959).

10 *The History of Parliament: The House of Commons, 1558–1603*, ed. P. W. Hasler, 3 vols

(London), 1981, II, 260–3. Excerpts from his speeches indicate a source from which Lady Southwell may have inherited her concern for feminine rights.

11 See Thompson Cooper, *A New Biographical Dictionary* (London, 1873).

12 For the long list of works by James I and the lack of works written by Charles I, see *A Short Title Catalogue*, 2nd edition, (London, 1976–91). Southwell mentions the *Demonology* in Precept 3, stanza 82.

13 London, British Library Additional MS 4820, fol. 98v. Raising another unsolved problem, the certificate lists only one daughter, not the two listed in later accounts.

14 *Burke's Genealogical and Heraldic History of the Landed Gentry*, 17th edition, ed. L. G. Pine, 3 vols (London, 1952), III, 2310; and *HMC De Lisle and Dudley*, III (1936), xxxiv–xxxv.

15 This quotation and those following are taken from *The Holy Bible and International Bible Encyclopedia and Concordance: Authorized or King James Version* (New York, 1940).

16 Suggested by Mary Ellen Lamb.

17 See the *Oxford English Dictionary*, 2nd edition (London & New York, 1998).

18 *HMC Salisbury*, xv (1930), 388.

19 Although no plaque marks the spot today, the chancel burial was cited by John Bowack, *The Antiquities of Middlesex; Being a Collection of the several church Monuments in that County* (London, 1705), pp. 51–52; see also Ballard, *Memoirs of British Ladies* (London, 1775); and Grosart, *The Lismore Papers* (London, 1886), II, 346.

20 Burke, 'Women and Early Seventeenth-Century Manuscript Culture: Four Miscellanies', *The Seventeenth Century*, 12, No. 2 (Autumn 1997), 143–4. T. Harper Smith, the present local historian of Acton, has also discussed the neighbourhood and its social gatherings in a paper by himself and A. Harper Smith, *Dr. Featley of Acton, Chelsea & Lambeth* (1990), pp. 9–10.

21 Robert Jones, *Vltimum Vale* (1605, XIV); Jones, *A Musicall Dreame* (1609, XV and XVII), and others in Klene, pp. 187–8; see also the explanation by Mary Hobbs that, 'as in a few other manuscripts of the 1620s and 1630s, the title "Sonnet" for a lyric poem often denotes, not the traditional stanza-form, but that it has been set to music', in 'Early Seventeenth-Century Verse Miscellanies and Their Value for Textual Editors', *English Manuscript Studies 1100–1700*, 1 (1989), 194.

22 *Calendar of State Papers Ireland 1625–32*, ed. Robert Pentland Mahaffey (London, 1900), p. 273.

23 Hasler, p. 261.

24 For examples of later publications, see Jean Cavanaugh, 'The Library of Lady Southwell and Captain Sibthorpe', *Studies in Bibliography*, 20 (1967), 243–54. Although the discussion needs to be updated with the more recent *Short-Title Catalogue*, it is still useful.

25 This was suggested by the way a colleague unconsciously puts periods between words as she begins in longhand to write a cautious student recommendation.

26 For more on the topos of female superiority and its derivation, see Linda Woodbridge, *Women and the English Renaissance: Literature and the Nature of Mankind 1540–1620* (Urbana, Illinois, 1984), pp. 38–44.

27 *The Rohan Book of Hours*, Bibliothèque Nationale, Paris (MS 9471), intro. by M. Meiss, commentary by M. Thomas, trans. by K. W. Carson (New York, 1973), Plate 13. I am indebted to Dolores Freeze for this reference.

28 For the Castlehavens, see Klene, pp. 190–1.

29 *Census of the Medieval and Renaissance Manuscripts in the United States and Canada*, by Seymour De Ricci with the assistance of W. J. Wilson (New York, 1935), I, 419, item 1669.1.

30 C. M. Briquet, *Les Filigranes* (1907), ed. Allan Stevenson (Amsterdam, 1968); and
    Edward Heawood, *Watermarks, Mainly of the 17th and 18th Centuries* (Hilversum, 1950).
31 Peter Beal, *Index of English Literary Manuscripts*, Vol. I, Part 1 (London & New York,
    1980), pp. 250–1; and Kelliher, who found that it can be identified as item 133 among
    'Manuscripts in Quarto' in the list at the end of Thoresby's *Ducatus Leodensis*, 2nd edi-
    tion (Leeds, 1816), Appendix, p. 85. I am grateful to Brett Dolman for aid in seeing
    the watermarks.
32 Lady Anne Southwell's 'Answere to the Court Newes', in response to Sir Thomas
    Overbury's 'Newes from Court', and her 'Answere to the very Countrey Newes', in
    response to John Donne's 'Newes from the very Countrey', first appeared in the 1614
    edition. Although the initials A.S. under the 'Answere to the Court Newes' were
    removed in subsequent editions, the verbal parallels between lines in the 'Answere'
    and in Southwell's other works leave no doubt about her authorship, as argued in
    Klene, pp. xxviii–xxxi. A facsimile edition by James E. Savage includes her
    'Answere to the Court Newes', pp. 225–7; her 'Answer to the very Countrey Newes',
    pp. 233–4; and the 'Certaine Edicts', which may possibly be by her, pp. 218–22.
    Savage also gives a useful explanation of the eccentric genre in *The 'Conceited Newes'*
    of Sir Thomas Overbury and His Friends: A Facsimile Reproduction of the Ninth Impression of
    1616 of 'Sir Thomas Ouerbury His Wife' (Gainesville, Florida, 1968), pp. lvi–lxii.

The Scribal Hands and Dating of
Lady Falkland: Her Life

Heather Wolfe

INTRODUCTION

The manuscript of *Lady Falkland: Her Life* recounts the life and conversion of Elizabeth, Lady Falkland (1586–1639) and the conversions of six of her eleven children.[1] It is known to exist in only one copy, which has been edited four times in the last one hundred fifty years.[2] Its discovery in the 1850s was the result of the Catholic convert Richard Simpson's (1820–76) search for documents representing the history of English Catholic 'refugees', a search undertaken because Simpson believed that English Protestant historians had misrepresented the religious heritage of the sixteenth and seventeenth centuries.[3] The manuscript's 'rediscovery' in the 1990s is a result of the interest in recovering the writings of early modern women.[4]

The authorship of this manuscript has been widely and inconclusively argued, while the question of when it was written has been all but ignored (see discussion below). The existing editions of *Lady Falkland: Her Life* do not represent the manuscript's revisions, additions, and deletions in a consistent manner, nor do the editors fully explain and consistently represent their interventions in terms of layout, punctuation, spelling, and paragraphing.[5] Through careful attention to the various hands in the manuscript, it is possible to determine the identities of the main scribe and two of its emenders, and when it was written and corrected.

THE MANUSCRIPT OF *LADY FALKLAND: HER LIFE*

The manuscript of *Lady Falkland: Her Life* (1645) is preserved in the Archives Départementales du Nord, in Lille, France, where it is catalogued as MS 20H9.[6] It is a quarto volume in a contemporary pasteboard binding, measuring 180 by 140mm. A green silk ribbon is sewn into the headband. On the first of two flyleaves 'The Lady Faulkland her Life' is written in a different hand from that of the text. The manuscript has been considerably trimmed on its three outer edges, so that some of the marginal additions have been made illegible. There are wormholes in the upper right and lower left corners which go through the entire manuscript, including the binding.

The manuscript has twelve gatherings of four leaves each, with one leaf tipped-in to quire three, between folios 11 and 12, in addition to two front flyleaves and two endleaves. The watermark on folios 1–48 consists of a bunch of grapes, with a countermark consisting of a pair of letters resembling 'BB'.[7] The horizontal chain lines and watermark-locations in folios 1–48 indicate that each gathering consists of two half-sheets, folded and quired. Catchwords are located at the end of every gathering. At the ends of gatherings 6, 7, 8, 9, 10, and 11, the catchwords are located on separate lines from the text. In two cases, the catchwords are slightly different from the first words on the following leaf, and in another case, the catchword is not repeated on the next leaf.[8]

The tipped-in leaf between folio 11 and folio 12 is smaller in size than the other leaves, but has the same watermark.[9] It is blank on its verso side. The hand of the tipped-in leaf is the same hand as the main scribe of the manuscript, but is smaller and denser.

The first front flyleaf has no watermark; the second front flyleaf has a watermark of a wreath with three circles in the center, in triangular formation, on horizontal chain lines. The watermark of the first endleaf consists of the pair of letters 'AM', and the second endleaf is a wreath. Both endleaves have vertical chain lines.

Provenance

The manuscript of *Lady Falkland: Her Life* was part of the library of Our Lady of Consolation, Cambrai, until 18 October 1793, when the French Republic seized the monastery on Rue des Anglaises during its revolutionary purge of foreigners. Dame Ann Teresa Partington's narrative of this calamity, written in 1796, after the community had settled in England, reveals that the nuns were informed that they 'should be totally out of their house in half a quarter of an hour and that they should take neither Trunk nor Box with them'. They were 'only allowed each one of them a small bundle'.[10]

Lady Falkland: Her Life did not make it into anyone's bundle. Along with the manuscripts of twelve other monasteries in Cambrai, it became national property, and was deposited, 'pêle-mêle', in 'les salles hautes du couvent hospitalier de Sainte-Agnès', under the care of M. Mallet, Notaire.[11] The books and manuscripts arrived there in a disorganized and dissheveled state and remained in disarray for some years, even after the government decided in 1794 to establish public libraries in each district in France, formed from the books of the suppressed religious establishments. The Musée de Cambrai was officially established in 1796.[12] 'Citoyen Pierre Joseph Houillon', the museum's first director, had been empowered to form the basis of the museum's collection from among the 'livres, tableaux et autres objets interessants' confiscated from Cambrai's monasteries and private non-citizens.[13] He would have had plenty of items from which to choose. Our Lady of Consolation's confiscated belongings included a library of 'about 1000 volumes', one hundred 'very valuable' volumes in the Confessor's apartment, and 'a small collection of useful Books' in the Abbess' apartment.[14] The catalogue of this collection, made by French officials in the early years of the republic, lists only a handful of seventeenth-century manuscripts.[15] One of the manuscripts listed is 'The writings of the most religious dame D. Magdalena [Lucy] Carie de St Cruce professed religious of the most holy order of St Benedict. In quarto (car. mod.)'.[16]

When the collection of printed books and manuscripts housed in the Cambrai Museum/Library was catalogued by André Le Glay in 1831, he discovered that some of the 'ouvrages importants' listed among the catalogues of the religious communities made at the time of the Revolution were missing, including seventeen volumes of the works of Father Augustine Baker.[17] Le Glay hypothesized (incorrectly) that the nuns of Our Lady of Consolation may have taken these manuscripts with them when they were forced to leave France—manuscripts including 'The writings of the most religious dame D. Magdalena Carie' and others 'que sont relatés à la fin du catalogue'.[18] In 1835, Le Glay, as director of Archives Départementales du Nord, a jurisdiction which included Cambrai, reminded the mayor of Cambrai that the papers of religious houses should officially be housed in the departmental archives at Lille, since they were national property. However, he would provisionally allow the manuscripts to stay in Cambrai, if the library's infrastructure were improved and if the catalogue of manuscripts conformed to the standards of the central archives at Lille.[19] The manuscripts at the Cambrai library continued to be neglected, however, and in November, 1884, many of them (most likely including *Lady Falkland: Her Life*) were transferred to Lille, where they were catalogued collectively as part of séries H in the Archives départementales du Nord.[20]

Based on a mistranslation of the first few pages of *Lady Falkland: Her Life* (which begins with an account of Lady Falkland's father, Sir

Lawrence Tanfield), Le Glay incorrectly described it in 1852 as the life
of Laurence Tanfield, 'wife' of Henry, Viscount Falkland, and 'mother'
of the celebrated Lucius, second Viscount Falkland. He stated that the
manuscript contained curious details about many politicians and
authors of the age, and that 'Lady Falkland se fit catholique, malgré tout
sa famille'.[21] In 1928, the French archivist Max Bruchet more accurately identified Lille MS 20H9 as 'Vie de Lady Faulkland', but incorrectly described the Lady Falkland in question as her daughter Lucy,
'Lucie-Madeleine Cary, fille de lord Faulkeland, vice-roi d'Irlande, née
en 1585', based on the presence of a fragment of Lucy's death notice
inserted inside the manuscript.[22] It was only in Richard Simpson's 1857
edition that the manuscript was first identified as the life of Elizabeth,
Lady Falkland.

Scribal Activity

According to the death notice of Lady Falkland's second-youngest
daughter, Lucy (Dame Magdalena), 'the relation' of Lady Falkland's life
was 'written by one who knew her well'.[23] Such ambiguity, like the fact
that the manuscript of *Lady Falkland: Her Life* is unsigned, was not
unusual in conventual writing. The seventh chapter of the Benedictine
Rule, 'Of Humility', states that a monk (or nun) should imitate Christ,
who 'came not to doe my owne will, but the will of him who sent me',[24]
a rule which would certainly include imputing to God whatever fruits
came from a nun's studies and writing. 'Of Humility' also specifies that
a monk was 'not only to have humility in his hart, but also to shew it in
his exteriour to all that behold him'.[25] Because her will was directed
toward God alone, it would have been lacking in humility, and indeed,
willful, for the author of *Lady Falkland: Her Life* to take individual credit
for her work, or for any other nun directly to attribute credit to her.
Such self-effacement characterises other manuscript life-writings at
Cambrai, whose authors are similarly anonymous: Dame Gertrude
More's death notice (d. 1633) referred anonymously to 'her life writ
more at large', and Dame Margaret Gascoigne's death-notice (d. 1637)
mentioned '*the* story of her life writ in another place'.[26] Authorial
anonymity is exemplified, too, in a catalogue of manuscripts belonging
to Cambrai's daughter house in Paris, which lists books not by the
author's name, but rather according to key words: collections compiled
by individual nuns are catalogued under *C*, Devotions under *D*,
Examples under *E*, Institutions under *I*, Lives under *L*, and so on.[27] It
was in keeping with monastic tradition, then, that the daughter who
wrote *Lady Falkland: Her Life* does not sign her work, and that she refers

to herself and her sisters collectively. The question of *Lady Falkland: Her Life*'s authorship was largely irrelevant to the nuns at Our Lady of Consolation, Cambrai because of their ideals of monastic humility and corporate identity. However, for twentieth century readers of the biography, the question of authorship *does* arise, since the author's reasons for writing a life of her mother provide insight into its purposes.

Lady Falkland's four Catholic daughters were nuns at the English Benedictine monastery of Our Lady of Consolation, Cambrai. This enclosed, contemplative community was founded in 1623 by Dame Gertrude More, the great-great granddaughter of Sir Thomas More. Lucy and Mary (Dame Magdalena and Dame Maria), Lady Falkland's two youngest daughters, were admitted to Cambrai on the same day as two other nuns, Barbara Constable and Justina Gascoigne, 31 August 1638.[28] Elizabeth and Anne (Dame Elizabetha and Dame Clementia), the older daughters, were admitted shortly thereafter, on 27 October 1638 and 8 March 1639, respectively. These six women, and a laysister who died a year later, would have been educated together in their first year, and were all professed in 1640. Known writings by this 'class of 1640' indicate that as a group, they were more prolific than any other group of nuns educated and professed together at Cambrai. Their work is notable for its quantity and range: original prose works, poems, sermons, letters, translations, and transcriptions.[29] Writing and transcribing for edifying purposes, or as a way to assemble useful texts for contemplation, was common practice among the Cambrai nuns, and was encouraged by their confessors. The nuns conceived of devotional reading (*lectio divina*) and writing, including the reading and writing of lives, as an early stage in the course towards mystical union with God.

All Cary scholars agree that the author of *Lady Falkland: Her Life* was one of Lady Falkland's four Catholic daughters.[30] Anne, the eldest surviving daughter, is the most popular choice, but the evidence for her authorship is altogether inadequate. Professor Donald Foster makes the most elaborate case, asserting that 'it is clear from a collation of the internal and external evidence that the biography cannot have been written by anyone but Anne Cary'.[31] He adds that besides *Lady Falkland: Her Life*, Anne 'preserved many, perhaps all, of her mother's writings', and cites a manuscript at Colwich Abbey which 'appears almost certainly to be the English translation of Blosius that Elizabeth Cary was working on during her last months'.[32] While it is correct to say that Anne was *one* of the transcribers of this Blosius manuscript, it might also be noted that she inscribed the *ex libris* of Our Lady of Good Hope, Paris, on the inside cover of the manuscript, and it is also clear that there were at least *three* other scribes at work on the manuscript. Furthermore, the manuscript is not 'almost certainly' Lady Falkland's translation: it is a transcription of a selection of Blosius's works, translated by Father Augustine Baker.[33]

At least four different hands contribute to the manuscript of *Lady Falkland: Her Life*. The ink used by the main scribe and all but one of the emending hands is now brown; the ink used by the unidentified emender is dark, almost black. The main scribe wrote the entire main text (including the tipped-in leaf between folios 11 and 12) and added marginal annotations written perpendicular to the text on folios 12, 15v, 16v, 21, and 29v. The nib has been changed or sharpened by the main scribe on a number of occasions, or there has been a gap between writing sessions (most apparently on folios 17v and 34) indicated by a slight shift in slant, scale, and ink. The other three hands appear in interlinear insertions and emendations, and marginal additions.

The main scribe writes in an unpractised hand, forming *z* and *k* with considerable awkwardness. The hand uses the *u/v* graph in an unconventional manner—for instance, writing *qv*- instead of *qu*-. It regularly transposes certain letter combinations (as in *wicth, forsowrne, frist*), and occasionally drops the terminal *e* (*prid, guid, sid, sincer*). Words are sometimes hyphenated in the middle of lines, suggesting that the scribe could be copying from an earlier version of the manuscript with different line endings. This hand appears in another manuscript formerly belonging to Our Lady of Consolation, a transcription of Father Augustine Baker's treatise, *Alphabet* (PLATE 1).[34]

Through a process of elimination based on hand analysis, it seems probable that the scribe of *Lady Falkland: Her Life* was Lucy. Anne's hand, explicitly identified in two manuscripts now at Colwich Abbey, is considerably different from the hand of the main scribe (PLATES 2 and 3).[35] Mary is not the main scribe either, although she does supply marginal annotations to the manuscript. Mary's hand can be determined from a marginal annotation which identifies three of the sisters as 'Mother Clementia, Dame Magdalena, and Sister Maria' (Anne, Lucy, and Mary) (PLATE 4). The Cambrai constitution states that the choir nuns are to refer to themselves in speech or writing as 'Sisters', to each other as 'Dames', and to the prioress and sub-prioress as 'Mother'.[36] This annotation, then, was written by 'Sister Maria'; that is, by Mary. Another marginal addition (not transcribed in Weller and Ferguson's 1994 edition of *Lady Falkland: Her Life*) corroborates this identification of Mary's hand, in that it names three sisters as Mother Clementia, Dame Augustina, and Dame Magdalena.[37] If one of the three named siblings had written this addition, she would have identified herself as 'Sister'.

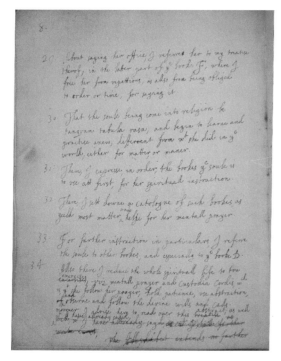

PLATE 1. *A page in a manuscript copy of Father Augustine Baker's* A Spiritual Alphabet: *Stratton-on-the-Fosse, Downside Abbey, Baker MS 29, p. 8 (Original page size 200 × 155mm.) Reproduced by permission of Downside Abbey.*

Again, Mary has written this marginal addition, and from these two examples, twenty-nine further marginal additions by Mary can be identified. Other extant Cambrai manuscripts in a hand which closely resembles Mary's include a fragment from a biography of Father Augustine Baker,[38] poetic paraphrases of the Psalms,[39] notes on the Benedictine Rule,[40] excerpts from the minor prophets (PLATE 5),[41] and the first half of a transcription of a treatise titled *The Mirror of Patience and Resignation*, dated July 1672—after the deaths of Lucy, in 1650, and Anne, in 1671.[42]

A third sibling can be tentatively ruled out as the main scribe. An autograph letter written by Elizabeth (Dame Elizabetha), Lady Falkland's second oldest daughter, at Cambrai in 1659, has many letter formations similar to those of the main scribe (PLATE 6).[43] However, Elizabeth's hand is smoother, more relaxed and more efficient than the

PLATE 2. *A page in the* XLth Book of Collec[tions]: *Colwich, Staffordshire, St Mary's Abbey, MS H23, p. 44 (Original page size 150 x 100mm.) Reproduced by permission of St Mary's Abbey, Colwich.*

unpractised hand of the manuscript, and some of her letter forms are entirely different.[44] It is not impossible that the differences between *Lady Falkland: Her Life* and Elizabeth's autograph letter reflect a natural maturation of style, since the biography was written approximately fourteen years earlier than Elizabeth's 1659 letter. This is the case with another Cambrai nun, Dame Barbara Constable, whose letter forms mature between 1644 and 1683.[45] However, the differences between the graph formations in *Lady Falkland: Her Life* and Elizabeth's in her 1659 letter are significant enough to suggest that Lucy, the only sister whose hand has not yet been positively identified, is the sister who penned the manuscript.

There are corrections and additions to the manuscript in at least three other contemporary hands. As described above, Mary identifies ambiguous pronouns by supplying proper names, and identifies

Scripture references in the margins of the manuscript. Patrick Cary, whose hand is identifiable by comparing it to autograph letters to the Earl of Clarendon, clarifies, corrects, and expands upon *Life*'s narrative, in particular concerning his father's time in Holland, and his own 'kidnapping' from Great Tew.[46] All but two of Patrick's marginal additions have been severely cropped (cropped additions appear on fols. 1, 39v, 41v, 44). I have not been able to identify the last hand, written in the darkest ink and thickest nib,[47] which supplies the surnames of English Benedictine monks referred to only by their first name or alias in the text.

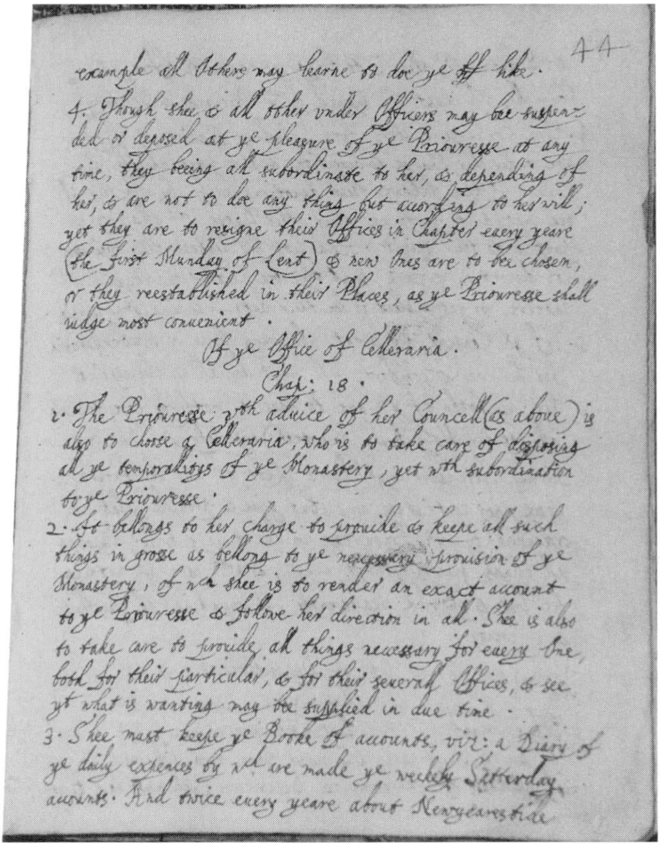
44

example all others may learne to doe ye the like.
4. Though shee & all other under Officers may bee suspen=
ded or deposed at ye pleasure of ye Prioresse at any
time, they beeing all subordinate to her, & depending of
her, & are not to doe any thing but according to her will;
yet they are to resigne their Offices in Chapter every yeare
(the first Munday of Lent) & new ones are to bee chosen,
or they reestablished in their Places, as ye Prioresse shall
iudge most conuenient.

Of ye Office of Celleraria.
Chap: 18.

1. The Prioresse with advice of her Councell (as aboue) is
also to chose a Celleraria, who is to take care of disposing
all ye temporalitys of ye Monastery, yet with subordination
to ye Prioresse.
2. It belongs to her charge to provide & keepe all such
things in grosse as belong to ye necessary provision of ye
Monastery, of wch shee is to render an exact account
to ye Prioresse & follow her direction in all. Shee is also
to take care to provide all things necessary for every one
both for their particular, & for their severall Offices, & see
yt what is wanting may bee supplied in due time.
3. Shee must keepe ye Booke of accounts, viz: a Diary of
ye daily expences by wch are made ye weekly Satterday
accounts. And twice every yeare about Newyearestide

PLATE 3. *A page in the* Constitution of Our Lady of Good Hope*: Colwich, Staffordshire, St Mary's Abbey,* MS *P2, fol. 44r (Original page size 190 × 150mm.) Reproduced by permission of St Mary's Abbey, Colwich.*

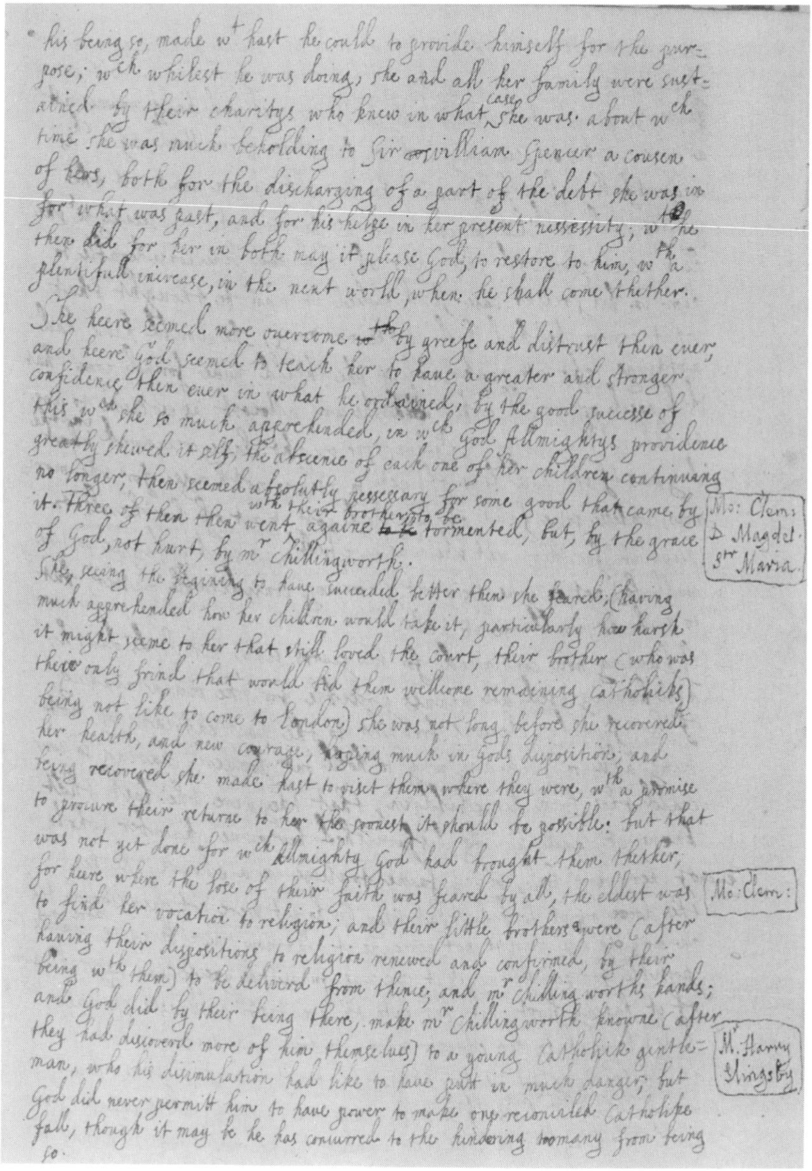

his being so, made wt hast he could to provide himself for the purpose; wch whilest he was doing, she and all her family were sust-
ained by their charitys who knew in what case she was. about wch
time she was much beholding to Sir William Spencer a cousen
of hers, both for the discharging of a part of the debt she was in
for what was past, and for his helpe in her present nessessity, wch he
then did for her in both may it please God, to restore to him, wth a
plentifull increase, in the next world, when he shall come thether.
She heere seemed more overcome wth by greefe and distrust then ever,
and heere God seemed to teach her to have a greater and stronger
confidence then ever in what he ordained, by the good successe of
this wch she so much apprehended, in wch God Allmightys providence
greatly shewed it self; the absence of each one of her children continuing
no longer, then seemed absolutly nessessary for some good that came by
it. Three of them then went againe wth their brother to be tormented, but, by the grace
of God, not hurt, by mr Chillingworth.
She, seeing the begining to have succeeded better then she feared; (having
much apprehended how her children would take it, particularly how harsh
it might seeme to her that still loved the court, their brother (who was
their only friend that would bid them wellcome remaining Catholiks)
being not like to come to London) she was not long before she recovered
her health, and new courage, relying much in Gods disposition; and
being recovered she made hast to visit them where they were, wth a promise
to procure their returne to her the soonest it should be possible: but that
was not yet done for wch Allmighty God had brought them thether,
for heere where the lose of their faith was feared by all, the eldest was
to find her vocation to religion; and their little brothers were (after
having their dispositions to religion renewed and confirmed, by their
being wth them) to be deliverd from thence, and mr Chillingworths hands;
and God did by their being there, make mr Chillingworth knowne (after
they had discoverd more of him themselves) to a young Catholik gentleman, who his dissimulation had like to have put in much danger; but
God did never permitt him to have power to make one reconciled Catholike
fall, though it may be he has concurred to the hindering so many from being
so.

Mo: Clem: D Magdel. Str Maria.

Mo: Clem:

Mr. Harry Slingsby

PLATE 4. *A page in* Lady Falkland: Her Life: *Lille, Archives Départementales du Nord,* MS *20H9, fol. 34v (Original page size 180 × 140mm.) Reproduced by permission of Archives Départementales du Nord. Photo: Jean-Luc Thieffry.*

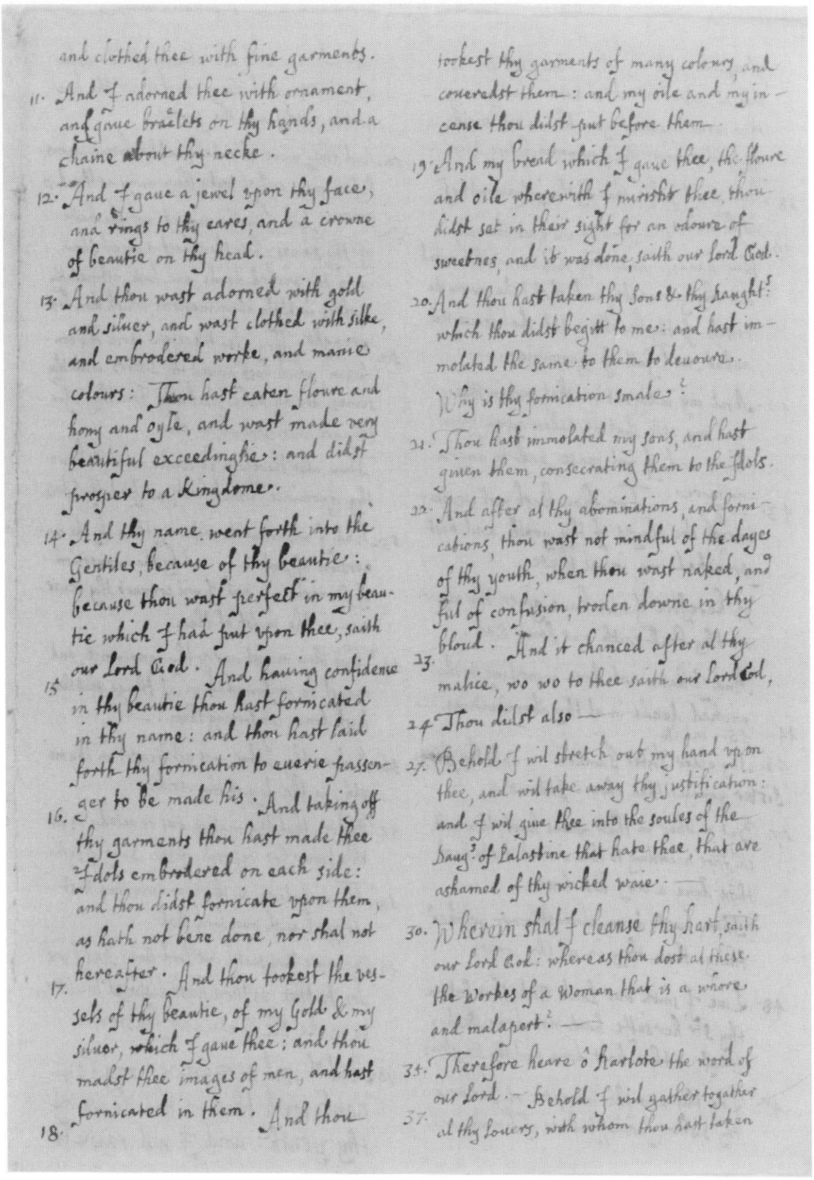

and clothed thee with fine garments.

11. And I adorned thee with ornament, and gaue bracelets on thy hands, and a chaine about thy necke.

12. And I gaue a jewel vpon thy face, and rings to thy eares, and a crowne of beautie on thy head.

13. And thou wast adorned with gold and siluer, and wast clothed with silke, and embrodered worke, and manie colours: Thou hast eaten floure and hony and oyle, and wast made very beautiful exceedinglie: and didst prosper to a kingdome.

14. And thy name went forth into the Gentiles, because of thy beautie: because thou wast perfect in my beautie which I had put vpon thee, saith our Lord God. And having confidence

15. in thy beautie thou hast fornicated in thy name: and thou hast laid forth thy fornication to euerie passenger to be made his. And taking off

16. thy garments thou hast made thee Idols embrodered on each side: and thou didst fornicate vpon them, as hath not bene done, nor shal not hereafter. And thou tookest the vessels

17. of thy beautie, of my gold & my siluer, which I gaue thee: and thou madst thee images of men, and hast fornicated in them. And thou

18.

tookest thy garments of many colours and coueredst them: and my oile and my incense thou didst put before them.

19. And my bread which I gaue thee, the floure and oile wherewith I nurisht thee, thou didst set in their sight for an odoure of sweetnes: and it was done, saith our Lord God.

20. And thou hast taken thy sons & thy daught{er} which thou didst begett to me: and hast immolated the same to them to deuoure. Why is thy fornication smale?

21. Thou hast immolated my sons, and hast giuen them, consecrating them to the Idols.

22. And after al thy abominations, and fornications thou wast not mindful of the dayes of thy youth, when thou wast naked, and ful of confusion, troden downe in thy bloud. And it chanced after al thy

23. malice, wo wo to thee saith our Lord God,

24. Thou didst also —

27. Behold I wil stretch out my hand vpon thee, and wil take away thy justification: and I wil giue thee into the soules of the daugh{ters} of Palastine that hate thee, that are ashamed of thy wicked waie.

30. Wherein shal I cleanse thy hart, saith our Lord God: whereas thou dost al these the workes of a woman that is a whore, and malapert? —

31. Therefore heare ò harlote the word of our Lord. — Behold I wil gather togather

37. al thy louers, with whom thou hast taken

PLATE 5. *A page in a manuscript of excerpts from the minor prophets: Lille, Archives Départementales du Nord, MS 20H39, part 11. (Original page size 200 × 148mm.) Reproduced by permission of Archives Départementales du Nord. Photo: Jean-Luc Thieffry.*

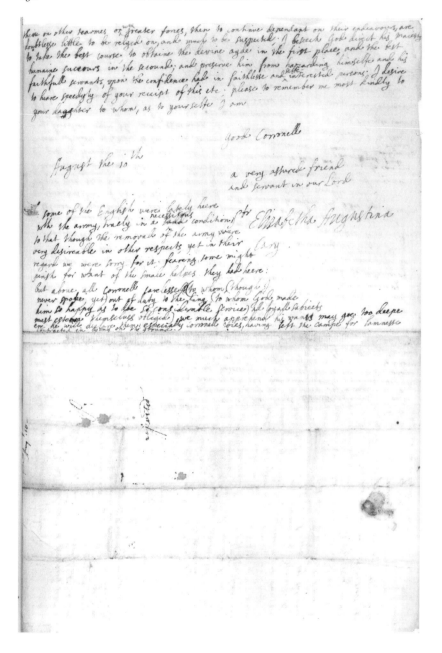

PLATE 6. *Autograph letter signed by Dame Elizabetha Cary, to Colonel Grace, 10 August 1659: Oxford, Bodleian Library, MS Clarendon 63, fol. 58v (Original page size 290 × 196mm.) Reproduced by permission of the Bodleian Library.*

Identifying the deleting hands in the manuscript of *Lady Falkland: Her Life* is a less straightforward process. The variety and occasional ambiguity of some of the deletions to the manuscript suggest that the revision process was never completed. It is difficult to assign the various kinds of deletions to a particular hand, but it is clear that they do not all come from the same hand (PLATE 7 shows two different kinds of deletions on the same page). Some of the passages appear to have been 'marked' as suggestions for deletions, but not all of these suggestions have been carried out. PLATES 8 and 9 show two leaves of *Lady Falkland: Her Life* that have material 'marked' for omission. In PLATE 8, the 'marked' passage has then been further deleted by strike-through, while in PLATE 9, only part of the suggested material has been further struck-through, although the beginning and end of the deletion has been altered more than once, and does not appear to have been finally resolved.[48]

Dating

Lady Falkland: Her Life is currently recognized as a *circa* 1655 copy of a manuscript text originally written between 1643 (after the death of Lucius in the Civil War) and 1650 (before the death of Lucy).[49] Evidence for the *circa* 1655 dating is wanting, however, and several references to events in the 1640s allow *Lady Falkland: Her Life* to be dated more precisely than 1643–50. The biography notes Dr Benjamin Laney's chaplaincy to Charles I, 'Docter Lany my lord Newburghs Chaplaine since the Kings', an appointment made in late January, 1644/5.[50] Three references to English Benedictine priests place the composition of *Lady Falkland: Her Life* before the General Chapter meeting of the English Benedictine Congregation in August, 1645: Dom Wilfrid Selby, who was made President of the English Benedictine Congregation in August, 1645, is referred to as, simply, 'Father Willfrid',[51] Dom Clement Reyner, who became Abbot of Lambspring in August 1645, is referred to as 'Father Clement, then President', referring to his tenure as President of the English Benedictine Congregation, 1635–40;[52] and finally, Dom Gabriel Brett is referred to as 'Reuerend Fa*ther* Gabriel, then Prior', referring to his Priorship at St Edmunds, Paris, 1633–40.[53] The only period during which Brett was not a prior of any monastery was between August 1643 and August 1645.[54] If *Lady Falkland: Her Life* was written after August 1645, Selby and Reyner would have been referred to by their present titles, President and Abbot, respectively, and Brett would have been referred to as 'Prior', rather than 'then Prior'. The style of their titling as an indication of a pre-August 1645 dating for *Lady Falkland: Her Life* is further supported by the

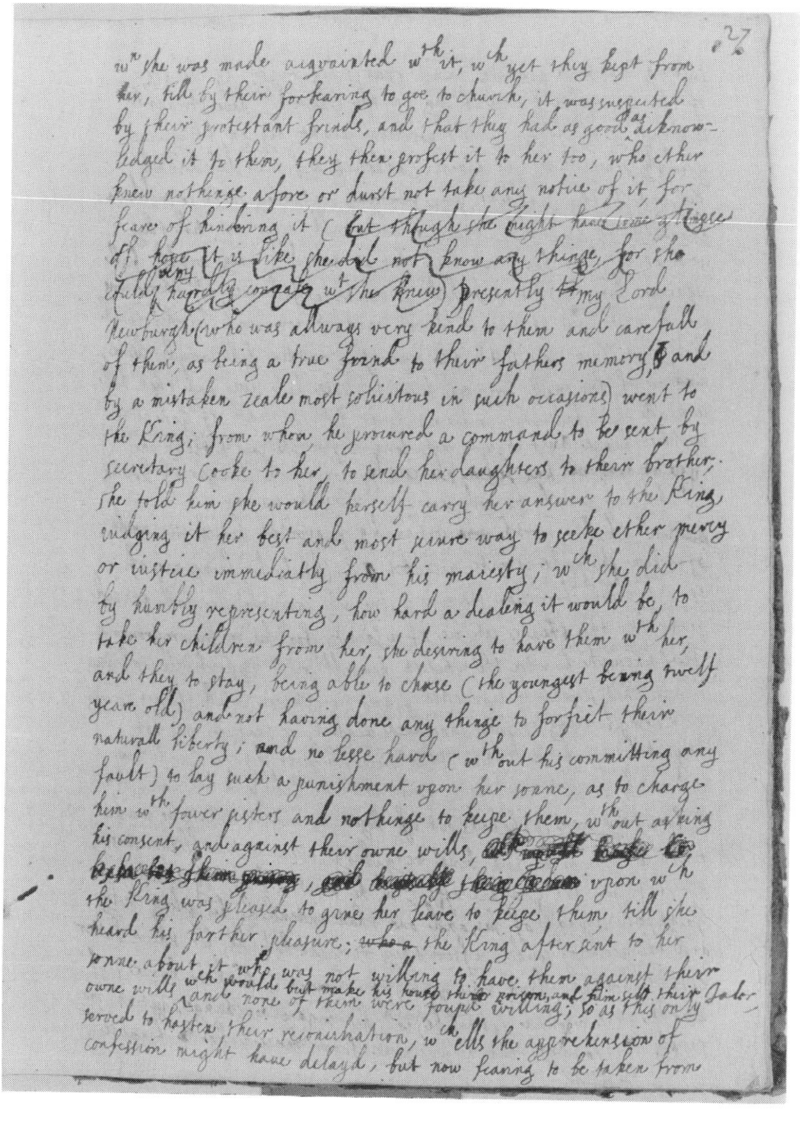

27

w[ch] she was made acquainted wth it, w[ch] yet they kept from
her, till by their forbearing to goe to church, it was suspected
by their protestant friends, and that they had as good acknowledged it to them, they then profest it to her too, who either
knew nothinge afore or durst not take any notice of it for
feare of hindring it (but though she might have done y[e] ???
of, how it is like she did not know any thinge, for she
could hardly conceale wth she knew) presently to my Lord
Newburgh (who was always very kind to them and carefull
of them, as being a true freind to their fathers memory, and
by a mistaken zeale most solicitous in such occasions) went to
the King; from whom he procured a command to be sent by
secretary Cooke to her, to send her daughters to their brother;
she told him she would herself carry her answer to the King,
iudging it her best and most pure way to seeke either mercy
or iustice immediatly from his maiesty; w[ch] she did
by humbly representing, how hard a dealing it would be, to
take her children from her, she desiring to have them w[th] her,
and they to stay, being able to chuse (the youngest being twelf
yeare old) and not having done any thinge to forfeit their
naturall liberty; and no lesse hard (w[th]out his committing any
fault) to lay such a punishment vpon her sonne, as to charge
him w[th] fower sisters and nothinge to keepe them, w[th]out asking
his consent, and against their owne wills, ~~??~~
~~??~~ vpon w[ch]
the King was pleased to giue her leaue to keepe them till she
heard his farther pleasure; when the King after sent to her
sonne, about it, who was not willing to have them against their
owne wills w[ch] would but make his house there ?? ?? their ??
serued to hasten their renunciation, wch ells the apprehension of
confession might have delayd, but now fearing to be taken from

PLATE 7. *A page in* Lady Falkland: Her Life: *Lille, Archives Départementales du Nord,* MS *20H9, fol. 26r (Original page size 180 × 140 mm.) Reproduced by permission of Archives Départementales du Nord. Photo: Jean-Luc Thieffry.*

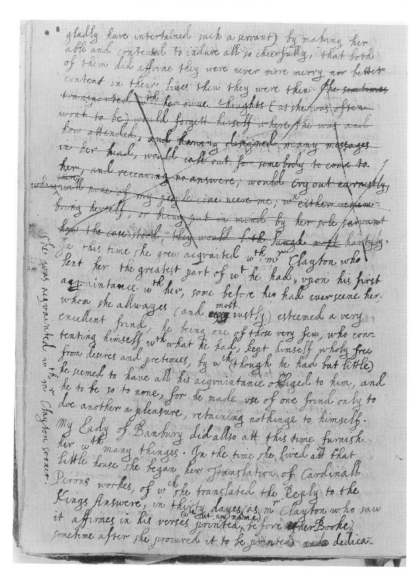

PLATE 8. *A page in* Lady Falkland: Her Life: *Lille, Archives Départementales du Nord,* MS *20H9, fol. 16v (Original page size 180 × 140mm.) Reproduced by permission of Archives Départementales du Nord. Photo: Jean-Luc Thieffry.*

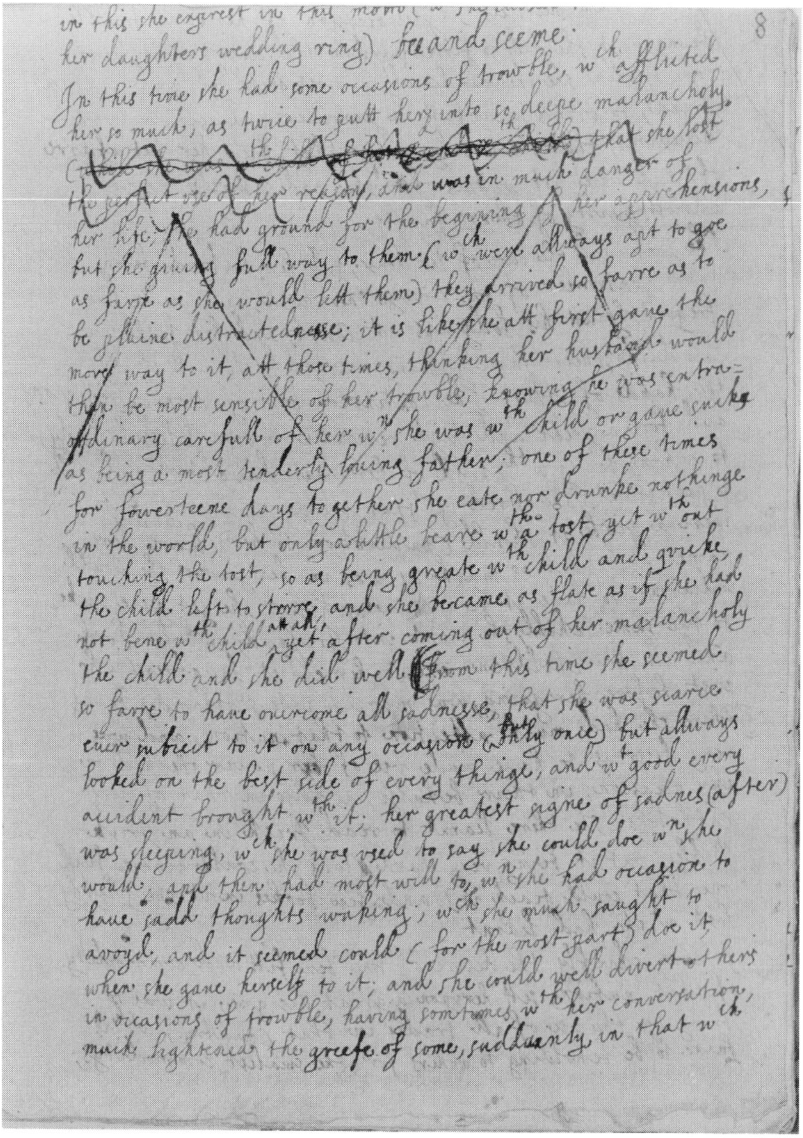

PLATE 9. *A page in* Lady Falkland: Her Life: *Lille, Archives Départementales du Nord,* MS *20H9, fol. 8r (Original page size 180 × 140mm.) Reproduced by permission of Archives Départementales du Nord. Photo: Jean-Luc Thieffry.*

manuscript's reference to Cambrai's chaplain from 1633–41, Dom John Meutisse, as 'Father ~~John~~ Prior of Doway that now is', and elsewhere, 'Father Prior of Doway', even though the biography is referring to him in his earlier capacity as chaplain at Cambrai.[55] Meutisse was prior at Douai from 1641–53. It is reasonable to infer, then, that *Lady Falkland: Her Life* was written between February and August 1645, after Laney was made chaplain to Charles I, and before the elections at the General Chapter of the English Benedictine Congregation.

Other topical references do not contradict this dating. Bessie Poulter, 'who now is . . . a quire Nun amongst the English Tersians att Antwerp' was received into the Antwerp Carmel in 1642, and was professed 9 October 1643.[56] *Lady Falkland: Her Life* mentions Walter Montagu's defence of Catholicism and Charles I 'for which he hath now the honer to suffer'.[57] Montagu was arrested in October 1643 and remained a prisoner until July 1647. Assuming his 'suffering' refers to his imprisonment, then it can be inferred that *Lady Falkland: Her Life* was completed before news of his July 1647 release reached Cambrai.[58] Further, *Lady Falkland: Her Life* does not note the death of Lady Falkland's daughter-in-law, Lettice, who died in January 1646/7, and observes that God will give Sir William Spencer 'a plentifull increase, in the next world, when he shall come thether'. He came 'thether' in May 1647.[59]

Marginal additions in the hand of Patrick Cary further make the *c.*1655 dating impossible. Patrick had converted to Catholicism in 1636, but was a married Protestant living in Dublin by the year 1655.[60] He (and his brother Henry) had been 'stolen' from Great Tew by Lady Falkland in 1636 and sent to St Edmund's, Paris, an English Benedictine monastery, where he lived until 1638. Patrick then went to Rome, where he remained until his pensions ran out in 1649. He returned to Great Tew to see if he could obtain an annuity from his nephew in 1649–50,[61] and probably went to Wickham at this time as well (home of his sister Victoria and her husband, Sir William Uvedale), since one of his manuscript poems contains the lines:

> Come (fayth) since I'me parting, & that God knowes when
> The walls of sweet *Wickham* I shall see aghen . . . [62]

He did not know when or if he would see Wickham again because he had decided to become a monk. A November 1649 letter from Henry Hammond to Gilbert Sheldon notes that Patrick had decided to return to Flanders,[63] and a letter from March 1649/50 places him in Brussels.[64] Patrick entered the English Benedictine monastery at Douai as a novice in May 1650, but after three months, decided that the monastic life was incompatible with his fragile health.[65] Patrick left the continent for good by September 1650, and a November 1650 letter from him to Lord Clarendon is dated from Wickham.[66] Soon after, he returned to the Protestant church and married Susan Uvedale, the niece of Sir William Uvedale (who had been with Patrick's father, Henry, first Viscount Falkland, in Holland). Patrick was admitted to Lincoln's Inn on 10 February 1651/2, and received his first appointment in Ireland in 1653. His first son (of three children) was born 30 October 1654, at Great Tew, and Patrick died in Dublin in March 1656/7.

It is more likely that Patrick made his corrections to the manuscript of *Lady Falkland: Her Life* after his trip to England in 1649 and before he became a novice, since he states in one of his corrections to the manuscript, 'Sir William Uvedale told me'.[67] His cropped addition, 'God be thanked there is some hope they died Catholics' suggests that he was still a Catholic when the manuscript came into his hands for correction.[68] Extant correspondence between Patrick and Lord Clarendon reveals that in the period between leaving England (by March 1650) and beginning at Douai (May 1650), he was in Brussels and Paris. At this time, he was in regular correspondence with Anne at Cambrai, and it is possible that he visited her there in March, 1649/50, since in a letter from Brussels dated 14 March 1649/50, Patrick informs Lord Clarendon that his 'Sisters' had been 'reporters of your Lordshippes propension towards our familye'.[69] In this letter, he also indicates his knowledge of a letter that Anne had written on his behalf to Lord Clarendon on 4 March 1649/50.[70] In June 1650, Anne writes to Lord Clarendon that her brother 'hath commanded' her to inform Clarendon of Patrick's decision to begin his noviciate, since the novice was not allowed to write letters himself.[71]

Lady Falkland: Her Life was bound after Patrick made his corrections, since many of them are cropped. The wreath watermark on the front flyleaf of *Lady Falkland: Her Life*, which would have been added at the time of binding, is identical to a watermark in a manuscript in the hand of Dame Barbara Constable, dated 1 March 1650.[72] Given that both the flyleaf and Dame Barbara's manuscript came from a similar stock of paper, it may be inferred that *Lady Falkland: Her Life* was bound near the time Dame Barbara completed her manuscript, in March 1650.[73] If so, then it was bound shortly after Patrick's corrections were added, perhaps also in March, shortly before beginning his noviciate at Douai.

WRITING AND SPIRITUALITY IN 1640s CAMBRAI

Written in 1631, the *Constitutions* of the Our Lady of Consolation, Cambrai, were quite specific concerning the ownership and consumption of books. They decreed that 'all *the* bookes must belong to *the* common librarie and . . . haue written on *them the* name of *the* Monastarie'; these library books were to 'be kept vnder lock' and were to be 'common to all indiffirentlie'.[74] The nuns should make a catalogue of the library's holdings, which the Vicarius would examine 'at euerie Visit, and at such time as the Ordinarie shall iudge fit' to ensure that their collection did not contain books, 'written or printed . . . that sauour not of a religious Monastical spirit'. While a nun could not claim ownership of a book, write her name on it, or say that she 'bought it or brought it', the Abbess would allow a nun to borrow a book 'for her vse in her celle as longe as she please'.[75] Extant books at Cambrai and their daughter-house at Paris show evidence of such book-borrowing in the form of nuns' names written on the pastedown, followed by the phrase, 'with leave'.

The monastic library at Cambrai was well-stocked with saints' lives, lives of medieval and counter-Reformation Catholics, and lives of continental Catholics and members of the English Benedictine Congregation, both in print and in manuscript, and in English, Latin, French, and Italian. An inventory of the monastery's confiscated library, compiled at the time of the French Revolution,[76] bears out the importance of hagiographical and exemplary lives and martyrologies to the nuns. It lists seventeenth-century lives of the Blessed Lady of Loreto,[77] Suor Maria Maddelena,[78] Marguerite de Lorraine,[79] Mary Stuart,[80] St Scholastica,[81] St Ignatius of Loyola,[82] St Teresa,[83] Tauler,[84] Thomas More,[85] Claude Bernarde,[86] Edmund Geinges,[87] St Bernard,[88] St Catherine,[89] and Mary Magdalene.[90] Father Augustine Baker, the spiritual director at Cambrai from 1624–33, was singlehandedly responsible for writing the copious lives of Dame Gertrude More and Dame Margaret Gascoigne, as well as *Life and Death of Mr. Francis Gascoigne*, written about 1638, and an autobiography written during the winter of 1637/38.[91] Of the three known lives of Father Augustine Baker written after his death—by Fathers Leander Prichard in 1643, Peter Salvin in 1646, and Serenus Cressy in 1650—two, the lives by Prichard and Salvin, were written at the explicit request of the Cambrai nuns.[92] *Lady Falkland: Her Life*, then, was composed in a place permeated with the lives of saints, martyrs, and other exemplary people. Though the text is not modelled after any one kind of life-writing—death notices, saints' lives, martyrologies, or secular lives—it shares certain resemblances with all of them.

The nuns would have had the opportunity to read saintly and exemplary lives during the short intervals for recreation or reflection in their cell, as well as in group work sessions, where the superiour 'maie cause some spirituall author to be read'.[93] In accordance with the Benedictine Rule, there was a particular emphasis placed on reading during Lent. The Rule suggested that 'each one take a booke out of the Librarie, reade it all ouer in order; and let these bookes be giuen them in the beginning of Lent'.[94] The Cambrai nuns encountered exemplary lives in the refectory as well, where the Catholic martyrology was read on a daily basis, and death notices of nuns were read 'after the reading of the Martyrologie the day before their Anniversarie'.[95] The Constitutions of the community state that death notices of fellow nuns were considered 'an example to posteritie' of 'All such things as happened in their lives, at their death, or after their death, worthy of note and memorie'.[96]

Nuns like Lucy, who led an 'infirme, sickly, and suffring life',[97] were excused from their daily offices to convalesce either in their cell or in the infirmary, during which time they often wrote. These writings, termed 'loose papers', were created outside of the times alloted for mental prayer and *lectio divina*, and concerned a nun's own 'particular conscience'.[98] A nun's loose papers often entered the library upon her death, if the Abbess deemed them useful for other nuns. The papers would be bound and titled, appearing under names such as 'Colections of Dame Eugenia Houltons', 'Eight Collection Bookes of . . . Mothere Clementia Cary . . . fower and parte of the fift are of her owne handwriting', 'a little book of Dame Mary Watsons Collections', and '2 Books of Reuerend Mother Bridget's More's Collections'.[99] Since *Lady Falkland: Her Life* was written in 1645, but not bound until 1650, the year of Lucy's death, it seems likely that the manuscript was part of her loose papers, gathered near the time of her death, and included among 'The writings of the most religious dame D. Magdalena Carie de St Cruce professed religious of the most holy order of St Benedict'.[100]

POSTSCRIPT: A NOTE ON ENGLISH NUNS' MANUSCRIPTS

Manuscripts relating to the English Benedictine nuns of Cambrai and Paris are now scattered across France (Lille, Cambrai, Nancy, Paris—Bibliothèque Mazarine, Bibliothèque Nationale, and Bibliothèque de l'Arsenal), England (the Bodleian Library, the British Library, Stanbrook Abbey, Colwich Abbey, Downside Abbey, Ampleforth Abbey, Douai Abbey, and Ushaw College), and the United States (the Beinecke Library). In addition to these two monasteries, nineteen other communities of English nuns were founded in France and what was then the Spanish Netherlands between the years 1598 and 1670.[101]

Year Founded	*Order*	*Location of Foundation*
1598	Benedictines	Brussels
1608/9	Poor Clares	Gravelines
1609	Austin Canonesses	Louvain
1618/9	Carmelites	Antwerp
1621	Franciscans	Bruges
1623	Benedictines	Cambrai
1624	Benedictines	Ghent
1629	Poor Clares	Aire
1629	Austin Canonesses	Bruges
1634	Austin Canonesses	Paris
1642	Sepulchrines	Liege
1644	Poor Clares	Rouen
1648	Carmelites	Lierre
1651	Benedictines	Paris
1652	Poor Clares	Dunkirk
1652	Benedictines	Boulogne
1658	Conceptionists	Paris
1661	Dominicans	Vilvorde
1662	Benedictines	Dunkirk
1665	Benedictines	Ypres
1670	Carmelites	Hoogstraeten

Manuscripts produced by these nuns are still extant—ranging from book-length devotional works and personal collections of assorted contemplative material (of religious verse, prose, song, drawings, and engravings) to letters, chapter speeches, medical receipts, and financial accounts. The fact that this wealth of material is virtually untrawled and often unrecognized supports Margaret Ezell's observation that recent work on early modern women's writings places an undue emphasis on the 'means of repression' rather than on 'the modes of production'.[102] It is to be hoped that recent microfilming and editing projects will make these manuscripts more widely available without disturbing the monasteries in which they are held, whose monks and nuns often lack the time, funds, people, and other resources to adminster their collections to the public.[103]

A bibliography of books and articles containing transcriptions of English nuns' manuscripts not mentioned in this article follows:

Arblaster, Paul (ed.), 'The Infanta and the English Benedictine Nuns: Mary Percy's Memories in 1634', *Recusant History*, 23.4 (1997), 508–27.

Burton, Catharine, *An English Carmelite the Life of Catharine Burton, Mother Mary Xaveria of the Angels, of the English Teresian Convent at Antwerp: Collected from her Own Writings and Other Sources*, ed. Thomas Hunter (London, 1876).

Calendar of the Clarendon State Papers Preserved in the Bodleian Library, ed. O. Ogle and W.H. Bliss, 5 vols (Oxford, 1869–70).

Clifford, Arthur (ed.), *Tixall Letters; or the Correspondence of the Aston Family, and Their Friends, During the Seventeenth Century* (London, 1815), II, 1–109.

Durrant, C.S., *A Link Between Flemish Mystics and English Martyrs* (London, 1925).

Forster, Ann M.C. (ed.), 'The Chronicles of the English Poor Clares of Rouen', *Recusant History*, 18 (1986), 59–102, 165–91.

Galgano, M.J., 'Negotiations for a Nun's Dowry: Restoration Letters of Mary Caryll, O.S.B. and Ann Clifton, O.S.B', *American Benedictine Review*, 24 (1973), 278–98.

Gillow, Joseph (ed.), 'Registers of the English Poor Clare Nuns at Gravelines, with Notes of Foundations at Aire, Dunkirk, and Rouen, 1608–1837', *Miscellanea 9*, Publications of the Catholic Record Society, 14 (London, 1914), 25–173.

——, and Richard Trappes-Lomax (eds), *Diary of the 'Blue Nuns', or Order of the Immaculate Conception of Our Lady at Paris, 1658–1810*, Publications of the Catholic Record Society, 8 (London, 1910).

Hamilton, Adam (ed.), *The Chronicle of the English Augustinian Canonesses Regular of the Lateran, at St Monica's in Louvain (now at St Augustine's Priory, Newton Abbot, Devon*, 2 vols (London, 1904–6).

——, 'The English Benedictine Nuns of Brussels and Winchester, 1598–1856', *Miscellanea 9*, Publications of the Catholic Record Society, 14 (London, 1914), 174–203.

A History of the Benedictine Nuns of Dunkirk, Now at St Scholastica's Abbey, Teignmouth, Devon, edited by the Community (London, 1958).

Knowles, David (ed.), *The Life of Lady Lucy Knatchbull, by Sir Tobie Matthew* (London, 1931).

Latz, Dorothy, '*Glow-Worm Light': Writings of Seventeenth Century English Recusant Women from Original Manuscripts*, Salzburg Studies in English

Literature (Salzburg: Institut für Anglistik und Amerikanistik Universitat, 1989).

——, 'The Mystical Poetry of Dame Gertrude More', *Mystics Quarterly*, 16.2 (1990), 66–82.

—— (ed.), *The Building of Divine Love, as Translated by Agnes More; Transcribed from the 17th century Manuscript* (Salzburg, 1992).

McCann, Justin (ed.), 'Some Benedictine Letters in the Bodleian', *Downside Review*, 49 (1931), 465–81.

Morris, John, *The Troubles of Our Catholic Forefathers Related by Themselves* (London, 1872: reprint 1970).

Orchard, Emmanuel, *Till God Will: Mary Ward Through Her Writings* (London, 1985).

Pasture, A. 'Documents concernant quelques monastères anglais aux Pays-Bas au XVIIe siècle', *Bulletin de l'Institute Historique Belge de Rome*, 10 (1930), 155–223.

Rumsey, Mary Justina (ed.), 'Abbess Neville's Annals of Five Communities of English Benedictine Nuns in Flanders, 1598–1687', *Miscellanea 5*, Publications of the Catholic Record Society, 6 (London, 1909), 1–72.

Trappes-Lomax, Richard (ed.), *The English Franciscan Nuns, 1619–1821 and the Friars Minor of the Same Province 1618–1761*, Publications of the Catholic Record Society, 24 (London, 1922).

Ward, Lady Abbess, and Community, 'Obituary Notices of the English Benedictine Nuns of Ghent in Flanders, and at Preston, Lancashire (now at Oulton, Staffordshire), 1627–1811', *Miscellanea 11*, Publications of the Catholic Record Society, 19 (London, 1917), 1–92.

NOTES

I am most grateful to Dr Phil West, Dr Marie Axton, Dame Margaret Truran OSB, and, above all, to the late Jeremy Maule, for their valuable advice on an earlier version of this paper, delivered at a meeting of the Trinity/Trent Colloquium in Nottingham, May 1998. I am further grateful to the English Benedictine communities at St Mary's Abbey (Colwich, Staffs.), Stanbrook Abbey, and Downside Abbey for their assistance and hospitality during my research in their libraries.

1 The six children of Lord and Lady Falkland who converted to Roman Catholicism were Anne (1614–71), Elizabeth (1617–82), Lucy (1619–50), Mary (1622–93), Patrick (1624–57), and Henry (1625–55). The other five children were Katherine (1609–25), Lucius (1610–43), Lorenzo (1613–42), Edward (1616–16), and Victoria (1620–94).

2 Richard Simpson, 'A Conversion from the Time of Charles I', *Rambler* 8 (1857), 173–89, 258–72; Richard Simpson, *The Lady Falkland, Her Life, from a Manuscript in the Imperial Archives at Lille* (London: Catholic Publishing and Bookselling Company, 1861); Georgiana Fullerton, *The Life of Elisabeth Lady Falkland 1585–1639*, Quarterly

Series, 43 (London: Burns and Oates, 1883); The Tragedy of Mariam The Fair Queen of Jewry *with* The Lady Falkland her Life *by one of her Daughters*, ed. Barry Weller and Margaret Ferguson (Berkeley, 1994).

3 Simpson edited the liberal Catholic journal the *Rambler* from February 1858 until autumn 1859. For Simpson as Catholic historian and polemicist, see Damian McElrath, *Richard Simpson 1820–1876: A Study in 19th Century English Liberal Catholicism* (Louvain, 1972); Josef Altholz, *The Liberal Catholic Movement in England: The 'Rambler' and its Contributors 1848–1864* (London, 1962); and Josef Altholz, Damian McElrath, and James Holland (eds), *The Correspondence of Lord Acton and Richard Simpson*, 3 vols (Cambridge, 1971–5).

4 *Lady Falkland: Her Life* has featured prominently in the work of Cary scholars as a biographical source, but has received little attention as an example of early modern life-writing. For a contextualization of *Lady Falkland: Her Life*, see Heather Wolfe, 'A Critical Edition of *Lady Falkland: Her Life* (1645) with Correspondence and Records of the Falkland Family (1625–1671)', (Dissertation, University of Cambridge, 1998).

5 For example, Simpson sometimes inserts the manuscript's marginal additions in the main text (in square brackets generally, but occasionally silently) and sometimes he places them in footnotes. Both he and Weller and Ferguson incorporate editorial comments in square brackets within the text without indicating that the addition belongs to them, rather than a contemporary emender. Weller and Ferguson silently and inconsistently incorporate marginal additions and interlinear insertions into their edition. In one marginal annotation, important for dating and identification, they transcribe 'The Bishop *the*n of Durham' as 'The Bishop of Durham'. They entirely omit a marginal addition (fol. 19) which is critical for confirming the identification of one of the marginal hands. For a discussion of the subjective editing of *Lady Falkland: Her Life*, see Jesse G. Swan, 'A Woman's Life as Ancillary Text: The Printed Texts of the Biography of Elizabeth Tanfield Cary', *The Journal of the Rocky Mountain Medieval and Renaissance Association* (forthcoming, 1999).

6 Weller and Ferguson (1994) misidentify the manuscript in the first paragraph of their introduction, calling it MS A.D.N.xx.(*ca*.1655).

7 My categorisation of watermarks is based on the categories in C.M. Briquet, *Les Filigranes*, ed. Allen Stevenson, 4 vols (Amsterdam, 1968), and Edward Heawood, *Watermarks, Mainly of the Seventeenth and Eighteenth Centuries* (Hilversum, 1950).

8 Commoditys/comoditys, at the end of quire 2 and the beginning of quire 3 (fols. 8v, 9r); withstanding/not withstanding, at the end of quire 7 and the beginning of quire 8 (fols. 28v, 29r). The catchword at the end of quire 10 (fol. 40v) is not repeated on the next leaf (fol. 41r).

9 The manuscript of *Life* is incorrectly foliated 1–49, in the upper right corner of each leaf (first in pencil, and then, between August 1994 and August 1997, traced over in blue ball-point pen). However, since fol. '12' is a tipped-in leaf, and not part of the gathering, it should be treated as an inserted leaf in between folios 11 and 12 (marked 13).

10 'Records of the Abbey of Our Lady of Consolation at Cambrai, 1620–1793', ed. Joseph Gillow, *Miscellanea 8*, Publications of the Catholic Record Society, 13 (London, 1913), 21, hereafter referred to as CRS 13. The community was imprisoned for eighteen months, during which time many of them died. The sixteen surviving nuns returned to England in 1796.

11 André Le Glay, *Mémoire sur les archives des églises et maisons religieuses du Cambrésis* (Lille, 1852), 5. A 1796 letter states that confiscated books from various monasteries were

also locked in the damp Chapel of the Virgin by 'le citoyen Mallet', who refused to give up the keys. In year 6 of the Republic (1799) these documents were still in the chapel, and in danger of ruin (Lille, Archives Départementales du Nord MS L4870).

12 Le Glay, *Notice sur les Archives du Département du Nord* (Lille, 1839), 34.

13 Lille, Archives Départementales du Nord MS L4873. Letters from the minister of the interior in Paris designated him as 'Commissaire bibliographe de Cambray;' he is also referred to as the 'bibliothècaire et conservateur du Musée de Cambray'. The museum's foundation was based on an order in 1796 from the 'Commission Executive de l'Instruction publique, Bureau des Musées'.

14 A document in French dated 1802, in Stanbrook Abbey, Annals 1.II, 504.

15 Cambrai, Médiathèque Municipale, MS B1004. Only one manuscript in this catalogue is now at Cambrai's Médiathèque Municipale: MS A1155, Dame Agnes More's translation of Dame Jean of Cambrai's *Treatise of the Ruin of Proper Love, and the Building of Divine Love*, transcribed by Dame Susanna Phillips. Four other manuscripts from the Cambrai community, not listed in MS B1004, are also at Cambrai: MSS A255, A1154, B910, B1361.

16 Cambrai, Médiathèque Municipale, MS B1004, p. 533, no. 3546.

17 Le Glay, *Catalogue descriptif et raisonné des Manuscrits de la bibliothèque de Cambrai* (Cambrai, 1831), 233-5. The seventeen volumes of Baker's autograph works are still missing.

18 Le Glay, *Catalogue*, 235. The catalogue he is referring to is the aforementioned Cambrai, Médiathèque Municipale, MS B1004.

19 Le Glay, *Histoire et Description des Archives Générales du Département du Nord, a Lille* (Paris, 1843), 65.

20 Le Glay, *Mémoire sur les archives des églises et maisons religieuses du Cambrésis* (Lille, 1852), 6. Many of the remaining manuscripts in the Musée de Cambrai were destroyed when the Hôtel de Ville was destroyed during the first World War (from private correspondence with Annie Fournier, Curator of Manuscripts and Rare Books, Médiathèque Municipale de Cambrai). Among the items known to be lost in the fire are 'extrait de l'obitier des dames bénédictines anglaises de Cambrai (1641-1683)', and 'Mémoires et pièces de procédure', listed in Edouard Gautier and André Lesort, *Inventaire Sommaire des Archives Communales Anterieures à 1790* (Cambrai, 1907). The manuscripts of Our Lady of Consolation are catalogued at Archives Départementales du Nord in Lille as MSS 20H1-20H59.

21 Le Glay, *Mémoire*, 41.

22 Max Bruchet, *Archives Départementales du Nord: Répertoire Numérique, Série H (Fonds Benedictins et Cisterciens)* (Lille, 1928).

23 Lille, Archives Départementales du Nord, MS 20H7, printed in CRS 13, 79.

24 The Cambrai nuns most likely used Father Cuthbert Fursden's (Lady Falkland's chaplain until his death in 1638) translation of the Benedictine Rule, which was printed posthumously and dedicated to Anne Cary, according to Fursden's wishes, by Anthony Batt (*The Second Book of the Dialogues of S. Gregorie the Greate . . . Containing the Life and miracles of our Holie Father S. Benedict. To which is Adioned the Rule of the Same Holie Patriarche, Translated into the Englishe Tongue by C.F. Priest and Monke of the Same Order* ([Douay], 1638), 30.

25 Fursden, 34.

26 CRS 13. Father Augustine Baker (d.1641) authored both of these *Lives. Life and Death of Dame Gertrude More* (*c*.1634-5) is extant in incomplete manuscript versions in Downside MSS 40-41, Stanbrook MS 5, Ampleforth MS 60, and Bodleian MS Rawl.c.460. See Justin McCann, 'Father Baker's Dame Gertrude', *Downside Review*

(May 1929), 157–67. The *Life and Death of Dame Margaret Gascoigne* (*c.*1636–7) is extant as Downside MS 42. I refer to the titles of Baker's manuscript works as established by Placid Spearritt, 'Survival of Medieval Spirituality among Exiled English Black Monks', *American Benedictine Review*, 25 (1974), 287–316, based on Justin McCann, 'Descriptive Catalogue of MSS in English and Foreign Libraries for the Works and Life of Father Augustine Baker, O.S.B.', *Memorials of Father Augustine Baker, O.S.B.*, ed. Justin McCann and Hugh Connolly, Publications of the Catholic Record Society, 33 (London, 1933), 274–93. This volume is hereafter referred to as CRS 33.

27 'A Catalogue of the Manuscript bookes belonging to the Liberary of the English Benedictine Nunnes of our Blessed Lady of Good Hope in Paris' (*c.*1690), Paris, Bibliothèque Mazarine, MS 4058.

28 CRS 13, 44–45.

29 Dame Justina Gascoigne was prioress of the Paris community 1665–90. Many of her chapter sermons are still extant (Colwich, St Mary's Abbey, MS H71, 2 vols).

30 Lewalski (1993) proposes Anne as the probable author, or perhaps Lucy (180, and n. 9); Louise Schleiner, *Tudor and Stuart Women Writers* (Bloomington and Indianapolis, 1994) proposes Anne or Elizabeth, based on reported dialogue, 190; Isobel Grundy proposes Anne, maybe Mary, 'Women's History? Writing by English Nuns', in *Women, Writing, History: 1640–1740*, ed. Grundy and Susan Wiseman (London, 1992), 126; Diane Purkiss proposes Mary, *Renaissance Women: The Plays of Elizabeth Cary, The Poems of Aemilia Lanyer* (London, 1994), ix; Weller and Ferguson propose Anne, or maybe Lucy, or neither, 1–2, 51–53; Dorothy Latz, '*Glow-worm Light*': *Writings of Seventeenth Century English Recusant Women from Original Manuscripts* (Salzburg, 1989) proposes Lucy, 9; Simpson 1857 proposes Lucy, 188; Simpson 1861 proposes 'one of Lady Falkland's four daughters'.

31 Donald Foster, 'Resurrecting the Author', *Privileging Gender in Early Modern England*, ed. Jean Brink (Kirksville, Mo, 1993), 145–6, n. 8.

32 Ibid.

33 Colwich, St Mary's Abbey, MS 36, *Sacellum Animae Fidelis* and *Margaritum Spiritulae* (extracts), a *Spiritual Table*, *Fire-steel of Divine Love*, *Of the Infinite Love of God*, and *A Compound of Instructions*.

34 This hand also makes corrections to the rest of *Alphabet*, which is part of Downside Abbey MS 29, pp. 7–8. *Alphabet* is paginated, while *Conversio Morum* is foliated. Dame Barbara Constable makes corrections to *Conversio Morum*. According to its *ex libris*, it was written at Cambrai, but later belonged to Our Lady of Good Hope (Paris), and then St Edmunds (the male English Benedictine monastery in Paris). Lucy also wrote a now-lost book of collections (a 'little book of collections of Dame Magdalene Cary'). This collection (listed in Bibliothèque Mazarine MS 4058, fol. 32) belonged to Our Lady of Good Hope (Paris), which her sister Anne had founded in 1651.

35 In Colwich, St Mary's Abbey, MS H23, p. 44 ('XLth Book of Collec[tions]', in many hands) and Colwich, St Mary's Abbey, MS P2 (the Constitution of Our Lady of Good Hope).

36 Cambrai Constitutions I, 3:14 (1631) (Lille, Archives Départementales du Nord MS 20H1). I am indebted to Dame Margaret Truran, OSB, of Stanbrook Abbey, for this observation.

37 This annotation on fol. 19 should appear on p. 217 of their edition.

38 The fragment of Mary's life of Baker is Stratton-on-the-Fosse, Downside Abbey MS A64, and is labelled as quire 11, pp. 151–66. I disagree with Justin McCann, who identified this manuscript as belonging 'very probably to a life written by Dame

Clementia Cary [Anne]', although I do not dispute his dating of it as 'the period 1645–50', in CRS 33, 154. This life of Baker is similar in style and exposition to Father Leander Prichard's Life of Baker (*c.*1643), also in *Memorials*, 53–154.

39 Lille, Archives Départementales du Nord, MS 20H39, part 5, consisting of poetical paraphrases of Psalms 70–78, 123–48. Dorothy Latz attributes these poems to Anne, based on her death notice, which states that she composed 'spirituall soungs . . . . for *the* solace of *the* sicke and infirme' (Colwich, St Mary's Abbey, MS R3, 'Perticuler Remarkes of our Venerable Mother-Beginners', p. 43, also printed in 'The English Benedictine Nuns of . . . Paris', *Miscellanea* 7, Publications of the Catholic Record Society, 9 (London, 1911), 334–41), and publishes a selection of them in her '*Glow-worm Light': Writings of Seventeenth Century English Recusant Women from Original Manuscripts* (1989), 81–93, as well as in '17th Century English Metaphysical Poetesses Gertrude More, Clementina (*sic.*) Cary, Gertrude Aston Thimelby and Katherine Thimelby Aston', Latz (ed.), *Neglected English Literature: Recusant Writings of the Sixteenth-Seventeenth Centuries* (Salzburg, 1997), 11–24.

40 Lille, Archives Départementales du Nord, MS 20H39, part 9.

41 Lille, Archives Départementales du Nord, MS 20H39, part 11.

42 Downside Abbey MS 68231.

43 To Colonel Grace, dated 10 August 1659; *f* and *z* are particularly similar, as is the unconventional use of the *u/v* graph (*i.e. qv* instead of *qu*).

44 *p* and *K* are formed differently in *Life*.

45 I am grateful to Dame Margaret Truran for this observation.

46 These corrections are in the same hand as his letters at the Bodleian Library (MSS Clarendon 39–41) and the British Library (Sloane MS 3299, fol. 177).

47 I have ruled out Dom Serenus Cressy and Dom Leander Prichard through hand comparisons. I have not ruled out Dom Placid (Henry) Cary, Lady Falkland's youngest son.

48 W.W. Greg makes a valuable distinction between deletions, suggestions for deletions, and unresolved deletions, in his edition of *The Book of Sir Thomas More*, in which he further explains that certain marks in the play are 'merely vague indications of what was objectionable and no attempt is made to sew the loose ends into decent continuity'. Thus, in his annotations to *The Book of Sir Thomas More*, Greg distinguishes between passages 'marked for omission', and passages 'marked for omission and crossed out'. He suggests that the former marks were probably supplied by a censor or 'a scribe under his influence': *The Book of Sir Thomas More*, ed. W.W. Greg, Malone Society Reprints (Oxford, 1911), xv. There is a large literature concerning *The Book of Sir Thomas More*. For recent studies of the revisions to this manuscript, see G. Melchiori and G. Vittorio, '*The Book of Sir Thomas More*: A Chronology of Revision', *Shakespeare Quarterly*, 37 (1986), 291–308.

49 Foster, Beilin, Lewalski, and Weller and Ferguson all accept the *c.*1655 dating.

50 Lille, Archives Départementales du Nord, MS 20H9, fol. 15 (Weller and Ferguson, 210). *Calendar of State Papers Domestic*, PRO 16/521/36, 3 May 1625, from Lord Conway to the Master and Fellows of Pembroke Hall, Cambridge, informs them that Sir Edward Barrett (later Lord Newburgh, uncle to the Cary sisters) had been appointed Resident Ambassador in France, and desired to take Laney as his household chaplain. Barrett never took up the post.

51 Lille, Archives Départementales du Nord, MS 20H9, fol. 42 (Weller and Ferguson, 262). Selby assisted Patrick in Rome, where he was Procurator of the English Benedictine Congregation from 1629 to 1645.

52 Lille, Archives Départementales du Nord, MS 20H9, fol. 44 (Weller and Ferguson,

266). From 1643 to 1645 Reyner was superior at Lambspring, a position not distinguished by a special title.

53 Lille, Archives Départementales du Nord, MS 20H9, fol. 42 (Weller and Ferguson, 262).

54 Brett was Prior of the English Benedictine monastery at St Malo from 1641 to 1643.

55 Lille, Archives Départementales du Nord, MS 20H9, fol. 44, fol. 47v (Weller and Ferguson, 266, 274).

56 Lille, Archives Départementales du Nord, MS 20H9, fol. 13v (Weller and Ferguson, 207); Anne Hardman, *English Carmelites in Penal Times* (London, 1936), 66, 193.

57 Lille, Archives Départementales du Nord, MS 20H9, fol. 44v (Weller and Ferguson, 269).

58 Elsie Duncan-Jones cites Montagu's release date from the Tower as 31 August 1649, but this was the date he was exiled from England ('Two Members of the Falkland Family, Victoria and Henry Cary', *Notes and Queries* (1955), 470, n. 8). The news of Montagu's release would not have taken long to reach Cambrai, since the English monasteries in France and the Spanish Netherlands were frequently visited by royalists, and used as mail drops for sensitive material.

59 G.E.C[okayne] (ed.), *Complete Baronetage*, 5 vols (Exeter, 1900–6), I, 69.

60 For details of Patrick's life and writing, see Pamela Willetts, 'Patrick Cary and his Italian Poems', *British Library Journal*, 2.2 (1976), 109–20; Willetts, 'Patrick Cary: a Sequel', *British Library Journal*, 4.2 (1978), 148–60; Veronica Delany, *The Poems of Patrick Cary* (Oxford, 1978); and John Horden, 'A New Emblem Manuscript by Patrick Cary (1623/4–1657)', *Word and Visual Imagination: Studies in the Interaction of English Literature and the Visual Arts*, ed. Karl Josef Höltgen, *et al.* (Erlangen, 1988), 147–81.

61 Patrick dates a September 1649 letter to Cardinal Barberini from Great Tew (Vatican Library, cod. Barb. Lat. 8620, fol. 182r, transcribed for me by Dr Fabio Bertolo).

62 Delany, 13–15, from a MS dated 20 August 1651 at Abbotsford Library ('Triuiall Ballades writt here in obedience to Mrs. Tomkins commands', consisting of twenty-three secular songs and thirteen religious poems). Other poems are extant in British Library Add. MS 58853 ('Parole di Gio. Patritio Carey messe in musica da diuersi Autori', consisting of eleven Italian songs), and in the Brotherton Collection at the University of Leeds, MS Lt 68 ('Ballades dedicated to The Lady Victoria Uvedale, by their Authour Iohn Patricke Carey', consisting of thirteen poems from the Abbotsford MS, with an emblematic picture and couplet epigram added to each one).

63 British Library, Harley MS 6942, fol. 71: Henry Hammond to Gilbert Sheldon, 4 November [1649]. Hammond dated his letters to Sheldon by day and month only, but 1649 can be deduced since he refers to the death of the third Viscount Falkland (in Montpelier, 27 September 1649) and his impending burial at Great Tew (7 November 1649).

64 Bodleian Library, MS Clarendon 39, fol. 92, 14 March 1649/50, Patrick Cary to Lord Clarendon.

65 Bodleian Library, MS Clarendon 40, fols 169–70, 30 August 1650, Patrick Cary to Lord Clarendon.

66 Bodleian Library, MS Clarendon 41, fol. 51.

67 Lille, Archives Départementales du Nord, MS 20H9, fol. 4 (Weller and Ferguson, 189).

68 Lille, Archives Départementales du Nord, MS 20H9, fol. 44 (Weller and Ferguson, 268).

69 Bodleian Library, MS Clarendon 39, fol. 92.

70 Bodleian Library, MS Clarendon 39, fols 75–76.

71 Bodleian Library, MS Clarendon 40, fols 13–14.

72 Dame Barbara Constable's transcription of Baker's *An Introduction or Preparative to a Treatise on the English Mission* (Downside Abbey, Baker MS 26).

73 The wide range of watermarks on extant manuscripts from Cambrai suggests that the supply came from a variety of sources. In recent years, scholars have cautioned against uncritical use of watermarks as dating evidence, since details about paper distribution, the lifespan of paper moulds, and the gap between the date of manufacture and date of use, are not well-established. Allen Stevenson notes that paper stock used for manuscripts might last for years, while printed books used up stock more rapidly. For paper and watermarks in the seventeenth century, see Allen Stevenson, 'Paper as Bibliographical Evidence', *The Library*, 5th ser. 17, (1962), 197–212; Stephen Spector (ed.), *Essays in Paper Analysis* (Washington, 1987); and Curt F. Bühler, 'Last Words on Watermarks', *Papers of the Bibliographical Society of America*, 67 (1973), 1–16.

74 Lille, Archives Départementales du Nord, MS 20H1, p. 5.

75 Lille, Archives Départementales du Nord, MS 20H1, p. 32.

76 Cambrai, Médiathèque Municipale, MS B1004.

77 Orazio Torsellino, *The history of our B. Lady of Loreto. Translated out of Latin into English*, trans. T[homas] P[rice] ([St Omer], 1608).

78 Cambrai owned three copies of Vincenzo Puccini, *The life of the holy and venerable mother Suor Maria Maddalena de Patsi, a Florentine lady, and religious of the order of the Carmelites . . . translated into English* ([St Omer], 1619).

79 Cambrai, Médiathèque Municipale, MS B1004 lists *La vie de Marguerite de Lorraine* (Douay: Pierre Auroy, 1628).

80 Cambrai, Médiathèque Municipale, MS B1004 dates this life 1630, possibly referring to one of the few seventeenth-century versions of her life, George Conn, *Vita Mariae Stuartae Scotiae Reginae* (Rome, 1624) (most lives of Queen Mary of Scots were written shortly after her death in 1587).

81 This life is listed in Cambrai, Médiathèque Municipale, MS B1004 as a manuscript called 'life of bl[esse]d mother st scolastic'.

82 Pedro de Ribadeneyra, *The life of the holy patriarch S. Ignatius of Loyola, authour, and founder of the Society of Iesus. Translated out of Spanish into English*, trans. [Michael Walpole] ([St Omer, 1622]).

83 [Michael Walpole?], trans., *The lyf of the mother Teresa of Iesus, foundresse of the monasteries of the descalced or bare-footed Carmelite nunnes and fryers, of the first rule. Written by herself, at the commaundement of her ghostly father, and now translated into English, out of Spanish* (Antwerp, 1611).

84 Listed in Cambrai, Médiathèque Municipale MS B1004 as a manuscript called 'translation out of the life works of tholerus by father baker'. Bibliothèque Mazarine MS 4058 has an entry, 'The Life conuersion and Death of Thoulerus' (fol. 143).

85 Possibly Cresacre More, *The life and death of Sir Thomas Moore* (Douai, 1630). Cresacre was the father of Cambrai's founder, Dame Gertrude More.

86 Possibly Jean-Pierre Camus, *Vie et eloge de pieté à la beite memoire de Mr. Claude Bernard, appelé le Pauvre Prestre . . .* 2nd. edn (Paris, 1641), or Jean Puget de la Serre, *La vie du P. Bernard* (Paris, 1642).

87 Cambrai had two copies of John Geninges, *The life and death of Mr. Edward Geninges priest, crowned with martyrdome at London 10 Nouember M.C.XCI* (St Omer, 1614).

88 Possibly Anthony Batt, *A hiue of sacred honie combes containing most sweet and heauenly counsel* (Douay, 1631), which was attributed to St Bernard.

89 Possibly D. Paleotti, *The rule . . . S. Clare. Togeather with the life of S. Catharine of Bologna*, trans. unknown ([St Omer], 1621).

90 Possibly J[ohn] S[weetnam], *S. Mary Magdalens pilgrimage to paradise. Wherein are liuely imprinted the footsteps of her excellent vertues, for sinners to follow, who desire to accompany her thither* (n.p., 1617).

91 For Francis Gascoigne's *Life*, extant as Downside Abbey MS 49, see Philip Jebb, 'A Hitherto Unnoticed Manuscript of the Venerable Augustine Baker', *Downside Review*, 104 (1986), 25–40. Augustine Baker's autobiography is in Bibliothèque Mazarine MS 1755 (*Quadrilogus*, which also includes lives of Baker by Fathers Serenus Cressy, Leander Prichard, and Peter Salvin, transcribed in the late seventeenth century by Dames Mechtilde Tempest, Maura Wytham, and two other scribes); for a printed version see 'The Treatise of the Venerable Father Augustin Baker concerning his own Life', CRS 33, 6–52. Cambrai, Médiathèque Municipale, MS B1004 lists 'the historical narration of life and death of the late Venerable Father Augustin Baker in octavo'.

92 Peter Salvin, 'What I have observed and noted through my own conversation with and relation to the Very Reverend and most Venerable Father, Father Augustine Baker: Concerning Him and his Doctrine', (April 8, 1646), *The Life of Father Augustine Baker, O.S.B.*, ed. Justin McCann (London, 1933), 3–49; Serenus Cressy, 'An historical narration of certain considerable passages of the life of the Venerable Father, Father Augustine Baker, and principally touching the manner and order of his prayer, as likewise of his writings, etc.', ibid, 53–153; Leander Prichard, 'The Second Treatise concerning the Life and Writings of the Venerable Father, F. Augustin Baker, preist of the Holy Order of S. Benet, Congregationis Anglicanae. Written by the Reverend Father, F. Leander Prichard, who had bin his Socio for severall years', CRS 33, 53–154.

93 Cambrai *Constitutions*, Lille, Archives Départementales du Nord, MS 20H1.

94 Fursden 88.

95 Cambrai *Constitutions*, Lille, Archives Départementales du Nord, MS 20H1, p. 20. J[ohn] W[ilson], *The English Martyrologe* ([St Omer], 1608).

96 Cambrai *Constitutions*, Lille, Archives Départementales du Nord, MS 20H1, p. 7. At Cambrai, the book of death-notices was called, 'A Catalogue of the names of the Religious Dames and sisters profes'd of this Conuent of our B*less*ed Lady of Consolation in Cambray who are dead Requiesiat in pace' (Lille, Archives Départementales du Nord, MS 20H7).

97 CRS 13, 79, from Lille, Archives Départementales du Nord, MS 20H7.

98 Cambrai *Constitutions*, Lille, Archives Départementales du Nord, MS 20H1, p. 42, and Paris *Constitutions*, Colwich, St Mary's Abbey, MS P2, p. 23.

99 Listed in Bibliothèque Mazarine, MS 4058, fols. 31–32.

100 Cambrai, Médiathèque Municipale, MS B1004, p. 354.

101 Most of the communities of English nuns moved to England in 1794–5; a few still exist in England and Ireland today. For a systematic but dated account of the movements of the communities, see Peter Guilday, *The English Catholic Refugees on the Continent, 1558–1795* (London, 1914).

102 Margaret J.M. Ezell, *Writing Women's Literary History* (Baltimore, 1993), 45.

103 For example, the Perdita Project, based at Nottingham Trent University, is systematically cataloguing and microfilming manuscript collections of seventeenth-century women. Claire Walker's article, 'Combining Martha and Mary: Gender

and Work in Seventeenth-Century English Cloisters', *Sixteenth Century Journal*, 30.2 (1999), 397–418, her forthcoming book, *Gender and Politics in Seventeenth Century English Convents* (Macmillan, 2000), her article, 'Prayer, Patronage, and Political Conspiracy: English Nuns and the Restoration', *Historical Journal*, 43 (2000), 1–23, and her PhD dissertation, 'Contemplative Communities: English Catholic Convents in France and the Low Countries, 1598–1700' (Dissertation, University of Western Australia, 1995), contribute greatly to our knowledge of early modern English nuns. See also Caroline Bowden's essay, 'The Abbess and Mrs. Brown: Lady Mary Knatchbull and Royalist Politics in Flanders in the late 1650s', *Recusant History* (May 1999), 288–308, and her forthcoming *DNB* articles on Mary Percy, Lettice Tredway, Lucy Knatchbull, Mary Knatchbull, and Susan Hawley. For a general survey of English nuns' writings of the seventeenth century, see Grundy 1992.

Elizabeth Jekyll's Spiritual Diary: Private Manuscript or Political Document?

Elizabeth Clarke

MS Osborn b 221 in the Beinecke Library at Yale is 60 pages long, and was probably once in a vellum binding: the present dark brown morocco binding is modern. It is catalogued, under the name of Elizabeth (Lake) Jekyll, as an autograph manuscript, a commonplace book, 1643–1652. However, all of these apparent facts recorded in the catalogue are inaccurate, including the dating. Like so many women's 'commonplace-books', there is no sense of engagement with traditional common places.[1] Moreover, the document is certainly not autograph, as we shall see. The modern cataloguer's mistake serves to demonstrate the success of the compiler of this document, who was not Elizabeth Jekyll, but someone who set out to create just this impression, of a woman writing only for herself. In fact, the manuscript has a life beyond the events it chronicles between 1643 and 1652, and has relevance within another turbulent period in English history, forty years later.

The document announces itself in true spiritual diary fashion as a record of the blessings of God, after the model of John Rogers, who, in his *Seven Treatises* of 1603, suggested remembering such marks of favour 'to learne experience by them against the times which shall come after'.[2] As with many spiritual diaries, the first entry includes a brief resumé of the subject's earlier life in terms of salvation history. This includes few of the personal details a researcher might hope for from autobiographical writing: as Ollive Cooper scornfully declared in her spiritual diary for 1704, the 'Temperall favours' of one's own life are 'but the dark side of gods goodness', deemed to be less valuable than what happens in the soul.[3] Consequently, the facts about this diarist's 'Temperall favours' have been painstakingly assembled from other sources. Elizabeth Jekyll was born Elizabeth Ward in 1624: 'Lake' is in fact a version of her mother-in-law's maiden name. Her grandmother, daughter of Sir John Clowes of Cheshire, had moved to London and married a citizen of substantial means. Elizabeth Ward's father George was a clothmaker. Her mother's cousin Thomas Clowes was milliner to the Queen in 1633 and Master of the Saddler's Company in 1639.[4] He was an influential Presbyterian member of the City's Common Council in the crucial years of 1647 and 1648.[5]

None of this personal history is evident on the first page, which in orthodox fashion appears to trace the mercies of God. However, in a move which becomes an interpretative key to the whole document, 'blessings' are immediately redefined as 'afflictions': they are 'mercies that hath [*sic*] done me good against my will'. Four events are specified as such: her bodily weakness, the loss of two children, her survival into redeemed adulthood, and her vocation: 'I desire to bless god that in fullness of time he was pleased to call me, and to leave them that were in the same family and of the same blood'. The repeated rhetorical formulation of the first page, 'I desire to bless God', insists on a particular personal allegiance: Elizabeth Jekyll is aware that this phrase is a distinguishing mark of radical Puritan culture, for she reports comment on her husband's use of it as 'the very speech of a Roundhead'. (p.4) The first entry is 'signed' and dated 1643, although, as we shall see, this signature cannot be authentic. The contents of the first page seem to serve as a kind of covenant with God 'at the beginning of this booke', a covenant to record a particular kind of information, that which can be classified as God's blessing and therefore turned to His praise, even if it involves some theological sophistication to do so.

The rationale for the spiritual journal is overwhelmingly spiritual and dogmatic, involving a selective recording of events that can be somewhat frustrating for a modern scholar reading in a spirit of historical enquiry. The principles for selection are determined by the statement of faith with which Elizabeth Jekyll heads page 2: 'Christ has an uncontrolable power at his pleasure whereby he dothe overrule the visible world'. As Calvin had insisted, there was no such thing as the operation of chance: all events were consciously willed by God.[6] This doctrine was the basis of the various permutations of providential thinking which, as Blair Worden has charted, dominated the interpretation of political as well as personal events in the seventeenth century.[7] Deliverance from fire and household accident were particularly easy to ascribe to a merciful God: the tendency of Stuart chimneys to fall down or flare up may be explained by the tractability of such events for the discipline of the spiritual journal, rather than by the realities of social history. Elizabeth Jekyll's family had their fair share of household mishaps: her eldest living son, Thomas, was particularly accident-prone, locking himself in a room with an open fire at the age of 18 months, and, at the age of three, falling into a water-butt and threatening to fall out of the highest window in the house. (pp. 14, 16, 17.) Happily he survived to become a well-respected clergyman.[8] However, the vicissitudes of everyday life did not always fit into the scheme requisite for theodicy. Childbirth, of course, was already scripted for women in numerous sermons and tracts, perhaps for the very reason that complications and peri-natal death resisted easy interpretation.[9] Events surrounding birth are given plenty of space in women's spiritual journals, probably because, on the authority of I Timothy 2.15, that event was regarded as having significance for a woman's spiritual life. For that reason, it is rare that an unorthodox sentiment is allowed to surface.[10] 'Delivery' in childbirth, with its connotations of God's saving intervention, can mean anything from a safe birth with no complications to death of both mother and child but amongst suitably holy manifestations which, in spiritual discourses of the seventeenth century, guarantee a passage into heaven.[11]

Elizabeth Jekyll has to perform this particular strategy of redefinition more than once. She seems to have suffered many miscarriages before bringing a live child into the world in 1643. God is thanked for 'his Wonderfull delivering me from the great pain and perril of childbirth': the baby, however, was dead (p. 6). The birth of twins in February 1645 looked like an unequivocal 'deliverance', producing two pages of outpourings of praise. One boy, however, only lived a month, and it was five days after his death that Elizabeth had a premonition about her surviving son John and rushed into the nurse's room at night just in time to save him from accidental smothering. This account, with its conventional formulation within providential blessing, serves to highlight her silence about the actual deaths of both children—John, rescued so miraculously, only lived a month longer. In spite of the death of Samuel earlier in this month, Elizabeth Jekyll ends the entry for March with her favourite formula, 'A Month of Mercie to Mee' (p. 11).

Elizabeth Jekyll's years of unsuccessful pregnancies coincided with the events of the first Civil War, and the recording of personal events is interspersed with news of the progress of the conflict, although in common with the policy of many of the Parliamentarian newsbooks she only records the successes of the Parliamentary army. David Underdown has suggested that she read such publications and used them for her account, but in fact the formulas she uses to record such victories have no equivalent either in the newsbooks or the pamphlets, and are distinctively her own: they are resonant of the rhetoric she uses for other entries in the journal.[12] 'In Aprill 1644, The mighty power of God was seen also in delivering of Selby'. 'It pleased God wonderfully to Look in Mercie upon this poor sinfull Kingdom . . . in delivering up Bridgewater

& Sherborne Castle which were very strong places' (p. 8, p. 12). Moreover, the 'spin' put on such news by Elizabeth Jekyll is not easily attributable to printed sources. Her vision of God's intervention in the capture of Bristol in September 1645 is distinctive.

> Sʳ Thomas treated with Prince Rupert which kept that City of Bristoll for the kings plundering use, But Prince Rupert was so high in terms that they could not agree, Sʳ Thomas offered him very fair this was upon monday being the 8th of September 1645, but he would not take it and so it pleased God to order it for the best, for yᵉ Parliament soon after that they agreed with him upon much lower and better termes then at first was offered him and So Prince Rupert delivered up the Citty of Bristoll on ffryday yᵉ 19th September 1645 thus we see the Lord can make his Enemies do what he sees best and so make them serve him in the way of his providence (p. 13).

This is an even stronger version of God's providence and partiality than is evident in the Parliamentarian newsbook accounts. Printed versions of the events of September 1645 tend to stress the mercy of Cromwell in storming Bristol at the point that he realised its Royalist garrison were plundering it.[13] Elizabeth Jekyll could have made her deductions about God's purpose from the detailed publication of the first terms offered to Rupert compared with the eventual terms on which the surrender took place, which is offered in *A Perfect Diurnall*.[14] She is fascinated by the revelation of God's hand in the particular negotiations of Royalist surrender, and clearly scoured printed accounts and newsbooks for details: Rupert's rashness in engaging battle on Marston Moor is attributed to the intervention of God because it occasioned the surrender of York upon lower terms (p. 8). Specific numbers of horse, troops and cannon captured are often quoted in this manuscript, such as in the description of the battle of Selby in April 1644: 'the Lord much Honoured Sʳ Thomas Fairfaxs and delivered the Towne into his hands wᵗʰ 500 horse & 1000 foot' (p. 8). These are probably taken from printed accounts and newsbooks for which such lists are favourite copy.[15] Elizabeth Jekyll, or the circle within which she discussed such news, favoured biblical parallels as a hermeneutic for contemporary events. She provides a Scriptural paradigm for the attempted storming of Plymouth by an overwhelmingly superior Royalist force on the 3rd of December 1643 (the date is mistranscribed in the manuscript). The story as she tells it is irresistibly reminiscent of Gideon's strategy in Judges 7, 16–23:

> in their distress it pleased God to put it into their harts to sound up six Drums (but had not one man to follow them), which when the Enimie

heard they were stricken with such Terror, that though they had gotten within their Workes, and had 2000 fresh men comeing to their Aide yet they took them to their feet and fled; thus you see if God stricks terror, the Enimie must fly when none pursued them (p.7).

The hermeneutical thrust of this striking story cannot be found in any printed accounts of the incident.

Elizabeth Jekyll's social life seems to have revolved around the radical City church of St Stephen Walbrook. She records visiting the house of Mr Juxon. The Juxon family figure largely in the parish records of St Stephen Walbrook: they were prosperous sugar-bakers, and Arthur Juxon & co. had to pay the third highest rates in Walbrook Ward in 1632.[16] Nicholas Juxon was churchwarden of St Stephen's in 1654: in 1646 the churchwarden was the radical merchant Peter Houblon, one of the famous Huguenot brothers, and he remained a faithful attender of the vestry meeting, as Elizabeth Jekyll's husband did, well into the 1660s.[17] It would not be surprising if this radical merchant community had their own distinctive view of events, formed from first-hand accounts rather than newsbooks. Elizabeth Jekyll tends to record battles from the north-east and south-west, and it was to these corners of the country that her husband John, son of a knight and wealthy freeman of the Fishmonger's Company, often travelled on business. One incident is treated twice in this manuscript, once as a brief entry and once as a more developed narrative, a common feature of the spiritual journal (pp. 6, 3–4). This is the arrest of John Jekyll in Bristol when the city was taken by Royalists in July 1643. He had gone to collect debts, but had the misfortune to be recognised and denounced, as 'the greatest Roundhead in all the parish' by a former neighbour now in the King's army, a sugar-baker named, appropriately, Worme. Although Jekyll was not allowed recourse to friends in Bristol, deliverance came from an unexpected quarter: a letter from the Royalist commander Sir Lewis Dyve secured his release. No information about possible prior connection between Dyve and the Jekyll family is offered, although the familiarity with the City merchant community demonstrated in Dyve's letters of 1646–7 does offer a context for such a relationship: it suits Elizabeth's purpose to stress the utter unlikelihood of such an event as being more likely to signify God's miraculous intervention.[18] The spiritually significant details of this special providence are, however, minutely traceable. 'They were not only limited in the Power of their hand, but in the power of there tounges' states Elizabeth, meaning, simply, that they asked him the wrong questions: they wanted to know whether he had been at the battle of Brentford when in fact he had been in Lincolnshire on business at the time. If they

had asked him whether he had taken the Covenant he would have had
to incriminate himself: he had taken it just the preceding Sunday (p. 4).
It is touching that God intervenes not only to save Jekyll from imprisonment but also to preserve his innocence.

This God is primarily interested in the spiritual development of His
people, and it is to this end that he manipulates kings, commanders, and
the circumstances of everyday life. When this grand narrative is not so
obvious, the diarist is in difficulties: after the end of the First Civil War
Elizabeth Jekyll apparently lost the plot. It may be that the responsibilities of a growing family—four births followed that of Thomas in 1646
at the rate of roughly one every summer—took precedence over politics
for a while. The diary offers evidence, however, that this period saw a
disillusionment in the Jekyll household. The entry headed 1648, the
year of Presbyterian/Independent conflict in the City, covers only personal blessings, and in contrast with the previous joyful formulation it is
ominously subscribed 'A year of publick troubles' (p. 15). In 1649 and
1650 only private blessings of an unproblematic sort are recorded, such
as Thomas' recovery from smallpox, and her husband's escape from
injury when he fell from a horse (p. 17). A note possibly copied from a
sermon laments 'O poor England how low art thou brought by the
pride of Ignorant Zealots' (p. 41). This sentiment places the Jekylls
firmly in line with the Presbyterian backlash in the City against the
Army, a suspicion confirmed by the very long and troubled entry for
1651, covering John Jekyll's arrest for involvement in the Presbyterian
Plot (pp. 18–23).[19]

The Jekyll family's appetite for news had continued unabated
throughout these difficult years, as John Jekyll's testimony at
Christopher Love's trial makes clear. Shortly after the execution of
Charles I a group of Presbyterian ministers and London citizens
shocked by this event had begun to meet at Love's house on Tuesdays,
to see friends, pray, and hear news in a kind of 'club' as co-defendant
John Gibbons, servant of Denzil Holles, called it.[20] In 1650 Jekyll was
churchwarden at St Stephen Walbrook where another of the conspira-
tors, and his lifelong friend, Thomas Watson, was minister. Christopher
Love, minister of St Lawrence Pountney, was later executed for his part
in this 'Presbyterian Plot' to bring back Charles II with the help of
Scottish Covenanters and Royalist sympathisers. It seems from evidence at Love's trial that Jekyll had been involved in a clandestine net-
work of communication using City shops as post-offices: letters left at
Captain Potter's apothecary shop in Blackfriars by the infamous
Colonel Bamfield were brought by him to Jekyll who opened them and
took them to Love.[21] These letters were from the Scottish Covenanter

leaders asking this wealthy group of London citizens for £10,000 for arms and shipping.[22] The very existence of these letters implied a conspiracy against the Commonwealth government, and Jekyll was clearly implicated. Elizabeth, in the throes of a difficult pregnancy, gropes for an understanding of God's providence here, but this circumstance resists interpretation. She tries to interpret the arrest in the light of his subsequent release, 'he bringeth into troubles that he may shew his power in delivering out of troubles'. However, this explanation is clearly too simple: Jekyll was released in return for his testimony, which was crucial to Love's conviction, and so was understandably 'under the Aspertion of Men'. 'Afflictions have A Voice', Elizabeth declares, but it takes her much soul-searching to decide what the voice is saying. Characteristically, she locates blame for her circumstance in her own sin in loving her husband too much:

> upon due Examination I found my hart to Much Sett upon my Deare Husband, who is Most dear to me and not without some plea for he is, to Avoyd particulars least my pen should do as my hart has done run beyound bounds; I only say he is worthy of all the Affections yt are lawfull to be given to a Creature, but here was and is too much my failing I did I fear look upon him in a higher Nature the Creature should be and for that cause I perswade my self that God hath Afflicted me (pp. 19–20).

This narrative closure seems to have brought her psychological release, or else she is striving very hard for the correct attitude of praise, for the last two pages of this entry consist of a more than usually rapturous recitation of Biblical verses of thanksgiving.

The dilemma for the keeper of the spiritual journal is when to assume that the meaning of events has been finally revealed, and to write the final version of the story. As Edward Gee wrote in 1650, 'The Argument from Providence is *ab Eventu* or from the issue of a thing; they then that will Conclude from this medium must tarry a while longer, even till the end be seene, and till the winding up of Providence'.[23] The description of unremittingly negative events is often delayed, because Providential thinking dictates that apparent tragedy has divine justification, and such a rationale, or rationalisation, is not always easy to arrive at. Romans 8:28 is the master-text here: 'All things shall work, yea, work together for good', as Anne Venn wrote to her sister in 1653.[24] The narrative and rhetorical patterns of the spiritual journal reveal the divine imperative to demonstrate the truth of this text, but chronology is often a casualty. There is no question of recording every event on the day that it happened, as in a conventional diary: for Elizabeth Jekyll, as for other compilers of spiritual journals, events were only recorded, or perhaps written into their final form, when their spiritual significance had become clear.[25] The exact date for Elizabeth Jekyll's entries for '1648' and '1651' is not given, but in both she is striving for a vision of events that will reveal God's purpose. The subsequent entry is completely undated, and masquerades as a theological reflection. It is headed 'What is Originall Sin', but it contains information about eleven tragedies in her life, nine of which we have not heard of before (pp. 25–28). For the first time we hear of her miscarriages, and the deaths of her parents and two brothers. The hermeneutic frame within which these disasters are finally voiced is that affliction is necessary 'to bring us out of Love with Sin': each of these tragedies is represented as God's attempt to correct her. This is entirely in line with the principle stated in the first page of her document, but the tone is different. The grim framework for God's dealings with her is perhaps the only one within which tragedy can be voiced: praise is not possible here. Her final note is dated and timed: 13th January 1652/3, 'being Thursday night' (p. 28: see PLATE 1). Here she records in a 'memorandum', perhaps to be

PLATE 1. *The 'final' memorandum of Elizabeth Jekyll in her spiritual diary, dated 13 January 1652[/3]: New Haven, Yale University, Beinecke Library, Osborn Collection b 221, pp. 28-29 (Original size 198 × 155mm.) Reproduced by permission of the James Marshall and Marie-Claire Osborn Collection, Beinecke Library, Yale University.*

copied up later into a more coherent entry like the others, the easing of the pain she was in. This is, in fact, the last page of her book: parish records show that she died at the beginning of March, a week after the baby to whom she had just given birth, at the age of 29.

The end of Elizabeth's life is not, however, the end of the document. Three poems, two on prayer and one on death, apparently signed with her name, presumably to indicate Elizabeth Jekyll's own authorship, follow neatly and immediately from the last diary entry: they are allowed a prominent place in the manuscript, as they are copied on one side of the double page only (pp. 31, 33, 35). The first poem is entitled 'upon Death' and 'signed' 'Elizabeth Jekyll 1652/ A year of great Mortality' (PLATE 2). It is 22 lines long, in rhyming couplets, with slightly irregular metre. The scribe has left a gap in Line 7 as if a word cannot be deciphered. It is a consolatory poem offering the orthodox sentiments of *memento mori*. The two poems that follow are entitled 'upon Prayer': the first is 20 lines long and is anti-Papist in sentiment, attacking Catholic practices of praying to saints and to Mary. The second is 14 lines long and is also dated 1652. The first two lines give an indication of the whole:

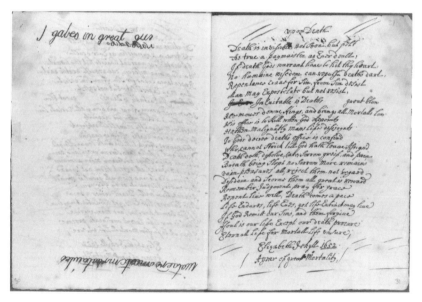

PLATE 2. *The poem 'vpon Death' appended to Elizabeth Jekyll's spiritual diary: New Haven, Yale University, Beinecke Library, Osborn Collection b 221, pp. 30-31 (Original size 198 × 155mm.) Reproduced by permission of the James Marshall and Marie-Claire Osborn Collection, Beinecke Library, Yale University.*

Ffear not to pray to god pray not cease
Till thou recieve both supply and Encrease.

This spiritually orthodox, rhetorically unsophisticated style of poetry is sometimes a feature of women's spiritual journals, but, perhaps surprisingly, the addition of one or more simple poems to a prose work is one of the features of religious writing by women beginning to move into published authorship. Often this type of poetry has the character of a psalm— it expresses gratitude in particular circumstances. What this discourse never does is pretend to rhetorical display. It is as if credentials are established by this biblical, orthodox, humble rhetorical form that help to add force to the accompanying prose work as similarly sincere and God-glorifying.[26] Elizabeth Jekyll's poetry may well have been copied from another notebook, but its transcription into a prose manuscript is entirely to be expected if Osborn MS b 221 is a product of scribal publication, rather than the autograph and private document it appears to be at first glance.

The fact of Elizabeth Jekyll's death is absent from the manuscript, as it would have been if she herself had been the scribe, but features of layout such as the lack of hiatus after the final diary entry, and the prominent position of the poems within the document, would of course have been impossible to achieve by Elizabeth Jekyll herself. Sermon notes and spiritual reflections continue the manuscript, which finishes, at the reverse end, with three lists of family records: one of the birthdates of her husband and his siblings, one of the deaths within her own family, and one of the birthdates of her surviving children. Suspicions that this is not an autograph document are aroused by slight errors characteristic of a copyist: the date of her father's death is given as 1649 rather than 1646, and a gap has been left where the copyist seems not to have been able to read the word 'Bradford' (p. 8).[27] What we know of women's manuscript practice indicates that spiritual diaries were often transcribed as fair copies by the writers themselves.[28] However, conclusive proof that this is not Elizabeth Jekyll's hand, nor that of a scribe she herself commissioned, is offered by the final entry, the only transcription of a printed text in the manuscript: 'The Lady Lyles "Dying Speech" ' (pp. 43–45). Alicia Lisle was one of the most famous 'Western Martyrs' of the Monmouth Rebellion, whose trials at the court of Judge Jeffreys, executions and dying words were publicised after the Glorious Revolution in several popular volumes.[29] This text, in an identical hand to the rest of the manuscript, must post-date 1685, when Alicia Lisle was executed. The whole document is thus definitely a transcription. Parish registers for St Stephen Walbrook show that Elizabeth Jekyll died in 1653, over thirty years before Alicia Lisle went to the scaffold.

At this point a complete reassessment of authorship, readership and significance of this manuscript has to be undertaken. As well as the internalised editing process which is a feature of the spiritual diary, this document has been subject to an external editor. Whoever transcribed these texts—the only 'signature' in this document is that of Elizabeth Jekyll—has put together a collection of religious writings with a peculiarly powerful signification. Osborn MS b 221 combines several forms of religious writing which were used as effective political propaganda in the seventeenth century. During the Civil Wars there had been a demand for a kind of secret knowledge about the main protagonists, a hidden narrative which would vindicate political and military action if it depicted complete moral integrity and a devout relationship with God. Hence the obsession with the discovery and publication of private letters during the Civil War.[30] The more 'private' the writing, the greater propaganda value it had when published. Hence also the importance of 'closet-writing', of which the spiritual journal is a classic example, which was read as if it retained a trace of the presence of God, assumed to be present in the closet, as no-where else except the deathbed, or scaffold. The validating criteria of privacy and piety line these discourses up with seventeenth-century ideals of female-authored writing, and, I have argued elsewhere, allow entry into political authorship for some women.[31]

However, for both women and men, the crucial element of privacy is compromised by an attempt to publish. Scribal publication seems to have been one way out of this dilemma. The Whig peer Lord Somers, whose sister married John Jekyll's son Joseph, collected political pamphlets, and included a manuscript copy of the Parliamentary general William Waller's prison writing, his 'Vindication', in his collection.[32] Confinement, including the restriction to manuscript, was not merely a condition of limitation, as Neil Keeble considers it for Lucy Hutchinson's *Life of Colonel Hutchinson*, but a source of its power as a persuasive document.[33] Several women with urgent if local political projects took advantage of the assumed status of their spiritual journals to persuade a limited audience. Both Alice Thornton and Anne Halkett had accusations of unchastity to refute, the latter with the notorious Colonel Bamfield. Alice Thornton obligingly records the success of her circulation of her 'Life', her name for her manuscript journal, amongst her enemies, who included members of the local aristocracy, and who took the document as absolute proof of her personal virtue.[34] Anne Halkett's fourteen volumes of devotions, alongside which her better-known 'Life' should be read, show a mastery of all discursive forms signifying of the sacred.[35] Elizabeth Jekyll's spiritual diary functions as a classic 'Exemplary Life'.

'Scribal publication' is a phrase which covers these acts of self-vindication, but it is also available for political uses of manuscript writing. However, it is difficult to assign to any document with certainty. It is an event born of the necessities of a particular moment in history, and in the absence of any testimony to the transcribing or reading of such a manuscript (such evidence is rare) the historical context has to be carefully reconstructed. The transcription of 'The Lady Lyles "Dying Speech" ' at the end of Osborn b 221 suggests an immediate context of 1680s Dissenting, and possibly Whig, activism for the manuscript as a whole. The 'Dying Speech', as a genre, had of course a religious and political function inherited from the discourse of martyrology: Peter Lake and Michael Questier have recently examined how it functioned early in the seventeenth century.[36] In 1683 the frantic attempts to undermine Lord William Russell's execution speech reveal how powerful such discourses were still considered as tools for propaganda. Melinda Zook has explained the post-1688 publishing phenomenon of 'Dying Speeches' as a strategy to forge a Whig tradition out of the equivocal and difficult events of the 1680s, taken on by the journalist John Tutchin, who was not averse to making up documents if he could not find them.[37] The version of the speech in this manuscript, however, is closer to that of an unlicensed pamphlet in the British Library dating probably from 1685, *The last Words of Coll. Richard Rumbold, Mad. Alicia Lisle, Alderman Henry Cornish, and Mr. Richard Nelthrop: Who were Executed in England and Scotland for High Treason in the Year 1685*. The context of the immediate aftermath of the Monmouth rebellion and the Jeffreys trials, when most of the Whig resistance to James had been rounded up or had fled to Holland, gives this manuscript an urgent political relevance.

Another aspect of this manuscript indicates its continuity with a feature of polemical publishing in the 1680s. At the end of the 'Dying Speech' is a list of the names of the jury who convicted Alicia Lisle. This does not appear in any printed version of the speech, and is not published until Howell's State Trials of 1719 (the result, as J. G. Muddiman would have it, of another Whig fabrication).[38] The list is slightly garbled as compared with the printed version, as if the names had been passed on orally: this factor supports a date for the transcription close to the events of the trial and execution.[39] Lists of juries are part of a particular persuasive form in the 1680s, in pamphlets addressed to them with advice or insult, or simply with the apparently neutral intention of making known who the individuals serving with them are. The 1681 pamphlet by 'Philononus', *Ignoramus Vindicated*, despite its title, is an indictment of the jury that failed to convict the Earl of Shaftesbury. It continues with a list of their names. This is the only political defence against the practice of 'packing' juries in which both sides, 'loyal' or 'fanatic', engaged, and which made sheriffs' elections the focus of so much contention, as they had the power of selection of juries. The effect of this 'naming and shaming' is to make members of juries personally responsible.[40] Alicia Lisle's last words as copied in this manuscript are these: 'I forgive him that desired to be taken off the Grand Jury and put on the petty Jury that he might be the more nearly concerned in my Death'. This apparent gesture of forgiveness is meant to heap coals of fire on the heads of the named individuals, and it was obviously seen as particularly effective: John Dunton included this extract in his 'edited highlights' of dying speeches, a 1701 volume called *The Merciful Assizes; or, a Panegyric on the late Lord Jeffreys*. Clearly the compiler of Osborn MS b 221 is augmenting the power of this persuasive form by publishing names of the jury which are missing from all the printed versions.

However, the main content of Osborn b 221, apparently transcribed at the same time as Alicia Lisle's speech, is Elizabeth Jekyll's diary, with its account of John Jekyll's activities. I have argued that some diaries are used as justification of the lives of their authors: but this document, I would suggest, functions to vindicate Elizabeth Jekyll's husband. John Jekyll died in 1690 at the age of 79, having completed at least four decades of radical political action in the City. He is almost unknown among historians, a feature of his talent for behind-the-scenes action, for in 1676 the mayor of Bristol was reported as saying that 'no man has more interest & favour here [*i.e.* the City of London] as Mr Jekel'.[41] Andrew Marvell spoke in his defence in the Commons in 1670, a further clue: as leader in the riots against the Conventicle Act he had refused to accept his arrest for riot as lawful and tried various legal manoeuvres, such as causing the Mayor to be arrested for wrongful imprisonment and taking his case to Parliament.[42] Despite being a loyal member of the vestry meeting, first at St Stephen Walbrook, 1649–1667, then at the City church of St Lawrence Jewry (where Henry Cornish was also a member), he is described as the 'sollicitor-general' and 'tresuar' for the four Nonconformist churches in Bristol—one Presbyterian, two Baptist, and one Independent.[43] It was to him they wrote when threatened with persecution in 1675, and with immediate result, for Jekyll's friends in the House of Lords authorised him to write a letter so intimidating that the nonconformists' enemies were drunk for the rest of the day.[44] He and his son John were prosecuted in the trial for riot at the shrieval elections of 1682 of fourteen prominent city figures that was the climax of the Exclusion Crisis for the City, and which, according to Bishop Burnet, nearly provoked full-scale rebellion against Charles II.[45] Letters to and from the Secretary of State in the 1670s and 80s show that he was constantly spied on, a focus for hatred and suspicion on the part of the 'loyal' party. His most recent foray into the political arena at the time of the unlicensed 'Dying Speech' pamphlet had been to appear as a witness for Henry Cornish, the sheriff doomed to be hanged, drawn and quartered for a patently ill-founded charge of complicity in the Rye House Plot. Jekyll was not much help as a witness: the judges remembered all too well his previous appearance with Henry Cornish when they were both convicted of riot in 1682.[46]

1685 was the nadir of Whig fortunes. The Royalist establishment had gained control of the printing press through which so much of Whig propaganda was effectively disseminated. The radical presses were, on the whole, silent: the Baptist printer Francis Smith, who had campaigned alongside Jekyll for the election of the Lord Mayor in 1681 and the sheriffs in 1682, was in prison.[47] A recently-introduced bylaw making it compulsory to declare the names of printers on every publication meant that those who produced pamphlets such as *The Last Words* were taking a huge risk, particularly as the Lord Chief Justice had wanted to supervise all publication in connection with the Cornish trial.[48] However, the Whigs were adept at the passing on of manuscript writing through the coffee houses and the Penny Post.[49] At John Starkey's bookshop, for a price, you could read a pamphlet on the premises or have a copy of it made.[50] It is scribal publication that I am suggesting is the mode for Elizabeth Jekyll's journal.

At the point that Elizabeth Jekyll's diary was probably transcribed, Jekyll was one of the few activists who had not fled abroad, or been imprisoned. The document reveals a much younger man in a different phase of his radical career, but it does testify to his spirituality and integrity, both qualities claimed by the Dissenting side as peculiarly their own. It shows him as motivated by religious principle, and his involvement in the Christopher Love plot gives him impeccable credentials as a very early Presbyterian Royalist, what in the 1680s Whig propaganda would call a 'true Royalist'. The diary helps to establish Jekyll as a model of Whig activism, and the aura of piety in which he is presented is characteristic of Nonconformist activists. Gervase Disney, the radical Nottingham Dissenter who was cousin to the unfortunate printer of Monmouth's 1685 *Declaration*, wrote an autobiographical document very similar to Elizabeth Jekyll's in the same year, also including poems and theological reflections, although it was not printed until after his death in 1692 (perhaps it was circulated in manuscript at an earlier date). It has the identical rhetorical function: to justify the subject's activism by demonstration of his absolute and private piety.

Osborn b 221, however, has a particular, feminine quality. David Underdown notes that Elizabeth Jekyll's diary with the repetition of her 'signature' is followed by Alicia Lisle's dying speech, selected from a pamphlet in which she is the only woman out of four Whig martyrs. Both these kinds of writing carry the signification of holiness, as I have suggested, but the effect is more powerful if the author is female: perhaps the more obvious choice from the volume would have been the speech of Henry Cornish, who was well known to the family. Even in the 1680s, women are still assumed to be incapable of explicitly political action: the wives of radical printers exploited their feminine immunity to carry on their husbands' businesses in difficult times.[51] Exemplary biography, with which these two genres is linked, exploits the perceived relation between feminine weakness and divine inspiration. One of the earliest exemplary lives of a woman, *The Christian Life and Death of Mistris Katherin Brettergh*, makes this connection, and its potential for propaganda, explicit.

> It must needs be a divine Religion and truth comming from God, that thus can fill the heart and mouth of a weake woman, at the time of death, with such admirable comfort. And a wretched conceit, and mere Antichristian, is that Religion, which so hateth and persecuteth this faith, which is thus able to leave the true-hearted professors thereof, with such unspeakeable peace unto their graves.[52]

This work went into 34 editions between 1591 and 1700, and must have gone some way towards forming the ideal of feminised Christian heroism in the seventeenth century. The assumption is that any bravery by a woman in the face of death has to be by a kind of divine inspiration, and this premise provides ultimate justification for her spiritual life, and, by extension, for her cause. Alicia Lisle was one of the favourite Western Martyrs because she was an old woman, and therefore assumed to be politically innocent (indeed, her defence rests on a plea of naivity) and physically weak. This portrayal does not fit with Bulstrode Whitelocke's view of the imperious wife of an important Commonwealth official with whom he had to share his house in the late 1640s, nor with the fact that she held conventicles in her house: but the courageous death of a powerless person is taken in the seventeenth century to signify the particular intervention of God to strengthen and inspire and therefore vindicate His chosen ones.[53] As we have seen, Elizabeth Jekyll's journal apparently finishes on a note of praise in the face of illness, desperate circumstances, and death. This is one of the features of exemplary biography, functioning to justify the subject's particular spiritual allegiance, as in Samuel Clarke's famous 1662 volume

of exemplary Lives. The polemical context of the genre is underlined by
the identification of an 'other' within such a text: *The Christian Life and
Death of Mistris Katherin Brettergh* names the collective enemy as 'Popish
Recusants, Church Papists, prophane Atheists, and carnall Protestants',
locating the tract in Elizabeth Jekyll's brand of religious rhetoric, the
terms of which were picked up and used in Whig propaganda at the end
of the century.

Wendy Wall has pointed out the symbolic capital to be gained for a
woman's writing if the author is actually dead.[54] The spiritual journal
of a dead woman is extremely powerful: it is purged of any self-publi-
cising impulse and carries with it a signification of truth and holiness. I
am sure David Norbrook is right to suggest that the Mrs Hutchinson
whose spiritual diary Lord Anglesey spent a whole morning reading in
that crucial year of 1682 is Lucy—to bequeath such a persuasive document to a powerful man is just the kind of thing she would do.[55] This is
why, I believe, no name other than Elizabeth Jekyll's appears as author,
compiler or scribe in Osborn b 221. It is important that the document
is linked with dead women rather than a scribe who may or may not be
female but who is probably still alive: it thus lays claim to a particular
kind of feminised spirituality which was perceived to have maximum
persuasive effectiveness.

There is one final piece of circumstantial evidence to support the
hypothesis that, rather than a document of private piety, this is a published discourse with political signification. In May 1685, about six
months before the date at which this manuscript was probably transcribed, James II directed the Court of Aldermen to take tough action
against 'the printing and dispensing of severall treasonous, Scandalous
and Sedicious books pamphletts and Libells'. The action proposed was
directed against all non-members of the Stationers' Company involved
in printing or bookselling. They had to leave their own livery and join
the Stationers' Company, thus coming under strict regulation: or cease
their trade in pamphlets. The first name on the list is John Jekyll. The
second name is John Junior, Elizabeth Jekyll's second son. Only a tiny
fraction of those named joined the Stationers' Company a fortnight
later, and the Jekylls were not among them.[56] In these circumstances,
continuation of any printing activity would have been extremely difficult, particularly as the Monmouth Rebellion intervened. John Jekyll
was arrested in June and released only after petitioning the King.[57]
However, it is unlikely that even under these unfavourable circumstances he abandoned his forty-year-long career in politics and propaganda: four years later, at the age of 78, he was standing again for
Chamberlain of the City. Selected scribal publication of his wife's diary,

that harmless, private, feminine form, is just one avenue a master-strategist might have taken at a dangerous time. The careful selection of the manuscript's contents, as well as the historical and social context in which it was compiled, would constitute effective propaganda in the difficult period between the Monmouth rebellion and the Glorious Revolution: its circulation in manuscript would ensure freedom from prosecution.

NOTES

Much of this article was written and researched during a Leverhulme Fellowship for the year 1999. I am grateful to the Leverhulme Foundation for making this possible.

1 Ann Moss does not believe that women kept authentic commonplace-books in this sense: *Printed Commonplace-Books and the Structuring of Renaissance Thought* (Oxford, 1996), p. viii.

2 Richard Rogers, *Seven Treatises, Containing such direction as is gathered out of the Holie Scriptures* (London, 1603), p. 335.

3 London, Dr Williams's Library MS 24.49, f. 19v.

4 Harleian Visitations of London, 1634 (London, 1880), I, 176; J. R. Woodhead, *The Rulers of London 1660–1689* (London, 1965), p. 49.

5 James Farnell, 'The Politics of the City of London, 1649–57' (unpublished PhD diss., University of Chicago, 1963), p. 356.

6 John Calvin, *The Institution of Christian Religion* (London, 1634), pp. 85–88.

7 Blair Worden, 'Providence and Politics in Cromwell's England', *Past and Present*, 109 (1985), 55–99.

8 See *DNB*, Thomas Jekyll 1646–1699, for an account of his life and the titles of his published sermons.

9 *A Handkercher for Parents Wet Eyes* (1630); John Flavel's *A Token for Mourners: or, the advice of Christ to a distressed Mother, bewailing the death of her dear and only Son* (1674); Jeremy Taylor, *The Rules and Exercises of Holy Living*, 7th edition (London, 1663), p. 135 (1st edition, 1650).

10 Ann Hulton, sister of Sarah Henry, did speculate, sinfully, on the wastefulness of pregnancy and labour if the child died very shortly afterwards: *The Diary of Mrs. Sarah Savage* (London, 1829), p. 327.

11 Blair Worden noted the peculiar variations in circumstances surrounding childbirth which could be subsumed into a providential scheme: see 'Providence and Politics in Cromwell's England', p. 83.

12 David Underdown, *A Freeborn People: Politics and the Nation in Seventeenth-Century England* (Oxford, 1996), p. 110.

13 See these newsbooks for early September 1645: *A Perfect Diurnall* no. 111: *Mercurius Veridicus* no. 21: *Kingdom's Weekly Intelligencer* nos. 116–117. Some newsbooks fail to report the outcome of the siege of Bristol, as sometimes happens when many printed accounts are circulating: for example, I. R., *A True Relation of the Storming of Bristol* (London, 13 September 1645); *Lieut. Generall Cromwells Letter to the House of Commons of all the Particulars of taking the City of Bristol* (London, 18 September 1645).

14 *A Perfect Diurnall* no. 111 (8–15 September 1645), p. 882.

15 *Mercurius Brittanicus* no 32 (15–22 April 1644), p. 253, has a (longer) list of arms taken at Selby.

16 *Calendar of State Papers Domestic, 1631–3*, p. 316.

17 London, Guildhall Library, Vestrybook, St Stephen Walbrook, pp. 13–20.

18 *The Tower of London Letter Book of Sir Lewis Dyve 1646–7*, ed. H. G. Tibbut (Bedford, 1958).

19 See Leland H. Carlson, 'A History of the Presbyterian Party from Pride's Purge to the Dissolution of the Long Parliament', *Church History*, 11 (1942), 83–122. Jekyll is wrongly assumed to be a minister.

20 *A Complete Collection of State Trials*, ed. T. B. Howell (London, 1811), V, 278.

21 Captain Potter, 'an honest fellow', had been replaced in the City regiments after the Army's occupation of London, according to a Presbyterian pamphlet of 1648, *A Paire of Spectacles for the City* (p. 12). In the confession of Thomas Cooke recorded in *The 13th Report of the Historical Manuscripts Commission*, Appendix 1, Potter is identified as 'a very active man in the cittie of London upon the Presbyterian interest, and one that had much acquaintance and correspondencie with the chiefe ministers in London' (p. 597). Potter became a witness for the prosecution at the Love trial and gave a great deal of information.

22 *State Trials*, V, 83.

23 Edward Gee, *A Plea for Non-Scribers* (London, 1650), Appendix, p. 15.

24 Anne Venn, *A Wise Virgins Lamp Burning; or, God's sweet incomes of love to a gracious soul waiting for him* (London, 1658), p. 70.

25 Dr Williams MS 24. 8., Eleanor Stockton's diary, one of the few which differing inks and deterioration in handwriting denote as the original notebook, has blank pages between entries. To the description of the death of her 19-year-old daughter she adds, many years later, a spiritual interpretation which rewrites incomprehensible tragedy as her own lack of faith (f. 19).

26 See, for example, the poems by the authors included at the beginning or end of these early published works by women: Dorothy Leigh, *The Mothers Blessing* (London, 1621); Alice Sutcliffe, *Meditations of Mans Mortalitie* (London, 1634); Elizabeth Richardson, *A Ladies Legacie to her Daughters* (London, 1645); Frances Cooke, *Mrs. Cookes Meditations, Being an Humble Thanksgiving to her Heavenly Father* (London, 1650).

27 I am indebted to Martyn Bennett for recognising the account of the battle from which the place name is missing as Bradford.

28 Alice Thornton writes and rewrites her diary in the thirty years after her husband's death, when it apparently finishes.

29 *The Protestant Martyrs: or the Bloody Assizes* (London 1689); *The Second and Last Collection of the Dying Speeches, Letters and Prayers &c.* (London, 1689); *The Dying Speeches of Several Excellent Persons* (London, 1689).

30 A French ambassador wrote in 1665 of the peculiar skills that the English had developed in intercepting correspondence: 'they have tricks to open letters more skilfully than anywhere in the world'. Quoted in Peter Fraser, *The Intelligence of the Secretaries of State and Their Monopoly of Licensed News 1660–1688* (Cambridge, 1956), p. 25.

31 Edmund Calamy used evidence of 'closet-writing' to prove the Earl of Warwick's holiness: *A Patterne for all, especially for Noble and Honourable Persons, to teach them how to die Nobly and Honourably* (London, 1658), pp. 34–35. Richard Baxter did the same for Elizabeth Baker: 'Some imitable passages of the life of Elizabeth, late Wife of Mr. Joseph Baker', attached to Richard Baxter, *A Treatise of Death* (London, 1660), p. 240. Anne Venn's 'closet-writing' was published with this validation (she died in 1654): *A wise virgin's lamp burning, written by her own hand and found in her closet at her death*. For more

politicised writing see Elizabeth Clarke, 'The Garrisoned Muse: Women's Use of the Religious Lyric in the Civil War Period' in *The English Civil Wars in the Literary Imagination*, ed. Claude Summers and Ted-Larry Pebworth (Columbia, 1999), pp. 130–43.

32 *A Catalogue of Valuable Manuscripts Collected at the Expense of the late Lord Somers. & since belonged to the Right Hon. Sir Joseph Jekyll knt* (London, 1739), p. 313.

33 N. H. Keeble, ' "The Colonel's Shadow": Lucy Hutchinson, women's writing and the Civil War' in *Literature and the English Civil War*, ed. J. Sawday and T. Healy (Cambridge, 1990), pp. 227–47.

34 'The Autobiography of Mrs. Alice Thornton', Surtees Society, 62 (1873), p. 259. The same criteria can be seen operating in reverse to prove someone reprobate in this verdict on Laud in *The Kingdoms Weekly Intelligencer* no.70, 27 August to 3 September 1644, p. 566: 'I do commend it to any judicious man, to read the Diary of his own life, which is now in print . . . and he that doubts of it, may reade the originall it selfe, *All of his own handwriting* . . . the man under his own hand condemnes himselfe to be a wicked instrument in church and Commonwealth'.

35 Edinburgh, National Library of Scotland, MSS 6849–6502.

36 Peter Lake and Michael Questier, 'Agency, Appropriation and Rhetoric Under The Gallows: Puritans, Romanists and the State in Early Modern England', *Past and Present*, 153 (1996), 64–107.

37 Melinda Zook, ' "The Bloody Assizes": Whig Martyrdom and Memory after the Glorious Revolution', *Albion*, 27.3 (1995), 273–96.

38 J. G. Muddiman, *The need for a new and revised edition of 'State Trials'* (Edinburgh, 1930).

39 *A Complete Collection of State Trials*, ed. T. B. Howell (London 1811), XI, 311.

40 This practice seems to have begun in the Civil War period. David Underdown notes the packing of the Grand Jury of Somerset: in response, the individual jurors' names were published in *A Perfect Diurnall* no. 247, pp. 17–24 April 1648: David Underdown, *Pride's Purge: Politics in the Puritan Revolution* (London, 1971), pp. 93–94.

41 Oxford, Bodleian Library, MS Tanner 40, f. 37.

42 *The Poems and Letters of Andrew Marvell*, ed. H. M. Margoliouth, 3rd edition (Oxford, 1971), II, 117–18, 317–18.

43 Bodleian Library, MS Tanner 40, f. 37.

44 *The Records of a Church of Christ in Bristol, 1640–87*, ed. Roger Hayden (Bristol, 1974), p. 177.

45 *Bishop Burnet's History of his Own Time: with the suppressed passages of the first volume and Notes by the Earle of Dartmouth and Hardanche and Speaker Onslow to which are added the Cursory Remarks of Swift* (London, 1823), p. 339.

46 *State Trials*, XI, 433.

47 See Timothy Crist, 'Francis Smith and the Opposition Press in England 1660–88' (unpub. Ph.D thesis, Cambridge, 1977), p. 176.

48 Crist, 'Francis Smith', 293: Corporation of London Record Office, Rep.90, f. 157.

49 Fraser, *The Intelligence of the Secretaries of State*, p. 120.

50 John Hetet, 'A Literary Underground in Restoration England: Printers and Dissenters in the Context of Constraints 1660–1689' (unpub. Ph.D thesis, Cambridge, 1987), p. 115.

51 Crist, 'Francis Smith', pp. 296–7.

52 William Harrison, *The Christian Life and Death of Mistris Katherin Brettagh* (London, 1641), p. 20.

53 *The Diary of Bulstrode Whitelocke 1605–1675*, ed. Ruth Spalding (London, 1990), p. 253.

54 Wendy Wall, *The Imprint of Gender: Authorship and Publication in the English Renaissance*

(Ithaca, 1993), p. 286. See the 'Approbation' to Elizabeth Joceline's *Mothers Legacie*, 1624, for the authorising link between God, closet, and death for the woman writer: 'Undauntedly looking death in the face, privatly in her Closet betweene God and her, she wrote these pious meditations.'

55 David Norbrook, 'Lucy Hutchinson's "Elegies" and the Situation of the Republican Woman Writer', *English Literary Renaissance*, 27 (1997), 485.

56 Corporation of London Record Office, Rep 90, ff. 81v–82r.

57 Dr Williams's Library, MS Roger Morrice Entring-Book, II, p. 476.

Swansongs: Reading voice in the poetry of Lady Hester Pulter

Mark Robson

'Which voice would speak of voice?'[1] The implications of Jean-Luc Nancy's question will resonate throughout this discussion, since one of my main concerns here is to introduce what will be for most people an unknown voice, that of the seventeenth-century royalist woman poet Lady Hester Pulter, née Ley.[2] The female voice has become a common concept in early modern and feminist studies, and is central to many discussions of the relationships between writing and subjectivity.[3] Voice, it has been suggested, also has a privileged relationship to manuscript text which print cannot match.[4] Yet to speak of Lady Hester Pulter's 'voice' is perhaps already too hasty, for there are many different tonalities in the manuscript which contains her work. Equally, it would not be wise to move forwards in reading this poetry without reflection on the extent to which the voice or voices that we hear in this work may be described, unequivocally, as 'hers'.[5]

Similarly, an emphasis on voice in lyric poetry is commonplace, but there are reasons to be cautious about collapsing too quickly the distinction between speech and writing. What Lady Hester Pulter's writings seem to demonstrate is that recourse to the referential security of a discourse which seeks to phenomenalize rhetorical figures (including the figure of the author) might lead us into problems that cannot simply be side-stepped. If this is in part a matter of *ethos* (in an Aristotelian sense), it is also a question of the relationships between rhetoric and politics.[6] For if the lyric is the poetic form most readily associated with subjectivity, then lyric poetry is the poetry of the subject, it is a 'subjective' genre. As such, its history partakes of the history of the subject, which is perhaps another way of saying that it is intimately linked to the project of modernity.[7] This question will remain a concern which guides these readings of voice in the poetry of Lady Hester Pulter.

Does my own presentation produce further problems? It will rapidly become apparent that the reading I offer here is not based upon an appeal to 'female experience' in any simple sense. I appreciate that there are debates around the question of reading women's writing, and that the approach taken here does not sit comfortably with aspects of these discussions. But what I wish to emphasise here is that this is precisely a matter for critical debate. Whilst I have no desire to diminish nor deny the specificity of the experience of a woman writer in the seventeenth century, I also wish to avoid a retreat from a reading of the poetry into areas of biography, cultural history or 'historicism', however conceived. Where such areas are indicated, this is done to throw into relief the distance between such readings and my own. Like Linda Charnes, I am concerned that the famous injunction, 'always historicise', is too often read in early modern studies as '*only* historicise'.[8]

I

University of Leeds, Brotherton Collection MS Lt q 32 consists of a single folio volume bound in seventeenth-century rough calf, and some loose sheets and smaller pieces. The manuscript contains almost one hundred and twenty poems, totalling over five thousand lines, and a prose romance of some thirty thousand words in two parts, the second of which is incomplete.[9] The poetry occupies 129 leaves, and seems from the evidence of the dates given in the manuscript itself to have been written between 1646 and 1665. The first folio bears the title *Poems Breathed Forth by the Noble Hadassas*. The prose romance, which occupies 36 leaves, is entitled *The Unfortunate Florinda*, and begins from the back of the volume (although folio numbering proceeds from the front of the volume and has been added in modern pencil). The text is predominantly in a clear scribal hand (see PLATE 1), with additions and corrections in two other hands. Of these three hands, the second, an apparently eighteenth-century hand, is responsible for the transcription of three whole poems in the bound volume (see PLATE 2), the fair copy of the second part of the romance, annotations to several poems in the bound volume, the Pulter and Ley family genealogies in the loose papers, a fragment in the loose papers which delineates the dramatis personae of the romance, and the transcript of the first stanza of a song, beginning 'There is one black & sullen hour', which appears in three places in the manuscript: once on a loose fragment, once at the end of the poems transcribed by the first scribe, and once on the reversed title-page of the romance. There are alterations in a third hand which might be that of Pulter herself, since these changes tend to improve the sense and perhaps mark errors of transcription. Fifteen poems show signs of

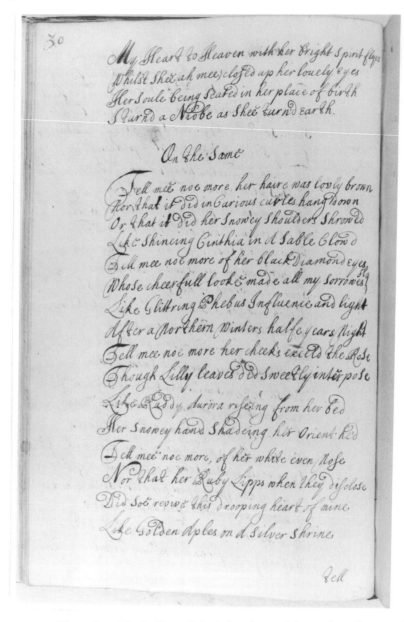

30

My Heart to Heaven with her bright Spirit flyes
Whilst Shee, ah mee, closed up her lovely eyes
Her Soule being seated in her place of birth
I turnd a Niobe as Shee turn'd earth.

On the Same

Tell mee noe more, her haire was lovely brown
Nor that it did in Curious curles hang downe
Or that it did her Snowey Shoulders Shrowed
Like Shineing Cinthia in A Sable Cloud
Tell mee noe more of her black Diamond eyes,
Whose cheerfull looke made all my Sorrowes fly
Like Glittring Phebus Influenie and light
After a Northern Winters halfe years night
Tell mee noe more her cheeks exceld the Rose
Though Lilly leaves did Sweetly interpose
Like Ruddy Aurora riseing from her bed
Her Snowey hand Shadeing her Orient Red
Tell mee noe more, of her white even Nose
Nor that her Ruby Lipps when they diselose
Did Soe revive this drooping heart of mine
Like Golden Aples on A Silver Shrine

Tell

PLATE 1. *The ending of Lady Hester Pulter's first elegy and the opening of her second elegy on the death of her daughter Jane, in the hand of the main amanuensis, in* Poems Breathed Forth by the Noble Hadassas: *University of Leeds, Brotherton Collection* MS Lt q 32, *fol. 17v. (Original size 280 × 180mm.) Reproduced by permission of the University of Leeds.*

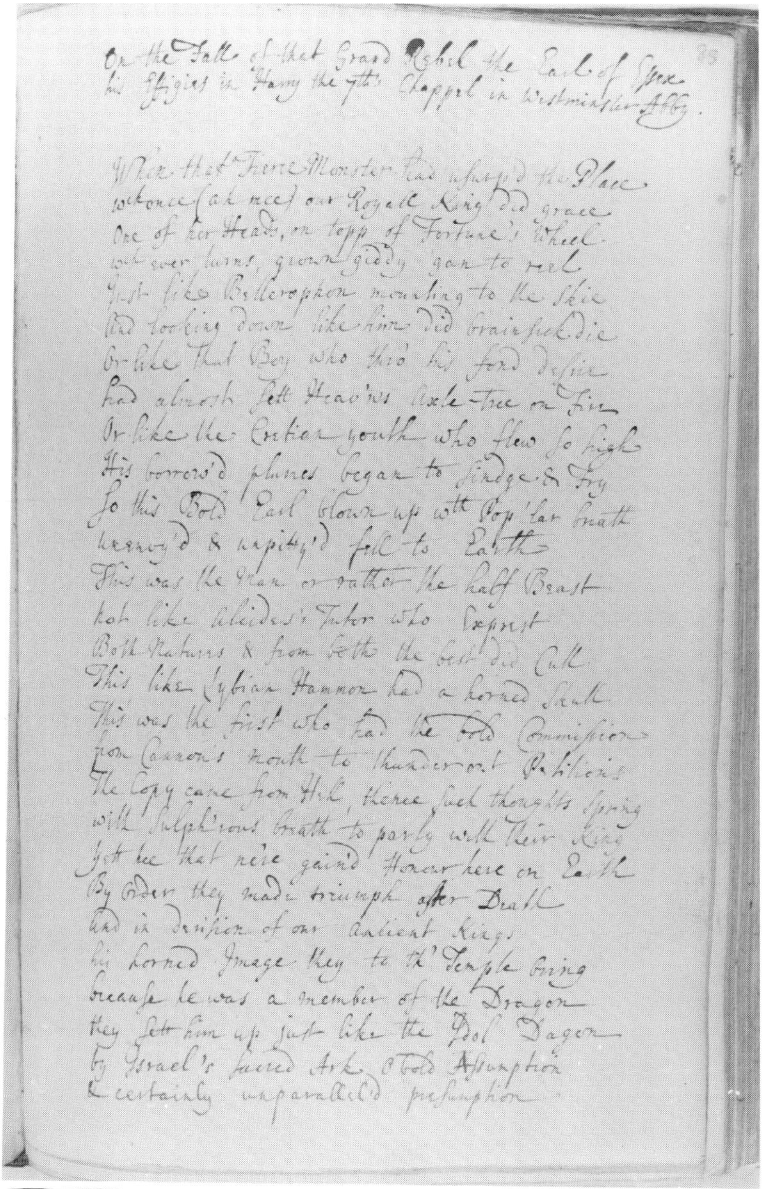
On the Fall of that Grand Rebel the Earl of Essex
his Effigies in Harry the 7th's Chappel in Westminster Abby.

When that Fierce Monster had usurp'd the Place
wch once (ah mee) our Royall King did grace
One of her Heads, on topp of Fortune's Wheel
wch ever turns, grown giddy gan to reel
Just like Bellerophon mounting to the Skie
And looking down like him did brainsick die
Or like that Boy who thro' his fond desire
had almost sett Heav'ns Axle-Tree on Fire
Or like the Cretian youth who flew so high
His borrow'd plumes began to sindge & fry
So this Bold Earl blown up wth Pop'lar breath
Unmoy'd & unpitty'd fell to Earth
This was the Man or rather the half Beast
Not like Alcides's Tutor who Exprest
Both Natures & from both the best did Cull
This like Lybian Hammon had a horned Skull
This was the first who had the bold Commission
from Cannon's mouth to thunder out Petitions
The Copy came from Hell, thence such thoughts spring
with Sulph'rous breath to parly with their King
Yett hee that neere gain'd Honour here on Earth
By Order they made triumph after Death
And in derision of our Antient Kings
his horned Image they to th' Temple bring
because he was a member of the Dragon
they sett him up just like the Idol Dagon
by Israel's sacred Ark A bold Assumption
& certainly unparallel'd presumption

PLATE 2. *The opening of Lady Hester Pulter's poem on the Earl of Essex, in the hand of a second scribe, in* Poems Breathed Forth by the Noble Hadassas: *University of Leeds, Brotherton Collection* MS *Lt q 32, fol. 85r. (Original size 280 × 180mm.) Reproduced by permission of the University of Leeds.*

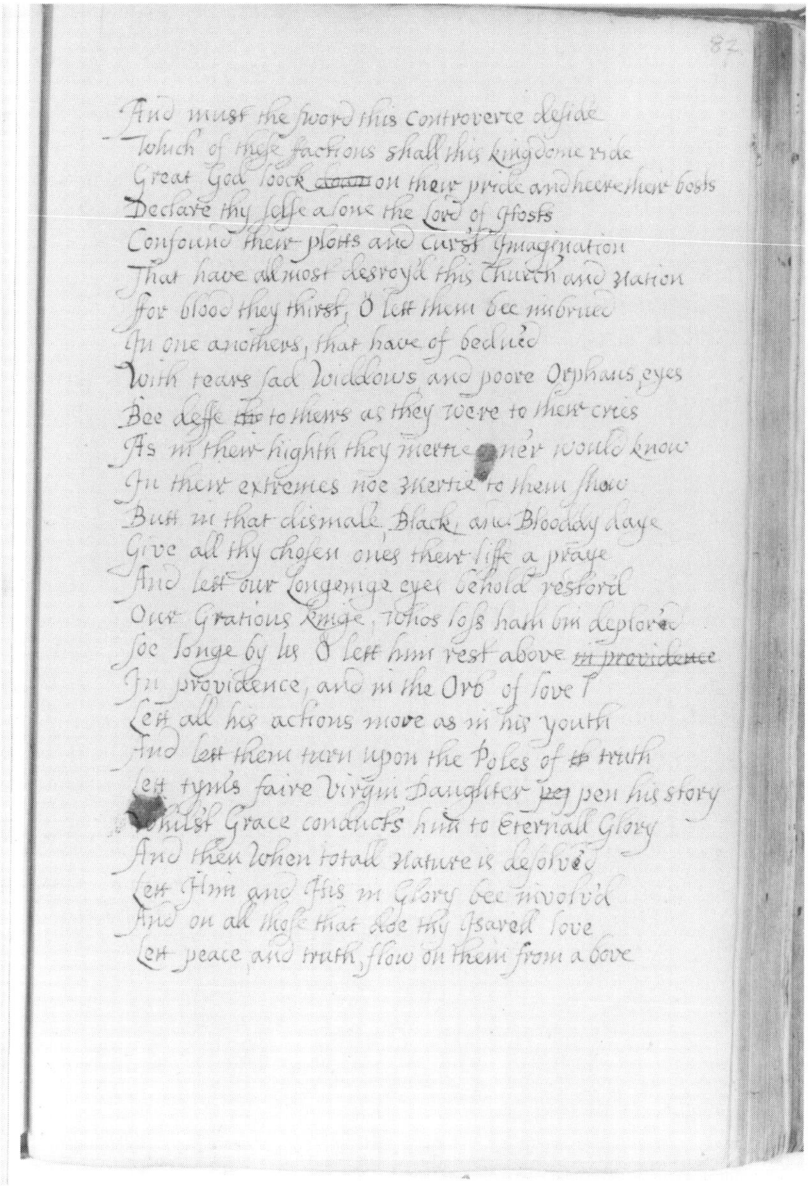

And must the sword this controverce deside
Which of these factions shall this kingdome ride
Great God looke downe on their pride and heere their bosts
Declare thy selfe alone the Lord of ghosts
Confound their plotts and curst ymagination
That have almost desroyd this Church and Nation
for blood they thirst, O lett them bee imbruec
In one anothers, that have of bedd
With tears sad Widdows and poore Orphans eyes
Bee lesse to theirs as they were to their cries
As in their highth they meet one would know
In their extremes noe mercie to them show
Butt in that dismale Black and Bloody daye
Give all thy chosen ones their life a praye
And lett our longeinge eyes behold restord
Our Gratious Kinge, whos loss hath bin deplored
Soe longe by us O lett him rest above
In providence, and in the Orb of love
Lett all his actions move as in his youth
And lett them turn upon the Poles of truth
Lett tymes faire Virgin Daughter pen his story
Whilst Grace conducts him to Eternall Glory
And then when totall Nature is desolvd
Lett Him and His in Glory bee involvd
And on all those that doe thy saved love
Lett peace and truth flow on them from above

PLATE 3. *Lady Hester Pulter's poem* 'And must the sword this controverce
deside', *in a third hand, possibly the author's, in* Poems Breathed Forth by the
Noble Hadassas: *University of Leeds, Brotherton Collection* MS Lt q *32, fol. 87r.
(Original size 280 × 180mm.) Reproduced by permission of the University of Leeds.*

some revision. These changes are largely minor, generally extending only to a single letter or word, although there are four poems (three in the volume and one on a loose sheet) which are seemingly also in this hand (see PLATE 3) as well as the draft of the second part of the romance, which is amongst the loose papers.

None of this material appears to have been printed. The poetry is attributed in the manuscript to Lady Hester Pulter, and this attribution is reinforced by the use of the name 'Hadassas', a biblical synonym for Esther, in the title of the volume. On the first folio of the manuscript there is a description of the poems as 'Hadassas chast fances Beeinge the fruett of solitary and many of them sad howers', and a couplet instructs the reader: 'Marvail not my names conceald / In beeinge hid itt is reve'ld'. This manuscript appears to be the unique extant record of her work.

Lady Hester Pulter was the daughter of James Ley, first Earl of Marlborough and Lord Treasurer. Born in 1596, she married Arthur Pulter of Bradfield or Broadfield in Hertfordshire. She outlived all but two of her fifteen children, and the records of Cottered in Hertfordshire show that she was buried on the 9th of April 1678, at the age of 82. Arthur Pulter, born at Hadham Hall in August 1603, was a Justice of the Peace, a Captain in the Militia, and High Sheriff of Hertfordshire in 1641. His mother was Penelope, daughter of Sir Arthur Capel of Hadham Hall, an ardent royalist. Arthur Pulter apparently withdrew from public life during the Civil War period, dedicating himself to the building of a house at Broadfield. As Sir Henry Chauncy puts it in *The Historical Antiquities of Hertfordshire*, published in 1700, Pulter 'shortly after the breaking forth of the late Civil War declin'd all publick Imployment, liv'd a retir'd Life, and thro' the importunity of his Wife, began to build a very fair House of Brick upon this Mannor [i.e. Broadfield], but dying he never finished it'.[10] Arthur Pulter died, having outlived all of his children, in February 1689, leaving a grandson James Forester (son of his daughter Margaret) as his heir. Forester was also unable to complete the house before his own death in 1696. The house no longer stands.

II

The poems in MS Lt q 32 encompass a wide variety of genres and there are dialogues, pastorals, polemics and laments, elegies, religious meditations, allegories and parables, satires, love poems, emblems, and praise for the royal family.

It is possible to distinguish three types of poetry in Pulter's writings. Much consists of responses to events of the Civil War period, and

subjects include the execution of Charles I; the deaths of Sir George
Lisle and Sir Charles Lucas, shot at Colchester in August 1648 for their
parts in the Kentish insurrection; Charles's imprisonment at Holmby in
1647, figured as a lament by the River Thames; the death of Arthur,
Lord Capel of Hadham; Sir William Davenant's loss of his nose
through syphilis; the suicide of a young woman at Oxford whose royalist lover was killed during the war; and the destruction of the effigy of
Robert Devereux, third Earl of Essex, in Westminster Abbey. This
political poetry is explicitly royalist, and is pervaded by a sense of anger
and loss. Pulter is often polemical, condemning what she describes as
the 'hydra' of the Parliamentarian 'mob' and the perceived chaos that
the war brought.

The other two categories are devotional and, for want of a better
term, 'domestic' poetry, and much of the latter is about or addressed to
Pulter's children. She explains in the titles of some of these poems that
she tended to write them during her 'confinement' periods. That she
had fifteen children might explain her relatively prolific poetic output.

Whilst Pulter's work does not seem to have been printed, this should
not be taken as an indication that this is 'private' poetry, nor is it indica-
tive of the texts' quality. As Margaret Ezell and others have argued, the
circulation of texts in manuscript should not be read only in terms of a
relationship to print. Arthur Marotti, for example, notes that a critical
tendency to judge the literature of the Civil War predominantly in
terms of printed texts has produced an inaccurate picture of cultural
production in the period.[11] Similarly, Ezell remarks on the unfortunate
consequences of this emphasis for the writing of women's literary history, in which writers prior to the eighteenth century are rendered far
less visible because the importance of manuscript texts is not sufficiently
appreciated.[12] It was not uncommon for writers' work to be transmitted in this manner, often among members of a 'coterie' audience, and
this can be seen in certain cases as a conscious choice. We should not
forget here the 'stigma' of print, particularly for aristocratic writers.[13]
Equally, in this period, the attempts to control print made by
Parliament may also be a determining factor.[14] Nor does this 'failure' to
publish apply only to the work of women. Donne and Sidney would be
the obvious examples of male writers whose work reached print only in
posthumous editions. The compilation of a manuscript such as Pulter's
implies a potential readership, even if that readership cannot be identified with any certainty. The most likely audience for this collection of
poetry is Pulter's family, and the presence of advice poems addressed to
Pulter's daughters suggests an emphasis on a female readership.

III

The two poems that I have chosen for these initial readings are inevitably going to be thought of as in some sense 'representative'. Obviously, the notion of one poem being representative of another is extremely problematic, and so all I can do here is gesture towards two of the types of poetry that are contained within the manuscript. Equally, these readings are far from 'complete'. There is not the space here to give anything more than an indication of certain areas to be explored in greater depth. I have chosen here two elegies, one satirical and political, the other more personal.[15] As I noted above, it has been suggested that manuscript texts have a privileged relationship to the idea of a 'voice' in (or behind) writing. These readings are guided by a similar concern for voices, but in the debate between Ong and Derrida that Harold Love interestingly sets up, the readings presented here would be much closer to the Derridean line than to that of Ong.[16]

The subject of the first of these poems is perhaps adequately described by its title, 'On the Fall of that Grand Rebel the Earl of Essex his Effigies in Harry the 7th's Chappel in Westminster Abby'.[17] Robert Devereux, third Earl of Essex, after Cromwell the most prominent Parliamentarian general, died after a stroke on 14 September 1646. As part of the grandest state funeral since the death of James I, an effigy of the Earl was constructed which was included in the procession. Following the funeral, this effigy of Devereux remained in Westminster Abbey, where it became the centrepiece of a Puritan shrine which attracted many visitors. The sermon which formed part of the funeral itself was given by Richard Vines and, by order of 'the House of Peeres', this sermon was published in October 1646, under the title *The Hearse of the Renowned, the Right Honourable Robert, Earle of Essex*.[18] In the sermon, Essex is compared to the biblical precedents Jonathan and Abner, linking their attempts to defend Israel to Essex's military role in the Parliamentarian cause, particularly at Edge Hill. Essex is described as a defender of the liberty and property of England, and his death is said to bring about a 'universall lamentation' (p. 3). Vines' conclusion is that: 'Hee lived *a good Generall*, Hee died *a Generall good*' (p. 36). Although the emphasis that Vines gives to his sermon centres on a theological rather than a political message, stressing the vanity of mortal fame and the inevitability of death ('Death is a fall from every thing but grace' (p. [12]), there are some phrases in the sermon which produce curious effects when viewed with the benefit of hindsight. Whilst towards the end of the text Vines claims of Essex's memory that 'it will be such a

Monument that every stone of it will speak a History' (p. 36), there is also the suggestion in 'The Epistle Dedicatory' (A3ᵛ) that, even in the cases of the great and good, 'their very Monuments are mortall'. In a retrospectively extraordinary passage towards the end of his text, Vines comments:

> the losse wee have susteined is great tho he never had wore Buff but onely Parliament Robes, & they say that when a limb or part of a man is cut off, *anima retrahitur*, the soule is retracted, I wish the Phylosophy may be verified in the retraction of his reality and faithfulnesse unto you; that so he may remayne among you in quintessence and vertue, being as it were divided among you, as they say of *Romulus*, that he was discerpt by the Senate, when he died, and every Senatour got a piece of him (p. 37).

This desire for a *metempsychosis*, in which the soul of Essex would be transported from him to the other Parliamentarians, is prompted by a perceived mutilation or dismemberment of Essex's dead body. The interest of this passage becomes more apparent when we realise what happened to the effigy of Essex. His monument did indeed seem to be 'mortal', and the figural dismemberment that Vines wishes for becomes literalized by the actions of one who did not share in the universal lamentation.

For on the night of 26 November 1646, the effigy of Essex was mutilated by the cavalier John White. White concealed himself in the Abbey, attacked the Inigo Jones-designed catafalque with an axe, slashed the effigy's clothing, which included a coat worn by Essex at Edge Hill, and chopped off the effigy's head. Finally, he stole a gilt sword. He was captured two weeks later, imprisoned in the Gatehouse, and questioned in the House of Lords, where he also admitted to accidentally breaking off the nose of a statue of William Camden, the antiquarian. Despite his pleas for clemency, White was allowed to starve in the Gatehouse. The effigy was restored and placed in a glass case to prevent further attacks, and it was only removed from the Abbey in 1661, by Charles II's order.[19] Although Essex's image was not submitted to further damage, he was the subject of numerous satires and polemics. One such is the poem to be found in Lady Hester Pulter's manuscript.

On the Fall of that Grand Rebel the Earl of Essex his Effigies in Harry
the 7th's Chappel in Westminster Abby

> When that Fierce Monster had usurp'd the Place
> Wᶜʰ once (ah mee) our Royall King did grace
> One of her Heads, on topp of Fortune's Wheel
> Wᶜʰ ever turns, grown giddy 'gan to reel

5 Just like Bellerophon mounting to the skie
 And looking down—like him did brainsick die
 Or like that Boy who thro' his fond desire
 had almost sett Heav'ns axle-tree on fire
 Or like the Cretian youth who flew soe high
10 His borrow'd plumes began to sindge & Fry
 So this Bold Earl blown up with Pop'lar breath
 Unenvy'd and unpitty'd fell to Earth
 This was the man or rather the half Beast
 Not like Alcides's Tutor who exprest
15 Both Natures & from both the best did Cull
 This like Lybian Hammon had a horned skull
 This was the first who had the bold Commision
 from Cannon's mouth to thunder out partitions
 The Copy came from Hell, thence such thoughts spring
20 With sulph'rous breath to parly with their King
 Yett hee that ne're gain'd Honour here on Earth
 By Order they made triumph after Death
 And in derision of our Antient Kings
 his horned Image they to th'Temple bring
25 because he was a member of the Dragon
 they sett him up just like the Idol Dagon
 by Israel's sacred Ark O bold Assumption
 & certainly unparallel'd presumption
 Butt down he fell loosing his hands & head
30 his Father serv'd so, living, hee so dead.
 such End such honour lett all Trayters have
 but our Augustus Heav'n protect & save.

This poem looks like a straightforward royalist polemic, celebrating the desecration of Essex's monument. Essex is described as an overreacher, with references to Bellerophon, Icarus, and others, and the well-worn topos of fortune's wheel. This is shown to be a familial trait, as the reference to the execution of the second Earl at the end of the poem suggests. Pulter's recurrent image of the Parliamentary supporters as a hydra appears here in the suggestion that Essex is one of the fierce monster's heads, and this prepares the way for the decapitation of the effigy. There is a recurrent movement between a use of third person description and the use of collective terms (such as hydra, our, they, and so on) which suggests that Essex, or at least his effigy, has a synecdochal significance. The destruction of the effigy thus becomes a symbolic victory against the Parliamentarians, and the link to the second Earl also produces the figure of a posthumous execution; the effigy, a figure of the body, is subject to the same punishment as a physical body. This might be connected to the practice of destroying effigies in cases where a criminal is seen to have escaped justice, but what also takes place is an inversion of the symbolism of the Parliamentarian funeral. John White's actions are figured in the poem as a literal reading of the effigy as a representation of Essex's body.

The hydra might also be read, however, as an image of the inhuman, or more precisely the not fully human, and it is not the only figure of this type to intervene in this poem. The connection made between Essex and the Lybian Hammon (l. 16), like the reference to the Idol Dagon (l. 26), is more than just an assertion of relationship between the effigy and idolatry. Hammon, or Ammon, is usually represented as half-man, half-beast, frequently with the head of a ram or a horned skull. Similarly, Dagon is commonly half-human, half-fish.[20] Such characterisations in Pulter's poem might be read as the adoption of a royalist poetic convention which shows the Parliamentarians as less than human. The horns of Ammon might also be read as the cuckold's horns, potentially becoming an allusion either to Essex's first marriage to Frances Howard, annulled amidst allegations of Essex's impotence and his wife's alleged adultery with Robert Carr, or else to his second, about which there were also suspicions that he had been cuckolded.[21] James Loxley notes the irony in the discrepancy between Essex's martial and marital reputations: 'That the military leader of the revolt should be the Earl of Essex, a man famously divorced for impotence, allowed royalist satire to locate emasculation in a figure who was the iconic centre of the Parliamentarian cause for most of the first civil war'.[22] The implication may be then not so much that Essex is less than fully human but that he is less than a man, with the emphasis on his masculinity.

Phenomenalization of the voice and subject is always necessarily implied in the lyric, but here it would seem that some strategy must be found for avoiding the full phenomenalization of Essex's body. The body of Pulter's text should not stand in for Essex's body, since this would make the text itself an effigy. Unlike the effigy used in the funeral procession, the poem is not intended to be a memorial of Essex, indeed it might best be read as the commemoration of a dismembered body, through its repetition of the dis-*figuring* of the effigy. This avoidance of the phenomenalization of Essex as textual monument is in part attempted through the creation of a less than fully human figure. The *broken* effigy thus remains as the accurate figuration of a human body which is itself incomplete.

The question of gender raised by this attention to masculinity takes us into an area that has not yet been taken into account in this reading of the poem. What of the fact that this is written by a woman? Pulter's adoption of an avowedly royalist poetic position seems to negate any sense of female passivity, particularly if we accept the connection made in so much royalist poetry between writing and fighting. The idea of writing as commitment, and more particularly as committed political action, stands in opposition to the notion of a cavalier withdrawal into drinking, friendship and *otium*. This might be read as a means of engagement for the non-combatant female writer. Yet the rhetoric of masculinity which underpins so much of this royalist writing, especially if conceived through an attack upon the masculine virtues of its opponents, must be disturbed by its inhabitation through a female voice. As Loxley has suggested: 'The corporeal agency such poetry demands is marked as biologically male, defined against a particularly physical lack'.[23]

As Loxley notes, however, this is to grant voice a privileged access to presence and corporeality. The gender difference that this royalist concentration on masculinity is attempting to assert and define is precisely rhetorical. A non-linguistic, corporeal origin must ground the claim for an actively masculine poetic, and yet the claims for poetry as activity and the definition of masculinity upon which this claim is grounded can only take place in the poetry itself. That which is posited as ontologically prior to its linguistic expression turns out to be itself a product of that expression, and the corporeal origin is dispersed into reiterated linguistic acts of positing. Any identification of Pulter's writing as an attempt to enter this discourse as a royalist female combatant necessarily threatens the royalist principle of poetry as action since it is predicated on masculinity.

It might then be possible to read Pulter's focus on the question of Essex's masculinity as a matter of deferral. The place of the woman writer within this masculine poetic convention is displaced, through the projection of a perceived physical lack onto the subject of the poem rather than the speaking persona.

And yet, this may also allow too much to the ontological claims of voice. In a very different poem to be found in the Pulter manuscript, it is possible to read a far less secure operation of voice. Whilst the Essex poem can be read as an attempt to avoid monumentalizing its subject, 'On the same' is an elegiac lament for the death of one of Lady Hester's daughters, Jane. The title refers to a poem which precedes this one in the manuscript, entitled 'Upon the death of my deare and lovely daughter J.P.', to which a note has been added: 'Jane Pulter, baptized May 1. 1625. Buried Oct. 8 1646 at 20'.[24]

On the same

Tell mee noe more her haire was lovly brown
Nor that it did in Curious curles hang down
Or that it did her snowey shoulders shrowed
Like shineing Cinthia in A sable Clowd
5   Tell mee noe more of her black Diamond eyes
Whose cheerfull looke made all my sorrowes fly
Like Glittring Phebus Influence and light
After a northern winters halfe years night
Tell mee noe more her cheeks exceld the Rose
10   Though Lilly leaves did sweetly interpose
Like Ruddy Aurora riseing from her bed
Her snowey hand shadeing her Orient he'd
Tell mee noe more of her white even nose
Nor that her Ruby Lipps when they disclose
15   Did soe revive this drooping heart of mine
Like Golden Aples on A silver shrine
Tell mee noe more her bre'sts were heaps of snow
White as the swans where Cristall Thams doth flow
Chast as Diana was her virgin Bre'st
20   Her noble Mind can never bee exprest
This but the Casket was of her rich[?] soule
Which now doth shine above the highest pole
Tell mee noe more of her perfection
Because it doth increase my hearts dejection
25   Nor tell mee that shee past here happy dayes
In singing Heavenly and the Museses layes
Nor like the swans on Cristall Poe
Shee sung her Dirges ere shee hence did goe
Noe never more tell my sad soule of Mirth
30   With her I lost most of my Joyes on earth
Nor can I ever raise my drooping spirit
Untill with her those Joyes I shall inherit
Those Glories which our finite thoughts transcend
Where wee shall praises sing World without end
35   To him that made both her and mee of Earth
And gave us spirits of Celestiall Birth
Tell me noe more of her Unblemished fame
Which doth I-mortalize her virgin name
Like fragrant odours Aromatick fumes
40   Which all succeeding Ages still perfumes

Nor why I mourn for her aske mee noe more
For all my life I shall her loss deplore
Till infinite power her dust and mine shall raise
To sing in Heaven his everlasting praise.[25]

This poem begins as an apostrophe to an unidentified interlocutor, to
one who seems to serve as an uncomfortable reminder of a daughter's
death. Who is this addressee? Several possibilities present themselves,
and attempts to make any identification naturally rest in part upon our
definition of lyric poetry and the figure of apostrophe.[26] Lyric poems
always imply a voice, speaking or singing, and necessarily imply someone or something to whom this voice speaks. It need not be a person,
fictional or otherwise. This unidentified interlocutor is precisely not
present, but neither in any strong sense is the author. We must preserve
the distinction between author and speaking persona, even or perhaps
especially in a poem which appears to be so evidently autobiographical.
The reader is thus a hearer, or perhaps, in John Stuart Mill's phrase,
someone who overhears.[27] This distinction might be important here,
since on one level it is impossible not to think of the reader as the
addressee. Yet it is also possible to think of the reader inhabiting the
position of the persona who speaks in the poem.

Apostrophe seeks to animate that which is inanimate. As Barbara
Johnson suggests:

Apostrophe is a form of ventriloquism through which the speaker throws
voice, life, and human form into the addressee, turning its silence into
mute responsiveness.[28]

The refrain of this poem—Tell mee noe more—seemingly enacts not so
much a desire for the voice of the other as a wish for silence. Response
in this case is to take the form of muteness. There are contrary impulses
here; an apostrophic address which calls the other to animation also
marks a conversation which is already in progress and that the discourse
of the poem seeks to end.

Of course, it is obvious that this is a poem about absence, about loss
and mourning.[29] Yet we should not be too quick to establish a strict
opposition between animate and inanimate. If apostrophe is a figure of
animation, and in particular the animation of the inanimate, then such
oppositions become hard to ground.

For Godsake hold your tongue, and let me mourn, might be an accurate summation of the tone of the beginning of this poem. The implied
dialogue that the poem enacts offers an apparent divergence between
two speakers which the reader may only hear as a single voice, and this

is accentuated by the call for the silence of the interlocutor. The repetition of the interlocutor's words, placing the blazon-like description of the daughter's qualities in invisible quotation marks, blurs any clear distinction between the supposedly antithetical positions. We also hear that these words are themselves repetitions; Tell mee *noe more*, not again, not now. I will return to the question of the temporality of this 'now'. The repetition of the descriptions makes the poem's apparent literal meaning untenable: the act of asking not to be reminded of the daughter's qualities is itself a reminder. Of course, for the reader, this a repetition which comes 'for the first time', it is an origin already marked by its secondarity, even without recourse to any mimetic notion of representation of the actual body of the deceased. Thus the desired muteness of the interlocutor is substituted for in the speaker's own locutions.

We might expect this act of mourning to be predicated on the loss of the human, yet the comparisons that are made are conventionally hyperbolic: Jane is 'Like shineing Cinthia', 'Like Glittring Phebus Influence and light', 'Like Ruddy Aurora', 'Chast as Diana', 'her cheeks exceld the Rose', 'her bre'sts *were* heaps of snow', and her body is merely the 'Casket' for her soul. Although such descriptions sound familiar as poetic conceits, we should be aware that most of these are rejected, they are the words that should not be repeated. Perhaps it is the movement into conceit that is the problem, the movement, marked by the repetition of 'like' away from the body itself (if we can use that word here). This presents the possibility of reading against the male love lyric.

The refrain is perhaps an echo of Carew's 'A Song', with its repeated response—Ask me no more—given to a series of impossible demands.[30] This aligns Pulter's poem with a rhetoric of love lyrics, and indeed if it were not for the title of the previous poem it would not be obvious from the opening lines of 'On the same' that this is an elegy. Unlike Lady Mary Wroth, Pulter does not make a clear effort to distance herself from a line of male love lyrics.[31]

The question of temporality becomes significant here. The emphasis on human corporeal finitude, on the need to transcend finite thoughts in favour of a recognition of infinite power and everlasting praise, opens the text to a reading as a memorial. Jane Pulter's body becomes monumentalized through the very act of repressing the memory of its component qualities. We might, then, think of this poem as an effigy. The substitution of a poetic text for an absent human body is not of course uncommon. The most famous examples are perhaps Ben Jonson's claim for 'his best piece of *poetrie*' in the elegy for his son, or Shakespeare's claim for the memorial quality of his sonnets.[32] Similarly, then, when Lady Hester remarks

Tell me noe more of her Unblemished fame
Which doth Imortalize her virgin name
Like fragrant odours Aromatick fumes
Which all succeeding Ages still perfumes

(ll. 37–40)

the immortalization is enacted in the utterance which requests its own
cancellation. The temporal location of the speaker's claim here should
be remarked; there is an implication that the speaker already knows
what the deceased's reputation will have been. There is an impossibly
transcendent position suggested here, but this attempt to move beyond
finite perfection is rejected. More pointedly, perhaps, fame immortal-
izes name, but it is not the name that is the object of mourning.

The sense of temporal dislocation that appears here is not restricted
to this moment in the text. The notion of the daughter singing a swan's
dirge (ll. 27–28) revives the classical conceit that swans are supposed to
sing but once, and that before their deaths. This familiar image, used by
Donne and by Shakespeare in both *Othello* and *Lucrece*, might be read as
the voice of the future anterior; it can only be interpreted, after the fact,
as that which will have announced death.[33] Is this poem, then, an apostrophe to death? Here might be another candidate for the unidentified
interlocutor, for there is another *telos* here, that of Lady Hester's own
death, and life in death.

The question of what it might mean to write an apostrophe to death,
what it might mean to attempt to animate death, or to see death as a
force capable of animation, is not one which could be answered too
quickly here. Donne's resort to paradox in the movement from 'Death
be not proud' to 'Death, thou shalt die' might exemplify the difficulties
inherent in such a project.[34] Jonathan Culler suggests that 'apostrophe
takes the crucial step of constituting the object as another subject with
whom the poetic subject might hope to strike up a harmonious relationship'.[35] Is it possible to have a harmonious relationship with death?
Given time, perhaps. Apostrophe is the trope which, through an obliter-
ation of temporality, attempts the instantiation of the poem as a hap-
pening, as an event in the ever-present 'now' of a reading. Culler
suggests that it is here that lyric is to be opposed to narrative. This is
perhaps where Pulter's poem itself, as memorial and as an instance of
voice, attempts to enact the transcendence of finitude.

This is then a *memento mori*, but it does not rest upon a strict division
between presence and absence.[36] Pulter might be seen to attempt to
dwell, to borrow a line from another of her poems, 'amongst the cav-
erns of the dead'.[37] Memory and memorial are always intended

towards the future, even if this must be figured in a future anterior. Just as identification with a royalist poetic cannot guarantee the production of a stable female voice of political engagement, neither can the border between the living voice and the dead voice be located, once and for all. The Muses' lays cannot bring back the dead, but neither can that song be simply silenced within memory. Jane Pulter's voice can also be heard, by the speaking persona at least, in this poem. It is her voice, as much as that of the interlocutor, which acts as a painful reminder. When Hamlet suggests that the rest is silence, he can give no guarantees; the rest of the play should already have told him that.

NOTES

Research for this paper took place at the Brotherton Library, University of Leeds, and the John Rylands Library, Manchester. I would like to thank the staff of both institutions. Versions of this piece have been delivered at the University of Leeds, at the Trinity/Trent Colloquium in the English Faculty at the University of Oxford in March 1998, and at the London Renaissance Seminar in April 1999. I am grateful to the organisers, Paul Hammond, Elizabeth Clarke, the late Jeremy Maule, and Thomas Healy, respectively, for invitations to speak. I would also like to express thanks to those who attended for their comments and suggestions. Since this is a paper about voice, it seems appropriate for some of the quality of the original oral form of the presentation to be retained.

1 The implications of this question are played out in Jean-Luc Nancy, 'Vox Clamans in Deserto', trans. Nathalia King, in *The Birth to Presence*, ed. Brian Holmes (Stanford, 1993), pp. 234–47. For this quotation see p. 236.
2 The poetry in question is contained in MS Lt q 32 in the Brotherton Collection at the University of Leeds. I am grateful to Leeds University Library for permission to use these texts. The texts presented here, and the biographical and bibliographical descriptions offered, are intended to facilitate the readings of the poems which will follow, and should not be taken as a final version.
3 The titles of some recent publications are all that can be cited here: for example, Elizabeth D. Harvey, *Ventriloquized Voices: Feminist Theory and English Renaissance Texts* (London, 1992); Jonathan Goldberg, *Voice Terminal Echo: Postmodernism and English Renaissance Texts* (London, 1986); Leslie Dunn and Nancy Jones (eds), *Embodied Voices: Representing Female Vocality in Western Culture* (Cambridge, 1994); and Kate Chedgzoy, Melanie Hansen and Suzanne Trill (eds), *Voicing Women* (Keele, 1997).
4 The suggestion is made in Walter J. Ong, *Orality and Literacy: The Technologizing of the Word* (London and New York, 1982), for example, p. 132. This is discussed in chapter 4 of Harold Love, *Scribal Publication in Seventeenth-Century England* (Oxford, 1993), especially pp. 141–4.
5 This article is not intended to be a source study. The question of Pulter's influences will, however, be addressed in my forthcoming edition of Pulter's poetry, to be published in the Leeds Texts and Monographs series.
6 See Aristotle's *Rhetoric*, Book 1.1365a. *Ethos* in this sense is related to persona and questions of authorial identity. The longevity of this concept may be indicated by

T. S. Eliot's 'The Three Voices of Poetry', in *On Poetry and Poets* (London, 1957), pp. 89–102, in which the Aristotelian notion of an original, organising voice linked to authorial intention is maintained.

7 On the political consequences of this shared 'experience', testified to by the work of Paul Celan, see Philippe Lacoue-Labarthe, *Poetry as Experience*, trans. Andrea Tarnowski (Stanford, 1999). For the definition of 'experience' as Lacoue-Labarthe uses it in this text, drawing upon its strict sense as 'a crossing through danger' rather than as something that is 'lived', see p. 18.

8 See Charnes, *Notorious Identity: Materializing the Subject in Shakespeare* (Cambridge, Mass., 1993), p. 15.

9 The manuscript was acquired by the Brotherton Collection at Christie's auction, 8 October 1975, lot 353. It was formerly the property of Sir Gilbert Inglefield, Bt.

10 Sir Henry Chauncy, *The Historical Antiquities of Hertfordshire* (London, 1700), p. 72.

11 Arthur F. Marotti, *Manuscript, Print, and the English Renaissance Lyric* (Ithaca & London, 1995), p. 73. Marotti's discussion of women's manuscripts occupies pp. 48–61.

12 Margaret J. M. Ezell, *Writing Women's Literary History* (Baltimore & London, 1993), pp. 37–38.

13 This was most notably argued in J. W. Saunders, 'The Stigma of Print: A Note on the Social Bases of Tudor Poetry', *Essays in Criticism*, 1 (1951), 139–64; but see also Steven W. May, 'Tudor Aristocrats and the Mythical "Stigma of Print" ', *Renaissance Papers 1980* (1981), 11–18.

14 These attempts, and the resistance to them, are discussed in the first chapter of Lois Potter, *Secret Rites and Secret Writing: Royalist Literature, 1641–1660* (Cambridge, 1989), pp. 1–37.

15 Marotti notes the popularity of death as a subject in manuscript collections: *Manuscript, Print, and the English Renaissance Lyric*, pp. 129–30.

16 See note 4 above. The texts of most relevance in Derrida's corpus would be *Of Grammatology*, trans. Gayatri Chakravorty Spivak (Baltimore, 1976); *Speech and Phenomena, and other essays on Husserl's theory of signs*, trans. David B. Allison (Evanston, 1973); although many other passages might be cited here.

17 MS Lt q 32, f. 85r–v.

18 Richard Vines, *The Hearse of the Renowned, the Right Honourable Robert, Earle of Essex* (London, 1646). The edition that I have consulted was printed for Abel Roper, and the connection with the House of Lords is given on the title-page.

19 Much of the following information is to be found in *Whole Proceedings of the Barbarous and Inhuman demolishing of the Earl of Essex Tomb on Thursday Night Last, November 26, 1646* (London, 1646); and Vernon F. Snow, *Essex the Rebel: The Life of Robert Devereux, the third Earl of Essex, 1591–1646* (Lincoln, Neb., 1970), especially p. 494.

20 The complaint about the proximity of the monument of Essex to Israel (l. 27) might also be a reference to the analogy drawn between Essex and the biblical defenders of Israel made in a text such as Vines's sermon.

21 On Essex and Frances Howard, see David Lindley, *The Trials of Frances Howard: Fact and Fiction at the Court of King James* (London, 1993). Ammon is also associated with Alexander the Great, and this may reinforce the critical attitude towards Essex's martial prowess. I am grateful to Peter Beal for this suggestion, and for his comments on this article as a whole.

22 James Loxley, 'Unfettered Organs: The Polemical Voices of Katherine Philips' (forthcoming), typescript, p. 13. I am grateful for the opportunity to read this text prior to publication. See also Loxley's *Royalism and Poetry in the English Civil Wars: The Drawn Sword* (Basingstoke, 1997).

23 Loxley, 'Unfettered Organs', p. 12.

24 Pulter, MS Lt q 32, f. 16v.

25 Pulter, MS Lt q 32, ff. 17v–18v.

26 For a discussion of lyric poetry which has influenced my approach here, see Timothy Bahti, *Ends of the Lyric: Direction and Consequence in Western Poetry* (Baltimore, 1996).

27 Mill, quoted in Bahti, p. 3.

28 Barbara Johnson, 'Apostrophe, Animation, and Abortion', in *A World of Difference* (Baltimore, 1987), pp. 184–99 (185).

29 For a useful recent discussion, see Matthew Greenfield, 'The Cultural Functions of Renaissance Elegy', *English Literary Renaissance*, 28.1 (1998), 75–94. For the status of particular genres in the Civil War period, including elegy, see Nigel Smith, *Literature and Revolution in England, 1640–1660* (New Haven & London, 1994).

30 It is to be noted that Henry King's 'Sonnet' begins with the phrase 'Tell me no more', but it does not maintain this in the manner of a refrain. Scott Nixon addresses the manuscript circulation of Carew's poem in ' "Aske me no more" and the Manuscript Verse Miscellany', *English Literary Renaissance*, 29.1 (1999), 97–130.

31 I am grateful to Michael Brennan for this suggestion.

32 Jonson, 'XLV On my First Sonne' from *Epigrammes*, in *Ben Jonson*, ed. C. H. Herford, Percy and Evelyn Simpson, 11 vols (Oxford, 1925–1952), VIII [1947], p. 41, l. 10.

33 Donne, 'An Anatomy of the World: The First Anniversary' [1611], in *The Complete English Poems*, ed. A. J. Smith (Harmondsworth, 1971 [1983]), p. 281, l. 407; Shakespeare, *Othello*, ed. Norman Sanders (Cambridge, 1984), 5.2.245–6; *Lucrece*, in *The Poems*, ed. F. T. Prince (London, 1969 [1990]), ll. 1611–12.

34 Donne, *Divine Meditations*, 'Holy Sonnet X' [1633], in *The Complete English Poems*, p. 313.

35 Jonathan Culler, 'Apostrophe', in *The Pursuit of Signs: Semiotics, Literature, Deconstruction* (London, 1981), pp. 135–54 (143).

36 Among many discussions of the function of the *memento mori* in England in this period, notable is Nigel Llewellyn, *The Art of Death: Visual Culture in the English Death Ritual c.1500–c.1800* (London, 1991), especially chapter 4.

37 Pulter, 'The complaints of Thames 1647 when the best of kings was imprisoned by the worst of Rebels at Holmbie', l. 108, MS Lt q 32, f. 10r. This poem also contains the image of the swan's dirge, l. 104.

Lucy Hutchinson and *Order and Disorder*: The Manuscript Evidence

David Norbrook

I

In the recent revival of interest in women's writing, Lucy Hutchinson (1620–81/2) has been relatively neglected. This may be in part because her failure to print her work (with the notable exception to which we shall come below) makes her seem more cautious and conventional than contemporaries like Behn and Philips, especially because she ascribed it to her inferior abilities as a woman. It has certainly made the reconstruction of her canon a complicated and uneven process. She left behind her a large body of manuscript writings, most of which passed to another branch of the Hutchinson family, and were recorded by Julius Hutchinson in his 1806 edition of *Memoirs of the Life of Colonel Hutchinson*. These papers were bequeathed by Julius Hutchinson to his solicitor, who left the country in financial difficulties, and though two of the manuscripts were printed in 1817, and others have found their way back into the archives, the manuscript of her autobiography, which contained a number of poems as well, remains unaccounted for. The other main manuscript known to date, the translation of Lucretius, passed down in the family of its dedicatee, Arthur Annesley, Earl of Anglesey, until its sale to the British Museum in 1853, and was not published until 1996.

The fact that the manuscripts were not printed does not of course mean that they did not receive some form of audience. As Margaret Ezell has pointed out, many women can be regarded as having 'published' even though the circulation was in manuscript form.[1] Hutchinson belongs to this group; and yet her particular political position made her unusually ambivalent about this situation, and her attitude towards the circulation of her writings was a complex one. Though she did assert in the dedication to her Lucretius translation that women should not venture into print, her wording was polemically edged:

'('though a masculine Witt hath thought it worth printing his head in a lawrell crowne for the version of one of these bookes) I am . . . farre from gloriing in my six'.[2] Hutchinson presents John Evelyn's printing of the first book of his own Lucretius translation as a vulgar ostentation, offensive to republican austerity (the title-page adapted an earlier portrait of Lucretius, appropriating the laurel crown for himself). Her female modesty emerges as morally superior to masculine ambition, even as she registers with pride her own achievement in having managed to translate all six books. She was well aware that self-deprecation was often a rhetorical formula: as she sardonically commented in a work addressed to her daughter, 'I write not for the presse, to boast my owne weaknesses to the world'.[3]

Paradoxically, if Hutchinson's strong Puritanism may to some extent have intensified her belief in a doctrine of female inferiority, it also emboldened her to become an outspoken critic of the state. Greatly complicating her relationship to the press was the fact that her writings were overtly seditious; they formed part of the republican 'underground' of figures like Edmund Ludlow and Algernon Sidney, whose works directly challenged the legitimacy of the Restoration and hence were closely confined in circulation. While the political reasons for this restriction were unwelcome, manuscript authorship did make it possible to circumvent the normal political compromises of print publication.[4] The more politically sensitive the material, the more closely guarded would have been the evidence about its circulation, but it is clear that Hutchinson did have attentive and influential readers. Shortly after her death, her friend the Earl of Anglesey, a champion of dissenters who had been recently dismissed as Lord Privy Seal, recorded the impression made by reading one of her manuscripts.[5] Since Anglesey was himself writing a history of Puritanism, it seems unlikely that Hutchinson did not confide to him her *Memoirs* of her husband, John Hutchinson, which were ostensibly addressed only to her children. She had a small circle of close friends and relatives with whom she was ready to trust her writings. New light on that circle has recently emerged.

In 1971 Yale University Library acquired a manuscript book containing a versification, some 8,500 lines in length, of the book of Genesis.[6] Headed simply 'Genesis Chap. 1.st Canto 1.st', the poem takes the Biblical story as far as Jacob's flight from Laban (chapter 31), where it breaks off in the middle of the twentieth canto. There is no indication of the poem's authorship, but a strong clue is provided by the shorter version which was published in five cantos in 1679, under the title of *Order and Disorder: Or; The World Made and Undone. Being Meditations upon the Creation and the Fall; as it is recorded in the beginning of GENESIS.*[7] As I have argued elsewhere[8], the phrasing of the preface to this edition is very close indeed to Lucy Hutchinson's dedication to the Earl of Anglesey of her translation of Lucretius, which she had given to him four years earlier. Moreover, some lines from *Order and Disorder* were copied out as Lucy Hutchinson's by Julius Hutchinson, son of her husband's half-brother, with the note that they had been 'transcribed out of my other Book' and were 'writ by Mrs Hutchinson on ye occasion of ye Coll: her Husbands being then a prisoner in ye Tower: 1664'.[9] (John Hutchinson was imprisoned in the Tower in 1663 and moved to Sandown Castle, where he died, in May 1664.) Julius Hutchinson had possession of most of Lucy Hutchinson's surviving manuscripts, but the 'other Book' has unfortunately not been traced. Perhaps it was the manuscript of poems to which Julius Hutchinson, the first editor of the *Memoirs*, had access in 1806 but which has since gone missing; since this contained lyric poems and an autobiographical fragment, it is unlikely to have had room for the whole of *Order and Disorder*.

It is easy to see why Julius Hutchinson might have mistaken the extract he copied for a speech in Lucy Hutchinson's own voice. Eve laments the expulsion from Eden and blames herself for causing her husband's downfall. Her lament is answered in a long speech by Adam, after which the narrator breaks out:

> Ah! can I this in *Adams* person say,
> While fruitless tears melt my poor life away? (page 75)

A personal note is not far beneath the surface. In her *Memoirs of the Life of Colonel Hutchinson*, Lucy Hutchinson repeatedly expressed her intense guilt at having compromised her husband by forging a letter of recantation in his name; an elegy for her husband portrayed her mental state as 'Fretting remorce & guilty dread' ('Elegies', viii.15). And other of her writings express guilt at her own actions. The Lucretius dedication is a fierce recantation of her own labours on an atheistic poem, effectively indicting herself as an instrument of corruption. In the religious treatise she addressed to her daughter, Barbara Orgil, she warns that 'the weaknesse of our sex' leaves it liable to become 'infected' by the Satanic errors of 'sect masters'.[10] The narrator of *Order and Disorder* sees Eve's fall more in intellectual than in sexual terms, as a lapse to 'Infectious counsel' (1679, page 51). In both passages, female overconfidence and neglect of a male friend lead to disaster. Eve's fall is linked with intellectual error, the kind of error for which Hutchinson belaboured herself in recanting her Lucretius translation; poem, prose treatise and the letter to Anglesey all quote from the same Pauline passage, 2 Tim. iii.6.

As for the date, it is likely that the date of 1664 appeared somewhere on the source Julius Hutchinson was quoting, for it appears also in the Yale manuscript. It is evident that he was not working directly from that manuscript, for he gives two lines which are not found in either printed or manuscript version:

> if on my sinn defiled self I gaze,
> my nakednesse & spotts do me amaze[.] ('Elegies', iiA.31–32)

Apparently Julius Hutchinson was working from some intermediate source, which shared with the Yale manuscript its date but not a sense that the speaker's voice might be different from the poet's.

II

I have argued elsewhere for Lucy Hutchinson's authorship of the poem[11], but since much of her writing remains in manuscript, some further illustrative material may help to confirm the attribution. Parallels can be found between *Order and Disorder* and all Hutchinson's known writings. An epic simile compares an advancing army to

> a furious torrent swell'd with raine
> Which in its violent passage overthrowes
> What ever doth the rapid streame oppose
> And falling down the hills with horrid noise
> All the plantations vines and Corne destroyes
> Carrying away the oxen stalls and fruites
> Resisting banks and trees torne from their rootes[.] (page 203)

Not only the phrasing but the rhyme-words here are strikingly close to Hutchinson's translation of Lucretius:

> But with no lesser force and fury goe
> The inundations which from mountains flow
> When store of raine the rapid torrent fills
> Whose violent streame descending the high hills
> Bears downe the groves, and vineyards, overthrows
> Bridges, whose vanquisht strength cannot oppose
> The suddaine furie of the waters fall,
> Which carries downe great stones, banks, rubbish all
> That in their passage lies; thus with loud noyse
> The rolling flood whatere it meetes destroys[.][12]

Descriptions of the end of the world in the two poems show close parallels: compare 'Loud fragors shall firm rocks in sunder rend' (1679, page 54) with a corresponding line from Hutchinson's translation of Lucretius, 'When the world falls, with horrid fragors rent' (ed. de Quehen, p. 146, v.118, rendering *De rerum natura* v.109, 'succidere horrisono posse omnia victa fragore').

There is a close parallel between a passage in her theological treatise:

a poore fleshly finite creature cannot ascend up to that inaccessible, incomprehensible light, wherein God dwells, to see or consider him as he is absolutely in himselfe; but by considering ourselves, as creatures produced in time, we are led to the knowledge of an eternall, uncreated Being before all time, who is the first cause . . .[13]

and the opening of *Order and Disorder*:

> And so, even that by which we have our sight,
> [God's] covering is, *He clothes himself with light*.
> Easier we may the winds in prison shut . . .
> Than stretch frail humane thought unto the height
> Of the great God, Immense, and Infinite . . .
> Yet as a hidden spring appears in streams,
> The Sun is seen in its reflected beams,
> Whose high embodied Glory is too bright,
> Too strong an object for weak mortal sight;
> So in Gods visible productions, we
> What is invisible, in some sort see;
> While we considering each created thing,
> Are led up to an uncreated spring,
> And by gradations of successive Time,
> At last unto Eternity do climb,
> As we in tracks of second causes tread
> Unto the first uncaused cause are led . . . (1679, page 3)

Both the poem and the prose passage cite as authorities the passage from Romans (i.20) that underlies the prefaces to *Order and Disorder* and the Lucretius translation, and another Pauline epistle, 1 Timothy vi.16: 'Who only hath immortality, dwelling in the light which no man can approach unto; whom no man hath seen, nor can see'. In discussing the fall of the angels, Hutchinson's treatise comments that: 'What that sinne was particularly, with other circumstances of their fall, the Scripture doth not positively informe us' (page 33); *Order and Disorder*, discussing the same topic, observes:

> But circumstances that we cannot know
> Of their rebellion and their overthrow
> We will not dare t'invent[.] (1679, page 46)

A number of verse fragments by Hutchinson seem to represent drafts for *Order and Disorder* or to spring from a related creative impulse. Though the basic sentiments can be regarded as religious and moral commonplaces, the parallels of phrasing and clusters of imagery are striking. Thus in one fragment the poet calls on her soul to turn away from the world:

> O sad benighted soule awake awake
> ~~And now at length thy glorious fetters breake~~
> ~~Vndoe lifes powerfull charms~~
> No more this brittle clay thy dwelling make
> Let the enchantment be dissolud & all
> ~~The seeming~~
> Its beauties end in their originall
> From dust all fleshly glory rose & must
> Againe resolue into its natiue dust
> Returne Returne to thy eternall rest
> There thy restored ~~ioyes~~ sence on pure ioyes feast[.][14]

The fetters of the deleted lines are also to be found in *Order and Disorder*:

> Men cannot from their golden fetters scape
> Till their coy Soules endure a holy rape[.] (MS, page 227[15])

The first, printed part of *Order and Disorder* ends with a similar self-dedication, likewise drawing on the same Biblical passage, Psalm cxvi.7 ('Return unto my rest, o my soul'):

> Return, return my soul to thy true rest,
> As young benighted birds unto their nest,
> There hide thyself under the wings of love
> Till the bright morning all thy clouds remove. (1679, page 78)

In similar terms, later in the poem the narrator invokes the divine wings that will bring fixity:

> Great ffather, when my soule shall fly away
> Out of this flesh, when thou this house of Clay
> Shalt with thy breath dissolve, O let me then
> The swift Wings of thy sacred Dove obtaine
> Which may beare vp my soule through empty Ayre
> To thy Celestiall Court and fix it there. (MS, page 165)

In the 'Elegies', John Hutchinson

> Soaring on wings of heauenly Loue
> Peirct Through his Clowds & fixt above[.] (ix.19–20)

'Fix' is one of Hutchinson's favourite words, its significance crystallized
in a poignant couplet on her husband:

> Hee's fixt aboue I by the wilde winds tost
> Am only in the hazard to be lost.[16]

The narrator of *Order and Disorder* can

> find
> Only the worlds first Chaos in my mind (page 2)

unless her 'rude conceptions' are aided by grace; in the 'Elegies' Lucy
Hutchinson can

> find
> In ye disordred passions of my mind

a parallel with her own and her garden's 'wild & rude' states in the
absence of her husband's ordering hand (vii, 31–32, 10).

The verse fragments and the 'Elegies' savagely attack the Restoration
political order and use the rural life, and sometimes in particular the
semi-paradisal, lost world of Owthorpe, as a political ideal of republican simplicity: in the country,

> Ambition wades not through the peoples blood
> To the affected glory of a throne [.][17]

Order and Disorder declares that

> all who to the high throne climb
> Must wade through blood and strife check at no Crime . . .
> With a guilt stained conscience hourely fight [.] (MS, page 284)

Both passages may recall the Lucretius translation:

> tis much better to obey,
> And in a subjects humble state to stand,
> Then to enjoy a crowne and vast command.
> Thus through ambitions glorious path in vaine
> Men, tired with sweate and blood, their passage gaine[.] [18]

(Such passages disturbed the royalist Evelyn, who found it necessary to
affirm 'against our poet, that the first Legislatiue power was not in the
people'.[19]) Both *Order and Disorder* and a manuscript poem now lost
emphasize in similar terms how the ruler's guilty conscience disturbs the
sleep that comes easily in the country.[20]

Order and Disorder outlines an anti-courtly poetics, correcting the false,
'unsteadie view' of worldly power: those who are dejected should take
heart, for they often

> dread what either never may arrive,
> Or not as seen in their false perspective;
> For in the crystal mirror of Gods grace
> All things appear with a new lovely face[.] (1679, page 77)

God's 'sight . . . penetrates into all shades all deepes' (MS, page 112). In similar terms, a poem in Hutchinson's theological manuscript declares that

> Tis true y^t through our fleshly (opticks) wee *of AS*
> All things in mists & in darke figures see
> But faiths cleare perspectiue makes heaven plaine
> To those who yet on distant earth remaine[.]²¹

A similar complex of ideas and phrases can be found in the 'Elegies':

> Out of ye Pile a Pheanix did arise
> Enlightned with quick penetrating Eies
> Which distant heauen into y:^e mind did draw
> And y:^e disguizd world in its owne forme saw . . .
> In prisons exile Sollitude disgrace
> And death it selfe beheld a louely face
> On God alone he fixt his steadfast looke
> Till God into himselfe his Creature tooke
> Who all Things elce w:^th God like eies now viewd
> And seeing y:^m in God Saw They were good
> Thus was delighted in The Creature Streames
> While They were guilt w:^th y:^e Creators beames
> But when y:^t heauenly Sun withdrew no more
> Did he The Inreflecting glasse adore
> Nor in y:^e Shadow Stayd but wheresoere
> The glorious substance pleasd next to appeare . . .
> This gaue Calamity a louely face
> And put on honours Crowne upon disgrace[.] (i.25–28, 37–48, 61–62)

Hutchinson's reluctance to hold back in her polemical denunciations helps to explain why great caution was needed in circulating her manuscripts. Yet she did circulate *Order and Disorder* and bring the earlier, less outspoken, cantos into print. Since the 1679 text differs in several ways from the Yale manuscript, and Hutchinson's putative text from both, we can assume that there were at least three manuscripts of the poem in part or in whole. However, the Yale manuscript is the fullest version remaining, and it needs a careful scrutiny.

III

How did the Countess of Rochester come to acquire the book? As was noted by the sales catalogue, 'Anne Rochester . . . probably acquired the manuscript through her friendship with Lucy Hutchinson, *née* Apsley'.[22] Kinship as well as friendship were at issue.[23] Anne Wilmot, Countess of Rochester, was the daughter of Sir John St John of Lydiard Tregoze, Wiltshire. Sir John was an elder brother of Lucy Hutchinson's mother, also named Lucy, who married Sir Allen Apsley in 1615. Lucy Hutchinson remained proud of her connections with the St John family, which she considered to have maintained a proud independence of courtly influence, and to some extent of the established church, even though like so many families its political allegiances divided during the Civil War. Anne St John became strongly associated with the royalist cause through her second marriage, to Henry Wilmot, Earl of Rochester, and after his death she used all the courtly connections she could to support the interests of the children by her two marriages. However, she had also gone out of her way at the Restoration to support Lucy Hutchinson in her campaign to save her husband from the death penalty.[24] She retained a strong vein of piety which constantly clashed with the libertine views of her son John, and played a leading part in encouraging his spectacular deathbed conversion. In 1676, between her preparation of the Lucretius manuscript and the publication of *Order and Disorder*, Lucy Hutchinson attended a gathering at the Earl of Anglesey's Oxfordshire house which was attended both by the young Earl of Rochester and his mother.[25] The young poet was already showing a strong interest in the poetry of Lucretius, as was his niece Anne Wharton. Whatever their political differences, the two women would have shared a preference for pious verse over Lucretian atheism, and it is possible that Lucy Hutchinson gave her the manuscript to fortify her in her views.

The connection with the Countess of Rochester, however, has served to confuse the authorship question. In the manuscript, as in the printed text, the poem is anonymous; and it was entered anonymously in the Term Catalogue. However, in his *Fasti Oxonienses* Anthony Wood attributed it to Lucy Hutchinson's brother, Sir Allen Apsley, and he has been followed by all later authorities. Wood was interested in Apsley, for he claimed to have been 'credibly enformed' that he had had an affair with the Countess of Rochester and was the real father of the young Earl of Rochester.[26] His attributions always need to be used with caution, however: W. R. Parker declared him 'almost wholly unreliable as

biographical source material' for Milton.[27] The only poem of Apsley's
yet traced is an eight-line lyric addressed to his wife.[28] Apsley was close
to his sister, who always speaks of him with great warmth in the *Memoirs*,
but in ideological terms they were a long way apart. Apsley had supported the king during the Civil War and at the Restoration became a
minor court functionary, serving as keeper of the royal hawks and later
as treasurer to the household of the Duke of York. He emphatically
defended the Restoration regime's punitive measures against dissenters,
acclaiming the arrest of Richard Baxter in 1661 as a victory in the war
against the Presbyterians.[29] An opposition tract branded him in 1677 as
one of 'the Principal Labourers, in the Great Designe of POPERY and
ARBITRARY POWER, &c', and as 'a Red Letter man [*i.e.* Papist], if
of any Religion'. He came under attack as an instrument of the Duke's
conversion to Catholicism.[30] He was also accused of general corruption: 'This gallant pimps it for his sonne'.[31] By 1679, when *Order and
Disorder* was licensed, the Exclusion Crisis was at its height and in the
elections for a new Parliament a wave of suspicion of the court toppled
Apsley from his seat. *Order and Disorder* is radically Puritan in spirit and
a highly unlikely poem for such a man to have written. Even his
favourite sport of hawking comes under attack in the poem, where
hawks and birds of prey are regularly associated with postlapsarian
tyranny and oppression (printed text, page 67, MS, pages 90, 143, 166).
(Lucy Hutchinson seems to have been a little uneasy about her husband's interest in hawking, recording that while he loved the sport in his
youth, he 'soone left it off', and that in the 1650s he again 'gave over his
hawkes' after a brief period.[32]) Apsley was part of the public world of
the Restoration; Lucy Hutchinson's political views as well as her gender
kept her out of that world, and her status as an author was unknown
outside a narrow circle. It is not surprising that Wood, learning of a relative of the Countess who wrote poetry, should have jumped to the conclusion that Apsley was the author, but he succeeded in misleading later
generations.

The inscription 'Anne Rochester her book' appears on the first leaf
of the Yale manuscript, followed on the next leaf by the beginning of
the text. In turning the book upside down one finds another signature,
'Rochester 1664', on the leaf attached to the binding at the back. The
date could thus conceivably appertain to the Countess of Rochester's
possession of the notebook rather than to the poem, which is copied
from the opposite direction. The manuscript is a leather-bound, gilt-
edged notebook measuring 303 × 188mm. The watermark is of a slung-
horn pattern common between the 1620s and the 1690s.[33] The poem
has no title, beginning merely 'Genesis Chap. 1.st Canto 1.st'. The title

of the printed edition is rather specifically tied to the period up to the
Fall, and though *Order and Disorder* is a convenient title, we cannot be
confident that Hutchinson would have used it for the entire poem.
The manuscript is in two different scribal hands: there is no sign of the
hands either of Lucy Hutchinson or of her brother, whose twice-
crossed 't's are a distinctive feature. The first, rather angular hand
takes the narrative from page 3 to page 174, towards the end of Canto
9, where a new scribe begins in mid-sentence. This second hand, more
elegant, hand carries the poem to page 324 and breaks off in mid-line.
Neither hand corresponds to either of the two scribal hands associated
with the other surviving manuscripts not in Hutchinson's own hand,
the Lucretius translation (British Library Additional MS 19333) and the
'Elegies' (Nottinghamshire Archives DD/HU2). The remaining thirty-
eight pages of the manuscript are blank. In addition to these two
hands, the manuscript contains evidence of corrections in different
hands, concentrated especially around the earliest and latest parts of
the poem.

What is the relationship between the manuscript and the 1679
printed text? The evidence is far from conclusive, but there are some
indications that the *Order and Disorder* manuscript represents an earlier
version of the poem. It appears that the scribe transcribing the first part
of the poem did not have access to the 1679 edition or to the manuscript
on which it was based, for on page 68, l. 6, a gap has been left for an
entire line, a gap which is filled in 1679, page 51: 'Hence learn pernicious councellors to shun'. On page 70, the line 'To be my helper and
associate', found in 1679 and necessary for a rhyme, has been omitted.
Some readings in 1679 seem evidently preferable: for example, on page
4 the verb 'Unite' is grammatically preferable to the manuscript's
'Vnitie' (page 6). On page 16, the reading 'wastes and grows' for the
moon is better than 'waites & growes' as in the MS (page 22), and on page
24, 'sacred Council' makes more sense than the manuscript's 'second
Councell' (page 31). The manuscript, page 37, claims that even the
noonday light 'could not penetrate' the thicker coverts of Eden; in 1679
(page 29) the reading 'scarcely' looks like a slightly pedantic correction.
The 1679 reading 'O're all the banks and all the flat ground spread'
(page 30) is clearly preferable to the manuscript's 'Ore all the ground,
and all the fat banks spread' (page 39). The context makes it clear that
the reference to the declining mother's 'vsefull grace' (MS, page 50) is
mistaken where 1679 reads 'youthful Grace' (p. 37). Some 36 lines are
found in 1679 and not in the manuscript. Most notably, the 1679 text
offers a much more elaborate account of the three persons of the
Trinity. Lucy Hutchinson was increasingly concerned in later life to

defend Calvinist orthodoxy against sceptical challenge, and the increasing popularity of anti-Trinitarian views may have led her to want to make this part of the poem more explicit. (Here, it may be noted, she differed sharply from Milton, whose account of the Trinity in *Paradise Lost* is sufficiently ambiguous to have been given orthodox and heterodox interpretations). Another divergence that can be explained on ideological grounds comes in a discussion of the status of the stars: such events as droughts, floods and wars are, the manuscript reads, 'Not only shewne but Caus'd' by the conjunction of the stars (page 23, line 5). The 1679 text reads that they are 'At least shewn, if not caus'd', making the stars signs but not causes. Such a careful emendation would seem to point to a growing authorial orthodoxy, consistent with what we know of Hutchinson. One of the most distinctive features of the 1679 printing is the cramming of the margins with Biblical proof-texts, making the whole poem an extended dialogue with Scripture. In the manuscript there is a sprinkling of marginal glosses in the first two cantos, and a few proof-texts are cited that are not found in 1679, but many more are omitted and in the later part of the poem the glosses largely disappear. The glosses sometimes point obliquely at politically sensitive areas, and it seems likely that Hutchinson amplified them for the poem's publication. Thus the passage on the stars' prophecies of doom is glossed with Judges 5, reminding us of Deborah's song of victory over Sisera, and this gives special force to the lines:

> For when God cuts the bloody Tyrant down,
> He will their lives with peace and blessings crown. (1679, page 18)

Assuming that the singular 'Tyrant' here is not merely a misprint, it becomes a bold challenge to Charles II, with a force lacking in the manuscript reading, 'Tyrants' (MS, page 24).

The differences between manuscript and printed text do not go one way, however: apart from the different formulations' of the Trinity passage, eight lines in the manuscript are not to be found in the printed text. One striking passage hits at the fashionable pastime of cockfighting, which was revived at the Restoration after attempts to ban it under the Protectorate:

> But Cocks more generous, murther'd not for food
> But for their Hono.ʳ spilt each others blood[.] (MS, page 90)

It is possible that the divergences can be explained by the manuscript's representing a later phase of revision which pruned down some lines and added others, though the weight of evidence seems to point the other way. What does seem clear is that the manuscript was read and revised over a lengthy period of time. The Countess inscribed the note-book in 1664; but a note which seems to be in her hand adds 'thus far printed' at the end of the fifth canto, thus dating the note post-1679 (PLATE 1). A frustratingly enigmatic note at the start of canto x (MS, page 190), possibly but not definitely in the second scribe's hand, reads 'There [*sic*] were copied out of the old notes after they were dead' (PLATE 2).[34] If 'they' were the Hutchinsons, the note must postdate Lucy Hutchinson's death in 1681 or early 1682. Though the note seems to imply that the sections of Cantos viii and ix copied out by the second scribe were done when 'they' were alive and from a different, more reli-able manuscript source, there is no sign of a break in ink or handwrit-ing at canto x. This evidence for a relatively late date for the latter part of the manuscript is hard to square with Anne Wilmot's date of 1664—unless that date referred to her acquisition of the manuscript book rather than the transcription of the poem.

The marks of revision are in several different hands, and involve dif-ferent kinds of correction. For the earlier part of the manuscript, in sev-eral places the manuscript has been brought to a wording closer to the state of the 1679 (pages 9, 10, 13, 15, 29, 46, 56, 57, 59, 64, 65, 75). The Trinity passage (MS, page 7; PLATE 3) is marked with a cross, and a for-mulation derived from the earlier version's account of the three sepa-rate persons, 'And were that Elohim', has been changed to 'was y^t great Elohim', bringing the text closer to 1679 though with a certain gram-matical forcing. Another passage containing a couplet not found in the 1679 text (page 9) is also marked with a cross. This process has not been carried through consistently, and a number of differences from the 1679 text remain. At one point, the hand that may be Rochester's firmly changes 'fallen natures' to 'fallen sinners', moving away from the printed text (MS, page 59; 1679, page 45). It is possible that the text was being collated with an earlier state of the version that became the 1679 text. It seems that at least one further version of the poem was in circu-lation, for the text of Eve's speech given by Julius Hutchinson has two lines not found in either 1667 or the Yale manuscript (see Appendix under MS pp. 93–94); the Yale manuscript and 1679 text differ less from each other than from this version.

Another set of corrections, most of them in what seem to be at least two different hands, appears to have been done without reference to any other text, guided rather by a desire—more characteristic of the later seventeenth century than of Hutchinson's age—for metrical tidi-ness, euphony and the precise rendering of elision. On page 22, line 19, the reviser has noticed that the line 'Their wandring Vessells on broad seas to quiet' does not rhyme with 'discried' in the following line and

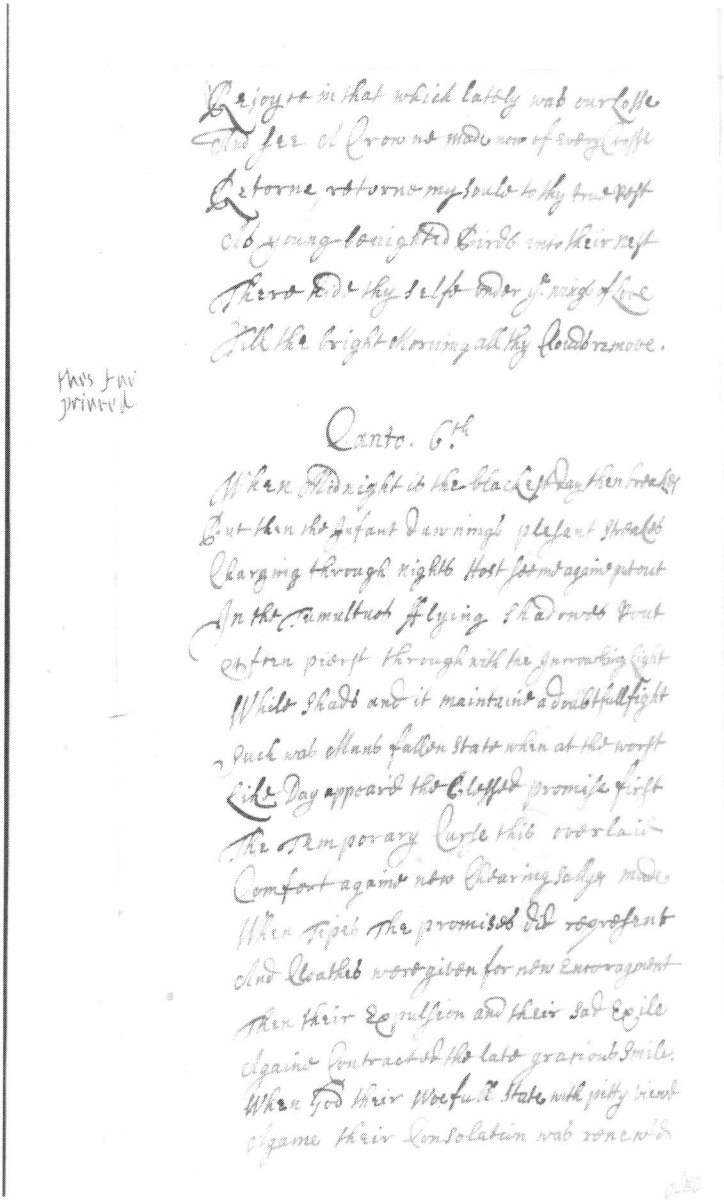
Rejoyce in that which lately was our losse
And see a Crowne made now of every Crosse
Returne returne my soule to thy true rest
As young-flighted Birds into their nest
There hide thy selfe under ye wings of Love
Till the bright Morning all thy clouds remove.

this far printed

Canto. 6th

When Midnight is the blackest day then breaks
But then the infant dawnings pleasant streaks
Charging through nights Host
In the tumultuous flying shadowes rout
Often pierst through with the increasing light
While shades and it maintaind a doubtfull fight
Such was Mans fallen State when at the worst
Like Day appeard the blessed promise first
The temporary Curse this overlaid
Comfort againe new Cheering sallys made
When Types the promises did represent
And Cloathes were given for new encouragement
Then their Expulsion and their sad Exile
Againe Contracted the late gracious smile.
When God their Woefull State with pitty view'd
Againe their Consolation was renew'd

PLATE 1. *The end of canto 5 and beginning of canto 6: New Haven, Yale University, Osborn Collection fb 100, p. 106 (Original size 303 × 188mm.) Reproduced by permission of the James Marshall and Marie-Claire Osborn Collection, Beinecke Library, Yale University.*

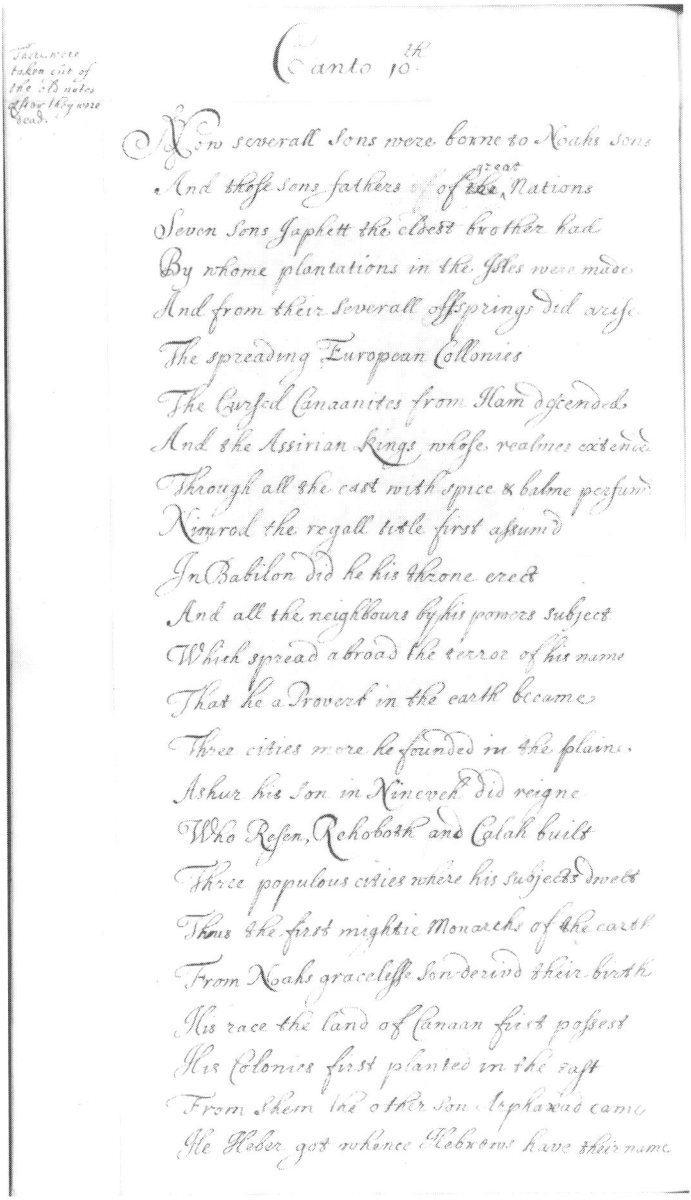

Canto 10th.

Thinge were
taken out of
the old notes
after they were
dead.

Now severall Sons were borne to Noahs Sons
And those Sons fathers of the great Nations
Seven Sons Japhett the eldest brother had
By whome plantations in the Isles were made
And from their severall offsprings did arise
The spreading European Collonies
The Cursed Canaanites from Ham descended,
And the Assirian kings, whose realmes extend
Through all the east with spice & balme perfum'd
Nimrod the regall title first assum'd
In Babilon did he his throne erect
And all the neighbours by his powers subject
Which spread abroad the terror of his name
That he a Proverb in the earth became
Three cities more he founded in the plaine.
Ashur his Son in Nineveh did reigne
Who Resen, Rehoboth and Calah built
Three populous cities where his subjects dwelt
Thus the first mightie Monarchs of the earth
From Noahs gracelesse Son derivd their birth
His race the land of Canaan first possest
His Colonies first planted in the east
From Shem the other Son Arphaxad came
He Heber got whence Hebrews have their name

PLATE 2. *The opening of canto 10: New Haven, Yale University, Osborn Collection fb 100, p. 190 (Original size 303 × 188mm.) Reproduced by permission of the James Marshall and Marie-Claire Osborn Collection, Beinecke Library, Yale University.*

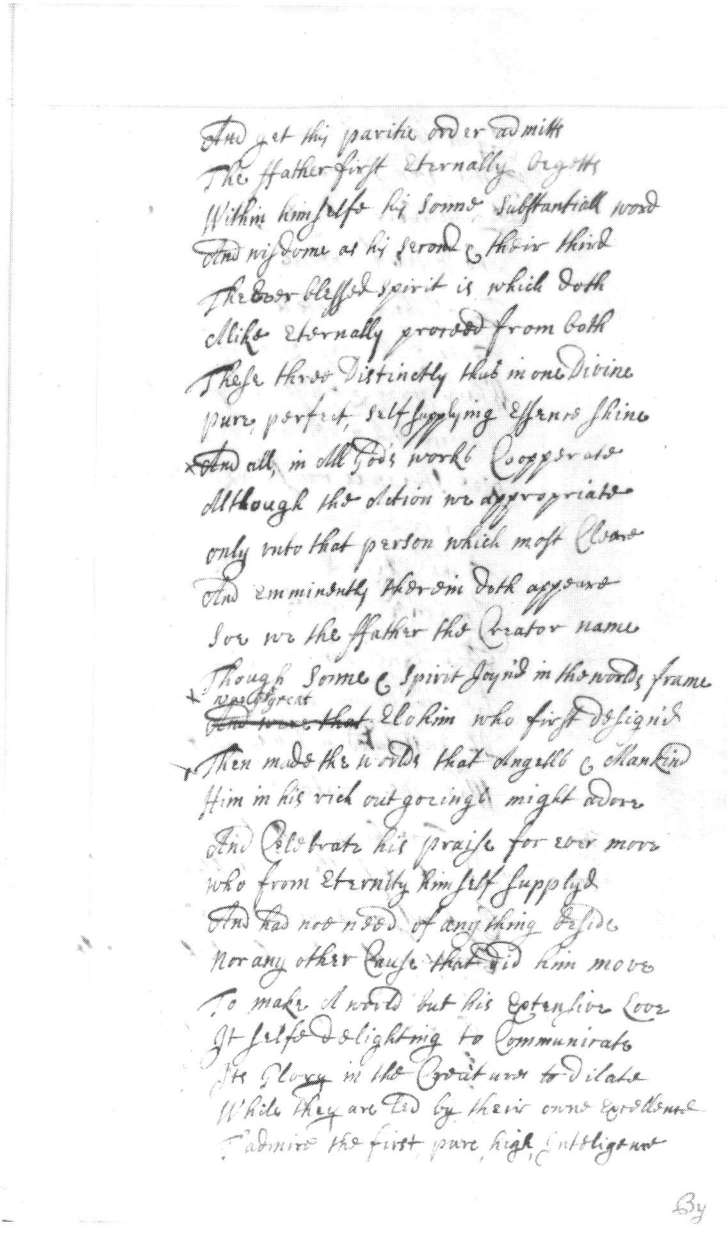

And yet this paritie order admitt
The ffather first eternally begetts
Within himselfe his Sonne substantiall word
And wisdome as his second & their third
The ever blessed spirit is which doth
Alike eternally proceed from both
These three Distinctly thus in one Divine
pure, perfect, selfsupplying Essence shine
And all in all Gods worke Cooperate
Although the action we appropriate
only unto that person which most Cleare
And eminently therein doth appeare
Soe we the ffather the Creator name
Though Sonne & spirit joyn'd in the worlds frame
was the great
that Elohim who first designd
Then made the worlds that Angells & Mankind
Him in his rich outgoeings might adore
And Celebrate his praise for ever more
who from Eternity himselfe supplyd
And had noe need of any thing beside
Nor any other Cause that did him move
To make A world but his extensive Love
It selfe delighting to Communicate
Its Glory in the Creatures to dilate
While they are led by their owne Excellence
T'admire the first pure, high, Intelligence

PLATE 3. *Canto 1, lines 97–122: New Haven, Yale University, Osborn Collection fb 100, p. 7 (Original size 303 × 188mm.) Reproduced by permission of the James Marshall and Marie-Claire Osborn Collection, Beinecke Library, Yale University.*

substituted 'ride'; but 1679 reads 'Their wandring vessels in broad seas to guide'. Page 10, line 4 of the manuscript originally read: 'Which doth both soule & body with full Joyes feast'. A different hand has deleted 'doth both' and inserted 'doth'. The motive here seems to have been to remove the awkward elision of 'body with'; but the change does not bring the line closer to 1679, which reads 'Which doth both soul and sense with full joys feast'. The revisions generally tend towards metrical regularity: thus on page 10, 'The spreading true Coelestiall vine' is made into a pentameter by changing 'The eternall' to 'Th'eternall', and 'This Heaven the third to vs within' is likewise reworked by inserting 'is' after 'Heaven'; on page 16, 'Like Hosts of various Creatures march' has 'spreading' added after the first word; on page 19, 'Then sprouted Grasse and hearbs and plants' is given an added foot with 'and Flow'rs'.[35] (The frequency of tetrameter lines in the poem, incidentally, may be taken as further confirmation of Lucy Hutchinson's authorship, for they are a conspicuous feature of her Lucretius translation.[36]) In the line 'Pious soules back to eternall rest convey' (MS, page 308), the scribe has emended to 't'eternall'. On page 256, 'There Israel's devout congregations joyn'd' becomes 'There Isra'lls pious congregations joyn'd'. This quest for euphony sometimes overlooks semantic factors. For example, on page 11 'This Heaven the third to vs within' becomes 'This Heaven is the third to vs within', which in reading 'Heaven' as disyllabic becomes a regular pentameter; the reviser has not noticed, however, that 'the third . . .' is an appositional phrase and that the 'is' is supplied two lines later. At one point different revisers register their disagreements: on page 9, line 26, the original reading 'Although the paradice of the faire world above', which corresponds verbatim to 1679 but was presumably objected to as unmetrical, is first changed to 'Though the faire paradice of the world above' and then another hand, possibly the Countess of Rochester's, deletes the resituated 'faire' and reinscribes the word above its original position in the line.

In the later parts of the poem, no printed text was available for comparison in any case, and the notes on the manuscript are clearly by a person or persons who had no direct knowledge of the author's intentions. On page 218 there is an additional note: 'what is at the end of this Canto seems to belong to this place', sensibly proposing that eight lines at the end of a canto should be inserted earlier on. The 'old notes' seem to have been in an unreliable state, and to have been unavailable by the time the annotation was made. An interesting deletion later in the poem may reflect the textual uncertainties. At one point towards the end of the poem, describing Isaac's anxieties about his wife's childlessness, the narrator makes an interjection in an apparently male voice:

> Such is my spouses beautie white and red
> Fresh healthy colours in her cheeks are spred
> And such mans wayward nature is, that one
> Felicitie denied, all else seeme none[.] (page 274)

The first two lines have been heavily deleted, possibly by the scribe. They do not seem quite to make sense in the context, and read more like a conventional allegorization of Christ's relationship to the church. In context, they seem to point to the speaker's being male rather than female; it is interesting that they were felt to stand out as inappropriate.

It is difficult at this stage to find a coherent pattern in this evidence. The 1664 date in the manuscript book, together with variants indicating that the text may be earlier than the 1679 printing, point to a relatively early date for the poem, and this would be consistent with the manuscript evidence on which Julius Hutchinson drew. On the other hand, if we accept his attribution to Lucy Hutchinson, we are left to explain the claim that the latter cantos were copied out after 'their death'. One explanation could be that the parts copied out by the second scribe were inserted at a later stage, after a period of interruption. This is not incompatible with external evidence. The later 1650s and early 1660s could be a possible date for Lucy Hutchinson to have composed the poem. By then she was being urged to desist from the Lucretius translation because the treatment of 'geniall things' did not become a lady.[37] Though she did finish the task, if she already felt the intense guilt about the project that can be seen in the 1675 dedication, she may have felt a need to turn to sacred verse as a form of penitence. This was a period of inner exile for the couple, initiated by Cromwell's dissolution of the Long Parliament in 1653, when John Hutchinson retired from public life to his 'rich fruitefull Vale' in Nottinghamshire (*Memoirs*, page 206) and intensified after the Restoration, when he had undertaken at his wife's urging to refrain from political activity in exchange for his life. The couple enjoyed a period of domestic tranquillity, albeit tinged with sadness at the loss of a new daughter-in-law, that is recalled with great warmth in the *Memoirs*. But John Hutchinson's work on his estate was in some ways a displacement of political energies, and he was also chafing at his enforced neutralization. Far from recanting the Good Old Cause, he was rereading secular documents and the Bible and 'the more he examin'd the cause from the first, the more he became confirm'd in it' (*Memoirs*, page 234). Lucy Hutchinson emphasized the intensity of her husband's reading of the Bible in the early 1660s; he had asked her to send a recent set of annotations to him in his prison, and complained that they were 'short'. He was constantly rereading Paul's epistles and a favoured set of psalms (*Memoirs*, pages 243, 270). At the end of the *Memoirs* manuscript Lucy Hutchinson copied out a long list of the passages her husband had marked in his Bible, with thematic headings linking his fate with the tyranny and ungodliness of the regime.[38] *Order and Disorder*, with its copious elaborations on the Biblical narrative, would have been appropriate reading for a household in which it was a major drawback of annotations to be short; and the detailed marginal glosses to the 1679 text correspond well to the passages most frequently marked by her husband.[39] The poem's sharp oscillations between lyricism, gentle meditation and prophetic outbursts would fit the rhythms of that period.

Of an earlier period of retirement Lucy Hutchinson wrote that her husband was like Moses in the wilderness at the time he wrote the book of Genesis (*Memoirs*, page 35). For her to have written her own account of Genesis during this new retreat would have been appropriate. During his final retreat John Hutchinson busied himself with 'opening springs and planting trees and dressing his plantations' (*Memoirs*, page 239), and in her elegies his wife returned again and again to the beauty of that carefully-cultivated landscape, presenting herself as one of the plants he had cultivated and lamenting its neglect now that weeds

> orerun all ye sweete fragrant bankes
> And [hide] what growes in better ord:rd rankes[.] (vii.29–30)

It is not so surprising that Julius Hutchinson, encountering Eve's speech amongst these poems, took it to be one more of her laments for the lost paradise of Owthorpe. This was also, of course, the period when Milton was completing his epic of Fall and restoration, under the similar political pressures of the promise and collapse of a millennial republican project. The birth of a child in 1662, however, must have impeded her progress on such an ambitious project, and it would certainly have been curtailed when her husband was suddenly and unexpectedly arrested in 1663. Over the following years she was intensely involved in trying to safeguard and eventually sell off her husband's estates, as well as with the composition of the life of her husband and an autobiography. The 1670s see a major turn in her writing towards directly devotional themes, with her translation from a Latin text of John Owen[40], whose congregation she attended, and a religious treatise addressed to her daughter. This may have been a period when she returned to *Order and Disorder*.

On the other hand, some factors point to the whole work's being composed at this later date. If, as John Shawcross argues, the poem is pervaded with allusions to *Paradise Lost*, it almost certainly postdated 1667—though in fact the evidence here does not seem conclusive.[41] The poem's treatment of the Fall is consistent with, but very much richer than, Hutchinson's treatment of the same topic in her statement of beliefs composed in 1667.[42] That year seems to have marked a period of intensified dedication to Biblical and theological studies and to Biblical verse. The theological notebook whose first dated item is from that year contains detailed annotations on Calvin's *Institutes* and verse fragments which, as has been seen, read like early drafts for *Order and Disorder*. A translation from Ovid (*Metamorphoses*, i.89–103) testifies to a general interest in creation narratives. In the theological treatise to her daughter, which must be dated after her marriage in 1668, there are some very close parallels with passages in *Order and Disorder*. Later composition would explain why only the first five cantos were printed in 1679, and why when she addressed her Lucretius translation to Anglesey in 1675 she could lament that 'I had not the capacity of making a worke, nor the good fortune of chusing a subject, worthy of being presented to your Lordship'.[43]

There is much that remains obscure about Lucy Hutchinson's later life. If she did not exactly go underground, her unrepentant defence of a regicide made her writings deeply sensitive, and some of the truth may never be known. What seems clear is that this confinement to manuscript circulation, even though as we have seen it did give her work far from negligible possibilities of circulation, could be a source of frustration to the author. Even in the self-deprecating dedication to the Lucretius translation, there is a clear undertow of a deep sense of poetic achievement: her verse, she writes, has gained some 'glory', her muse is 'aspiring'. In presenting her translation to a friend and giving him the option of burning it, she was of course evoking the models of Virgil's *Aeneid* and Sidney's *Arcadia*. In the humanist tradition in which her unusual education had initiated her, bringing one of the great classical epics into a vernacular language was a supreme achievement. English had waited a long time for its Lucretius. Anglesey himself registered the achievement by endorsing his copy 'by the worthye *author* [emphasis added] Mrs. Lucie Hutchinson' (de Quehen edition, page 17). In preparing the Lucretius, she had a scribe carefully copy out her translation, even giving it line numbers as if in a classic text, and when she became frustrated by scribal errors impatiently completed the copying herself. And she chooses her words very carefully: she asks Anglesey to 'preserve, wherever your Lordship shall dispose this booke, this record with it'. There would be no point in writing the preface at all if she did not anticipate that the manuscript would in fact be further circulated:

she declares that she has 'sett up this seamarke, to warn incautious travellers' (de Quehen edition, page 26), a powerfully charged antidote to the work it accompanies. She ends by saying that she depends on his 'protection against all the censures a booke might expose me to' (de Quehen edition, page 27). Paradoxically, by rounding so strongly on Lucretius in the dedication she has just about made it possible to see its circulation as legitimate. The main reason she is offering the manuscript is a fear that a 'lost copie' was circulating. The fear was understandable, for the manuscript could easily be used against her. Here was the widow of a former regicide circulating the ideas of a godless epicurean: what could be a more classic example of the hypocrisy for which puritans and republicans were regularly denounced? And yet a careful reading of the Lucretius dedication suggests that she may have been envisaging circulation not only in manuscript but also in print. Anglesey, it may be noted, had played a significant part in introducing controversial manuscript works to the printed sphere—including Marvell's *The Rehearsal Transpros'd* and Milton's *History of Britain*. Despite all her intense ambivalence about the Lucretius translation, by the 1670s Lucy Hutchinson was chafing at the constraints of keeping it silent. The self-division of the preface could be resolved if poetry could be shown to be not just an instrument of idolatry but a means of gaining access to lost divine truths. In composing, or completing, *Order and Disorder* in the later 1670s she could claim to have helped to redeem poetry as well as her own personal career as a writer. The preface ends not with an attack on false myths but with a celebration of poetry's power to evoke the divine order, the true origins of things, and the poem itself, for all its satirical vengefulness, is infused also with a sense of exhilaration at the taking flight of a free, redeemed muse. Anonymous printing enabled Hutchinson to elude official identification yet still address a wider audience, some of whom, the preface makes quite clear, were expected to guess her identity.

It is then not so surprising to find her venturing into print (PLATE 4). Though we need not expect any special link between seventeenth-century writers and their publishers, the publisher of *Order and Disorder*, Henry Mortlock, did have a striking number of Nottinghamshire connections. A native of Stanton in Derbyshire, Mortlock seems to have had family connections with Nottinghamshire nonconformists which are reflected in some of the works he printed. He had been questioned by the authorities earlier in the decade for allegedly selling pamphlets defending the regicides.[44] Some of his books were printed to be sold by Nottingham booksellers, one of whom, John Mortlock, seems to have been a relative and the son of a noted Nottingham Presbyterian.[45] Two

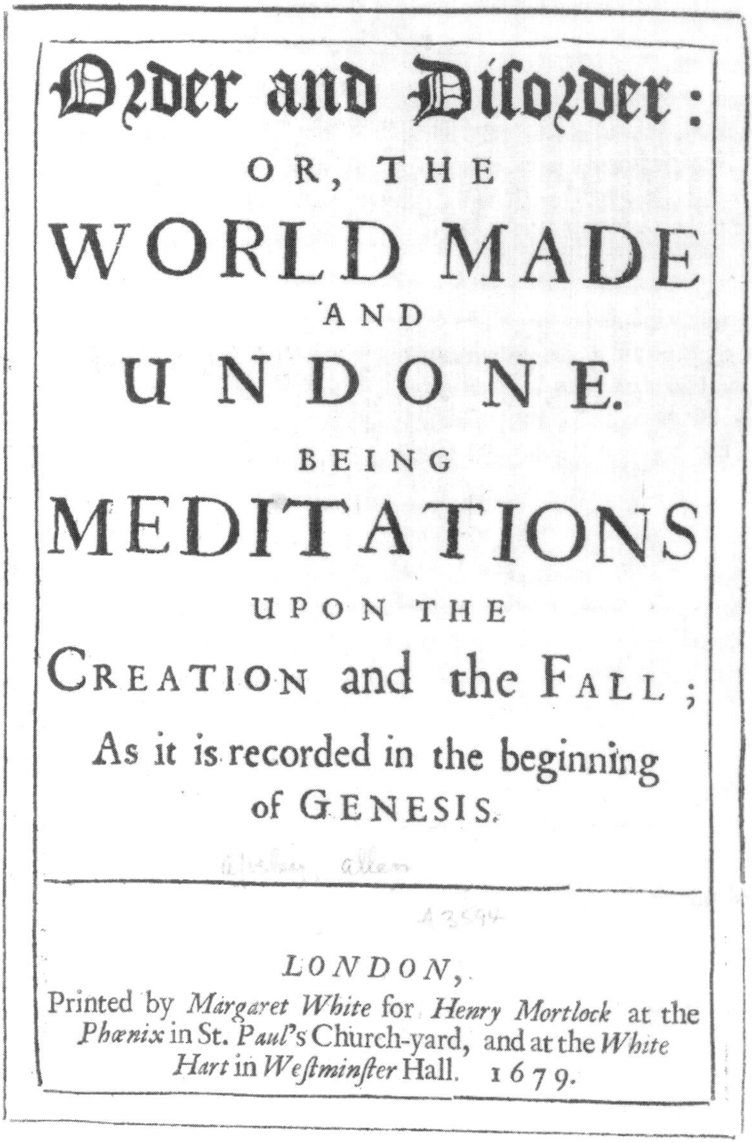

𝕺𝖗𝖉𝖊𝖗 𝖆𝖓𝖉 𝕯𝖎𝖘𝖔𝖗𝖉𝖊𝖗:

OR, THE

WORLD MADE

AND

UNDONE.

BEING

MEDITATIONS

UPON THE

CREATION and the FALL ;

As it is recorded in the beginning
of GENESIS.

allen

A 3594

LONDON,

Printed by *Margaret White* for *Henry Mortlock* at the
Phœnix in St. *Paul's* Church-yard, and at the *White
Hart* in *Weſtminſter* Hall.   1 6 7 9.

PLATE 4. *Title-page of* Order and Disorder, *1679. Reproduced by permission of
the James Marshall and Marie-Claire Osborn Collection, Beinecke Library, Yale
University.*

years before *Order and Disorder* appeared, Henry Mortlock had published
the first great work of Nottinghamshire history, Robert Thoroton's *The
Antiquities of Nottinghamshire*, which is advertised along with some of his
other books at the back of *Order and Disorder*. Thoroton, though himself
a scourge of Dissenters, kept his political views in the background in this
work. He had taken the suggestion for his project from Gervase Pigott,
a Nottinghamshire friend and political ally of the Hutchinsons.
Thoroton's *Antiquities* discreetly mentions John Hutchinson's tomb at
Owthorpe, whose outspoken inscription had been composed by his
wife.[46] Pigott had contributed an elegy to a commemorative volume to
the Nottinghamshire Presbyterian Francis Pierrepont which was published by Mortlock[47]; another contributor, Edward Stillingfleet, who
had tutored Pierrepont, was to become the author most published by
Mortlock, who sealed the connection in 1677 by marrying Stillingfleet's
niece. Stillingfleet had supported movements towards a broadly-based
church under the Protectorate and though he was later taxed by his former allies, now Dissenters, for supporting the Anglican settlement, he
tried to keep channels of communication open. Thus in 1680, in publishing a controversial sermon against separation, he dedicated it to Sir
Robert Clayton, a figure sympathetic to Dissenters whom Lucy
Hutchinson had petitioned for a position for her son, and who as Lord
Mayor of London was mustering Protestant forces in the Exclusion
Crisis; his publisher was as usual Henry Mortlock.[48] Later Mortlock was
to publish a topographical work by Richard Franck, a Puritan who had
been arrested in Nottingham at the same time as John Hutchinson for
alleged involvement in the 1663 Northern Rising.[49] Mortlock, then,
would have been an obvious person for Lucy Hutchinson to approach
on deciding to publish her poem.

Far from dying in total obscurity, then, Lucy Hutchinson was moving into a new phase of authorship in her last years. Even before she
ventured into print, her manuscript writings enjoyed a wider circulation
than has so far been recognized, and much remains to be done in recon-
structing the manuscript culture in which she was involved.

APPENDIX

Major Substantive Variants

Manuscript page number and reading are given first, followed by reading and page number in the 1679 text; deleted or raised text indicates
an emendation in a hand other than the principal scribe's, recorded

only where there is a difference from the 1679 text. The marginal citations from the Bible are too numerous for inclusion here.

MS p. 3, l. 2 *desires*] admires (p. 1)

l. 12 *Which yet he by opposeing doth fullfill*] Which tho' opposing he must yet fulfill
(p. 2)

l. 15 *whilest*] while (p. 2)

l. 23 *struck in*] struck with (p. 2)

p. 4, l. 2 *vnperfect*] imperfect (p. 2)

l. 3 *forme*] forms (p. 2)

l. 13 *Mortall*] mortals (p. 2)

p. 5, l. 1 *His essence wrap'd vp in Misterious Clouds / While he himselfe in dazling Glory
shrouds* [not in 1679]

l. 9 *vaine* frail] (p. 3)

l. 16 *mortalls*] mortal (p. 3)

p. 6, l. 9 *Vnitie*] Unite (p. 4)

l. 11 *Derived*] Divided (p. 4)

l. 19 *In which*] Wherein (p. 4)

l. 22 *happynesse*] blessedness (p. 4)

l. 23 *latter*] Later (p. 4)

p. 7, l. 9

And all, in All God's works Coopperate

Although the Action we appropriate

Only vnto that person which most Cleare

And emminently therein doth appeare

Soe we the ffather the Creator name

Though Sonne & Spirit Joyn'd in the worlds frame

~~*And were that*~~ *Was ye great Elohim who first design'd*

[crosses in margin at l. 9 and l. 15]

And all cooperate in all works done
Exteriourly, yet so, as every one,
In a peculiar manner suited to
His Person, doth the common action do.
Herein the Father is the Principal,
Whose sacred counsels are th'Original
Of every Act; produced by the Son,
By'the Spirit wrought up to perfection.
I'the Creation thus, by'the Fathers wise decree,
Such things should in such time, and order be,
The first foundation of the world was laid.
The Fabrique, by th'Eternal Word, was made
Not as th'instrument, but joynt actor, who

Joy'd to fulfill the counsels which he knew.
By the concurrent Spirit all parts were
Fitly dispos'd, distinguisht, rendred fair,
In such harmonious and wise order set,
As universal Beauty did compleat.
This most mysterious Triple Unitie,
In Essence One, and in subsistence Three,
Was that great *Elohim*, who first design'd,

pp. 4–5

p. 8, l. 7 *Where power, Love, Wisdome, Justice, Mercy shine*] Where Power, Love,
Justice, and Mercy shine (p. 5)

p. 10, l. 4 *Which doth both soule & body with full Joyes doth feast*] Which doth both
soul and sense with full joys feast (p. 7)

l. 20 *hopes & thoughts*] thoughts and hopes (p. 7)

l. 21 *saftie*] safe rest (p. 7)

l. 24 *the Deity*] that Deity (p. 7)

p. 11, l. 4 *Royall*] Regal (p. 7)

l. 9 *not being*] being not (p. 8)

l. 11 *where a*] when no (p. 8)

l. 12 *Doth not into*] Doth into (p. 8)

l. 15 *Heaven is*] heaven (p. 8)

l. 18 *him that*] him who (p. 8)

l. 24 *Consumeing*] devouring (p. 8)

p. 12, l. 11 *Who not*] He not (p. 8)

p. 13, l. 1 *Some raised to Thrones & principalities / Some power, some Dominion Excercise*
[not in 1679; each line marked with a cross]

l. 12 *poore*] mean (p. 9)

p. 14, l. 2 *Mountaines*] mountain (p. 10)

l. 7 *Heights*] height (p. 10)

l. 17 *his radiant*] its radiant (p. 10)

l. 23 *determin'd by*] agreed among (p. 10)

p. 15, l. 1 *Dampning*] Damping (p. 10)

l. 2 *Shadow*] shadows (p. 10)

l. 26 *earthly*] earthy (p. 11)

p. 16, Canto 2, l. 2 *make*] made (p. 12)

l. 8 *Magazine*] magazines (p. 12)

l. 10 *Thunders*] thunder (p. 12)

l. 12 *Like spreading Hosts of various Creatures march*] Like hosts of various formed
creatures march (p. 12)

l. 13 *scene*] Scenes (p. 12)

l. 18 *shoot*] fire (p. 12)

p. 17, l. 5 *delights*] delight (p. 12)

l. 7 *erected*] heav'd (p. 13)

after l. 12 [MS lacks couplet in 1679:]

Not quenching, nor drunk up by that bright wall/Of fire, which neighbouring them, encircles all. (p. 13)

l. 14 *Windores*] windows (p. 13)

l. 20 *pearle*] Pearls (p. 13)

l. 24 *Thunders*] thunder (p. 13)

p. 18, l. 20 *the vast*] that vast (p. 14)

l. 27 *fixt on*] fixt in (p. 14)

p. 19, l. 1 *first A . . . A*] first the . . . the (p. 14)

l. 11 *Then sprouted Grasse and hearbs* ^and Flow'rs *and plants*] Then sprouted Grass and Herbs and Plants (p. 14)

l. 14 *Revive their Spirits and Cure their Maladies*] Revive their spirits, cure their maladies (p. 14)

l. 19 *mist*] mists (p. 15)

l. 25 *suns rise*] Sun-rise (p. 15)

p. 20, l. 1 *Rather the fields then painted Courts Admire*] Then rather Fields than painted Courts admire (p. 15)

l. 24 *which lead*] that lead (p. 16)

p. 21, l. 11 *flameing Radiant*] radiant flaming (p. 16)

l. 14 *Heat & Light*] light and heat (p. 16)

l. 23 *this orbe*] its Orb (p. 16)

p. 22, l. 5 *waites*] wastes (p. 16) [asterisk in margin]

l. 19 *Their wandring Vessells ~~on~~ ^on broad seas to ~~quiet~~ ^ride*] Their wandring vessels in broad seas to guide (p. 17)

p. 23, l. 5 *Not only shewne but Caus'd*] At least shewn, if not caus'd (p. 17)

l. 24 *all the world*] the whole word (p. 18)

p. 24, l. 5 *Tyrants*] Tyrant (p. 18)

l. 15 *Come . . . meet*] Comes . . . greet (p. 18)

l. 20 *passeth*] passes (p. 18)

l. 21 *Theatre*] Threatre (p. 18)

p. 25, l. 5 *prepar'd but*] prepar'd; Yet (p. 19.)

l. 16 *bid*] bade (p. 19)

l. 17 *each shell fish*] all shell-fish (p. 19)

l. 21 *amongst the billows*] among the billows (p. 19)

l. 23 *greater or lesser*] less or greater (p. 19)

p. 26, l. 6 *mount to'wards*] mounted (p.19)

l. 15 *most deare*] own dear (p. 20)

p. 27, l. 22 *Turtles would teach vs*] We might from some learn (p. 20)

l. 24 *Storks piety, Conjugall kindnesse Swans/ Would teach, paternall Bounty pellycans*] Conjugal kindess of the paired Swans,/ Paternal Bounty of the Pelicans (p. 21)

p. 28, after l. 3 [MS lacks the following passage found in 1679:]

Wisdome of those who when storms threat the Skie,

In thick assemblies to their shelter flie,

And those who seeing devourers in the air,

To the safe covert of the wing repair. (p. 21)

l. 3 *will teach*] would teach (p. 21)

l. 24 *the sixth day rose*] rose the sixth day (p. 21)

p. 29, l. 4 *these Creatures*] the creatures (p. 21)

ll. 5–6 *And did in their prepared Mansions dwell/Like Hermits* some *Made hollow Rocks their Cell*] Like Hermits some made hollow rocks their Cell,/And did in their prepared mansions dwell (p. 22)

l. 8 *hid in Trees*] hid in clefts of trees (p. 22)

l. 10 *Beast*] beasts (p. 22)

thickest] thickets (p. 22)

l. 23 *some Docillitie*] and docility (p. 22)

ll. 25–26 *Some past things, long in Memory doe keepe/Some have a ffancey working in their sleepe* [not in 1679, p. 22]

p. 30, l. 3 *prudence*] memory (p. 22)

l. 12 *Tigers*] Tygres (p. 22)

after l. 16 [MS lacks reading in 1679:]

The Kingly Lion in his bosome hath

The fiery seed of self-provoking wrath,

(p. 23)

p. 31, Canto 3, l. 4 *second*] sacred (p. 24)

l. 17 *Live rise*] life ris' (p. 24)

p. 32, l. 16 *desire*] require (p. 25)

l. 22 *wool*] Woolls (p. 25)

p. 33, ll. 7–8

Which Ayd to all the other Members give/And Gods rich bounties for the rest receive] Which Gods rich bounties for the rest receive,/And aid to all the other members give (p. 25)

l. 10 *or*] and (p. 25)

l. 22 *phansey, wit, Invention*] Fancy and Invention (p. 26)

p. 34, l. 1 *with*] by (p. 26)

l. 5 *Thousand*] thousands (p. 26)

l. 8 *windores*] windows (p. 26)

l. 13 *As*] At (p. 26)

l. 16 *Conspires*] Conspire (p. 26)

p. 35, l. 7 *Curtaine*] curtains (p. 27)

l. 12 *sets*] set (p. 27)

l. 20 *thickest*] thick set (p. 27)

p. 37, l. 4 *frame*] feign (p. 28)

l. 16 *tall pines and growing Cedars*] tall growing Pines and Cedars (p. 29)

l. 18 *not*] scarcely (p. 29)

p. 38, l. 12 *Hebrew Captives*] captiv'd Hebrews (p. 29)

l. 14 *their grace*] the grace (p. 29)

p. 39, l. 11 *Ore all the ground, and all the fat banks spread*] O're all the banks and all the flat ground spread (p. 30)

l. 18 *as in*] as on (p. 30)

p. 40, l. 1 *And the*] And they (p. 30)

l. 4 *points*] prints (p. 30)

p. 41, l. 14 *Nor these*] Nor those (p. 31)

l. 19 *feathers*] feather (p. 31)

p. 42, l. 13 *embraceth*] embraces (p. 32)

l. 17 *'tempt*] attempt (p. 32)

l. 19 *Invests*] invades (p. 32)

p. 43, l. 6 *Joy, & Saftey*] joy, safety (p. 32)

p. 44, l. 17 *Creations*] Creators (p. 33)

l. 22 *to one Brest had bin Confin'd*] had been to one brest confin'd (p. 33)

p. 45, l. 19 *be*] lie (p. 34)

l. 24 *black*] dark (p. 34)

p. 46, l. 4 *heat*] good (p. 34)

l. 6 *A retreat*] to retreat (p. 34)

l. 19 *As sweet*] For sweet (p. 35)

p. 47, l. 8 *cast*] casts (p. 35)

ll. 13–14

'Till Conversation doe it Current make/And it through much Exchange a brightnesse take]

Till it through much exchange a brightnesse take/And Conversation doth it current make (p. 35)

p. 48, l. 15 *shall Cleave*] doth cleave (p. 36)

p. 49, l. 19 *raiseth*] raises (p. 37)

l. 26 *wast*] wastes (p. 37)

p. 50, l. 1 *vsefull*] youthful (p. 37)

l. 6 *ffor of best things Corruptions still y.ᵉ worst*] For of best things, still the corruption's worst (p. 37)

l. 9 *out of sleeping formed² Adamᵗ thus*] out of sleeping *Adam* formed thus (p. 37)

p. 51, l. 12 *Life, Merit*] merit, life (p. 38)

l. 22 *Tipes & figures*] types and shadows (p. 39)

p. 52, l. 11 *their head quarter*] the head quarter (p. 39)

l. 23 *And the seaventh*] The seventh (p. 39)

p. 53, l. 8 *Interrupt*] intermit (p. 40)

l. 27 *same that*] same which (p. 40)

p. 54, l. 8 *last of all*] last (p. 41)

l. 18 *Extended*] Ascended (p. 41)

l. 21 *till*] until (p. 41)

l. 25 *his Rest*] Gods rest (p. 41)

p. 55, l. 1 *Sabboth*] Sabbaths (p. 41)

l. 5 *worke*] works (p. 41)

l. 9 *our hearts*] all hearts (p. 41)

l. 15 *Raines descend*] rain descends (p. 42)

l. 16 *In it*] On it (p. 42)

l. 17 *their hives*] the hive (p. 42)

l. 18 *provision*] provisions (p. 42)

l. 26 *soe rich*] such rich (p. 42)

p. 57, l. 4 *Cultures*] culture (p. 43)

l. 8 *Inclosure*] enclosures (p. 43)

l. 10 *Instruction*] intrusions (p. 43)

l. 13 *deligts*] delight (p. 43)

l. 21 *ffed with faire* ^hope^ *led with desire the fruite*] Led by desire, fed with fair hope, the fruit (p. 43)

p. 58, l. 2 *Constant*] continual (p. 43)

l. 9 *there y^e^*] then the (p. 44)

p. 59, Canto 4, l. 10 *In the bold Rebells torturing flame seeme bright*] In the Rebels torturing flames seem bright (p. 45)

l. 15 *Beauty*] brightness (p. 45)

p. 60, after l. 4 [MS lacks couplet in 1679:] Turns to a noisome, dead, and poysonous Lake,/

Infecting all who the foul waters take: (p. 46)

p. 61, l. 4 *truth*] truths (p. 46)

l. 8 *doth steere*] steer (p. 46)

p. 63, l. 14 *bands*] bonds (p. 48)

l. 15 *ever can*] never can (p. 48)

p. 64, l. 10 *villaines*] villain (p. 49)

l. 21 *Through*] Thorough (p. 49)

p. 65, l. 14 *that all*] not all (p. 49)

p. 67, l. 17 *Her vnbeleeveing quencht*] Her unbelief quenching (p. 51)

l. 21 *applying*] applies (p. 51)

p. 68, l. 3 *pleasures*] pleasure (p. 51)

l. 6 [left blank in MS] Hence learn pernicious councellors to shun (p. 51)

l. 12 *Thy punishment for this accursed fact*] A punishment on thee, for this accursed fact (p. 52)

p. 69, l. 6 *mighty*] mightier (p. 52)

l. 11 *compasseth*] compasses (p. 52)

l. 13 *And Curtains of broad fig leaves they divise*] And curtains of broad thin Fig-leaves devise (p. 52)

l. 18 *Body*] bowels (p. 52)

p. 70, l. 23 *learned or*] learned and (p. 53)

p. 71, l. 16 *that dread*] their dread (p. 54)

p. 72, l. 15 *God them*] God then (p. 54)

p. 73, l. 7 *its absence*] their absence (p. 55)

l. 9 *Whiles*] While (p. 55)

after l. 20 [MS lacks these lines in 1679:]

When Christs all-heating softning spirit, hath

Their Furnance [*sic*] been, and his pure blood their Bath. (p.55)

p. 74, l. 3 *frightned*] frighted (p. 56)

l. 4 *that never*] who never (p. 56)

l. 17 *hope of Light*] light of hope (p. 56)

p. 75, Canto 5, l. 13 *selfe Judg'd Criminalls*] Criminals (p. 57)

p. 76, l. 3 *Among*] Amongst (p. 57)

after line 9 [MS lacks the following line in 1679:] To be my helper and associate, (p. 58)

l. 17 *sinfulls*] sinful (p. 58)

p. 77, l. 4 *Woman which*] woman *That* (p. 58)

p.78, l. 4 *art Curst*] accurst (p. 59)

l. 8 *shall bruise*] shalt bruise (p. 59)

l. 19 *take place*] takes place (p. 59)

p. 79, l. 5 *Champion*] champions (p. 59)

l. 19 *Angells which*] Angels whom (p. 60)

p. 80, l. 14 *Woe and losse*] loss and woe (p. 60)

p. 81, l. 12 *wifes*] wives (p. 61)

l. 17 *Though golden*] Yet golden (p. 61)

l. 20 *galling those*] galling them (p. 61)

l. 21 *their Rule*] the rule (p. 61)

p. 82, l. 2 *And by their Wishes, sorrowes Contribute*] And their own wishes to their sorrows contribute. (p. 61)

l. 3 *their fruit*] the fruit (p. 61)

l. 23 *good which*] good, who (p. 62)

p. 83, l. 4 *fall*] falls (p. 62)

l. 16 *sin*] sins (p. 62)

p. 84, l. 5 *Cures*] curses (p. 63)

p. 85, l. 3 *fight*] fights (p. 63)

12 *hurts*] hurt (p. 63)

p. 86, l. 5 *employ*] implie (p. 64)

l. 16 *Triumph*] trample (p. 64)

p. 88, l. 13 *earthly*] earthy (p. 66)

l. 15 *alsoe least he*] lest he also (p. 66)

l. 16 *and Imortallitie*] and an Immortal be (p. 66)

l. 18 *farther*] further (p. 66)

p. 89, l. 2 *Mountaine*] mountains (p. 66)

l. 7 *revisiting*] returning to (p. 66)

l. 15 *his grace*] whose grace (p. 66)

p. 90, l. 12 *Battallions*] Battalia's (p. 67)

ll. 17–20

> *But Cocks more generous, murther'd not for food*
> *But for their Hono.ʳ spilt each others blood*
> *Through Lust and Jealousy the Gulls Contend*
> *Till flight or Death the Cruell Combate End*

[not in 1679, p. 67]

l. 23 *resistlesse*] restless (p. 67)

p. 91, l. 6 *engage*] ensnare (p. 67)

l. 10 *Mischiefe*] mischiefs (p. 67)

l. 18 *should share*] shall share (p. 68)

l. 19 *then to our parents sad*] to our parents, then, sad (p. 68)

p. 92, l. 6 *bosome*] bosomes (p. 68)

l. 7 *dround*] drown (p. 68)

l. 19 *Insult on*] insult o're (p. 68)

l. 20 *Soveraigne*] Soveraigns (p. 68)

p. 93, l. 1 *Wood*] woods (p. 69)

l. 2 *Excerciz'd*] exercise (p. 69)

l. 4 *in such*] with such (p. 69)

l. 5 *his*] its (p. 69)

l. 14 *Hope & Comfort*] MS, 1679; hopes & comforts 'Elegies'

l. 16 *At once to take*] MS, 1679; To take at once 'Elegies'

l. 20 *worme*] MS, 1679; flie 'Elegies'

l. 21 *gripeing Hunger*] MS, 1679; hungar 'Elegies'

l. 22 *amongst*] MS, 1679; among 'Elegies'

p. 94, after l. 12 [MS and 1679 lack two lines found in the 'Elegies':]

if on my sinn defiled self I gaze,/my nakednesse & spotts do me amaze

l. 14 *doth*] MS, 1679; does 'Elegies'

l. 15 *lov'd*] MS, 1679; Love 'Elegies'

p. 95, l. 8 *Just and wise*] wise, and just (p. 70)

l. 11 *Cause*] case (p. 70)

l. 20 *plagu'd*] plung'd (p. 70)

p. 96, l. 12 *Consummation*] consummations (p. 71)

p. 97, l. 4 *their sad*] those sad (p. 71)

p. 98, ll. 5–6 *If Heaven doth frowne above the angry Clowds/God sitts and sees through all y.ᵉ blackest shrouds*] Doth Heaven frown? Above the sullen shrouds/God sits, and see through all the blackest clouds (p. 72)

l. 11 *lightning*] lightnings *stormes*] storm (p. 72)

p. 99, l. 9 *Though gapeing Monsters, Horrid dangers stand*] Though dangers then, like gaping monsters stand (p. 73)

l. 10 *every hand*] either hand (p. 73)

l. 12 *canot*] can nor (p. 73)

l. 20 *In hast*] With hast (p. 73)

p. 100, l. 2 *nibbling*] nibblings (p. 73)

l. 7 *Who at*] Which at (p. 73)

p. 101, l. 13 *Let's not each other now in vaine vpbraid*] Let's not in vain each other now upbraid (p. 74)

p. 102, l. 6 *Joyes*] joy (p. 75)

p. 103, l. 8 *health*] healths (p. 76)

l. 10 *food*] fruit (p. 76)

l. 16 *Men doe rejoyce*] Many do joy (p. 76)

l. 19 *with free*] by free *their*] that (p. 76)

p. 104, l. 11 *feares*] tears (p. 76)

l. 12 *dround*] drown (p. 76)

l. 17 *passion*] passions (p. 77)

p. 105, l. 3 *Enervateing the Soules powers when they shou'd*] Unnerving the souls powers, then, when they shou'd (p. 77)

l. 7 *Casuall are*] casual is (p. 77)

l. 20 *Tempests*] tempest (p. 77)

l. 21 *Which either dread what never may arrive*] Which dread what either never may arrive, (p. 77)

p. 106, l. 2 *made now*] made up (p. 78)

NOTES

1 Margaret J. M. Ezell, *The Patriarch's Wife: Literary Evidence and the History of the Family* (Chapel Hill & London, 1987), chapter 3.

2 *Lucy Hutchinson's Translation of Lucretius: De rerum natura*, ed. Hugh de Quehen (London, 1996), p. 23.

3 Lucy Hutchinson, *On the Principles of the Christian Religion, addressed to her daughter, and On Theology* (London, 1817), p. 91. The manuscript of the treatise to her daughter is now in the Northamptonshire Record Office (Fitzwilliam Misc. vol. 793).

4 Harold Love, *Scribal Publication in Seventeenth-Century England* (Oxford, 1993), pp. 184–91.

5 British Library Additional MS 18730 (Anglesey's diary), fol. 100v, 8 October 1682. Since Hutchinson gave him a copy of her Lucretius translation, it is not unlikely that he received other manuscript material, but no more has so far been traced.

6 The manuscript (Osborn Collection fb100) is cited by permission of the Beinecke Rare Book and Manuscript Library, Yale University. The manuscript was bought from the booksellers Hofmann and Freeman, who had acquired it in November 1970 from Bernard Quaritch Ltd. (information courtesy of Mr Theodore Hofmann); I have not yet been able to determine its provenance, or to consult the 'paper of

some writings and papers in my one custody' by the Countess of Rochester cited in *Sotheby's Catalogue of Autograph Letters*, 20 November 1973, lot 11 (sold to Graham Greene). There is no reference to the manuscript in James William Johnson, ' "My dearest sonne": Letters from the Countess of Rochester to the Earl of Lichfield', *The University of Rochester Library Bulletin*, 28 (1974), 25–32, and the letters by the Countess in the Public Record Office, C104/89.

7 Licensed on 10 March 1679, the poem was listed in the Term Catalogue in June: *The Term Catalogues, 1668–1709 A.D.*, ed. Edward Arber, 3 vols. (London, 1903), I, 359.

8 David Norbrook, 'A devine Originall: Lucy Hutchinson and the "woman's version" ', *Times Literary Supplement*, 19 March 1999, pp. 13–15.

9 Nottinghamshire Archives, DD/HU2, pp. vi–vii, cited by David Norbrook, 'Lucy Hutchinson's "Elegies" and the Situation of the Republican Woman Writer (with text)', *English Literary Renaissance*, 27 (1997), 468–521 (pp. 490–1). Future citations of the 'Elegies' are from this edition.

10 Lucy Hutchinson, *On the Principles of the Christian Religion*, pp. 5, 3.

11 In work in progress by John Burrows and Hugh Craig, extensive stylistic texts using frequent word analysis, drawing on a large database of later seventeenth-century poetry, have found very close correlations between *Order and Disorder* and Hutchinson's known writings.

12 *Lucy Hutchinson's Translation of Lucretius*, ed. de Quehen, p. 36 (i. 287–96).

13 Hutchinson, *On the Principles of the Christian Religion*, p. 10.

14 Nottinghamshire Archives, DD/HU3, p. 3; cited by permission of Mrs Hugh Priestley and of the Principal Archivist, Nottinghamshire Archives.

15 The manuscript has no pagination but a later hand has numbered the first page of text as p. 3; I continue this numbering for the rest of the manuscript.

16 Nottinghamshire Archives, DD/HU3, p. 277.

17 Nottinghamshire Archives, DD/HU3, p. 1.

18 *Lucy Hutchinson's Translation of Lucretius*, ed. de Quehen, p. 170 (*De rerum natura*, v.1127–31).

19 Commentary on his translation of Lucretius, currently British Library Evelyn MS 34, fol. 106r.

20 MS, p. 303; Lucy Hutchinson, *Memoirs of the Life of Colonel Hutchinson*, ed. Julius Hutchinson (London, 1806), p. 445.

21 Nottinghamshire Archives, DD/HU3, p. 277.

22 Hofmann and Freeman sale catalogue No. 32 (February 1971).

23 See *The Surviving Works of Anne Wharton*, ed. G. Greer and S. Hastings (Stump Cross, 1997), pp. 8ff, 48ff. I am grateful to Dr Greer for help on the Wilmot connection.

24 *Memoirs of the Life of Colonel Hutchinson*, ed. C. H. Firth (London, 1906), pp. 449–50.

25 British Library Additional MS 18730 (diary of the Earl of Anglesey), fols. 15v–16r, 2 September 1676.

26 Anthony Wood, *Athenae Oxonienses* (London, 1691), col. 830; *The Life and Times of Anthony Wood*, ed. Andrew Clark, 5 vols. (Oxford, 1861–1900), II, 492.

27 On Wood as source see W. R. Parker, 'Wood's *Life of Milton*: Its Sources and Significance', *Papers of the Bibliographical Society of America*, 52 (1958), 1–22 (p. 3), and Nicholas von Maltzahn, 'Wood, Allam, and the Oxford Milton', *Milton Studies*, 31 (1994), 155–77. Wood does not seem to have corresponded with Apsley, who died in 1683, four years after the poem's appearance. His later notes in the Bodleian copy of the *Athenae* (Wood 431a) do not mention the poem and draw their information from Bulstrode Whitelocke's *Memorials* (1682). His attribution apparently postdates the index he compiled to his copies of the Term Catalogues, Bodleian MS Wood 36,

which contains no entry for Sir Allen; his copy of the relevant issue, *A Catalogue of Books*, No. 20 (Trinity Term 1679; Bodleian Wood 658), fol. 112r, contains markings for other books but not for *Order and Disorder*. (I am indebted to Nicholas von Maltzahn for help with Wood.)

28 A. B. Bathurst, *History of the Apsley and Bathurst Families* (Cirencester, 1903), p. 43.

29 Letter to Horatio, Baron Townshend, 28 September 1661, Folger Shakespeare Library, MS Add. 906.

30 *The History of Parliament: The House of Commons 1660–1690*, ed. Basil Duke Henning, 3 vols., I (1983), 541–3; *A Seasonable Argument to Perswade . . . for a New Parliament* (Amsterdam, 1677), p. 13; Thomas Jones, *Elymas the Sorcerer: or, A Memorial towards the Discovery of the Bottom of this Popish-Plot* (London, 1682), pp. 19, 32; a note in Wood's copy, Bodleian Wood 427(47), at p. 32, identifies 'A. A.' as 'Sʳ Allen Apsley' (I owe this reference to Professor N. Riessling).

31 'On the Duke's Servants', Yale University Library, Osborn Collection, fb 140, p. 22.

32 *Memoirs of the Life of Colonel Hutchinson*, ed. James Sutherland (London, 1973), pp. 4, 207. Quotations in the texts are from this edition.

33 W. A. Churchill, *Watermarks in Paper in Holland, England, France, etc., in the XVII and XVIII Centuries* (Amsterdam, 1935), p. ccxlix, No. 315.

34 Peter Beal has suggested that 'There' could be the Scottish form for 'these' (*OED*, 'Thir').

35 Cf. changes on MS p. 199, 'Thou likest ᵗᵒ'ⁱⁿʰᵃᵇⁱᵗᵉ if on the right hand'; p. 283, 'His fathers league with Abraham ᵐᵃᵈᵉ, then sent'.

36 *Lucy Hutchinson's Translation of Lucretius*, ed. de Quehen, p. 14.

37 Aston Cokayne, *Small Poems of Divers Sorts* (London, 1658), p. 204.

38 Nottinghamshire Archives, DD/HU4, pp. [423–79].

39 The books most cited in the *Order and Disorder* annotations are the Psalms, Matthew, Revelation and Romans, all favoured texts of John Hutchinson's. Though, of course, such texts were favoured by Puritans generally, one or two seem to be inserted gratuitously to give them a polemical edge. For example, the concluding passage of Adam's speech, p. 76, is glossed with Revelation 20.4, 'I saw the souls of them that were beheaded for the witness of Jesus, and for the word of God, and which had not worshipped the beast, neither his image', a favourite text with the supporters of the martyred regicides. A reference to the 'just threats' of the stars to tyrants is glossed with the victory song of Deborah and Barak (Judges 5), p. 18.

40 Katherine Narveson, 'The Sources for Lucy Hutchinson's *On Theology*', *Notes and Queries*, NS 36 (1989), 40–41. The current location of this manuscript, which was printed in 1817, has not been traced.

41 John T. Shawcross, *Milton: A Bibliography for the Years 1624–1700* (Binghamton, 1984), p. 251, claims: 'Influence from *Paradise Lost*, passim'. Shawcross is perhaps thinking of such phrases as 'the race of time' (1679, p. 2; cf. *Paradise Lost*, xii.554), and 'Natural tears' (p. 76; cf. *Paradise Lost*, xii.645). In the manuscript we twice find 'wandring steps' (pp. 247, 249; cf. Paradise Lost, xii.648). However, both poets were drawing on a common store of Biblical poetry, notably Du Bartas' *Divine Weeks and Works*, in which the phrase 'wandring steps' can be found: *The Divine Weeks and Works of Guillaume de Saluste Sieur du Bartas*, ed. Susan Snyder, 2 vols (Oxford, 1979), I, 483 (2.2.4.567). The manuscript, p. 104, gives 'Naturall feares'. Some passages, however, take on the air of a critique of Milton by ostentatiously refusing to go beyond Scripture. We do not know, the narrator tells us, just how the angels fell, and whether Adam asked for a mate (1679, pp. 46, 33)—both topics on which Milton confidently expatiated. Henry Mortlock, publisher of *Order and Disorder*, was listed as

one of the booksellers on the title-page of the 1668 *Paradise Lost*.

42 Nottinghamshire Archives, DD/HU3, pp. 69–74.

43 *Lucy Hutchinson's Translation of Lucretius*, ed. de Quehen, p. 23.

44 Richard L. Greaves, *Deliver us from Evil: The Radical Underground in Britain, 1660–1663* (Stanford, 1986), p. 224 (though I have been unable to trace a reference to Mortlock in the sources there given).

45 See Edward Reyner, *The Being and Well-being of a Christian* (London, 1669), which was printed for Mortlock and for Samuel Richards, a bookseller at Nottingham, and John Twells, *An Explanation of the Additional Rules, for the Genders of Nouns* (London, printed for Hen. Mortlock at the Phoenix in St. Paul's Churchyard, and sold by John Mortlock Bookseller in Nottingham, and in his shop at Newark, 1695). Reyner was a Presbyterian ejected from his living in 1662; for John Mortlock see Nottinghamshire Archives, DDP37/3, fol. 199r. I am grateful to the late D. F. McKenzie, the late Michael Treadwell, and Stuart Jennings for help with the Mortlock family.

46 Robert Thoroton, *The Antiquities of Nottinghamshire* (London, 1677), p. 79. Mortlock published several books by the Presbyterian divine Thomas Hall, who was expelled from his living in 1662; Hall dedicated his *An Exposition of the Prophet Amos* (London, 1661) to Pigot in terms of high praise (I owe this reference to Dr G. F. Nuttall).

47 *Elegies On the much Lamented Death of the Honourable and Worthy Patriot, Francis Pierepont, Esq.* (London, 1658), sigs. B1^{r-v}, B2^{v}–3^{r}.

48 Edward Stillingfleet, *The Mischief of Separation* (London, 1680); Lucy Hutchinson to Sir Robert Clayton, 16 May 1675; British Library Additional MS 63788B, fol. 143r.

49 Richard Franck, *Northern Memoirs* (London, 1694).

Manuscripts at Auction:
January 1999 to December 1999

A. S. G. Edwards

This list is intended to provide a summary of manuscript items copied or owned in the British Isles between 1100 and 1700 that have appeared for sale at the major auction houses in London and New York, and in other auction house or booksellers' catalogues, where these have been available to the compiler. I would be pleased to receive notice of any auction or booksellers' catalogues containing relevant items for the period from January 1999.

The list cannot claim to be exhaustive but is offered as a guide to these materials. Where known, the names of purchasers and/or prices paid (including the buyers' premium) have been given, and also the present locations of the manuscripts or their subsequent appearance in booksellers' catalogues.

Items which can be dated, in whole or in part, approximately to before 1500 are indicated by an asterisk (*) before the lot or item number.

All medieval manuscripts written or illuminated in the British Isles have been included, as have manuscripts written or illuminated abroad but which can be shown to have been in the British Isles before 1700. Charters, grants and other items judged to be mainly of archival interest have generally been excluded.

For the later period, 1500–1700, manuscripts chiefly of literary, rather than historical interest have been included. Royal letters and documents are generally omitted, as are single letters written by statesmen, ecclesiastics and other public figures. Maps and surveys, miscellaneous heraldic manuscripts, cookery books and collections of recipes are also generally excluded. Prices and buyers for mixed collections of leaves sold as a single lot and only partly comprising English manuscripts are given after the last relevant item in each lot.

Abbreviations
ALs(s)   Autograph letter(s) signed

attrib.	attributed to
Ds(s)	Document(s) signed
ill.	illuminated
Ls(s)	Letter(s) signed

LONDON

Bloomsbury Book Auctions

6 May 1999

4 GEORGE COTTON: Translation of Diego de Estella, *The Contempt of the World*; *c.*1600. Copied from a printed edition (Rouen, 1584: STC 10541). Unsold.

9 PREACHER'S NOTEBOOK; 1662 and later. £299 to Lachman.

136 SAMUEL PEPYS: ALs to Lord Yarmouth, 27 April 1678. £460 to Wiche.

10 June 1999

*33 BREVIARY: on vellum, in Latin, ill., Sarum use; *c.*1450. £10,350 to Griffon.

147 HENRY SPELMAN: *Glossarium Archeologium*; 1606. £1,395 to Harrop.

159 ELIZABETH & WILLIAM ELSTOB: Eighteenth-century transcripts of eleventh-century Anglo-Saxon laws in BL Cotton Nero A. I. £2,800 to Christopher Edwards. Now in a private collection in Japan.

11 November 1999

38 JOHN MILTON: Letter in Latin signed by Oliver Cromwell, to Leopold, Archduke of Austria, the text probably composed by Milton, 16 February 1654/5. Unsold.

105 RICHARD LEE: Visitations of Oxfordshire, on vellum; 1574. £368 to Oxfordshire Record Office.

106 HENRY BALL (d.1687): *Baronagium Angliae*, genealogies of Scotland, subsequently owned by Peter Le Neve. £1,035 to a private buyer.

110 HERMES TRISMEGISTUS: 'His First Booke', on paper; [?1650]. £8,050 to Estates of Mind.

113 HERALDRY: Notes for a treatise on blazonry; late seventeenth-early eighteenth century. £1,380 to Christopher Edwards.

Bonham's

8 June 1999

435 HENRY ELSYNGE: *The First Booke of Modus Tenendi Parliamentum*; 1626.
£3,105.

Christie's

2 June 1999

32 SWAN ROLL: on vellum, in Middle English, illustrated, (?) Norwich;
*c.*1500. £43,700.

158 ASTROLOGY: London; 1643. £6,900.

29 November 1999

9 ASTROLOGICAL AND MEDICAL COMPENDIUM: in Middle English, on vellum, in prose and verse. £285,000.

237 WILLIAM SHAKESPEARE: Commonplace book of the Danby family of
Kirby Knowle, North Yorkshire, including two quotations from
Othello; early-seventeenth-century. £19,550.

Phillips

12 March 1999

129 JOHN TOLE: Religious meditations, ill.; 1662. £5,060 to Quaritch.
Now in Lambeth Palace Library.

286 HERALDRY: Armorial trees, watercolour; late-seventeenth-century.
£276 to a private buyer

11 June 1999

249 ROBERT DEVEREUX, SECOND EARL OF ESSEX: Forty-three ALss to
Elizabeth I; October 1590 to January/February 1601. £165,750 to
Quaritch. Now in the British Library, Add. MS 74286.

250 ROBERT DEVEREUX, SECOND EARL OF ESSEX: Discourse on the Cadiz
Expedition of 1596, autograph; early August 1596. £20,700 to
Quaritch. Now in the British Library, Add. MS 74287.

257 HERALDRY: Dictionary of Arms in the hand of Henry Chitting
(d.1638),Chester Herald; *c.*1600. £414 to a private buyer.

258 HERALDRY: Caroline Armorial, four hundred and forty illuminated
coats of arms on vellum; *c.*1630–40. £2,185 to a private buyer.

Sotheby's

22 June 1999

*6(a) PETER LOMBARD: *Collectanea in Epistolas Pauli*, on vellum, single leaf; second half of twelfth century.

*(b) BREVIARY: bifolium, on vellum, *c.*1180–1200. £1,700 to Quaritch.

*54 MISSAL + ROYAL SUMMONSES, etc: on vellum and paper, English or Irish, in Latin and Middle English; mid-fifteenth and second half of sixteenth century. £2,800 to Quaritch. Now in Trinity College Dublin.

15 July 1999

6 HERALDRY: *A Catalogue of the fiue Conquerors of this Island and theire Armes*, ill. on vellum; former owners include one 'Edmd. Waller' ; *c.*1606. £1,380 to Roy Davids. = Roy Davids, Catalogue VI.

7 HERALDRY: *Armorial of English family*, *olim* Phillipps MSS 10869 and 13953; mid-seventeenth-century. £1,495 to a private buyer.

8 SIR HENRY HERBERT: Collection of documents relating to Ribbesford. £805 to Quaritch. Now in the British Library, Add. Ch. 77026–77037.

7 December 1999

2(c) LATIN BIBLE: Single leaf on vellum; second half of thirteenth century; in a collection. £1,610.

7(b) LECTIONARY: Single leaf on vellum; first half of thirteenth century; in a collection. £1,150 to a private buyer.

8 PSALTER: bifolium on vellum; first half of fourteenth century. £1,955 to Sam Fogg.

34 BOETHIUS: *De Consolatione Philosophiae*, on vellum; first half of fourteenth century. £17,250 to Sam Fogg.

6 December 1999 (Pencarrow sale)

32 THOMAS HOBBES: ALs to William Cavendish, third Earl of Devonshire, 23 July/2 August 1641. £12,500 to Quaritch. Now in a private collection in the U.S.A.

8 December 1999 (Fermor-Hesketh sale)

291 SPENCER COWPER: 'Poems upon Several Occasions', some addressed to 'Orinda'; 1694. £14,950 to Maggs. Now in the Huntington Library.

292 HENRY VIII: *A Necessary Doctrine and Erudition for any Christen man*, on paper; mid-sixteenth-century. £2,070 to Arthur Freeman.

294 HERALDRY: Genealogies of families of Huntingdonshire,

Bedfordshire and Buckinghamshire, on paper, *olim* Phillipps MS
18162; *c.*1566. £4,025.

295 HERALDRY: Collection of papers of Sir Henry St George the
younger (1625–1715), Garter King of Arms, including designs for the
Union Flag in 1707. £63,250 to Heywood Hill Ltd.

297 NORTHAMPTONSHIRE: *A New Ballad called the Northamptonshire High
Cunstable*, on paper, *olim* Phillipps MS 12089. £4,600 to Maggs. Now
in the Huntington Library.

BOOKSELLERS' CATALOGUES

Roy Davids

Catalogue VI (1999)

45 HERALDRY: Ill. grant of arms to Edward Sebrighte by Robert Cooke,
Clarenceux, and William Dethick, Garter, 1 April 1580. £3,000.

71 HERALDRY = Sotheby's, 15 July 1999, lot 6.

Sam Fogg Rare Books and Manuscripts

Illuminated Manuscripts (January 1999)

*5 PSALTER: on vellum, German with added English calendar, six full-
page initials, other ill. initials of varying sizes throughout. Previously
sold Sotheby's, 9 November 1990, lot 99. $90,000.

*16 SAXBY HOURS: on vellum, Latin, with Middle English verse and
prose, twenty large historiated initials and full-page frontispiece,
southern England, possibly London; *c.*1430–50. Previously sold
Sotheby's, 21 June 1998, lot 67. $250,000.

Maggs Bros. Ltd

Catalogue 1272 (1999)

27 SIR THOMAS BROWNE: *Concerning Artificiall mounts and raised hills without
fortificaetions attending them*, on paper in a secretarial hand with
Browne's autograph subscription and signature, 27 October 1658.
£22,500.

66 ILLUMINATOR'S RECIPES: Late sixteenth-century paper leaf used as
binder's waste. £2,400.

78 ANDREW HORNE: *La Somme Appell* [*etc*], on paper, from a transcript
made by Francis Tate (1560–1616); *c.*1615–30. £2,500.

132 SHELTON FAMILY ARMORIAL: on vellum; *c.*1600 with later seventeenth-century additions. £2,300. = Sotheby's, 20 July 1989, lot 261.

164 VILLIERS FAMILY PEDIGREE: Vellum roll with 125 ill. coats of arms and other illumination; *c.*1637. £ 6,500.

Notes on Contributors

SYLVIA BROWN is Assistant Professor of English at the University of Alberta. She is editor of *Women's Writing in Stuart England: The Mothers' Legacies of Dorothy Leigh, Elizabeth Joscelin, and Elizabeth Richardson* (1999).

VICTORIA E. BURKE is a Research Fellow at Nottingham Trent University working on the Perdita Project on Early Modern Women's Manuscript Compilations. She has published, and is publishing, various articles on early modern women's writing, including their reading practices, the commonplace book, and the manuscripts of Anne, Lady Southwell.

ELIZABETH CLARKE is Research Lecturer at Nottingham Trent University, where she leads the Perdita Project for Early Modern Women's Compilations. She is author of *Theory and Theology in George Herbert's Poetry: 'Divinitie, and Poesie, Met'* (1997) and of articles on early-modern women's manuscripts

A.S.G. EDWARDS is currently Helen Cam Fellow at Girton College, Cambridge. He has most recently been one of the editors of Volume I of the Yale edition of *The English Works of St Thomas More* and has published, with Julia Boffey, a facsimile of Bodleian Library MS Arch. Selden B. 24. He is also collaborating with Dr Boffey on a revision of the *Index of Middle English Verse*.

MARGARET P. HANNAY is Professor of English Literature at Siena College. She is author of *Philip's Phoenix: Mary Sidney, Countess of Pembroke* (1990), and, with Noel J. Kinnamon and Michael G. Brennan, has edited *The Collected Works of Mary Herbert, Countess of Pembroke* (2 vols, 1998). She has edited, with Susanne Woods, *Teaching Tudor and Stuart Women Writers* (2000) and is currently editing, with N. Kinnamon and M. Brennan, *Selected Correspondence of Robert Sidney, Earl of Leicester*.

JEAN KLENE is Professor of English at Saint Mary's College, Notre Dame, Indiana. She has published *The Southwell-Sibthorpe Commonplace Book: Folger MS. V.b.198* (1997) and articles on Lady Southwell, Chaucer and Shakespeare.

STEVEN W. MAY is Professor of English at Georgetown College, Kentucky. He has published books and articles on Elizabethan literature. He is currently compiling the *Bibliography and First-Line Index of*

English Verse, 1559–1603, and his continuing research interests include the transmission of literary texts in manuscript at the Elizabethan court.

DAVID NORBROOK is Professor of English at the University of Maryland. His publications include *Poetry and Politics in the English Renaissance* (1984) and *Writing the English Republic: Poetry, Rhetoric and Politics, 1627–1660* (1999). He is currently editing *Order and Disorder* for Blackwell Publishers.

MARK ROBSON is Lecturer in English at the University of Nottingham. He has published articles on Thomas More, women's writing, biography and autobiography, and critical theory, and is co-editor of *The Limits of Death* (forthcoming, Manchester University Press). His edition of the poetry of Lady Hester Pulter will be published in the Leeds Texts & Monographs series.

JANE STEVENSON teaches in the Centre for British and Comparative Cultural Studies at the University of Warwick. She has worked extensively on women's writing from late antiquity to the present day, particularly on Latin texts. She is currently engaged, notably, on *The Oxford Book of Early Modern Women Poets*, with Peter Davison, and *Poetissae: Women and the Language of Authority*, on women writers of Latin verse.

FRANCES TEAGUE is Professor of English at the University of Georgia. She has published work on Renaissance drama, including Shakespeare, and on early women writers, including Bathsua Makin, Queen Elizabeth, and 'Judith Shakespeare Reading'.

ANNEKE TJAN-BAKKER is an independent researcher who has taught English Literature at Leiden University and at the VU (Free University) in Amsterdam. She is currently working on a study of Esther Inglis's life and work.

HEATHER WOLFE, having just received a Ph D from the University of Cambridge and an MLIS from the University of California, Los Angeles, is a newly-appointed Assistant Curator of Manuscripts at the Folger Shakespeare Library. She is currently preparing an edition of *Lady Falkland: Her Life* and of the letters of Lady Falkland and her family, as well as editing a collection of essays on Lady Falkland.

GEORGIANNA ZIEGLER is Reference Librarian at the Folger Shakespeare Library, Washington, D.C. She has published essays on women and Renaissance literature, and has articles forthcoming on Esther Inglis and on researching early modern women.

Index of Manuscripts

This index lists the present repositories of manuscripts and annotated books mentioned in the text (excluding the footnotes), listed alphabetically by location, together with the present locations (where known) of items in Manuscripts at Auction on pp. 292–7.

General Index

This index contains proper names appearing in the the volume, including the section on Manuscripts at Auction (except generally for names of characters in the Bible and classical mythology, and recent owners or buyers of manuscripts). It excludes the footnotes and names of modern scholars.